DEATH VALLEY

IN '49

W Leebanly

DEATH VALLEY

IN '49

An Autobiography of a Pioneer
Who Survived the California Desert

BY WILLIAM LEWIS MANLY

Skyhorse Publishing

First Skyhorse Publishing edition 2016

Skyhorse Publishing books may be purchased in bulk at special discounts for sales promotion, corporate gifts, fund-raising, or educational purposes. Special editions can also be created to specifications. For details, contact the Special Sales Department, Skyhorse Publishing, 307 West 36th Street, 11th Floor, New York, NY 10018 or info@skyhorsepublishing.com.

Skyhorse® and Skyhorse Publishing® are registered trademarks of Skyhorse Publishing, Inc.®, a Delaware corporation.

Visit our website at www.skyhorsepublishing.com.

10 9 8 7 6 5 4

Library of Congress Cataloging-in-Publication Data is available on file.

Cover design by Rain Saukas

Print ISBN: 978-1-63450-440-9
Ebook ISBN: 978-1-5107-0033-8

Printed in the United States of America

TO
THE PIONEERS OF CALIFORNIA,
THEIR CHILDREN AND GRANDCHILDREN,
THIS BOOK IS DEDICATED,
WITH THAT HIGH RESPECT AND REGARD
SO OFTEN EXPRESSED IN ITS PAGES,
BY THE AUTHOR.

CONTENTS.

CHAPTER VIII.

CHAPTER IX.

CHAPTER X.

CHAPTER XI.

CHAPTER XII.

CHAPTER XIII.

CHAPTER XIV

CHAPTER XV

CHAPTER I.

St- Albans, Vermont is near the eastern shore of Lake Champlain, and only a short distance south of "Five-and-forty north degrees" which separates the United States from Canada, and some sixty or seventy miles from the great St. Lawrence River and the city of Montreal, Near here it was, on April 6th, 1820, I was born, so the record says, and from this point with wondering eyes of childhood I looked across the waters of the narrow lake to the slopes of the Adirondack mountains in New York, green as the hills of my own Green Mountain State.

The parents of my father were English people and lived near Hartford, Connecticut, where he was born. While still a little boy he came with his parents to Vermont. My mother's maiden name was Phœbe Calkins, born near St. Albans of Welch parents, and, being left an orphan while yet in very tender years, she was given away to be reared by people who provided food and clothes, but permitted her to grow up to womanhood without knowing how to read or write. After her marriage she learned to do both, and acquired the rudiments of an education.

Grandfather and his boys, four in all, fairly carved a farm out of the big forest that covered the cold rocky hills. Giant work it was for them in such heavy timber—pine, hemlock, maple, beech and birch—the clearing of a single acre being a man's work for a year. The place where the maples were thickest was reserved for a sugar grove, and from it was made all of the sweet material they needed, and some besides. Economy of the very strictest kind had to be used in every direction. Main strength and muscle were the only things dispensed in plenty. The crops raised consisted of a small flint corn, rye oats, potatoes and turnips. Three cows, ten or twelve sheep, a few pigs and a yoke of strong oxen comprised the live stock—horses, they had none for many years. A great ox-cart was the only wheeled vehicle on the place, and this, in winter, gave place to a heavy sled, the runners cut from a tree having a natural crook. and roughly, but strongly, made.

In summer there were plenty of strawberries, raspberries, whortleberries and blackberries growing wild, but all the cultivated fruit was apples. As these ripened many were peeled by hand, cut in quarters, strung on long strings of twine and dried before the kitchen fire for winter use. They had a way of burying up some of the best keepers in the ground, and opening the apple hole was quite an event of early spring.

The children were taught to work as soon as large enough. I remember they furnished me with a little wooden fork to spread the heavy swath of grass my father cut with easy swrings of the scythe, and when it was dry and being loaded on the great ox-cart I followed closely with a rake gathering every scattering spear. The barn was built so that every animal was housed comfortably in winter, and the house was such as all settlers built, not considered handsome, but capable of being made very warm in winter and the great piles of hard wood in the yard enough to last as fuel for a year, not only helped to clear the land, but kept us comfortable. Mother and the girls washed, carded, spun, and wove the wool from our own sheep into good strong cloth. Flax was also raised, and I remember how they pulled it, rotted it by spreading on the green meadow, then broke and dressed it, and then the women made linen cloth of various degrees of fineness, quality, and beauty. Thus, by the labor of both men and women, we were clothed. If an extra fine Sunday dress was desired, part of the yarn was colored and from this they managed to get up a very nice plaid goods for the purpose.

In clearing the land the hemlock bark was peeled and traded off at the tannery for leather, or used to pay for tanning and dressing the hide of an ox or cow which they managed to fat and kill about every year. Stores for the family were either made by a neighboring shoe-maker, or by a traveling one who went from house to house, making up a supply for the family—whipping the cat, they called it then. They paid him in some-thing or other produced upon the farm, and no money was asked or expected.

Wood was one thing plenty, and the fireplace was made large enough to take in sticks four feet long or more, for the more they could burn the better, to get it out of the way. In an outhouse, also provided with a fireplace and chimney, they made shingles during the long winter evenings, the shavings making plenty of fire and light by which to work. The shingles sold for about a dollar a thousand. Just beside the fireplace in the house was a large brick oven where mother baked great loaves of bread, big pots of pork and beans, mince pies and loaf cake, a big turkey or a young pig on grand occasions. Many of the dishes used were of tin or pewter; the milk pans were of earthenware, but most things about the house in the line of furniture were of domestic manufacture.

The store bills were very light. A little tea for father and mother, a few spices and odd luxuries were about all, and they were paid for with surplus eggs. My father and my uncle had a sawmill, and in winter they hauled logs to it, and could sell timber for $8 per thousand feet.

The school was taught in winter by a man named Bowen, who managed forty scholars and considered sixteen dollars a month, boarding himself, was pretty fair pay. In summer some smart girl would teach the small scholars and board round among the families.

When the proper time came the property holder would send off to the collector an itemized list of all his property, and at another the taxes fell due. A farmer who would value his property at two thousand or three thousand dollars would find he had to pay about six or seven dollars. All the money in use then seemed to be silver, and not very much of that. The whole plan seemed to to be to have every family and farm self-supporting as far as possible. I have heard of a note being given payable in a good cow to be delivered at a certain time, say October 1, and on that day it would pass from house to house in payment of a debt, and at night only the last man in the list would have a cow more than his neighbor. Yet those were the days of real independence, after all. Every man worked hard from early youth to a good old age. There were no millionaires, no tramps, and the poorhouse had only a few inmates.

I have very pleasant recollections of the neighborhood cider mill. There were two rollers formed of logs carefully rounded and four or five feet long, set closely together in an upright position in a rough frame, a long crooked sweep coming from one of them to which a horse was hitched and pulled it round and

round,   One roller had mortices in it, and projecting
wooden teeth on the other fitted into these, so that, as
they both slowly turned together, the apples were
crushed,   A huge box of coarse slats, notched and
locked together at the corners, held a vast pile of the
crushed apples while clean rye straw was added to
strain the flowing juice and keep the cheese from
spreading too much;   then the ponderous screw and
streams of delicious cider.   Sucking cider through a
long rye straw inserted in the bung-hole of a barrel was
just the best of fun, and cider taken that way ''awful''
good while it was new and sweet.

The winter ashes, made from burning so much fuel
and gathered from the brush-heaps and log-heaps, were
carefully saved and traded with the potash men for potash or sold for a small price.   Nearly every one went
barefoot in summer, and in winter wore heavy leather
mocassins made by the Canadian French who lived
near by.

CHAPTER II.

ABOUT 1828 people began to talk about the far West. Ohio was the place we heard most about, and the most we knew was, that it was a long way off and no way to get there except over a long and tedious road, with oxen or horses and a cart or wagon. More than one got the Western fever, as they called it, my uncle James Webster and my father among the rest, when they heard some traveler tell about the fine country he had seen; so they sold their farms and decided to go to Ohio. Uncle James was to go ahead, in the fall of 1829 and get a farm to rent, if he could, and father and his family were to come on the next spring.

Uncle fitted out with two good horses and a wagon; goods were packed in a large box made to fit, and under the wagon seat was the commissary chest for food and bedding for daily use, all snugly arranged. Father had, shortly before, bought a fine Morgan mare and a light wagon which served as a family carriage, having wooden axles and a seat arranged on wooden springs, and they finally decided they would let me take the horse and wagon and go on with uncle, and father and mother would come by water, either by way of the St. Lawrence river and the lakes or by way of the new canal recently built, which would take them as far as Buffalo.

So they loaded up the little wagon with some of the mentioned things and articles in the house, among which I remember a fine brass kettle, considered almost indispensable in housekeeping. There was a good lot of bedding and blankets, and a quilt nicely folded was placed on the spring seat as a cushion.

As may be imagined I was the object of a great deal of attention about this time, for a boy not yet ten years

old just setting out into a region almost unknown was
a little unusual. When I was ready they all gathered
round to say good bye and my good mother seemed
most concerned. She said—"Now you must be a good
boy till we come in the spring. Mind uncle and aunt
and take good care of the horse, and remember us.
May God protect you." She embraced me and kissed
me and held me till she was exhausted. Then they
lifted me up into the spring seat, put the lines in my
hand and handed me my little whip with a leather strip
for a lash. Just at the last moment father handed me
a purse containing about a dollar, all in copper cents—
pennies we called them then. Uncle had started on
they had kept me so long, but I started up and they
all followed me along the road for a mile or so before
we finally separated and they turned back. They
waved hats and handkerchiefs till out of sight as they
returned, and I wondered if we should ever meet
again.

I was up with uncle very soon and we rolled down
through St. Albans and took our road southerly along
in sight of Lake Champlain. Uncle and aunt often
looked back to talk to me; "See what a nice cornfield!"
or, "What nice apples on those trees," seeming to
think they must do all they could to cheer me up, that
I might not think too much of the playmates and home
I was leaving behind.

I had never driven very far before, but I found the
horse knew more than I did how to get around the big
stones and stumps that were found in the road, so that
as long as I held the lines and the whip in hand I was
an excellent driver.

We had made plans and preparations to board ourselves on the journey. We always stopped at the farm
houses over night. and they were so hospitable that
they gave us all we wanted free. Our supper was

generally of bread and milk, the latter always furnished gratuitously, and I do not recollect that we were ever turned away from any house where we asked shelter. There were no hotels, or taverns as they called them, outside of the towns.

In due time we reached Whitehall, at the head of Lake Champlain, and the big box in Uncle's wagon proved so heavy over the muddy roads that he put it in a canal boat to be sent on to Cleveland, and we found it much easier after this for there were too many mud-holes, stumps and stones and log bridges for so heavy a load as he had. Our road many times after this led along near the canal, the Champlain or the Erie. and I had a chance to see something of the canal boys' life. The boy who drove the horses that drew the packet boat was a well dressed fellow and always rode at a full trot or a gallop, but the freight driver was generally ragged and barefoot, and walked when it was too cold to ride, threw stones or clubs at his team, and cursed and abused the packet-boy who passed as long as he was in hearing. Reared as I had been I thought it was a pretty wicked part of the world we we were coming to.

We passed one village of low cheap houses near the canal. The men about were very vulgar and talked rough and loud, nearly every one with a pipe, and poorly dressed, loafing around the saloon, apparently the worse for whisky. The children were barefoot, bare headed and scantly dressed, and it seemed awfully dirty about the doors of the shanties. Pigs, ducks and geese were at the very door, and the women I saw wore dresses that did not come down very near the mud and big brogan shoes, and their talk was saucy and different from what I had ever heard women use before. They told me they were Irish people—the first I had ever seen.

It was along here somewhere that I lost my little
whip and to get another one made sad inroads into the
little purse of pennies my father gave me. We traveled slowly on day after day. There was no use to
hurry for we could not do it. The roads were muddy,
the log ways very rough and the only way was to take
a moderate gait and keep it. We never traveled on
Sunday. One Saturday evening my uncle secured the
privilege of staying at a well-to do farmer's house until Monday. We had our own food and bedding, but
were glad to get some privileges in the kitchen, and
some fresh milk or vegetables. After all had taken
supper that night they all they all sat down and made
themselves quiet with their books, and the children
were as still as mice till an early bed time when all retired. When Sunday evening came the women got
out their work—their sewing and their knitting, and
the children romped and played and made as much
noise as they could, seeming as anxious to break the
Sabbath as they had been to have a pious Saturday
night. I had never seen that way before and asked
my uncle who said he guessed they were Seventh Day
Baptists.

After many days of travel which became to me quite
monotonous we came to Cleveland, on Lake Erie, and
here my uncle found his box of goods, loaded it into
the wagon again, and traveled on through rain and
mud, making very slow headway, for two or three
days after, when we stopped at a four-corners in
Medina county they told us we were only 21 miles from
Cleveland. Here was a small town consisting of a
hotel, store, church, schoolhouse and blacksmith shop,
and as it was getting cold and bad, uncle decided to
go no farther now, and rented a room for himself and
aunt, and found a place for me to lodge with Daniel
Stevens' boy close by. We got good stables for our

horses.

I went to the district school here, and studied reading, spelling and Colburn's mental arithmetic, which I mastered. It began very easy—"How many thumbs on your right hand?" "How many on your left?" "How many altogether?" but it grew harder further on.

Uncle took employment at anything he could find to do, Chopping was his principal occupation. When the snow began to go off he looked around for a farm to rent for us and father to live on when he came, but he found none such as he needed. He now got a letter from father telling him that he had good news from a friend named Cornish who said that good land nearly clear of timber could be bought of the Government in Michigan Territory, some sixty or seventy miles beyond Detroit, and this being an opportunity ot

We then gave up the idea of staying here and preget what land they needed with their small capital, they would start for that place as soon as the waterways were thawed out, probably in April.

pared to go to Michigan as soon as the frost was out of the ground. Starting, we reached Huron River to find it it swollen and out of its bank, giving us much trouble to get across, the road along the bottom lands being partly covered with logs and rails, but once across we were in the town and when we enquired about the road around to Detroit, they said the country was all a swamp and 30 miles wide and in Spring impassible. They called it the Maumee or Black Swamp. We were advised to go by, water when a steamboat came up the river bound for Detroit we put our wagons and horses on board, and camped cn the lower deck ourselves. We had our own food and were very comfortable, and glad to have esaped the great mudhole.

CHAPTER III.

We arrived in Detroit safely, and a few minutes answered to land our wagons and goods, when we rolled outward in a westerly direction. We found a very muddy roads, stumps and log bridges plenty, making our rate of travel very slow, When out upon our road aboui 30 miles, near Ypsilanti, the thick forest we had been passing through grew thinner, and the trees soon dwindled down into what they called oak openings, and the road became more sandy. When we reached McCracken's Tavern we began to enquire for Ebenezer Manley and family, and were soon directed to a large house near by where he was stopping for a time.

We drove up to the door and they all came out to see who the new comers were. Mother saw me first and ran to the wagon and pulled me off and hugged and kissed me over and over again, while the tears ran down her cheeks, Then she would hold me off at arm's length, and look me in the eye and say—"I am so glad to have you again"; and then she embraced me again and again. "You are our little man," said she, "You have come over this long road, and brought us our good horse and our little wagon." My sister Polly two years older than I, stood patiently by, and when mother turned to speak to uncle and aunt, she locked arms with me and took me away with her. We had never been separated before in all our lives and we had loved each other as good children should, who have been brought up in good and moral principles. We loved each other and our home and respected our good father and mother who had made it so happy for us.

We all sat down by the side of the house and talked pretty fast telliug our experience on our long journey by land and water, and when the sun went down we were called to supper, and went hand in hand to surround the bountiful table as a family again. During the conversation at supper father said to me—"Lewis, I have bought you a smooth bore rifle, suitable for either ball or shot." This, I thought was good enough for any one, and I thanked him heartily. We spent the greater part of the night in talking over our adventures since we left Vermont, and sleep was forgotten by young and old.

Next morning father and uncle took the horse and little wagon and went out in search of Government land. They found an old acquaintance in Jackson county and Government land all around him, and, scarching till they found the section corner, they found the number of the lots they wanted to locate on —200 acres in all. They then went to the Detroit land office and secured the pieces they had chosen.

Father now bought a yoke of oxen, a wagon and a cow, and as soon as we could get loaded up our little emigrant train started west to our future home, where we arrived safely in a few days and secured a house to live in about a mile away from our land. We now worked with a will and built two log houses and also hired 10 acres broken, which was done with three or four yoke of oxen and a strong plow. The trees were scattered over the ground and some small brush and old limbs, and logs which we cleared away as we plowed. Our houses went up very fast—all rough oak logs, with oak puncheons, or hewed planks for a floor, and oak shakes for a roof, all of our own make. The shakes were held down upon the roof by heavy poles, for we had no nails, the door of split stuff hung with

wooden hinges, and the fire place of stone laid up with
the logs, and from the loft floor upward the chimney
was built of split stuff plastered heavily with mud.
We have a small four-paned window in the house.
We then built a log barn for our oxen, cow and horse
and got pigs, sheep and chickens as fast as a chance
offered.

As fast as possible we fenced in the cultivated land,
father and uncle splitting out the rails, while a younger
brother and myself, by each getting hold of an end of
one of them managed to lay up a fence four rails high,
all we small men could do.   Thus working on, we had
a pretty well cultivated farm in the course of two or
three years, on which we produced wheat, corn and
potatoes, and had an excellent garden. We found
plenty of wild cranberries and whortleberries, which
we dried for winter use.   The lakes were full of good
fish, black bass and pickerel, and the woods had deer,
turkeys, pheasants, pigeons, and other things. and I
became quite an expert in the capture of small game
for the table with my new gun. Father and uncle
would occasionally kill a deer, and the Indians came
along and sold vension at times.

One fall after work was done and preparations were
made for the winter, father said to me:—"Now Lewis,
I want you to hunt every day—come home nights—
but keep on till you kill a deer." So with his permission I started with my gun on my shoulder, and with
feelings of considerable pride. Before night I started
two deer in a brushy place, and they leaped high over
the oak bushes in the most affrighted way.   I brought
my gun to my shoulder and fired at the bounding animal when in most plain sight. Loading then quickly,
I hurried up the trail as fast as I could and soon came
to my deer, dead, with a bullet hole in its head. I was
really surprised myself, for I had fired so hastily at the

almost flying animal that it was little more than a random shot. As the deer was not very heavy I dressed it and packed it home myself, about as proud a boy as the State of Michigan contained. I really began to think I was a capital hunter, though I afterward knew it was a bit of good luck and not a bit of skill about it.

It was some time after this before I made another lucky shot. Father would once in a while ask me:— "Well can't you kill us another deer?" I told him that when I had crawled a long time toward a sleeping deer, that I got so trembly that I could not hit an ox in short range. "O," said he, "You get the buck fever—don't be so timid—they won't attack you." But after awhile this fever wore off, and I got so steady that I could hit anything I could get in reach of.

We were now quite contented and happy. Father could plainly show us the difference between this country and Vermont and the advantages we had here. There the land was poor and stony and the winters terribly severe. Here there were no stones to plow over, and the land was otherwise easy to till. We could raise almost anything, and have nice wheat bread to eat, far superior to the "Rye-and-Indian" we used to have. The nice white bread was good enough to eat without butter, and in comparison this country seemed a real paradise.

The supply of clothing we brought with us had lasted until now—more than two years—and we had sowed some flax and raised sheep so that we began to get material of our own raising, from which to manufacture some more. Mother and sister spun some nice yarn, both woolen and linen, and father had a loom made on which mother wove it up into cloth, and we were soon dressed up in bran new clothes again. Domestic economy of this kind was as necessary here as it was in Vermont, and we knew well how to practice it.

About this time the emigrants began to come in very fast, and every piece of Government land any where about was taken.   So much land was ploughed, and so much vegetable matter turned under and decaying that there came a regular epidemic of fever and ague and bilious fever, and a large majority of the people were sick.   At our house father was the first one attacked, and when the fever was at its height he was quite out of his head and talked and acted like a crazy man.   We had never seen any one so sick before, and we thought he must surely die, but when the doctor came he said:—"Don't be alarmed.   It is only 'fever 'n' agur,' and no one was ever known to die of that."   Others of us were sick too, and most of the neighbors, and it made us all feel rather sorrowful. The doctor's medicines consisted of calomel, jalap and quinine, all used pretty freely, by some with benefit, and by others to no visible purpose, for they had to suffer until the cold weather came and froze the disease out.   At one time I was the only one that remained well, and I had to nurse and cook, besides all the outdoor work that fell to me.   My sister married a man near by with a good farm and moved there with him, a mile or two away.   When she went away I lost my real bosom companion and felt very lonesome, but I went to see her once in a while, and that was pretty often, I think.   There was not much going on as a general thing.   Some little neighborhood society and news was about all.   There was, however, one incident which occured in 1837, I never shall forget, and which I will relate in the next chapter.

CHAPTER IV.

ABOUT two miles west father's farm in Jackson county Mich., lived Ami Filley, who moved here from Connecticut and settled about two and a half miles from the town of Jackson, then a small village with plenty of stumps and mudholes in its streets. Many of the roads leading thereto had been paved with tamarac poles, making what is now known as corduroy roads. The country was still new and the farm houses far between.

Mr. Filley secured Government land in the oak openings, and settled there with his wife and two or three children, the oldest of which was a boy named Willie. The children were getting old enough to go to school, but there being none, Mr. Filley hired one of the neighbor's daughters to come to his house and teach the children there, so they might be prepared for usefulness in life or ready to proceed further with their education—to college, perhaps in some future day.

The young woman he engaged lived about a mile a half away—Miss Mary Mount—and she came over and began her duties as private school ma'am, not a very difficult task in those days. One day after she had been teaching some time Miss Mount desired to go to her father's on a visit, and as she would pass a huckleberry swamp on the way she took a small pail to fill with berries as she went, and by consent of Willie's mother, the little boy went with her for company. Reaching the berries she began to pick, and the little boy found this dull business, got tired and homesick and wanted to go home. They were about a mile from Mr. Filley's and as there was a pretty good foot trail over which they had come, the young woman took the boy to it, and turning him toward home told him to follow it carefully and he would soon see his mother. She then filled her pail with berries, went on to her own home, and remained there till nearly sundown, when she set out to return to Mr. Filley's, reaching there yet in the early twilight. Not seeing Willie, she inqired for him and was told that he had not returned, and that they supposed he was safe with her. She then hastily related how it happened that he had started back toward home, and that she supposed he had safely arrived.

Mr. Filley then started back on the trail, keeping close watch on each side of the way, for he expected he would soon come across Master Willie fast asleep. He called his name every few rods, but got no answer nor could he discover him, and so returned home again, still calling and searching, but no boy was discovered. Then he built a large fire and put lighted candles in all the windows, then took his lantern and went out in the woods calling and looking for the boy. Sometimes he thought he heard him, but on going where the sound came from nothing could be found. So he looked and called all night, along the trail and all about the woods, with no success. Mr. Mount's home was situated not far from the shore of Fitch's Lake, and the trail went along the margin, and in some places the ground was quite a boggy marsh, and the trail had been fixed up to make it passably good walking.

Next day the neighbors were notified, and asked to assist, and although they were in the midst of wheat harvest, a great many laid down the cradle and rake and went out to help search. On the third day the whole county became excited and quite an army of earchers turned out ,coming from the whole country miles around.

Mr. Filley was much excited and quite worn out and

beside himself with fatigue and loss of sleep. He could not eat. Yielding to entreaty he would sit at the table, and suddenly rise up, saying he heard Willie calling, and go out to search for the supposed voice, but it was all fruitless, and the whole people were sorry indeed for the poor father and mother.

The people then formed a plan for a thorough search. They were to form in a line so near each other that they could touch hands and were to march thus turning out for nothing except inpassable lakes, and thus we marched, fairly sweeping the county in search of a sign. I was with this party and we marched south and kept close watch for a bit of clothing, a foot print or even bones, or anything which would indicate that he had been destroyed by some wild animal. Thus we marched all day with no success, and the next went north in the same careful manner, but with no better result. Most of the people now abandoned the search, but some of the neighbors kept it up for a long time.

Some expressed themselves quite strongly that Miss Mount knew where the boy was, saying that she might have had some trouble with him and in seeking to correct him had accidentally killed him and then hidden the body away—perhaps in the deep mire of the swamp or in the muddy waters on the margin of the lake. Search was made with this idea foremost, but nothing was discovered. Rain now set in, and the grain, from neglect grew in the head as it stood, and many a settler ate poor bread all winter in consequence of his neighborly kindness in the midst of harvest. The bread would not rise, and to make it into pancakes was the best way it could be used.

Still no tidings ever came of the lost boy. Many things were whispered, about Mr. Mount's dishonesty of character and there were many suspicions about him, but no real facts could be shown to account for the boy. The neighbors said he never worked like the rest of them, and that his patch of cultivated land was altogether too small to support his family, a wife and two daughters, grown. He was a very smooth and affable talker, and had lots of acquaintances. A few years afterwards Mr. Mount was convicted of a crime which sent him to the Jackson State Prison, where he died before his term expired. I visited the Filley family in 1870, and from them heard the facts anew and that no trace of the lost boy had ever been discovered.

CHAPTER V.

THE second year of sickness and I was affected with the rest, though it was not generally so bad as the first year. I suffered a great deal and felt so miserable that I began to think I had rather live on the top of the Rocky Mountains and catch chipmuncks for a living than to live here and be sick, and I began to have very serious thoughts of trying some other country. In the winter of 1839 and 1840 I went to a neigboring school for three months, where I studied reading, writing and spelling, getting as far as Rule of Three in Daboll's arithmetic. When school was out I chopped and split rails for Wm. Hanna till I had paid my winter's board. After this, myself and a young man named Orrin Henry, with whom I had become acquainted, worked awhile scoring timber to be used in building the Michigan Central Railroad which had just then begun to be built. They laid down the ties first (sometimes a mudsill under them) and then put down four by eight wooden rails with a strips of band iron half an inch thick spiked on top. I scored the timber and Henry used the broad axe after me. It was pretty hard work and the hours as long as we could see, our wages being $13 per month, half cash.

In thinking over our prospect it seemed more and more as if I had better look out for my own fortune in some other place. The farm was pretty small for all of us. There were three brothers younger than I, and only 200 acres in the whole, and as they were growing up to be men it seemed as if it would be best for me, the oldest, to start out first and see what could be done to make my own living. I talked to father and mother about my plans, and they did not seriously object, but gave me some good advice, which I remember to this day—"Weigh well every thing you do;

shun bad company; be honest and deal fair; be truthful and never fear when you know you are right.''
But, said he, "Our little peach trees will bear this
year, and if you go away you must come back and
help us eat them; they will be the first we ever raised
or ever saw.'' I could not promise.

Henry and I drew our pay for our work. I had five
dollars in cash and the rest in pay from the company's
store. We purchased three nice whitewood boards,
eighteen inches wide, from which we made us a boat
and a good sized chest which we filled with provisions
and some clothing and quilts. This, with our guns
and ammunition, composed the cargo of our boat.
When all was ready, we put the boat on a wagon and
were to haul it to the river some eight miles away
for embarkation. After getting the wagon loaded,
father said to me;—"Now my son, you are starting
out in life alone, no one to watch or look after you.
You will have to depend upon yourself in all things.
You have a wide, wide world to operate in—you will
meet all kinds of people and you must not expect to
find them all honest or true friends. You are limited
in money, and all I can do for you in that way is to
let you have what ready money I have.'' He handed
me three dollars as he spoke, which added to my own
gave me seven dollars as my money capital with which
to start out into the world among perfect strangers,
and no acquaintances in prospect on our Western
course.

When ready to start, mother and sister Polly came
out to see us off and to give us their best wishes, hoping we would have good health, and find pleasant
paths to follow. Mother said to me:—"You must be
a good boy, honest and law-abiding. Remember our
advice, and honor us for we have striven to make you
a good and honest man, and you must follow our

teachings, and your conscience will be clear. Do nothing to be ashamed of; be industrious, and you have no fear of punishment." We were given a great many "Good byes" and "God bless you's" as with hands, hats and handkerchiefs they waved us off as far as we could see them. In the course of an hour or so we were at the water's edge, and on a beautiful morning in early spring of 1840 we found ourselves floating down the Grand River below Jackson.

The stream ran west, that we knew, and it was west we thought we wanted to go, so all things suited us. The stream was small with tall timber on both sides, and so many trees had fallen into the river that our navigation was at times seriously obstructed. When night came we hauled our boat on shore, turned it partly over, so as to shelter us, built a fire in front, and made a bed on a loose board which we carried in the bottom of the boat. We talked till pretty late and then lay down to sleep, but for my part my eyes would not stay shut, and I lay till break of day and the little birds began to sing faintly.

I thought of many things that night which seemed so long. I had left a good dear home, where I had good warm meals and a soft and comfortable bed. Here I had reposed on a board with a very hard pillow and none too many blankets, and I turned from side to side on my hard bed, to which I had gone with all my clothes on. It seemed the beginning of another chapter in my pioneer life and a rather tough experience. I arose, kindled a big fire and sat looking at the glowing coals in still further meditation.

Neither of us felt very gleeful as we got our breakfast and made an early start down the river again. Neither of us talked very much, and no doubt my companion had similar thoughts to mine, and wondered what was before us. But I think that as a pair we were at that moment pretty lonesome. Henry had rested better than I but probably felt no less keenly the separation from our homes and friends. We saw plenty of squirrels and pigeons on the trees which overhung the river, and we shot and picked up as many as we thought we could use for food. When we fired our guns the echoes rolled up and down the river for miles making the feeling of loneliness still more keen, as the sound died faintly away. We floated along generally very quietly. We could see the fish dart under our boat from their feeding places along the bank, and now and then some tall crane would spread his broad wings to get out of our way.

We saw no houses for several days, and seldom went on shore. The forest was all hard wood, such as oak, ash, walnut, maple, elm and beech. Farther down we occasionally passed the house of some pioneer hunter or trapper, with a small patch cleared' At one of these a big green boy came down to the bank to see who we were. We said "How d'you do," to him, and, getting no response, Henry asked him how far is was to Michigan, at which a look of supreme disgust came over his features as he replied—"'Taint no far at all."

The stream grew wider as we advanced along its downward course, for smaller streams came pouring in to swell its tide. The banks were still covered with heavy timber. and in some places with quite thick undergrowth. One day we saw a black bear in the river washing himself, but he went ashore before we were near enough to get a sure shot at him. Many deer tracks were seen along the shore, but as we saw very few of the animals themselves, they were probably night visitors.

One day we overtook some canoes containing Indians, men, women and children. They were poling

their craft around in all directions spearing fish.
They caught many large mullet and then went on
shore and made camp, and the red ladies began scaling
the fish. As soon as their lords and masters had unloaded the canoes, a party started out with four of the
boats, two men in a boat, to try their luck again.
They ranged all abreast, and moved slowly down the
stream in the still deep water, continually beating the
surface with their spear handles, till they came
to a place so shallow that they could see the bottom easily, when they suddenly turned the canoes
head up stream, and while one held the craft steady by
sticking his spear handle down on the bottom, the
other stood erect, with a foot on either gunwale so he
could see whatever came down on either side. Soon
the big fish would try to pass, but Mr. Indian had too
sharp an eye to let him escape unobserved, and when
he came within his reach he would turn his spear and
throw it like a dart, seldom missing his aim. The
poor fish would struggle desperately, but soon came to
the surface, when he would be drawn in and knocked
in the head with a tomahawk to quiet him, when the
spear was cut out and the process repeated. We
watched them about an hour, and during that time
some one of the boats was continually hauling in a fish.
They were sturgeon and very large. This was the first
time we had ever seen the Indian's way of catching fish
and it was a new way of getting grub for us. When
the canoes had full loads they paddled up toward their
camp, and we drifted on again.

When we came to Grand Rapids we had to go on
shore and tow our boat carefully along over the many
rocks to prevent accident. Here was a small cheap
looking town. On the west bank of the river a water
wheel was driving a drill boring for salt water, it
seemed through solid rock. Up to this time the cur-

rent was slow, and its course through a dense forest.
We occasionally saw an Indian gliding around in his
canoe, but no houses or clearings. Occasionally we
saw some pine logs which had been floated down some
of the streams of the north. One of these small rivers
they called the "Looking-glass," and seemed to be
the largest of them.

Passing on we began to see some pine timber, and
realized that we were near the mouth of the river
where it emptied into Lake Michigan. There were
some steam saw mills here, not then in operation, and
some houses for the mill hands to live in when they
were at work. This prospective city was called Grand
Haven. There was one schooner in the river loaded
with lumber, ready to sail for the west side of the lake
as soon as the wind should change and become favorable, and we engaged passage for a dollar and a half each.
While waiting for the wind we visited the woods in
search of game, but found none. All the surface of
the soil was clear lake sand, and some quite large pine
and hemlock trees were half buried in it. We were
not pleased with this place for it looked as if folks
must get their grub from somewhere else or live on
fish.

Next morning we were off early, as the wind had
changed, but the lake was very rough and a heavy
choppy sea was running. Before we were half way
across the lake nearly all were sea-sick, passengers and
sailors. The poor fellow at the helm stuck to his post
casting up his accounts at the same time, putting on
an air of terrible misery.

This, I thought was pretty hard usage for a land-
lubber like myself who had never been on such rough
water before. The effect of this sea-sickness was to
cure me of a slight fever and ague, and in fact the cure
was so thorough that I have never had it since. As

we neared the western shore a few houses could be seen, and the captain said it was Southport. As there was no wharf our schooner put out into the lake again for an hour or so and then ran back again, lying off and on in this manner all night. In the morning it was quite calm and we went on shore in the schooner's yawl, landing on a sandy beach. We left our chest of clothes and other things in a warehouse and shouldered our packs and guns for a march across what seemed an endless prairie stretching to the west. We had spent all our lives thus far in a country where all the clearing had to be made with an axe, and such a broad field was to us an entirely new feature. We laid our course westward and tramped on. The houses were very far apart, and we tried at everv one of them for a chance to work, but could get none, not even if we would work for our board. The people all seemed to be new settlers, and very poor, compelled to do their own work until a better day could be reached. The coarse meals we got were very reasonable, generally only ten cents, but sometimes a little more.

As we travelled westward the praries seemed smaller with now and then some oak openings between. Some of the farms seemed to be three or four years old, and what had been laid out as towns consisted of from three to six houses, small and cheap, with plenty of vacant lots. The soil looked rich, as though it might be very productive. We passed several small lakes that had nice fish in them, and plenty of ducks on the surface.

Walking began to get pretty tiresome. Great blisters would come on our feet, and, tender as they were, it was a great relief to take off our boots and go barefoot for a while when the ground was favorable. We crossed a wide prairie and came down to the Rock river where there were a few houses on the east side

but no signs of habitation on the west bank. We
crossed the river in a canoe and then walked seven
miles before we came to a house where we staid all
night and inquired for work. None was to be had
and so we tramped on again. The next day we met
a real live Yankee with a one-horse wagon, peddling
tin ware in regular Eastern style. We inquired of
him about the road and prospects, and he gave us an
encouraging idea—said all was good. He told us
where to stop the next night at a small town called
Sugar Creek. It had but a few houses and was being
built up as a mining town, for some lead ore had been
found there. There were as many Irish as English
miners here, a rough class of people. We put up at
the house where we had been directed, a low log
cabin, rough and dirty, kept by Bridget & Co. Supper was had after dark and the light on the table was
just the right one for the place, a saucer of grease,
with a rag in it lighted and burning at the edge of the
saucer. It at least served to made the darkness apparent and to prevent the dirt being visible. We had
potatoes, beans and tea, and probably dirt too, if we
could have seen it. When the meal was nearly done
Bridget brought in and deposited on each plate a good
thick pancake as a dessert. It smelled pretty good,
but when I drew my knife across it to cut it in two,
all the center was uncooked batter, which ran out
upon my plate, and spoiled my supper.

We went to bed and soon found it had other occupants beside ourselves, which, if they were small were
lively and spoiled our sleeping. We left before breakfast, and a few miles out on the prairie we came to a
house occupied by a woman and one child, and we
were told we could have breakfast if we could wait to
have it cooked. Everything looked cheap but cheery,
and after waiting a little while outside we were called

in to eat. The meal consisted of corn bread, bacon, potatoes and coffee. It was well cooked and looked better than things did at Bridget's. I enjoyed all but the coffee, which had a rich brown color, but when I sipped it there was such a bitter taste I surely thought there must be quinine in it, and it made me shiver. I tried two or three times to drink but it was too much for me and I left it. We shouldered our loads and went on again. I asked Henry what kind of a drink it was. "Coffee," said he, but I had never seen any that tasted like that and never knew my father to buy any such coffee as that.

We labored along and in time came to another small place called Hamilton's Diggings where some lead mines were being worked. We stopped at a long, iow log house with a porch the entire length, and called for bread and milk, which was soon set before us. The lady was washing and the man was playing with a child on the porch. The little thing was trying to walk, the man would swear terribly at it—not in an angrv way, but in a sort of careless, blasphemous style that was terribly shocking. I thought of the child being reared in the midst of such bad language and reflected on the kind of people we were meeting In this far away place. They seemed more wicked and profane the farther west we walked. I had always lived in a more moral and temperate atmosphere, and I was learning more of some things in the world than I had ever known before. I had little to say and much to see and listen to and my early precepts were not forgotten. No work was to be had here and we set out across the prairie toward Mineral Point, twenty miles away. When within four miles of that place we stopped at the house of Daniel Parkinson, a fine looking two-story building, and after the meal was over Mr. Henry hired out to him for $16 per

month, and went to work that day. I heard of a job
of cutting cordwood six miles away and went after it,
for our money was getting very scarce, but when I
reached the place I found a man had been there half
an hour before and secured the job. The proprietor,
Mr. Crow, gave me my dinner which I accepted with
many thanks, for it saved my coin to pay for the next
meal. I now went to Mineral Point, and searched
the town over for work. My purse contained thirty-
five cents only and I slept in an unoccupied out house
without supper. I bought crackers and dried beef for
ten cents in the morning and made my first meal since
the day before, felt pretty low-spirited. I then went
to Vivian's smelting furnace where they bought lead
ore, smelted it, and run it into pigs of about 70 pounds
each. He said he had a job for me if I could do it
The furnace was propelled by water and they had a
small buzz saw for cutting four-foot wood into blocks
about a foot long. These blocks they wanted split up
in pieces about an inch square to mix in with charcoal in smelting ore. He said he would board me
with the other men, and give me a dollar and a quarter a cord for splitting the wood. I felt awfully poor,
and a stranger, and this was a beginning for me at
any rate, so I went to work with a will and never lost
a minute of daylight till I had split up all the wood and
filled his woodhouse completely up. The board was
very coarse—bacon, potatoes, and bread—a man cook,
and bread mixed up with salt and water. The old log
house where we lodged was well infested with troublesome insects which worked nights at any rate,
whether they rested days or not, and the beds had a
mild odor of pole-cat. The house was long, low and
without windows. In one end was a fireplace, and
there were two tiers of bunks on each side, supplied
with straw only. In the space between the bunks was

a stationary table, with stools for seats. I was the only American who boarded there and I could not well become very familiar with the boarders.

The country was rolling, and there were many beautiful brooks and clear springs of water, with ferile soil. The Cornish miners were in the majority and governed the locality politically. My health was excellent, and so long as I had my gun and ammunition I could kill game enough to live on, for prairie chickens and deer could be easily killed, and meat alone would sustain life, so I had no special fears of starvattion. I was now paid off, and went back to see m companion, Mr. Henry. I did not hear of any more work, so I concluded I would start back toward my old home in Michigan, and shouldered my bundle and gun, turning my face eastward for a long tramp across the prairie. I knew I had a long tramp before me, but I thought best to head that way, for my capital was only ten dollars, and I might be compelled to walk the whole distance. I walked till about noon and then sat down in the shade of a tree to rest for this was June and pretty warm. I was now alone in a big territory, thinly settled, and thought of my father's home, the well set table, all happy and well fed at any rate, and here was my venture, a sort of forlorn hope. Prospects were surely very gloomy for me here away out west in Wisconsin Territory, without a relative, friend or acquaintance to call upon, and very small means to travel two hundred and fifty miles of lonely road—perhaps all the way on foot. There were no laborers required, hardly any money in sight, and no chance for business. I knew it would be a safe course to proceed toward home, for I had no fear of starving, the weather was warm and I could easily walk home long before winter should come again. Still the outlook was not very pleasing to one in my circumstances.

I chose a route which led me some distance north of the one we travelled when we came west, but it was about the same. Every house was a new settler, and hardly one who had yet produced anything to live upon. In due time I came to the Rock River, and the only house in sight was upon the east bank. I could see a boat over there and so I called for it, and a young girl came over with a canoe for me. I took a paddle and helped her hold the boat against the current, and we made the landing safely. I paid her ten cents for ferriage and went on again. The country was now level, with burr-oak openings. Near sundown I came to a small prairie of about 500 acres surrounded by scattering burr-oak timber, with not a hill in sight, and it seemed to me to be the most beautiful spot on earth. This I found to belong to a man named Meachem, who had an octagon concrete house built on one side of the opening. The house had a hollow column in the center, and the roof was so constructed that all the rain water went down this central column into a cistern below for house use. The stairs wound around this central column, and the whole affair was quite different from the most of settlers' houses. I staid here all night, had supper and breakfast, and paid my bill of thirty-five cents. He had no work for me so I went on again. I crossed Heart Prairie, passed through a strip of woods, and out at Round Prairie. It was level as a floor with a slight rise in one corner, and on it were five or six settlers. Here fortune favored me, for here I found a man whom I knew, who once lived in Michigan, and was one of our neighbors there for some time. His name was Nelson Cornish. I rested here a few days, and made a bargain to work for him two or three days every week for my board as long as I wished to stay. As I

got acquainted I found some work to do and many of
my leisure hours I spent in the woods with my
gun, killing some deer, some of the meat of which I
sold. In haying and harvest I got some work at fifty
cents to one dollar per day, and as I had no clothes to
buy, I spent no money, saving up about fifty dollars
by fall. I then got a letter from Henry saying that I
could get work with him for the winter and I thought
I would go back there again.

Before thinking of going west again I had to go to
Southport on the lake and get our clothes we had left
in our box when we passed in the spring. So I
started one morning at break of day , with a long cane
in each hand to help me along, for I had nothing to
carry, not even wearing a coat. This was a new road,
thinly settled, and a few log houses building. I got a
bowl of bread and milk at noon and then hurried on
again. The last twenty miles was clear prairie, and
houses were very far apart, but little more thickly settled as I neared Lake Michigan. I arrived at the
town just after dark, and went to a tavern and inquired about the things. I was told that the warehouse had been broken into and robbed, and the proprietor had fled for parts unknown. This robbed me
of all my good clothes, amd I could now go back as
lightly loaded as when I came. I found I had walked
sixty miles in that one day, and also found myself very
stiff and sore so that I did not start back next day,
and I took three days for the return trip—a very un-
profitable journey.

I was now ready to go west, and coming across a
pet deer which I had tamed, I knew if I left it it
would wander away with the first wild ones that came
along, and so I killed it and made my friends a present of some venison- I chose still a new route this
time, that I could see all that was possible of this big

territory when I could do it so easily. I was always a great admirer of Nature and things which remained as they were created, and to the extent of my observation, I thought this the most beautiful and perfect country I had seen between Vermont and the Mississippi River. The country was nearly level, the land rich, the prairies small with oak openings surrounding them, very little marsh land and streams of clear water. Rock River was the largest of these, running south. Next west was Sugar River, then the Picatonica. Through the mining region the country was rolling and abundantly watered with babbling brooks and health-giving springs.

In point of health it seemed to me to be far better than Michigan. In Mr. Henry's letter to me he had said that he had taken a timber claim in "Kentuck Grove," and had all the four-foot wood engaged to cut at thirty-seven cents a cord. He said we could board ourselves and save a little money and that in the spring he would go back to Michigan with me. This had decided me to go back to Mineral Point. I stopped a week or two with a man named Webb, hunting with him, and sold game enough to bring me in some six or seven dollars, and then resumed my journey.

On my way I found a log house ten miles from a neighbor just before I got to the Picatonica Piver. It belonged to a Mr. Shook who, with his wife and three children, lived on the edge of a small prairie, and had a good crop of corn. He invited me to stay with him a few days, and as I was tired I accepted his offer and we went out together and brought in a deer. We had plenty of corn bread, venison and coffee, and lived well. After a few days he wanted to kill a steer and he led it to a proper place while I shot it in the head. We had no way to hang it up so he rolled the intestines out, and I sat down with my side against the steer and helped him to pull the tallow off.

It was now getting nearly dark and while he was splitting the back bone with an axe, it slipped in his greasy hands and glancing, cut a gash in my leg six inches above the knee. I was now laid up for two or three weeks, but was well cared for at his house. Before I could resume my journey snow had fallen to the depth of about six inches, which made it rather unpleasant walking, but in a few days I reached Mr. Henry's camp in "Kentuck Grove," when after comparing notes, we both began swinging our axes and piling up cordwood, cooking potatoes, bread, bacon, coffee and flapjacks ourselves, which we enjoyed with a relish.

I now went to work for Peter Parkinson, who paid me thirteen dollars per month, and I remained with him till spring. While with him a very sad affliction came to him in the loss of his wife. He was presented by her with his first heir, and during her illness she was cared for by her mother, Mrs. Cullany, who had come to live with them during the winter. When the little babe was two or three weeks old the mother was feeling in such good spirits that she was left alone a little while, as Mrs. Cullany was attending to some duties which called her elsewhere. When she returned she was surprised to see that both Mrs. Parkinson and the babe were gone. Everyone turned out to search for her. I ran to the smoke house, the barn, the stable in quick order, and not finding her a search was made for tracks, and we soon discovered that she had passed over a few steps leading over a fence and down an incline toward the spring house, and there fallen, face downward, on the floor of the house which was covered only a few inches deep with water lay the unfortunate woman and her child, both dead. This was doubly distressing to Mr. Parkinson and saddened the whole community. Both were buried in one grave, not far from the house, and a more impressive funeral I never beheld.

I now worked awhile again with Mr. Henry and we sold our wood to Bill Park, a collier, who made and sold charcoal to the smelters of lead ore. When the ice was gone in the streams, Henry and I shouldered our guns and bundles, and made our way to Milwaukee, where we arrived in the course of a few days. The town was small and cheaply built, and had no wharf, so that when the steamboat came we had to go out to it in a small boat. The stream which came in here was too shallow for the steamer to enter. When near the lower end of the lake we stopped at an island to take on food and several cords of white birch wood. The next stopping place was at Michilamackanac, afterward called Mackinaw. Here was a short wharf, and a little way back a hill, which seemed to me to be a thousand feet high, on which a fort had been built. On the wharf was a mixed lot of people—Americans, Canadians, Irish, Indians, squaws and pappooses. I saw there some of the most beautiful fish I had ever seen. They would weigh twenty pounds or more, and had bright red and yellow spots all over them. They called them trout, and they were beauties, really. At the shore near by the Indians were loading a large white birch bark canoe, putting their luggage along the middle lengthways, and the pappooses on top. One man took a stern seat to steer, and four or five more had seats along the gunwale as paddlers and, as they moved away, their strokes were as even and regular as the motions of an engine, and their crafts danced as lightly on the water as an egg shell. They were starting for the Michigan shore some eight or ten miles away. This was the first birch bark canoe I had ever seen and was a great curiosity in my eyes.

We crossed Lake Huron during the night, and through its outlet, so shallow that the wheels stirred up the mud from the bottom; then through Lake St. Clair and landed safely at Detroit next day. Here we took the cars on the Michigan Central Railroad, and on our way westward stopped at the very place where we had worked, helping to build the road, a year or more before. After getting off the train a walk of two and one half miles brought me to my father's house, where I had a right royal welcome, and the questions they asked me about the wild country I had traveled over, how it looked, and how I got along— were numbered by the thousand.

I remained at home until fall, getting some work to do by which I saved some money, but in August was attacked with bilious fever, which held me down for several weeks, but nursed by a tender and loving mother with untiring care, I recovered, quite slowly, but surely. I felt that I had been close to death, and that this country was not to be compared to Wisconsin with its clear and bubbling springs of health-giving water. Feeling thus, I determined to go back there again.

CHAPTER VI.

WITH the idea of returning to Wisconsin I made plans for my movements. I purchased a good outfit of steel traps of several kinds and sizes, thirty or forty in all, made me a pine chest, with a false bottom to separate the traps from my clothing when it was packed in traveling order, the clothes at the top. My former experience had taught me not to expect to get work there during winter, but I was pretty sure something could be earned by trapping and hunting at this season, and in summer I was pretty sure of something to do. I had about forty dollars to travel on this time, and quite a stock of experience. The second parting from home was not so hard as the first one. I went to Huron, took the steamer to Chicago, then a small, cheaply built town, with rough sidewalks and terribly muddy streets, and the people seemed pretty rough, for sailors and lake captains were numerous, and knock downs quite frequent. The country for a long way west of town seemed a low, wet marsh or prairie.

Finding a man going west with a wagon and two horses without a load, I hired him to take me and my baggage to my friend Nelson Cornish, at Round Prairie. They were glad to see me, and as I had not yet got strong from my fever, they persuaded me to stay a while with them and take some medicine, for he was a sort of a doctor. I think he must have given me a dose of calomel, for I had a terribly sore mouth and could not eat any for two or three weeks. As soon as I was able to travel I had myself and chest taken to the stage station on the line for the lake to Mineral Point. I think this place was called Geneva. On the

tage I got along pretty fast, and part of the time on a
new road. The first place of note was Madison the
capital of the territory, situated on a block of land
nearly surrounded by four lakes, all plainly seen from
the big house. Further on at the Blue Mounds I left
the stage, putting my chest in the landlord's keeping
till I should come or send for it.

I walked about ten miles to the house of a friend
named A. Bennett, who was a hunter and lived on the
bank of the Picatonica River with his wife and two
children. I had to take many a rest on the way, for I
was very weak.

Resting the first few days, Mrs. Bennett's father,
Mr. J. P. Dilly, took us out about six miles and left
us to hunt and camp for a few days. We were quite
successful, and killed five nice, fat deer, which we
dressed and took to Mineral Point, selling them
rapidly to the Cornish miners for twenty-five cents a
quarter for the meat. We followed this business till
about January first, when the game began to get poor,
when we hung up our guns for a while. I had a little money left yet. The only money in circulation
was American silver and British sovereigns. They
would not sell lead ore for paper money nor on credit.
During the spring I used my traps successfully, so
that I saved something over board and expenses.

In summer I worked in the mines with Edwin Buck
of Bucksport, Maine, but only found lead ore enough
to pay our expenses in getting it. Next winter I
chopped wood for thirty-five cents per cord and
boarded myself. This was poor business; poorer than
hunting. In summer I found work at various things,
but in the fall Mr. Buck and myself concluded that as
we were both hunters and trappers, we would go
northward toward Lake Superior on a hunting expedition, and, perhaps remain all winter. We replenished

our outfit, and engaged Mr. Bennett to take us well
up into the north country. We crossed the Wisconsin
River near Muscoda, went then to Prairie du Chien,
where we found a large stone fur trading house, owned
by Mr. Brisbois, a Frenchman, from whom we obtained some information of the country further on. He
assured us there was no danger from the Indians if we
let them alone and treated them fairly.

We bought fifty pounds of flour for each of us, and
then started up the divide between the Wisconsin and
Mississippi Rivers. On one side flowed the Bad River,
and on the other the Kickapoo. We traveled on this
divide about three days, when Mr, Bennett became
afraid to go any further, as he had to return alone and
the Indians might capture him before he could get
back to the settlement. We camped early one night
and went out hunting to get some game for him. I
killed a large, black bear and Mr. Bennett took what
he wanted of it, including the skin, and started back
next morning.

We now cachéd our things in various places, scattering them well. Some went in hollow logs, and
some under heaps of brush or other places, where
the Indians could not find them. We then built a
small cabin about six by eight feet in size and four feet
high, in shape like a Λ. We were not thoroughly
pleased with this location and started out to explore
the country to the north of us, for we had an idea that
it would be better hunting there.

The first day we started north we killed a bear, and
filled our stomachs with the fat, sweet meat. The
next night we killed another bear after a little struggling. The dog made him climb a tree and we shot
at him; he would fall to the ground as if dead, but
would be on his feet again in an instant, when, after
the dog had fastened to his ham, he would climb the

tree again. In the third trial he lay in the fork and had a good chance to look square at his tormenter. I shot him in the head, and as he lay perfectly still, Buck said:—"Now you have done it—we can't get him." But in a moment he began to struggle, and soon came down, lifeless.

Here we camped on the edge of the pine forest, ate all the fat bear meat we could, and in the morning took separate routes, agreeing to meet again a mile or so farther up a small brook. I soon saw a small bear walking on a log and shot him dead. His mate got away, but I set my dog on him and he soon had to climb a tree. When I came up to where the dog was barking I saw Mr. Bear and fired a ball in him that brought him down. Just then I heard Mr. Buck shoot close by, and I went to him and found he had killed another and larger bear. We stayed here another night, dressed our game and sunk the meat in the brook and fastened it down, thinking we might want to get some of it another time.

We were so well pleased with this hunting ground that we took the bear skins and went back to camp. When we got there our clothes were pretty well saturated with bear's oil, and we jokingly said it must have soaked through our bodies, we had eaten so much bear meat. I began to feel quite sick, and had a bad headache. I felt as if something must be done, but we had no medicine. Mr. Buck went down by the creek and dug some roots he called Indian Physic, then steeped them until the infusion seemed as black as molasses, and, when cool told me to take a swallow every fifteen minutes for an hour, then half as much for another hour as long as I could keep it down. I followed directions and vomited freely and for a long time, but felt better afterward, and soon got well. It reminded me some of the feelings I had when I was seasick on

Lake Michigan.

It may be interesting to describe how we were dressed to enter on this winter campaign. We wore mocassins of our own make. I had a buckskin jumper, and leggins that came up to my hips. On my head a drab hat that fitted close and had a rim about two inches wide. In fair weather I went bare-headed, Indian fashion. I carried a tomahawk which I had made. The blade was two inches wide and three inches long—the poll two inches long and about as large round as a dime; handle eighteen or twenty inches long with a knob on the end so it would not easily slip from the hand. Oiled patches for our rifle balls on a string, a firing wire, a charger to measure the powder, and a small piece of leather with four nipples on it for caps—all on my breast, so that I could load very rapidly. My bed was a comfort I made myself, a little larger than usual. I lay down on one side of the bed and with my gun close to me, turned the blanket over me. When out of camp I never left my gun out of my reach. We had to be real Indians in custom and actions in order to be considered their equals. We got our food in the same way they did, and so they had nothing to ask us for. They considered themselves the real kings of the forest.

We now determined to move camp, which proved quite a job as we had to pack everything on our backs; which we did for ten or fifteen miles to the bank of a small stream where there were three pine trees, the only ones to be found in many miles. We made us a canoe of one of them. While we were making the canoe three Indians came along, and after they had eaten some of our good venison, they left us. These were the first we had seen, and we began to be more cautious and keep everything well hid away from camp and make them think we were as poor as they were, so they might not be tempted to molest us.

We soon had the canoe done and loaded, and embarked on the brook down stream. We found it rather difficult work, but the stream grew larger and we got along very well. We came to one place where otter signs seemed fresh, and stopped to set a trap for them. Our dog sat on the bank and watched the operation, and when we started on we could not get him to ride or follow. Soon we heard him cry and went back to find he had the trap on his fore foot. To get it off we had to put a forked stick over his neck and hold him down, he was so excited over his mishap. When he was released he left at full speed and was never seen by us after.

When we got well into the pine woods we camped and cachéd our traps and provisions on an island, and made our camp further down the stream and some little distance from the shore. We soon found this was very near a logging camp, and as no one had been living there for a year, we moved camp down there and occupied one of the empty cabins. We began to set dead-fall traps in long lines in many different directions, blazing the trees so we could find them if the snow came on. West of this about ten miles, where we had killed some deer earlier, we made a Λ-shaped cabin and made dead falls many miles around to catch fishes, foxes, mink and raccoons. We made weekly journeys to the places and generally staid about two nights.

One day when going over my trap lines I came to a trap which I had set where I had killed a deer, and saw by the snow that an eagle had been caught in the trap and had broken the chain and gone away. I followed on the trail he made and soon found him. He tried to fly but the trap was too heavy, and he could only go slowly and a little way. I fired and put a ball

in him and he fell and rolled under a large log on the
hillside. As I took the trap off I saw an Indian coming down the hill and brought my gun to bear on him.
He stopped suddenly and made signs not to shoot, and
I let him come up. He made signs that he wanted
the feathers of the bird which I told him to take, and
then he wanted to know where we slept. I pointed
out the way and made him go ahead of me there, for I
did not want him behind me. At camp he made signs
for something to eat, but when I showed him meat he
shook his head. However he took a leg of deer and
started on, I following at a good distance till satisfied
that he would not come back.

We had not taken pains to keep track of the day of
the week or month; the rising and setting of the sun
and the changes of the moon were all the almanacs we
had. Then snow came about a foot deep, and some days
were so cold we could not leave our camp fire at all.
As no Indians appeared we were quite successful and
kept our bundle of furs in a hollow standing tree some
distance from camp, and when we went that way we
never stopped or left any sign that we had a deposit
there.

Some time after it was all frozen up solid, some
men with two yoke of oxen came up to cut and put
logs in the river to raft down when the ice went out.
With them came a shingle weaver, with a pony and a
small sled, and some Indians also. We now had to take
up all of our steel traps, and rob all our dead-falls and
quit business generally—even then they got some of
our traps before we could get them gathered in. We
were now comparatively idle.

Until these loggers came we did not know exactly
where we were situated, but they told us we were on
the Lemonai river, a branch of the Wisconsin, and
that we could get out by going west till we found the

Mississippi river and then home. We hired the shəngle man with his pony to take us to Black River, further north which we reached in three days, and found a saw mill there in charge of a keeper. Up the river farther we found another mill looked after by Sam Ferguson. Both mills were frozen up. The Indians had been here all winter. They come from Lake Superior when the swamps froze up there, to hunt deer, till the weather gets warm, then they returned to the Lake to fish,

Of course the presence of the Indians made game scarce, but the mill men told us if we would go up farther into the marten country they thought we would do well. We therefore made us a hand sled, put some provisions and traps on board, and started up the river on the ice. As we went the snow grew deeper and we had to cut hemlock boughs for a bed on top of the snow. It took about a half a cord of wood to last us all night, and it was a trouble to cut holes in the ice to water, for it was more than two feet thick. Our fire kindled on the snow, would be two or three feet below on the ground, by morning. This country was heavily timbered with cedar, or spruce and apparently very level.

One day we saw two otters coming toward us on the ice. We shot one, but as the other gun missed fire, the other one escaped, for I could not overtake it in the woods. We kept on up the river till we began to hear the Indians' guns, and then we camped and did not fire a gun for two days, for we were afraid we might be discovered and robbed, and we knew we could not stay long after our grub was gone. All the game we could catch was the marten or sable, which the Indians called *Waubusash*. The males were snuff color and the female much darker. Mink were scarce, and the beaver, living in the river bank, could not be got at till the ice went out in the spring.

We now began to make marten traps or dead-falls, and set them for this small game. There were many cedar and tamarack swamps, indeed that was the principal feature, but there were some ridges a little higher where some small pines and beech grew. Now our camp was one place where there was no large timber caused by the stream being dammed by the beaver. Here were some of the real Russian Balsam trees, the most beautiful in shape I had ever seen. They were very dark green, the boughs very thick, and the tree in shape like an inverted top. Our lines of trips led for miles in every direction marked by blazed trees. We made a trap of two poles, and chips which we split from the trees. These were set in the snow and covered with brush, We sometimes found a porcupine in the top of a pine tree. The only signs of his presence were the chips he made in gnawing the bark for food. They never came down to the ground as we saw. They were about all the game that was good to eat. I would kill one, skin it and drag the carcass after me all day as I set traps, cutting off bits for bait, and cooking the rest for ourselves to eat. We tried to eat the marten but it was pretty musky and it was only by putting on plenty of salt and pepper that we managed to eat them. We were really forced to do it if we remained here. We secured a good many of these little fellows which have about the the best fur that is found in America.

We were here about three weeks, and our provisions giving out and the ice becoming tender in the swamp were two pretty strong reasons for our getting out, so we shouldered our packs of fur and our guns and, getting our course from a pocket-compass, we started out. As we pushed on we came to some old windfalls that were troublesome to get through. The dense timber seemed to be six feet deep, and we would sometimes climb over and sometimes crawl under, the fallen trees were so thickly mixed and tangled.

Mr. Buck got so completely tired that he threw away his traps. We reached our starting place at O'Neil's saw-mill after many days of the hardest work, and nearly starved, for we had seen no game on our trip. We found our traps and furs all safe here and as this stream was one of the tributaries of the Mississippi, we decided to make us a boat and float down toward that noted stream, We secured four good boards and built the boat in which we started down the river setting traps and moving at our leisure. We found plenty of fine ducks, two bee trees, and caught some cat-fish with a hook and line we got at the mill. We also caught some otter, and, on a little branch of the river killed two bears, the skin of one of them weighing five pounds. We met a keel boat being poled up the river, and with the last cent of money we possessed bought a little flour of them.

About the first of May we reached Prairie du Chien. Here we were met with some surprise, for Mr. Brisbois said he had heard we were killed or lost. He showed us through his warehouses and pointed out to us the many bales of different kinds of furs he had on hand. He told us we were the best fur handlers he had seen, and paid us two hundred dollars in American gold for what we had. We then stored our traps in the garret of one of his warehouses, which was of stone, two stories and an attic, as we thought of making another trip to this country if all went well.

We now entered our skiff again and went on down the great river till we came to a place nearly opposite Mineral Point, when we gave our boat to a poor settler, and with guns and bundles on our backs took a atraight shoot for home on foot. The second day

about dark we came in the edge of the town and were
seen by a lot of boys who eyed us closely and with
much curiosity, for we were dressed in our trapping
suits.   They followed us, and as we went along the
crowd increased so that when we got to Crum. Lloyd's
tavern the door was full of boys' heads looking at us
as if we were a circus.   Here we were heartily wel-
comed, and every body was glad to see us, as they
were about to start a company to go in search of their
reported murdered friends.   It seems a missionary got
lost on his way to Prairie La Crosse and had come
across our deserted cabin, and when he came in he reported us as no doubt murdered.

I invested all of my hundred dollars in buying eighty
acres of good Government land.   This was the first
$100 I ever had and I felt very proud to be a land
owner.   I felt a little more like a man now than I had
ever felt before, for the money was hard earned and
all mine.

CHAPTER VII.

MR. BUCK and myself concluded we would try our luck at lead mining for the summer and purchased some mining tools for the purpose. We camped out and dug holes around all summer, getting just about enough to pay our expenses—not a very encouraging venture, for we had lived in a tent and had picked and shoveled and blasted and twisted a windlass hard enough to have earned a good bit of money.

In the fall we concluded to try another trapping tour, and set out for Prairie du Chien. We knew it was a poor place to spend money up in the woods, and when we got our money it was all in a lump and seemed to amount to something. Mr· Brisbois said that the prospects were very poor indeed, for the price of fur was very low and no prospect of a better market. So we left our traps still on storage at his place and went back again. This was in 1847, and before Spring the war was being pushed in Mexico. I tried to enlist for this service, but there were so many ahead of me I could not get a chance.

I still worked in the settlement and made a living, but had no chance to improve my land. The next winter I lived with Mr A. Bennett, hunted deer and sold them at Mineral Point, and in this way made and saved a few dollars.

There had been from time to time rumors of a better country to the west of us and a sort of a pioneer, or western fever would break out among the people occasionally. Thus in 1845 I had a slight touch of the disease on account of the stories they told us about Oregon. It was reported that the Goverment would give a man a good farm if he would go and settle, and

make some specified improvement. They said it was
in a territory of rich soil, with plenty of timber, fish
and game and some Indians, just to give a little spice
of adventure to the whole thing. The climate was
very mild in winter, as they reported, and I concluded
it would suit me exactly. I began at once to think
about an outfit and a journey, and I found that it
would take me at least two years to get ready. A trip
to California was not thought of in those days, for it
did not belong to the United States.

In the winter of 1848–49 news began to come that
there was gold in California, but not generally believed
till it came through a U. S. officer, and then, as the
people were used to mines and mining, a regular gold
fever spread as if by swift contagion. Mr. Bennett
was aroused and sold his farm, and I felt a change in
my Oregon desires and had dreams at might of digging up the yellow dust. Nothing would cure us
then but a trip, and that was quickly decided on.

As it would be some weeks yet before grass would
start, I concluded to haul my canoe and a few traps
over to a branch of the Wisconsin, and make my way
to Prairie du Chien, do a little trapping, get me an Indian pony on which to ride to California. There were
no ponies to be had at Mineral Point. Getting a ride
up the river on a passing steamboat I reached Prairie
La Crosse, where the only house was that of a Dutch
trader from whom I bought a Winnebago pony, which
he had wintered on a little brushy island, and I
thought if he could winter on brush and rushes he
must be tough enough to take me across the plains.
He cost me $30, and I found him to be a poor, lazy
little fellow. However, I thought that when he got
some good grass, and a little fat on his ribs he might
have more life, and so I hitched a rope to him and
drove him ahead down the river. When I came to

the Bad Axe river I found it swimming full, but had
no trouble in crossing, as the pony was as good as a
dog in the water.

Before leaving Bennett's I had my gun altered over
to a pill lock and secured ammunition to last for two
years. I had tanned some nice buckskin and had a
good outfit of clothes made of it, or rather cut and
made it myself. Where I crossed the Bad Axe was a
the battle ground where Gen. Dodge fought the Winnebago Indians. At Prairie du Chien I found a letter
from Mr. Bennett, saying that the grass was so backward he would not start up for two or three weeks,
and I had better come back and start with them; but
as the letter bore no date I could only guess at the exact time. I had intended to strike directly west from
here to Council Bluffs and meet them there, but now
hought perhaps I had better go back to Mineral Point
and start out with them there, or follow on rapidly
after them if by any chance they had already started.

On my way back I found the Kickapoo river too
high to ford, so I pulled some basswood bark and
made a raft of a couple of logs, on which to carry my
gun and blanket; starting the pony across I followed
after. He swam across quickly, but did not seem to
like it on the other side, so before I got across, back
he came again, not paying the least attention to my
scolding. I went back with the raft, which drifted a
good way down stream, and caught the rascal and
started him over again, but when I got half way
across he jumped and played the same joke on me
again. I began to think of the old puzzle of the story
of the man with the fox, the goose and a peck of corn,
but I solved it by making a basswood rope to which I
tied a stone and threw across, then sending the pony
over with the other end. He staid this time, and after three days of swimming streams and pretty hard

travel reached Mineral Point, to find Bennett had been gone two weeks and had taken my outfit with him as we first planned.

I was a little troubled, but set out light loaded for Dubuque, crossed the river there and then alone across Iowa, over wet and muddy roads, till I fell in with some wagons west of the Desmoines River. They were from Milwaukee, owned by a Mr. Blodgett, and I camped with them a few nights, till we got to the Missouri River.

I rushed ahead the last day or two and got there before them. There were a few California wagons here, and some campers, so I put my pony out to grass and looked around. I waded across the low bottom to a strip of dry land next to the river, where there was a post office, store, and a few cabins. I looked first for a letter, but there was none. Then I began to look over the cards in the trading places and saloons, and read the names written on the logs of the houses, and everywhere I thought there might be a trace of the friends I sought. No one had seen or knew them. After looking half a day I waded back again to the pony—pretty blue. I thought first I would go back and wait another year, but there was a small train near where I left the pony, and it was not considered very safe to go beyond there except with a pretty good train. I sat down in camp and turned the matter over in my mind, and talked with Chas. Dallas of Lynn, Iowa, who owned the train. Bennett had my outfit and gun, while I had his light gun, a small, light tent, a frying pan, a tin cup, one woolen shirt and the clothes on my back. Having no money to get another outfit, I about concluded to turn back when Dallas said that if I would drive one of his teams through, he would board me, and I could turn my pony in with his loose horses; I thought it over, and

finally put my things in the wagon and took the ox
whip to go on. Dallas intended to get provision here,
but could not, so we went down to St. Jo, following
the river near the bluff. We camped near town and
walked in, finding a small train on the main emigrant
road to the west. My team was one yoke of oxen and
one yoke of cows. I knew how to drive, but had a
little trouble with the strange animals till they found
I was kind to them, and then they were all right.

This was in a slave state, and here I saw the first
negro auction. One side of the street had a platform
such as we build for a political speaker. The auc-
tioneer mounted this with a black boy about 18 years
old, and after he had told all his good qualities and
had the boy stand up bold and straight, he called for
bids, and they started him at $500. He rattled away
as if he were selling a steer, and when Mr. Rubi-
deaux, the founder of St. Jo bid $800, he went 11
higher and the boy was sold. With my New England
notions it made quite an impression on me.

Here Dallas got his supplies, and when the flour
and bacon was loaded up the ferryman wanted $50 to
take the train across. This Dallas thought too high
and went back up the river a day's drive, where he
got across for $30. From this crossing we went across
the country without much of a road till we struck the
road from St. Jo, and were soon on the Platte bottom.

We found some fine strawberries at one of the camps
across the country. We found some hills, but now
the country was all one vast prairie, not a tree in sight
till we reached the Platte, there some cottonwood and
willow. At the first camp on the Platte I rolled up
in my blanket under the wagon and thought more
than I slept, but I was in for it and no other way but
to go on. I had heard that there were two forts, new
Ft. Kearny and Ft. Laramie, on the south side of the

river, which we must wass before we reached the
South Pass of the Rocky Mountains, and beyond there
there would be no place to buy medicine or food. Our
little train of five wagons, ten men, one woman and
three children would not be a formidable force against
the indians if they were disposed to molest us, and it
looked to me very hazardous, and that a larger train
would be more safe, for Government troops were seldom molested on their marches.

If I should not please Mr. Dallas and get turned off
with only my gun and pony I should be in a pretty
bad shape, but I decided to keep right on and take
the chances on the savages, who would get only my
hair and my gun as my contribution to them if they
should be hostile. I must confess, however, that the
trail ahead did not look either straight or bright to me,
but hoped it might be better than I thought. So I
yoked my oxen and cows to the wagon and drove on.
All the other teams had two drivers each, who took
turns, and thus had every other day off for hunting if
they chose, but I had to carry the whip every day and
leave my gun in the wagon.

When we crossed Salt Creek the banks were high
and we had to tie a strong rope to the wagons and
with a few turns around a post, lower them down easily, while we had to double the teams to get them up
the other side.

Night came on before half the wagons were over,
and though it did not rain the water rose before morning so it was ten feet deep. We made a boat of one of
the wagon beds, and had a regular ferry, and when
they pulled the wagons over they sank below the surface but came out all right. We came to Pawnee Village, on the Platte, a collection of mud huts, oval in
shape, and an entrance low down to crawl in at. A
ground owl and some prairie dogs were in one of them,

and we suspected they might be winter quarters for the Indians.

Dallas and his family rode in the two-horse wagon, Dick Field was cook, and the rest of us drove the oxen. We put out a small guard at night to watch for Indians and keep the stock together so there might be no delay in searching for them. When several miles from Ft. Kearney I think on July 3rd, we camped near the river where there was a slough and much cottonwood and willow. Just after sundown a horse came galloping from the west and went in with our horses that were feeding a little farther down. In the morning two soldiers came from the fort, inquiring after the stray horse, but Dallas said he had seen none, and they did not hunt around among the willows for the lost animal. Probably it would be the easiest way to report back to the fort—"Indians got him." When we hitched up in the morning he put the horse on the off side of his own, and when near the fort, he went ahead on foot and entertained the officers while the men drove by, and the horse was not discovered. I did not like this much, for if we were discovered, we might be roughly handled, and perhaps the property of the innocent even confiscated. Really my New England ideas of honesty were somewhat shocked.

Reaching the South Platte, it took us all day to ford the sandy stream, as we had first to sound out a good crossing by wading through ourselves, and when we started our teams across we dare not stop a moment for fear the wagons would sink deep into the quicksands. We had no mishaps in crossing, and when well camped on the other side a solitary buffalo made his appearance about 200 yards away and all hands started after him, some on foot. The horsemen soon got ahead of him, but he did not seem inclined to get out of their way, so they opened fire on him. He still

kept hi feet and they wentnearer, Mr. Rogers, being
on a horse with a blind bridle, getting near enough to
fire his Colt's revolver at him, when he turned, and the
horse, being unable to see the animal quick enough to
get out of the way, suffered the force of a sudden attack
of the old fellow's horns, and came out with a gash in
his thigh six inches long, while Rogers went on a flying expedition over the horse's head, and did some
lively scrambling when he reaced the ground. The res
them worried him along for about half a mile, and
finally, after about forty shots he lay down but held
his head up defiantly, receiving shot after shot with an
angry shake, till a side shot laid him out. This game
gave us plenty of meat, which though tough, was a
pleasant change from bacon. I took no part in this
battle except as an observer. On examination it was
found that the balls hadbeen many of them stopped by
the matted hair about the old fellow's head and none
of them had reached the skull.

A few days after this we were stopped entirely by a
herd of buffaloes crossing our road. They came up
from the river and were moving south. The smaller
animals seemed to be in the lead, and the rear was
brought up by the old cows and the shaggy, burly
bulls. All were moving at a smart trot, with tongues
hanging out, and seemed to take no notice of us,
though we stood within a hundred yards of them. We
had to stand by our teams and stock to prevent a
stampede, for they all seemed to have a great wonder,
and somewhat of fear at their relatives of the plains.
After this we often saw large droves of them in the
distance. Sometimes we could see what in the distance
seemed a great patch of brush, but by watching
closely we could see it was a great drove of these animals. Those who had leisure to go up to the bluffs
often reported large droves in sight. Antelopes were

also seen, but these occupied the higher ground, and
it was very hard to get near enough to them to shoot
successfully. Still we managed to get a good deal of
game which was very acceptable as food.

One prominent land mark along the route was
what they called Court House Rock, standing to the
south from the trail and much resembled an immense
square building, standing high above surrounding
country. The farther we went on the more plentiful
became the large game, and also wolves and prairie
dogs, the first of which seemed to follow the buffaloes
closely.

About this time we met a odd looking train going
east, consisting of five or six Mormons from Salt Lake,
all mounted on small Spanish mules. They were
dressed in buckskin and mocassins, with long spurs
jingling at their heels, the rowels fully four inches
long, and each one carried a gun, a pistol and a big
knife. They were rough looking fellows with long,
matted hair, long beards, old slouch hats and a generally back woods get-up air in every way. They had
an extra pack mule, but the baggage and provisions
were very light. I had heard much about the Mormons, both at Nauvoo and Salt Lake, and some way
or other I could not separate the idea of horse thieves
from this party, and I am sure I would not like to
meet them if I had a desirable mule that they wanted,
or any money, or a good looking wife. We talked
with them half an hour or so and then moved on.

We occasionally passed by a grave along the road,
and often a small head board would state that the poor
unfortunate had died of cholera. Many of these had
been torn open by wolves and the blanket encirling
the corpse partly pulled away. Our route led a few
miles north of Chimney Rock, standing on an elevated
point like a tall column, so perfect and regular on all

sides, that from our point it looked as if it might be
the work of the stone cutters. Some of the party went
to see it and reported there was no way to ascend it,
and that as far as a man could reach, the rocks were
inscribed with the names of visitors and travelers who
passed that way.

At Scott's Bluffs, the bluffs came close to the river,
so there was considerable hill climbing to get along,
the road in other places finding ample room in the bottom. Here we found a large camp of the Sioux Indians on the bank of a ravine, on both sides of which
were some large cottonwood trees. Away up in the
large limbs platforms had been made of poles, on
which were laid the bodies of their dead, wrapped in
blankets and fastened down to the platform by a sort
of a network of smaller poles tightly lashed so that
they could not be dragged away or disturbed by wild
animals. This seemed a strange sort of cemetery, but
when we saw the desecrated earth-made graves we
felt that perhaps this was the best way, even if it was
a savage custom.

These Indians were fair-sized men, and pretty good
looking for red men. Some of our men went over to
their camp, and some of their youths came down to
ours, and when we started on they seemed quite
proud that they had learned a little of the English language, but the extent of their knowledge seemed to
be a little learned of the ox-drivers, for they would
swing their hands at the cattle and cry out "Whoa!
haw, g—d d—n." Whether they knew what was
meant, I have my doubts. They seemed pretty well
provided for and begged very little, as they are apt to
do when they are hard pressed.

We saw also some bands of Pawnee Indians on the
move across the prairies. They would hitch a long,
light pole on each side of a pony, with the ends drag-

ging behind on the ground, and on a little platform at
the hind end the children sat and were dragged along.

As we passed on beyond Scott's Bluff the game began to be preceptibly scarcer, and what we did find
was back from the traveled road, from which it had
apparently been driven by the passing hunters.

In time we reached Ft. Laramie, a trading post,
where there were some Indian lodges, and we noticed
that some of the occupants had lighter complexions
than any of the other Indians we had seen. They had
cords of dried buffalo meat, and we purchased some.
It was very fat, but was so perfectly cured that the
clear tallow tasted as sweet as a nut. I thought it was
the best dried meat I had ever tasted, but perhaps a
good appetite had something to do with it.

As we passed Ft. Laramie we fell in company with
some U. S. soldiers who were going to Ft. Hall and
thence to Oregon. We considered them pretty safe to
travel with and kept with them for some time, though
their rate of travel was less than ours. Among them
were some Mormons, employed as teamsters, and in
other ways, and they told us there were some
Missourians on the road who would never live to see
California. There had been some contests between the
Missourians and the Mormons, and I felt rather glad
that none of us hailed from Pike county.

We turned into what they called the Black Hills,
leaving the Platte to the north of us. The first night
on this road we had the hardest rain I ever experienced, and the only one of any account on our journey. Our camp was on a level piece of ground on the
bank of a dry creek, which soon became a very wet
creek indeed, for by morning it was one hundred
yards wide and absolutely impassable. It went down,
however, as quickly as it rose, and by ten o'clock it
was so low that we easily crossed and went on our

way. We crossed one stream where there were great drifts or piles of hail which had been brought down by a heavy storm from higher up the hills. At one place we found some rounded boulders from six to eight inches in diameter, which were partly hollow, and broken open were found to contain most beautiful crystals of quartz, clear as purest ice. The inside was certainly very pretty, and it was a mystery how it came there. I have since learned that such stones are found at many points, and that they are called geodes.

We came out at the river again at the mouth of Deer Creek, and as there was some pretty good coal there quite easy to get, we made camp one day to try to tighten our wagon tires, John Rogers acting as blacksmith. This was my first chance to reconoitre, and so I took my gun and went up the creek, a wide, treeless bottom. In the ravines on the south side were beautiful groves of small fir trees and some thick brush, wild rose bushes I think. I found here a good many heads and horns of elk, and I could not decide whether they had been killed in winter during the deep snow, or had starved to death.

There was a ferry here to cross the river and go up along north side. Mr. Dallas bought the whole outfit for a small sum and when we were safely over he took with him such ropes as he wanted and tied the boat to the bank The road on this side was very sandy and led over and among some rolling hills. In talking with the men of the U. S. troops in whose company we still were, I gathered much information concerning our road further west. They said we were entirely too late to get through to California, on account of crossing the Sierra Nevada mountains, which, they said would be covered with snow by November, or even earlier, and that we would be compelled to winter at Salt Lake. Some of the drivers overheard Mr.

Dallas telling his family the same thing, and that if he should winter at Salt Lake, he would discharge his drivers as soon as he arrived, as he could not afford to board them all winter.

This was bad news for me, for I had known of the history of them at Nauvoo and in Missouri, and the prospect of being thrown among them with no money to buy bread was a very sorry prospect for me. From all I could learn we could not get a chance to work, even for our board there, and the other drivers shared my fears and disappointment. In this dilemma we called a council, and invited the gentleman in to have an understanding. He came and our spokesmam stated the case to him, and our fears, and asked him what he had to say to us about it. He flew quite angry at us, and talked some and swore a great deal more, and the burden of his speech was:—''This train belongs to me and I propose to do with it just as I have a mind to, and I don't care a d—n what you fellows do or say. I am not going to board you fellows all winter for nothing, and when we get to Salt Lake you can go where you please, for I shall not want you any longer.'' We talked a little to him and under the circumstances to talk was about all we could do. He gave us no satisfaction and left us apparently much offended that we had any care for ourselves.

Then we had some talk among ourselves, at the time, and from day to day as we moved along. We began to think that the only way to get along at all in Salt Lake would be to turn Mormons. and none of us had any belief or desire that way and could not make up our minds to stop our journey and lose so much time, and if we were not very favored travelers our lot might be cast among the sinners for all time.

We were now on the Sweetwater River, and began to see the snow on the Rocky Mountains ahead of us,

another reminder that there was a winter coming and
only a little more than half our journey was done. We
did not feel very happy over it, and yet we had to
laugh once in a while at some of the funny things that
would happen.

The Government party we were with had among
them a German mule driver who had a deal of
trouble with his team, but who had a very little knowledge of the English language. When the
officers tried to instruct him a little he seemed to get
out of patience and would say something very like
Sacramento. We did not know exactly what this
meant. We had heard there was a river of that name
or something very near like that; and then again some
said that was the Dutch for swearing. If this latter
was the truth then he was a very profane mule driver
when he got mad.

The Captain of the company had a very nice looking
lady with him, and they carried a fine wall tent which
they occupied when they went into camp. The company cook served their meals to them in the privacy
of their tent, and they seemed to enjoy themselves
very nicely. Everybody though the Captain was very
lucky in having such an accomplished companion,
and journey along quietly to the gold fields at government expense.

There seemed to be just a little jealousy between
the Captain and the Lieutenant, and one day I saw
them both standing in angry attitude before the Captain's quarters, both mounted, with their carbines
lying across their saddles before them. They had
some pretty sharp, hot words, and it looked as if they
both were pretty nearly warmed up to the shooting
point. Once the Lieutenant moved his right hand a
little, and the Captain was quick to see it, shouting;
—"Let your gun alone or I will make a hole through

you,'' at the same time grasping his own and pointing
it straight at the other officer. During all this time
the Captain's lady stood in the tent door, and when
she saw her favorite had the drop on the Lieutenant
she clapped her delicate, little hands in a gleeful manner:—''Just look at the Captain! Ain't he spunky?''
and then she laughed long and loud to see her lord
show so much military courage. She seemed more
pleased at the affair than any one else. I don't know
exactly what the others thought, but I never could believe that the lady and the Captain were ever married.

The Lieutenant was no coward, but probably thinking that prudence was the better part of valor, refrained from handling his gun, and the two soon rode
away in opposite directions.

We passed a lone rock standing in the river bottom
on the Sweetwater, which they named Independence
Rock. It was covered with the names of thousands of
people who had gone by on that road. Some were
pretty neatly chiseled in, some very rudely scrawled,
and some put on with paint. I spent all the time I
could hunting Mr. Bennett's name, but I could not
find it anywhere. To have found his name, and thus
to know that he had safely passed this point would
have been a little re-assuring in those rather doubtful
days. Some had named the date of their passing, and
some of them were probably pretty near the gold
fields at this time.

All along in this section we found alkali water near
the road, some very strong and dangerous for man or
beast to use. We traveled on up the Sweetwater for
some time, and at last came to a place where the road
left the river, and we had a a long, hard hill to pull
up. When we reached the top of this we were in the
South Pass of the Rocky Mountains, the backbone of
the American continent. To the north of us were

some very high peaks white with snow, and to the south were some lower hills and valleys. The summit of the mountains was not quite as imposing as I expected, but it was the summit, and we were soon surely moving down the western side, for at Pacific Springs the water ran to the westward, toward the Pacific coast. The next day we came to the nearly dry bed of the river—the Big Sandy. The country round about seemed volcanic, with no timber. but plenty of sage brush, in which we were able to shoot an occasional sage hen. The river bed itself was nothing but sand, and where there was water enough to wet it, it was very miry and hard traveling over it. There are two streams, the Big Sandy and Little Sandy, both tributaries to Green River, which we soon reached and crossed.

It was a remarkable clear and rapid stream and was now low enough to ford. One of the Government teams set out to make the crossing at a point where it looked shallow enough, but before the lead mules reached the opposite shore, they lost their footing and were forced to swim. Of course the wagon stopped and the team swung round and tangled up in a bad shape. They were unhitched and the wagon pulled back, the load was somewhat dampened, for the water came into the wagon box about a foot. We camped here and laid by one day, having thus quite a little chance to look around.

When we came to the first water that flowed toward the Pacific Coast at Pacific Springs, we drivers had quite a little talk about a new scheme. We put a great many "ifs" together and they amounted to about this:—If this stream were large enough; if we had a boat; if we knew the way: if there were no falls or bad places; if we had plenty of provisions; if we were bold enough set out on such a trip, etc., we

might come out at some point or other on the Pacific
Ocean. And now when we came to the first of the
"ifs," a stream large enough to float a small boat; we
began to think more strongly about the other "ifs".

In the course of our rambles we actually did run
across the second "if" in the shape of a small ferry
boat filled up with sand upon a bar, and it did not
take very long to dig it out and put it into shape to
use, for it was just large enough to hold one wagon at
a time. Our military escort intended to leave us at
this point, as their route now bore off to the north of
ours. I had a long talk with the surgeon who seemed
well informed about the country, and asked him about
the prospects. He did not give the Mormons a very
good name. He said to me:—"If you go to Salt Lake
City, do not let them know you are from Missouri, for
I tell you that many of those from that State will
never see California. You know they were driven
from Missouri, and will get revenge if they can."
Both the surgeon and the captain said the stream
came out on the Pacific Coast' and that we had no obstacles except cataracts, which they had heard were
pretty bad. I then went to Dallas and told him what
we proposed doing and to our surprise he did not offer
any objections, and offered me $60 for my pony. He
said he would sell us some flour and bacon for provisions also.

We helped them in crossing the river, which was
somewhat difficult, being swift, with boulders in the
bottom but we got all safely over and then made the
trade we had spoken of. Dallas paid me for my pony
and we took what flour and bacon he would let go.
He gave us some ropes for head and stern lines to our
boat and a couple of axes, and we laid these, and our
provisions in a pile by the roadside. Six of us then
gave up our whips. Mr. S. McMahon, a driver, hesi-

tated for some time, but being pressed by Dallas for a decision, at last threw down his whip and said:—"I will go with the boys." This left Dallas with only one driver, but he took a whip himself, and with the aid of the children and his wife who drove the two-horse wagon, they got along very well. I paid for such provisions as we had taken , as the rest of the fellows had almost no money.

So we parted company, the little train slowly moving on its way westward. Our military captain, the soldier boys, and the gay young lady taking the route to Oregon, and we sitting on the bank of the river whose waters flowed to the great Pacific. Each company wished the other good luck, we took a few long breaths and then set to work in earnest to carry out our plans.

CHAPTER VIII.

ABOUT the first thing we did was to organize and select a captain, and, very much against my wishes, I was chosen to this important position. Six of us had guns of some sort, Richard Field, Dallas's cook, was not armed at all. We had one regular axe and a large camp hatchet, which was about the same as an axe, and several very small hatchets owned by the men. All our worldly goods were piled up cn the bank, and we were alone.

An examination of the old ferry boat showed it to be in pretty good condition, the sand with which it had been filled keeping it very perfectly. We found two oars in the sand under the boat, and looked up some poles to assist us in navigation. Our cordage was rather scant but the best we could get and all we could muster. The boat was about twelve feet long and six or seven feet wide, not a very well proportioned craft, but having the ability to carry a pretty good load. We swung it up to the bank and loaded up our goods and then ourselves. It was not a heavy load for the craft, and it looked as if we were taking the most sensible way to get to the Pacific, and almost wondered that everybody was so blind as not to see it as we did.

This party was composed of W. L. Manley, M. S McMahon, Charles and Joseph Hazelrig, Richard Field, Alfred Walton and John Rogers. We untied the ropes, gave the boat a push and commenced to move down the river with ease and comfort, feeling much happier than we would had we been going toward Salt Lake with the prospect of wintering there.

At the mouth of Ham's Fork we passed a camp of

Indians, but we kept close to the opposite shore to
avoid being boarded by them. They beckoned very
urgently for us to come ashore, but I acted as if I did
not understand them, and gave them the go-by.

As we were floating down the rapid stream it became more and more a rapid, roaring river, and the
bed contained many dangerous rocks that were difficult to shun. Each of us had a setting-pole, and we
ranged ourselves along the sides of the boat and tried
to keep ourselves clear from the rocks and dangers.
The water was not very deep and made such a dashing noise as the current rushed among the rocks that
one had to talk pretty loud to be heard. As we were
gliding along quite swiftly, I set my pole on the bottom
and gave the boat a sudden push to avoid a boulder,
when the pole stuck in the crevice between two rocks,
and instead of losing the pole by the sudden jerk I
gave, I was the one who was very suddenly yanked
from the boat by the spring of the pole, and landed in
the middle of the river. I struck pretty squarely
on my back, and so got thoroughly wet, but swam for
shore amid the shouts of the boys, who waved their
hats and hurrahed for the captain when they saw he
was not hurt. I told them that was nothing as we
were on our way to Califofnia by water any way, and
such things must be expected.

The next day after this I went on shore and sighted
a couple of antelope, one of which I shot, which gave
us good grub. and good appetites we already had. As
near as we could estimate we floated about thirty miles
a day, which beat the pace of tired oxen considerably.
In one place there was a fringe of thick willows along
the bank, and a little farther back a perpendicular
bluff, whicl between the two was a strip of fine green
grass. As we were passing this we scared up a band
of elk in this grass meadow, and they all took a run

down the river like a band of horses. One of them turned up a small ravine with walls so steep he could not get out, so we posted a guard at the entrance, and three of us went up the cañon after him, and after the others had each fired a shot, I fired the third and brought him down. This was about the finest piece of Rocky Mountain beef that one could see. We took the carcass on board and floated on again.

Thus far we had a very pleasant time, each taking his turn in working the boat while the others rested or slept. About the fifth day when we were floating along in very gently running water, I had lay down to take a rest and a little sleep. The mountains here on both sides of the river were not very steep, but ran gradually for a mile or so. While I was sleeping the boat came around a small angle in the stream, and all at once there seemed to be a higher, steeper range of mountains right across the valley. The boys thought the river was coming to a rather sudden end and hastily awoke me, and for the life of me I could not say they were not right, for there was no way in sight for it to go to. I remembered while looking over a map the military men had I found a place named Brown's Hole, and I told the boys I guessed we were elected to go on foot to California after all, for I did not propose to follow the river down any sort of a hole into any mountain. We were floating directly toward a perpendicular cliff, and I could not see any hole any where, nor any other place where it could go. Just as we were within a stone's throw of the cliff, the river turned sharply to the right and went behind a high point of the mountain that seemed to stand squarely on edge. This was really an immense crack or crevice, certainly 2000 feet deep and perhaps much more, and seemed much wider at the bottom than it did at the top, 2000 feet or more above our heads. Each wall seemed to lean in toward the water as it rose.

We were now for some time between two rocky walls between which the river ran very rapidly, and we often had to get out and work our boat over the rocks, sometimes lifting it off when it caught. Fortunately we had a good tow line, and one would take this and follow along the edge when it was so he could walk. The mountains seemed to get higher and higher on both sides as we advanced, and in places we could see quite a number of trees overhanging the river, and away up on the rocks we could see the wild mountain sheep looking down at us. They were so high that they seemed a mile away, and consequently safe enough. This was their home, and they seemed very independent, as if they dared us fellows to come and see them. There was an old cottonwood tree on bank with marks of an axe on it, but this was all the sign we saw that any one had ever been here before us. We got no game while passing through this deep cañon and began to feel the need of some fresh provisions very sorely.

We passed many deep, dark cañons coming into the main stream, and at one place, where the rock hung a little over the river and had a smooth wall, I climbed up above the high water mark which we could clearly see, and with a mixture of gunpowder and grease for paint, and a bit of cloth tied to a stick for a brush, I painted in fair sized letters on the rock, CAPT. W. L. MANLEY, U. S. A. We did not know whether we were within the bounds of the United States or not, and we put on all the majesty we could under the circumstances. I don't think the sun ever shone down to the bottom of the cañon, for the sides were literally sky-high, for the sky, and a very small portion of that was all we could see.

Just before night we came to a place where some

huge rocks as large as cabins had fallen down from the mountain, completely filling up the river bed, and making it completely impassible for our boat. We unloaded it and while the boys held the stern line, I took off my clothes and pushed the boat out into the torrent which ran around the rocks, letting them pay the line out slowly till it was just right. Then I sang out to—"Let go"—and away it dashed. I grasped the bow line, and at the first chance jumped overboad and got to shore, when I held the boat and brought it in below the obstructions. There was some deep water below the rocks; and we went into camp. While some loaded the boat, others with a hook and line caught some good fish, which resembled mackerel.

While I was looking up toward the mountain top, and along down the rocky wall, I saw a smooth place about fifty feet above where the great rocks had broken out, and there, painted in large black letters, were the words "ASHLEY, 1824." This was the first real evidence we had of the presence of a white man in this wild place, and from this record it seems that twenty-five years before some venturesome man had here inscribed his name. I have since heard there were some persons in St. Louis of this name, and of some circumstances which may link them with this early traveler.

When we came to look around we found that another big rock blocked the channel 300 yards below, and the water rushed around it with a terrible swirl. So we unloaded the boat again and made the attempt to get around it as we did the other rocks. We tried to get across the river but failed. We now, all but one, got on the great rock with our poles, and the one man was to ease the boat down with the rope as far as he could, then let go and we would stop it with our poles and push it out into the stream and let it go over, but the current was so strong that when the boat

struck the rock we could not stop it, and the gunwale
next to us rose, and the other went down, so that in a
second the boat stood edgewise in the water and the
bottom tight against the big rock, and the strong current pinned it there so tight that we could no more
move it than we could move the rock itself.

This seemed a very sudden ending to our voyage
and there were some very rapid thoughts as to whether
we would not safer among the Mormons than out in
this wild country, afoot and alone. Our boat was
surely lost beyond hope, and something must be done.
I saw two pine trees, about two feet through, growing
on a level place just below, and I said to them that
we must decide between going afoot and making some
canoes out of these pine trees. Canoes were decided
on, and we never let the axes rest, night or day till
we had them completed. While my working shift
was off, I took an hour or two, for a little hunting,
and on a low divide partly grown over with small
pines and juniper I found signs, old and new, of many
elk, and so concluded the country was well stocked
with noble game. The two canoes, when completed
were about fifteen feet long and two feet wide, and
we lashed them together for greater security. When
we tried them we found they were too small to carry
our load and us, and we landed half a mile below,
where there were two other pine trees—white pine—
about two feet through, and much taller than the ones
we had used. We set at work making a large canoe
of these. I had to direct the work for I was the only
one who had ever done such work. We worked night
and day at these canoes, keeping a big fire at night
and changing off to keep the axes busy. This canoe
we made twenty-five or thirty feet long, and when
completed they made me captain of it and into it
loaded the most valuable things, such as provisions,

ammunition, and cooking utensils. I had to take the lead for I was the only skillful canoeist in the party. We agreed upon signals to give when danger was seen, or game in sight, and leading off with my big canoe we set sail again, and went flying down stream.

This rapid rate soon brought us out of the high mountains and into a narrow valley when the stream became more moderate in its speed and we floated along easily enough. In a little while after we struck this slack water, as we were rounding a point, I saw on a sand bar in the river, five or six elk, standing and looking at us with much curiosity. I signaled for those behind to go to shore, while I did the same, and two or three of us took our guns and went carefully down along the bank, the thick brush hiding us from them, till we were in fair range, then selecting our game we fired on them. A fine doe fell on the opposite bank, and a magnificent buck which Rogers and I selected, went below and crossed the river on our side. We followed him down along the bank which was here a flat meadow with thick bunches of willows, and soon came pretty near to Mr. Elk who started off on a high and lofty trot. As he passed an opening in the bushes I put a ball through his head and he fell. He was a monster. Rogers, who was a butcher, said it would weigh five hundred or six hundred pounds. The horns were fully six feet long, and by placing the horns on the ground, point downwards, one could walk under the skull between them. We packed the meat to our canoes, and staid up all night cutting the meat in strips and drying it, to reduce bulk and perserve it, and it made the finest kind of food, fit for an epicure.

Starting on again, the river lost more and more of of its rapidity as it came out into a still wider valley, and became quite sluggish. We picked red berries that grew on bushes that overhung the water. They were sour and might have been high cranberries. One day I killed an otter, and afterward hearing a wild goose on shore, I went for the game and killed it on a small pond on which there were also some mallard duck. I killed two of these. When I fired, the ones not killed did not fly away, but rather swam toward me. I suppose they never before had seen a man or heard the report of a gun. On the shore around the place I saw a small bear track, but I did not have time to look for his bearship, and left, with the game already killed, and passed on down through this beautiful valley.

We saw one place where a large band of horses had crossed, and as the men with them must have had a raft, we were pretty sure that the men in charge of them were white men. Another day we passed the mouth of a swollen stream which came in from the west side. The water was thick with mud, and the fish, about a foot long, came to the top, with their noses out of water. We tried to catch some, but could not hold them. One night we camped on an island, and I took my gun and went over toward the west side where I killed a deer. The boys hearing me shoot, came out, guns in hand, thinking I might need help, and I was very glad of their assistance. To make our flour go as far as possible we ate very freely of meat, and having excellent appetites it disappeared very fast.

It took us two or three days to pass this beautiful valley, and then we began to get into a rougher country again, the cañons deeper and the water more tumultuous. McMahon and I had the lead always, in the big canoe. The mountains seemed to change into bare rocks and get higher and higher as we floated along. After the first day of this the river be-

came so full of boulders that many times the only way
we could do was to unload the canoes and haul them
over, load up and go ahead, only to repeat the same
tactics in a very short time again. At one place where
the river was more than usually obstructed we found
a deserted camp, a skiff and some heavy cooking
utensils, with a notice posted up on an alder tree saying that they had found the river route impracticable,
and being satisfied that the river was so full of rocks
and boulders that it could not be safely navigated,
they had abandoned the undertaking and were about
to start overland to make their way to Salt Lake. I
took down the names of the parties at the time in my
diary, which has since been burned, but have now forgotten them entirely. They were all strangers to me.
They had taken left such heavy articles as could not
be carried on foot. This notice rather disconcerted
us, but we thought we had better keep on and see for
ourselves, so we did not follow them, but kept on down
the rocky river. We found generally more boulders
than water, and the down grade of the river bed was
heavy.

Some alders and willows grew upon the bank and
up quite high on the mountains we could see a little
timber. Some days we did not go more than four or
five miles, and that was serious work, loading and unloading our canoes, and packing them over the
boulders, with only small streams of water curling
around between them. We went barefoot most of the
time, for we were more than half of the time in the
water which roared and dashed so loud that we could
hardly heard each other speak. We kept getting more
and more venturesome and skillful, and managed to
run some very dangerous rapids in safety.

On the high peaks above our heads we could see the
Rocky Mountain sheep looking defintly at us from their

mountain fastnesses, so far away they looked no larger
than jack rabbits. They were too far off to try to
shoot at, and we had no time to try to steal up any
nearer for at the rate we were making, food would be
the one thing needful, for we were consuming it very
fast. Sometimes we could ride a little ways, and then
would come the rough-and-tumble with the rocks
again.

One afternoon we came to a sudden turn in the
river, more than a right angle, and, just below, a fall
of two feet or more. This I ran in safety, as did the
rest who followed and we cheered at our pluck and
skill. Just after this the river swung back the other
way at a right angle or more, and I quickly saw there
was danger below and signaled them to go on shore
at once, and lead the canoes over the dangerous
rapids. I ran my own canoe near shore and got by
the rapid safely, waiting for the others to come also.
They did not obey my signals but thought to run the
rapid the same as I did. The channel here was
straight for 200 yards, without a boulder in it, but
the stream was so swift that it caused great, rolling
waves in the center, of a kind I have never seen anywhere else. The boys were not skillful enough to nav-
gate this stream, and the suction drew them to the
center where the great waves rolled them over and
over, bottom side up and every way. The occupants
of our canoe let go and swam to shore. Fields had
always been afraid of water and had worn a life per-
server every day since we left the wagons. He threw
up his hands and splashed and kicked at a terrible
rate, for he could not swim, and at last made solid
ground. One of the canoes came down into the eddy
below, where it lodged close to the shore, bottom up.
Alfred Walton in the other canoe could not swim, but
held on to the gunwale with a death grip, and it went

on down through the rapids. Sometimes we could
see the man and sometimes not, and he and the canoe
took turns in disappearing. Walton had very black
hair, and as he clung fast to his canoe his black head
looked like a crow on the end of a log. Sometimes
he would be under so long that we thought he must
be lost, when up he would come again still clinging
manfully.

McMahon and I threw everything out of the big
canoe and pushed out after him. I told Mc. to kneel
down so I could see over him to keep the craft off the
rocks, and by changing his paddle from side to side as
ordered, he enabled me to make quick moves and
avoid being dashed to pieces. We fairly flew, the
boys said, but I stood up in the stern and kept it clear
of danger till we ran into a clear piece of river and
overtook Walton clinging to the overturned boat; Mc-
Mahon seized the boat and I paddled all to shore, but
Walton was nearly dead and could hardly keep his
grasp on the canoe. We took him to a sandy place
and worked over him and warmed him in the sun till
he came to life again, then built a fire and laid him
up near to it to get dry and warm. If the canoe had
gone on 20 yards farther with him before we caught
it, he would have gone into another long rapid and
been drowned. We left Walton by the fire and crossing the river in the slack water, went up to where the
other boys were standing, wet and sorry-looking, say-
that all was gone and lost. Rogers put his hand in
his pocket and pulled out three half dollars and said
sadly:—"Boys, this is all I am worth in the world."
All the clothes he had were a pair of overalls and a
shirt. If he had been possessed of a thousand in gold
he would have been no richer, for there was no one to
buy from and nothing to buy. I said to them: "Boys,
we can't help what has happened, we'll do the best we

can.   Right your canoe, get the water out, and we'll
go down and see how Walton is.''   They did as I told
them, and lo and behold when the canoe rolled right
side up, there were their clothes and blankets safe
and sound.   These light things had floated in the
canoe and were safe.   We now tried by joining hands
to reach out far enough to recover some of the guns,
but by feeling with their feet they fouud the bottom
smooth as glass and the property all swept on below,
no one knew where.   The current was so powerful
that no one could stand in it where it came up above
his knees.   The eddy which enabled us to save the
first canoe with the bedding and clothes was caused
by a great boulder as large as a house which had fallen
from above and partly blocked the stream.   Everything that would sink was lost.

We all got into the two canoes and went down to
Walton, where we camped and staid all night for
Walton's benefit.   While we were waiting I took my
gun and tried to climb up high enough to see how
much longer this horrible cañon was going to last, but
after many attempts, I could not get high enough to
see in any direction.   The mountain was all bare
rocks in terraces, but it was impossible to climb from
one to the other, and the benches were all filled with
broken rocks that had fallen from above.

By the time I got back to camp, Walton was dry and
warm and could talk.   He said he felt better, and
pretty good over his rescue.   When he was going
under the water, it seemed sometimes as if he never
would come to the top again, but he held on and
eventually came out all right.   He never knew how
he got to shore, he was so nearly dead when rescued.

The next morning Walton was so well we started
on.   We were now very poorly armed.   My rifle and
McMahon's shotgun were all the arms we had for

seven of us, and we could make but a poor defence if attacked by man or beast, to say nothing of providing ourselves with food. The mountains on each side were very bare of timber, those on the east side particularly so, and very high and barren. Toward night we were floating along in a piece of slack water, the river below made a short turn around a high and rocky point almost perpendicular from the water. There was a terrace along the side of this point about fifty feet up, and the bench grew narrower as it approached the river. As I was coming down quite close under this bank I saw three mountain sheep on the bench above, and, motioning to the boys, I ran on shore and, with my gun in hand, crept down toward them, keeping a small pine tree between myself and the sheep. There were some cedar bushes on the point, and the pines grew about half way up the bank. I got in as good a range as possible and fired at one of them which staggered around and fell down to the bottom of the cliff. I loaded and took the next largest one which came down the same way. The third one tried to escape by going down the bend and then creeping up a crevice, but it could not get away and turned back, cautiously, which gave me time to load again and put a ball through it. I hit it a little too far back for instant death, but I followed it up and found it down and helpless, and soon secured it. I hauled this one down the mountain, and the other boys had the two others secure by this time. McMahon was so elated at my success that he said: "Manley, if I could shoot as you do I would never want any better business." And the other fellows said they guessed we were having better luck with one gun than with six, so we had a merry time after all. These animals were of a bluish color, with hair much finer than deer, and resembled a goat more than a sheep. These

three were all females and their horns were quite
straight, not curved like the big males.   We cut the
meat from the bones and broke them up, making a
fine soup which tasted pretty good.   They were in
pretty good order, and the meat like very good mut-
ton.

We kept pushing on down the river.   The rapids
were still dangerous in many places, but not so frequent nor so bad as the part we had gone over, and we
could see that the river gradually grew smoother as
we progressed.

After a day or two we began to get out of the cañons,
but the mountains and hills on each side were barren
and of a pale yellow caste, with no chance for us to
climb up and take a look to see if there were any
chances for us further along.   We had now been
obliged to follow the cañon for many miles, for the
only way to get out was to get out endwise, climbing the banks being utterly out of the question.   But
these mountains soon came to an end, and there was
some cottonwood and willows on the bank of the river,
which was now so smooth we could ride along without the continual loading and unloading we had been
forced to practice for so long.   We had begun to get
a little desperate at the lack of game, but the new
valley, which grew wider all the time, gave us hope
again, if it was quite barren everywhere except back
of the willow trees.

We were floating along very silently one day, for
none of us felt very much in the mood for talking,
when we heard a distant sound which we thought was
very much like the firing of a gun.   We kept still,
and in a short time a similar sound was heard, plainer
and evidently some ways down the stream.   Again and
again we heard it, and decided that it must be a gun
shot, and yet we were puzzled to know how it could

be.   We were pretty sure there were no white people
ahead of us, and we did not suppose the Indians in
this far-off land had any firearms.   It might be barely
possible that we were coming now to some wagon
train taking a southern course, for we had never heard
that there were any settlements in this direction and
the barren country would preclude any such thing, as
we viewed it now.   If it was a hostile band we could
not do much with a rifle and a shot gun toward defending ourselves or taking the aggressive.   Some of the
boys spoke of our scalps ornamenting a spear handle,
and indulged in such like cheerful talk which com-
forted us wonderfully.

Finally we concluded we did not come out into that
wild country to be afraid of a few gunshots, and determined to put on a bold front, fight if we had to, run
away if we could not do any better, and take our
chances on getting scalped or roasted.   Just then we
came in sight of three Indian lodges just a little back
from the river, and now we knew for certain who had
the guns.   McMahon and I were in the lead as usual,
and it was only a moment before one of the Indians
appeared, gun in hand, and made motions for us to
come on shore.   A cottonwood tree lay nearly across
the river, and I had gone so far that I had to go around
it and land below, but the other boys behind were
afraid to do otherwise than to land right there as the
Indian kept his gun lying across his arm.   I ran our
canoe below to a patch of willows, where we landed
and crawled through the brush till we came in sight
of the other boys, where we stood and waited a moment to see how they fared, and whether our red men
were friends or enemies.   There were no suspicious
movements on their part, so we came out and walked
right up to them.   There was some little talk, but I
am sure we did not understand one another's language,

and so we made motions and they made motions, and
we got along better. We went with them down to
the tepee, and there we heard the first word that was
at all like English and that was "Mormonee," with
a sort of questioning tone. Pretty soon one said
"Buffalo," and then we concluded they were on a big
hunt of some sort. They took us into their lodges
and showed us blankets, knives, and guns, and then,
with a suggestive motion, said all was "Mormonee,"
by which we understood they had got them from the
Mormons. The Indian in the back part of the lodge
looked very pleasant and his countenance showed a
good deal of intelligence for a man of the mountains.
I now told the boys that we were in a position where
we were dependent on some one, and that I had seen
enough to convince me that these Indians were perfectly friendly with the Mormons, and that for our own
benefit we had better pass ourselves off for Mormons,
also. So we put our right hand to our breast and said
"Mormonee," with a cheerful countenance, and that
act conveyed to them the belief that we were chosen
disciples of the great and only Brigham and we became
friends at once, as all acknowledged. The fine-look-
ing Indian who sat as king in the lodge now, by motions and a word or two, made himself known as Chief
Walker, and when I knew this I took great pains to
cultivate his acquaintance.

I was quite familiar with the sign language used by
all the Indians, and found I could get along pretty
well in making him understand and knowing what he
said. I asked him first how many "sleeps" or days
it was from there to "Mormonee." In answer he put
out his left hand and then put two fingers of his right
astride of it, making both go up and down with the
same motion of a man riding a horse. Then he shut
his eyes and laid his head on his hand three times, by

which I understood that a man could ride to the Mormon settlement in three sleeps or four days. He then wanted to know where we were going, and I made signs that we were wishing to go toward the setting sun and to the big water, and I said "California." The country off to the west of us now seemed an open, barren plain, which grew wider as it extended west. The mountains on the north side seemed to get lower and smaller as they extended west, but on the south or east side they were all high and rough. It seemed as if we could see one hundred miles down the river, and up to the time we met the Indians we thought we had got through all our troublesome navigation and could now sail on, quietly and safely to the great Pacific Ocean and land of gold.

When I told Chief Walker this he seemed very much astonished, as if wondering why we were going down the river when we wanted to get west across the country. I asked him how many sleeps it was to the big water, and he shook his head, pointed out across the country and then to the river and shook his head again; by which I understood that water was scarce, out the way he pointed. He then led me down to a smooth sand bar on the river and then, with a crooked stick, began to make a map in the sand. First he made a long crooked mark, ten feet long or so, and pointing to the river to let me know that the mark in the sand was made to represent it. He then made a straight mark across near the north end of the stream, and showed the other streams which came into the Green river which I saw at once was exactly correct. Then he laid some small stones on each side of the cross mark, and making a small hoop of a willow twig, he rolled it in the mark he had made across the river, then flourished his stick as if he were driving oxen. Thus he represented the emigrant road. He traced

the branches off to the north where the soldiers had
gone, and the road to California, which the emigrants
took, all of which we could see was correct. Then
he began to describe the river down which we had
come. A short distance below the road he put some
small stones on each side of the river to represent
mountains. He then put down his hands, one on
each side of the crooked mark and then raised them
up again saying e-e-e-e-e-e as he raised them, to say
that the mountains there were very high. Then he
traced down the stream to a place below where we
made our canoes; when he placed the stone back from
the river farther, to show that there was a valley there;
then he drew them in close again farther down, and
piled them up again two or three tiers high, then
placing both fists on them he raised them higher than
the top of his head, saying e-e-e-e-e-e and looking still
higher and shaking his head as if to say :- "Awful bad
cañon", and thus he went on describing the river till
we understood that we were near the place where we
now were, and then pointed to his tepee, showing that
I understood him all right. It was all correct, as I
very well knew and assured me that he knew all about
the country.

I became much interested in my new found friend,
and had him continue his map down the river- He
showed two streams coming in on the east side and
then he began piling up stones on each side of the river
and then got longer ones and piled them higher and
higher yet. Then he stood with one foot on each side
of his river and put his hands on the stones and then
raised them as high as he could, making a continued
e-e-e-e-e-e as long as his breath would last, pointed to
the canoe and made signs with his hands how it would
roll and pitch in the rapids and finely capsize and throw
us all out. He then made signs of death to show us

that it was a fatal place.   I understood perfectly plain
from this that below the valley where we now were
was a terrible cañon, much higher than any we had
passed, and the rapids were not navigable with safety.
Then Walker shook his head more than once and
looked very sober, and said "Indiano" and reaching
for his bow and arrows, he drew the bow back to it's
utmost length and put the arrow close to my breast,
showing how I would get shot.   Then he would draw
his hand across his throat and shut his eyes as if in
death to make us understand that this was a hostile
country before us, as well as rough and dangerous.

I now had a description of the country ahead and believed it to be reliable.   As soon as I could conviently after this, I had a council with the boys, who had looked
on in silence while I was holding the silent confab
with the chief.   I told them where we were and what
chances there were of getting to California by this
route, and that for my part I had as soon be killed by
Mormans as by savage Indians, and that I believed
the best way for us to do was to make the best of our
way to Salt Lake.   "Now" I said, "Those of you who
agree with me can follow — and I hope all will."

Mc. Mahon said that we could not understand a
word the old Indian said, and as to following his trails,
I don't believe a word of it, and it don't seem right.

He said he had a map of the conntry, and it looked
just as safe to him to go on down the river as to go
wandering across a dry and desolate country which
we knew nothing of.   I said to Mc. Mahon — "I
know this sign language pretty well.   It is used by
almost all the Indians and is just as plain and certain
to me as my talk is to you.   Chief Walker and his
forefathers were borne here and know the country as
well as you know your father's farm, and for my
part, I think I shall take one of his trails and go to Salt

Lake and take the chances that way. I have no objections to you going some other way if you wish to
and think it is best". McMahon and Fields concluded they would not follow me any farther.

I then went to Chief Walker and had him point
out the trail to "Mormonie" as well as he could. He
told me where to enter the mountains leading north,
and when we got part way he told me we would come
to an Indian camp, when I must follow some horse
tracks newly made; he made me know this by using
his hands like horse's forefeet, and pointed the way.

Some of the young men motioned for me to come
out and shoot at a mark with them, and as I saw it
would please them I did so and took good care to
beat them every time too. Then they wanted to swap
(narawaup) guns with me which I declined doing.
After this the Chief came to me and wanted me to go
and hunt buffalo with them. I told him I had no
horse, and then he went and had a nice gray one
brought up and told me I could ride him if I would go.
He took his bow and arrow and showed me how he
could shoot an arrow straight through a buffalo just
back of his short ribs and that the arrow would go
clear through and come out on the other side without
touching a bone. Those fellows were in fine spirit,
on a big hunt, and when Walker pointed out his route
to me he swung his hand around to Salt Lake.

They all spoke the word buffalo quite plainly. I
took his strong bow and found I could hardly pull it
half way out, but I have no doubt he could do as he said
he could. I hardly knew how to refuse going with him.
I asked him how long it would be before he would get
around his long circuit and get to Salt Lake, to which
he replied by pulverizing some leaves in his hands and
scattering them in the air to represent snow, which
would fall by the time he got to "Mormonee". I shiv-

ered as he said this and by his actions I saw that I
understood him right·

I told him I could not go with him for the other boys
would depend on me to get them something to eat,
and I put my finger into my open mouth to tell him
this. I think if I had been alone I should have accepted his offer and should have had a good time. I
gave them to understand that we would swap (narawaup) with them for some horses so he brought up a
pair of nice two year-old colts for us. I offered him
some money for them, he did not want that, but would
take clothing of almost any kind. We let them have
some that we could get along without, and some one
let Walker have a coat. He put it on, and being
more warmly dressed than ever before, the sweat ran
down his face in streams. We let them have some
needles and thread and some odd notions we had to
spare. We saw that Walker had some three or four
head of cattle with him which he could kill if they
did not secure game at the time they expected.

McMahon and Field still persisted they would not
go with us and so we divided our little stock of flour
and dried meat with them as fairly as possible and decided we would try the trail. When our plans were
settled we felt in pretty good spirits again, and one of
the boys got up a sort of corn-stalk fiddle which made
a squeaking noise and in a little while there was a sort
of mixed American and Indian dance going on in
which the sqaws joined in and we had a pretty jolly
time till quite late at night. We were well pleased
that these wild folks had proved themselves to be true
friends to us.

The morning we were to start I told the boys a dream
I had in which I had seen that the course we had de-
cided on was the correct one, but Mc. Mahon and
Field thought we were foolish and said they had rath-

er take the chances of going with the Indians, or going on down the river. He seemed to place great
stress on the fact that he could not understand the
Indians.

Said He:—"This Indian may be all right, and may-
be he will lead us all into a dreadful trap. They are
treacherous and revengeful, and for some merely fancied wrong done by us, or by some one else of whom
we have no control or knowledge, they may take our
scalps, wipe us out of existence and no one will ever
know what became of us. Now this map of mine
don't show any bad places on this river, and I believe
we can get down easily enough, and get to California
some time. Field and I cannot make up our minds so
easily as you fellows. I believe your chances are
very poor.

The boys now had our few things loaded on the two
colts, for they had fully decided to go with me, and I
was not in the least put back by McMahon's dire
forbodings. We shook hands with quivering lips as
we each hoped the other would meet good luck, and
find enough to eat and all such sort of friendly talk,
and then with my little party on the one side and
McMahon and Field, whom we were to leave behind,
on the other, we bowed to each other with bared
heads, and then we started out of the little young cottonwoods into the broad plain that seemed to get wider and wider as we went west.

The mountains on the northern side grew smaller
and less steep as we went west, and on the other hand
reached down the river as far as we could see. The
plain itself was black and barren and for a hundred
miles at least ahead of us it seemed to have no end.
Walker had explained to us that we must follow some
horse tracks and enter a cañon some miles to the
northwest. He had made his hands work like horses'

feet, placing then near the ground as if following a
trail, We were not much more than a mile away
when on looking back, we saw Chief Walker coming towards us on a horse at full speed; and motioning
for us to stop. This we did, though some of the boys
said we would surely be marched back and scalped.
But it was not for that he came. He had been watching us and saw that we had failed to notice the tracks
of the horses he told us about so he rode after us, and
now took us off some little distance to the right, got
off his horse and showed us the faint horse tracks which
we were to follow and said "Mormonie". He pointed
out to us the exact cañon we were to enter when we
reached the hills; and said after three "sleeps" we
would find an Indian camp on top of the mountain.
He then bade us good bye again and galloped back
to his own camp.

We now resumed our journey, keeping watch of
the tracks more closely, and as we came near the
spurs of the mountain which projected out into the
barren valley we crossed several well marked trails
running along the foot hills, at right angles to our
own. This we afterwards learned was the regular trail
from Santa Fé to Los Angeles. At some big rocks
further on we camped for the night, and found water
in some pools or holes in the flat rocks which held
the rain.

Reading people of to-day, who know so well the geography of the American continent, may need to stop
and think that in 1849 the whole region west of the
Missouri River was very little known, the only men
venturesome enough to dare to travel over it were
hunters and trappers who, by a wild life had been
used to all the privations of such a journey, and
shrewd as the Indians themselves in the mysterious
ways of the trail and the chase. Even these fellows

had only investigated certain portions best suited to
their purpose.

The Indians here have the reputation of being blood
thirsty savages who took delight in murder and tor-
ture, but here, in the very midst of this wild and desolate country we found a Chief and his tribe, Walker
and his followers who were as humane and kind to
white people as could be expected of any one. I have
often wondered at the knowledge of this man respect-
ing the country, of which he was able to make us a
good map in the sand, point out to us the impassable
cañon, locate the hostile indians, and many points
which were not accurately known by our own explorers for many years afterward. He undoubtedly saved
our little band from a watery grave, for without his
advice we had gone on and on, far into the great
Colorado cañon, from which escape would have been
impossible and securing food another impossibility,
while destruction by hostile indians was among the
strong probabilities of the case. So in a threefold way
I have for these more than forty years credited the
lives of myself and comrades to the thoughtful interest
and humane consideration of old Chief Walker.

In another pool or pond near the one where we
were camped I shot a small duck. Big sage was plenty
here for fuel and we had duck for supper. Our party
consisted of five men and two small ponies only two
years old, with a stock of provisions very small including that the old chief had given us. We started on
in the morning, following our faint trail till we came to
the cañon we had in view, and up this we turned as
we had been directed, finding in the bottom a little
running stream. Timber began to appear as we ascended, and grass also. There were signs of deer and
grouse but we had no time to stop to hunt, for I had
the only gun and while I hunted the others must lie

idly by. We reached the summit at a low pass, and just above, on the north side of the higher mountains were considerable banks of snow. Following the Chief's instructions we left the trail and followed some horse tracks over rolling hills, high on the mountain side. We found the Indian camp exactly as the Chief had described, consisting of two or three lodges. The men were all absent hunting, but the women were gathering and baking some sort of a root which looked like a carrot. They made a pile of several bushels and covered it with earth, then made a fire, treating the pile some as a charcoal burner does his pit of coal. When sufficiently cooked they beat them up and made the material into small cakes which were dried in the sun. The dried cakes were as black as coal and intended for winter use. These roots before roasting were unfit for food, as they contained a sort of acrid juice that would make the tongue smart and very sore but there was a very good rich taste when cooked. The woman pointed to our horses and said "Walker", so we knew they were aware that we got them of him, and might have taken us for horse thieves for aught I know. As it was not yet night when we came to the camp, we passed on and camped on a clear mountain brook where grew some pine trees.. After a little some of the Indians belonging to the camp we had passed came in, bringing some venison, for which we traded by giving them some needles and a few other trinkets. I beat these fellows shooting at a mark, and then they wanted to trade guns, which I declined. This piece of meat helped us along considerably with our provisions, for game was very scarce and only some sage hens had come across our trail. One day I scared a hawk off the ground, and we took the sage hen he had caught and was eating, and made some soup of it.

After being on this trail six or seven days we began
to think of killing one of our colts for food, for we had
put ourselves on two meals a day and the work was
very hard; so that hunger was all the time increasing.
We thought this was a pretty long road for Walker to
ride over in three sleeps as he said he could, and we
began also to think there might be some mistake
somewhere, although it had otherwise turned out just
as he said.   On the eighth day our horse-tracks came
out into a large trail which was on a down grade leading in a northward direction.   On the ninth day we
came into a large valley, and near night came in sight
of a few covered wagons, a part of a train that intended going on a little later over the southern route to
Los Angeles but were waiting for the weather to get
a little cooler, for a large part of the route was over
almost barren deserts.   We were very glad to find
these wagons, for they seemed to have plenty of food
and the bountiful supper they treated us to was the
very thing we needed.   We camped here and told
them of the hardships we had passed through.   They
had hired a guide, each wagon paying him ten dollars
for his service.   Our little party talked over the situation among ourselves, and concluded that as we were
good walkers we must allow ourselves to be used in
any way so that we had grub and concluded as
many of us as possible would try to get some service
to do for our board and walk along with the party.
John Rogers had a dollar and a half and I had thirty
dollars, which was all the money we had in our camp.
We found out we were about 60 miles south of Salt
Lake City.   Some of the boys next day arranged to
work for their board, and the others would be taken
along if they would furnish themselves with flour and
bacon.   This part of the proposition fell to me and
two others, and so Hazelrig and I took the two colts

and started for the city, where they told us we could
get all we needed with our little purse of money.
We reached Hobble Creek before night, near Salt
Lake where there was a Mormon fort, and were also
a number of wagons belonging to some prospecting
train. There seemed to be no men about and we were
looking about among the wagons for some one to inquire of, when a woman came to the front of the last
wagon and looked out at us, and to my surprise it was
Mrs. Bennett, wife of the man I had been trying to
overtake ever since my start on this long trip Bennett
had my entire outfit with him on this trip and was all
the time wondering whether I would ever catch up
with them. We stayed till the men came in with their
cattle towards night, and Bennett was glad enough
to see me, I assure you. We had a good substantial
supper and then sat around the campfire nearly all
night telling of our experience since leaving Wisconsin. I had missed Bennett at the Missouri River.
I knew of no place where people crossed the river except Council Bluff, here I had searched faithfully, finding no trace of him, but it seems they had crossed
farther up at a place called Kanesville, a Mormon
crossing, and followed up the Platte river on the north
side. Their only bad luck had been to loose a fine
black horse, which was staked out, and when a herd
of buffaloes came along he broke his rope and followed
after them. He was looked for with other horses, but
never found and doubtless became a prize for some
enterprizing Mr. Lo. who was fortunate enough to
capture him. Hazelrig and I told of our experiance
on the south side of the Platte; why we went down
Green River; what a rough time we had; how we
were stopped by the Indians and how we had come a-
cross from the river, arriving the day before and were
now on our way to Salt Lake to get some flour and ba-

con so we could go on with the train when it started
as they had offered to haul our grub for our service if
we could carry ourselves on foot.

Mr. Bennett would not hear of my going on to Salt
Lake City, for he said there must be provisions
enough in the party and in the morning we were able
to buy flour and bacon of John Philips of Mineral
Point Wis. and of Wm. Philips his brother. I think
we got a hundred pounds of flour and a quantity of bacon and some other things. I had some money which
I had received for my horse sold to Dallas, but as the
others had none I paid for it all, and told Hazelrig to
take the ponies and go back to camp with a share of
the provisions and do the best he could. I had now
my own gun and ammunition, with some clothing
and other items which I had prepared in Wisconsin
before I started after my Winnebago pony, and I
felt I ought to share the money I had with the other
boys to help them as best I could. I felt that I was
pretty well fixed and had nothing to fear.

Mr. Bennett told me much of the trip on the north
side of the Platte. He said they had some cholera, of
which a few people died, and related how the outer if
not the inner nature of the men changed as they left
civilization, law and the courts behind them. Some
who had been raised together, and lived together all
their lives without discord or trouble, who were considered model men at home and just the right people
to be connected with in such an expedition, seemed to
change their character entirely out on these wild
wastes. When anything excited their displeasure
their blood boiled over, and only the interference of
older and wiser heads on many occasions prevented
bloodshed. Some dissolved the solemn contract they
had made to travel together systematically and in order
and to stand, by, even unto death, and when they

reached the upper Platte, the journey only half over, talked of going back, or splitting up the outfit and join others they had taken a fancy to. Some who could not agree upon a just division of a joint outfit, thinking one party was trying to cheat, would not yield but would cut their wagons in two lengthwise just for spite so that no carts could be made and the whole vehicle spoiled for both parties. The ugly disagreements were many and the cloven foot was shown in many ways. Guns were often drawn and pointed but some one would generally interfere and prevent bloodshed. Others were honest and law abiding to the last degree beyond law and churches, and would act as harmoniously as at home, obeying their chosen captain in the smallest particular without any grumbling or dissension, doing to every one as they would be done by. These were the pride of the train. The trains were most of them organized, and all along the river bottom one was hardly ever out of sight of some of the wagons, all going west. Buffalo and antelope were plenty and in great droves, followed always by wolves great and small, who were on the lookout for crippled or dead animals with which to fill their hungry stomachs. Buffalo meat was plenty and much enjoyed while passing this section of the road and this opportunity of replenishing, enabled the stock to last them over more desolate regions where game was scarce.

After Bennett had told his stories, and I had related more of our own close escapes I began to ask him why he went this way which seemed to be very circuitous and much longer than the way they had first intended to go. He said that it was too late in the season to go the straight-road safely, for there was yet 700 miles of bad country to cross and do the best they could it would be at the commencement of the rainy season before the Sierra Nevada mountains could be reached and in those mountains there was often a snow fall of 20 feet or more, and anyone caught in it would surely perish. If they tried to winter at the base of the mountains it was a long way to get provisions, and no assurance of wild game, and this course was considered very hazardous for any one to undertake. This they had learned after consulting mountaineers and others who knew about the regions, and as there was nothing doing among the Latter Day Saints to give employment to any one, it was decided best to keep moving and go the southern route by way of Los Angeles. No wagons were reported as ever getting through that way, but a trail had been traveled through that barren desert country for perhaps a hundred years, and the same could be easily broadened into a wagon road.

After days of argument and camp-fire talks, this Southern route was agreed upon, and Capt. Hunt was chosen as guide. Capt. Hunt was a Mormon, and had more than one wife, but he had convinced them that he knew something about the road. Each agreed to give him ten dollars to pilot the train to San Bernardino where the Mormon Church had bought a Spanish grant of land, and no doubt they thought a wagon road to that place would benefit them greatly, and probably gave much encouragement for the parties to travel this way. It was undoubtedly safer than the northern mountain route at this season of the year. It seemed at least to be a new venture for west-bound emigrant trains, at least as to ultimate success, for we had no knowledge of any that had gone through safely.

Some western people remembered the history of the Mormons in Illinois and Missouri, and their doings there, feared somewhat for their own safety now that they were so completely under their power, for they

knew the Mormons to be revengeful and it was considered very unsafe for any traveler to acknowledge
he was from Missouri. Many a one who had been
born there, and lived there all his life, would promptly
claim some other state as his native place. I heard
one Mormon say that there were some Missourians on
the plains that would never reach California. "They
used us bad," said he, and his face took on a really
murderous look.

These Mormons at Salt Lake were situated as if on
an island in the sea, and no enemy could reach any
adjoining state or territory if Brigham Young's band
of destroying angels were only warned to look after
them.

At a late hour that night we lay down to sleep, and
morning came clear and bright. After breakfast Mr.
Bennett said to me:—"Now Lewis I want you to go
with me; I have two wagons and two drivers and four
yoke of good oxen and plenty of provisions. I have
your outfit yet, your gun and ammunition and your
two good hickory shirts which are just in time for
your present needs. You need not do any work. You
just look around and kill what game you can for us,
and this will help as much as anything, you can do." I
was, of course glad to accept this offer, and thanks to
Mr. Bennett's kind care of my outfit, was better fixed
then any of the other boys.

We inquired around among the other wagons as to
their supply of flour and bacon; and succeeded to
getting flour from Mr. Philips and bacon from some
of the others, as much as we supposed the other boys
would need, which I paid for, and when this was
loaded on the two colt,s Hazelrig started back alone
to the boys in camp. As I was so well provided for
I gave him all my money for they might need some,
and I did not:

The wagons which composed the intended train were very much scattered about, having moved out from Salt Lake at pleasure, and it was said to be too early to make the start on the southern route, for the weather on the hot, barren desert was said to grow cooler a little later in the season, and it was only at this cool season that the south west part of the desert could be crossed in safety. The scattering members of the train began to congregate, and Capt. Hunt said it was necessary to have some sort of system about the move, and that before they moved they must organize and adopt rules and laws which must be obeyed. He said they must move like an army, and that he was to be a dictator in all things except that in case of necessity a majority of the train could rule otherwise. It was thought best to get together and try a march out one day, then go in camp and organize.

This they did, and at the camp there was gathered one hundred and seven wagons, a big drove of horses and cattle, perhaps five hundred in all. The train was divided into seven divisions and each division was to elect its own captain. Division No. 1 should lead the march the first day, and their men should take charge of the stock and deliver them to the wagons in the morning, and then No. 1 should take the rear, with No. 2 in the lead to break the road. The rear division would not turn a wheel before 10 o'clock the next day, and it would be about that time at night before they were in camp and unyoked. The numbers of animals cleaned out the feed for a mile or two each side of the camp and a general meeting was called for the organization of the whole. Mr. L. Granger got up so he could look over the audience and proceeded to explain the plan and to read a preamble and resolutions which had been prepared as

the basis for government.   I remember that it begun
thus:—"This Organization shall be known and designated as   the Sand Walking Company, and shall
consist of   seven divisions   etc," detailing the
manner of marching as we have recited. Capt J.
Hunt was chosen commander and guide, and his
orders must be obeyed.   All possible trouble that we
could imagine might come was provided against in
our written agreement, and all promised to live up to
it.

CHAPTER IX.

We moved off in good style from this camp. After a day or two and before we reached what is called Little Salt Lake, an attempt was made to make a short cut, to save distance. The train only went on this cut off a day or two when Capt. Hunt came back from the front and said they had better turn back to the old trail again, which all did. This was a bad move, the train much broken and not easy to get them into regular working order again. We were now approaching what they called the Rim of the Basin. Within the basin the water all ran to the north or toward Great Salt Lake, but when we crossed the rim, all was toward the Colorado River, through which it reached the Pacific Ocean. About this time we were overtaken by another train commanded by Capt. Smith. They had a map with them made by one Williams of Salt Lake a mountaineer who was represented to know all the routes through all the mountains of Utah, and this map showed a way to turn off from the southern route not far from the divide which separated the waters of the basin from those which flowed toward the Colorado, and pass over the mountains, coming out in what they called Tulare valley, much nearer than by Los Angeles.

This map was quite frequently exhibited and the matter freely discussed in camp, indeed speeches were made in the interest of the cut-off route which was to be so much shorter. A clergyman, the Rev. J. W. Brier, was very enthusiastic about this matter and discaused learnedly and plausibly about it. The more the matter was talked about the more there were who were converted to the belief that the short road would be the best. The map showed every camp on the road and showed where there was water and grass, and as to obstacles to the wagons it was thought they could easily be overcome. A general meeting was called for better consideration of the question. Capt. Hunt said: "You all know I was hired to go by way of Los Angeles, but if you all wish to go and follow Smith I will go also. But if even one wagon decides to go the original route, I shall feel bound to go with that wagon."

A great many were anxious to get the opinion of Capt. Hunt on the feasibility of the new route for he was a mountain man and could probably give us some good advice. He finally consented to talk of it, and said he really knew no more then the others about this particular route, but he very much doubted if a white man ever went over it, and that he did not consider it at all safe for those who had wives and children in their company to take the unknown road. Young men who had no family could possibly get through, and save time even if the road was not as good as Los Angeles road. But said he "If you decide to follow Smith I will go will go with you, even if the road leads to Hell."

On the route from near Salt Lake to this point we found the country to grow more barren as we progressed. The grass was thinner, and sage brush took the place of timber. Our road took us in sight of Sevier Lake, and also, while going through the low hills, passed Little Salt Lake, which was almost dry, with a beach around it almost as white as snow. It might have had a little more the dignity of a lake in wet weather, but it was a rather dry affair as we saw it.

At one point on this route we came into a long narrow valley, well covered with sage brush, and before we had gone very far we discovered that this was a great place for long eared rabbits, we would call them Jack Rabbits now. Every one who had a gun put it into service on this occassion, and there was much popping and shooting on every side. Great clouds of smoke rolled up as the hunters advanced and the rabbits ran in every direction to get away. Many ran right among the horses, and under the feet of the cattle and under the wagons, so that the teamsters even killed some with a whip. At the end of the valley we went into camp, and on counting up the game found we had over 500, or about one for every person in camp. This gave us a feast of fresh meat not often found.

It was on this trip that one of Mr. Bennett's ox drivers was taken with a serious bowel difficulty, and for many days we thought he would die, but he eventually recovered. His name was Silas Helmer.

It was really a serious moment when the front of the train reached the Smith trail. Team after team turned to the right while now and then one would keep straight ahead as was at first intended. Capt. Hunt came over to the larger party after the division was made, and wished them all a hearty farewell and a pleasant happy journey. My friend Bennett whose fortune I shared was among the seceders who followed the Smith party. This point, when our paths diverged was very near the place afterward made notorious as Mountain Meadows, where the famous massacre took place under the direction of the Mormon generals. Our route from here up to the mountain was a very pleasant one, steadily up grade, over rolling hills, with wood, water and grass in plenty. We came at last to what seemed the summit of a great mountain, about three days journey on the new trail. Juniper trees grew about in bunches, and my experience with this timber taught me that we were on elevated ground.

Immediately in front of us was a cañon, impassible for wagons, and down into this the trail descended. Men could go, horses and mules, perhaps, but wagons could no longer follow that trail, and we proposed to camp while explorers were sent out to search a pass across this steep and rocky cañon. Wood and bunch grass were plenty, but water was a long way down the trail and had to be packed up to the camp. Two days passed, and the parties sent out began to come in, all reporting no way to go farther with the wagons. Some said the trail on the west side of the cañon could be ascended on foot by both men and mules, but that it would take years to make it fit for wheels.

The enthusiasm about the Smith cut-off had begun to die and now the talk began of going back to follow Hunt. On the third morning a lone traveler with a small wagon and one yoke of oxen, died. He seemed to be on this journey to seek to regain his health. He was from Kentucky, but I have forgotten his name. Some were very active about his wagon and, some thought too much attention was paid to a stranger. He was decently buried by the men of the company.

This very morning a Mr. Rynierson called the attention of the crowd and made some remarks upon the situation. He said: ''My family is near and dear to me. I can see by the growth of the timber that we are in a very elevated place. This is now the seventh of November, it being the fourth at the time of our turning off on this trail. We are evidently in a country where snow is liable to fall at any time in the winter season, and if we were to remain here and be caught in a severe storm we should all probably perish. I, for one, feel in duty bound to seek a safer way than this. I shall hitch up my oxen and return at once to the old trail. Boys (to his teamsters) get

the cattle and we'll return." This was decisive, and
Mr. Rynierson would tarry no longer. Many others
now proceeded to get ready and follow, and as Mr.
Rynierson drove out of camp quite a respectable train
fell in behind him. As fast as the hunters came in
and reported no road available, they also yoked up
their oxen and rolled out. Some waited awhile
or companions yet in the fields, and all were about
ready to move, when a party came in with news that
the pass was fonnd and no trouble could be seen
ahead. About twenty-seven wagons remained when
this news came, and as their proprietors had brought
good news they agreed to travel on westward and not
go back to the old trail.

Mr. Bennett had gone only a short distance out when
he had the misfortune to break the axle of his wagon
and he then went back to camp and took an axle out
of the dead man's wagon and by night had it fitted
into his own. He had to stay until morning, and
there were still a few others who were late in getting a
start, who camped there also. Among these were
J. B. Arcane, wife and child; two Earhart brothers
and sons and some two or three other wagons.

When all was ready we followed the others who had
gone ahead. The route led at first directly to the
north and a p asswas said to be in that direction. Of
the Green River party only Rodgers and myself remained with this train. After the wagons straightened
out nicely, a meeting was called to organize, so as to
travel systematically. A feeling was very manifest
that those without any families did not care to bind
themselves to stand by and assist those who had
wives and children in their party and there was considerable debate, which resulted in all the family
wagons being left out of the arrangements.

A party who called themselves "The Jayhawkers"

passed us, and we followed along in the rear, over rolling hills covered with juniper timber, and small grassy valleys between where there was plenty of water and went well, for those before us had broken out the road so we could roll along very pleasantly.

At the organization Jim Martin was chosen captain. Those who were rejected were Rev. J. W. Brier and, his family, J. B. Arcane and family, and Mr. A. Bennett and family, Mr. Brier would not stay put out, but forced himself in, and said he was going with the rest, and so he did. But the other families remained behind. I attended the meeting and heard what was said, but Mr. Bennett was my friend and had been faithful to me and my property when he knew not where I was, and so I decided to stand by him and his wife at all hazards.

As I had no team to drive I took every opportunity to climb the mountains along the route, reaching the highest elevations even if they were several miles from the trail. I sometimes remained out all night. I took Mr. Arcane's field glass with me and was thus able to see all there was of the country. I soon became satisfied that going north was not taking us in the direction we ought to go. I frequently told them so, but they still persisted in following on. I went to the leaders and told them we were going back toward Salt Lake again, not making any headway toward California. They insisted they were following the directions of Williams, the mountaineer; and they had not yet got as far north as he indicated. I told them, and Mr. Bennett and others, that we must either turn west, or retrace our steps and get back into the regular Los Angeles road again. In the morning we held another consultation and decided to turn west here, and leave the track we had been following.

Off we turned at nearly right angles to our former

course, to the west now, over a piece of table land
that gave us little trouble in breaking our own road.
When we camped, the oxen seemed very fond of a white
weed that was very plenty, and some borrowed a good
deal of trouble thinking that perhaps it might be
poison. I learned afterwards that this plant was the
nutritious white sage, which cattle eat freely, with
good results. We now crossed a low range and a
small creek running south, and here were also some
springs. Some corn had been grown here by the
Indians. Pillars of sand stone, fifteen feet high and
very slim were round about in several places and
looked strange enough. The next piece of table land
sloped to the east, and among the sage grew also a
bunch grass a foot high, which had seeds like broom-
corn seeds. The Indians had gathered the grass and
made it in piles of one hundred pounds or so, and
used it for food as I found by examining their camps.

One day I climbed a high mountain where some pine
grew, in order to get a view of the country. As I
neared its base I came to a flat rock, perhaps fifty feet
square. I heard some pounding noise as I came near,
but what ever it was, it ceased on my approach.
There were many signs of the rock being used as a
camp, such as pine burrs, bones of various kinds of
animals, and other remains of food which lay every
where about and on the rock. Near the center was a
small oblong stone fitted into a hole. I took it out
and found it covered a fine well of water about three
feet deep and was thus protected against any small
animal being drowned in it. I went on up the
mountain and from the top I saw that the land west
of us looked more and more barren.

The second night the brave Jayhawkers who had
been so firm in going north hove in sight in our rear.
They had at last concluded to accept my advice and had

came over our road quite rapidly. We all camped together that night, and next morning they took the lead
again. After crossing a small range they came to a
basin which seemed to have no outlet, and was very
barren. Some of the boys in advance of the teams
had passed over this elevation and were going quite
rapidly over the almost level plain which sloped into
the basin, when they saw among the bunches of sage
brush behind them a small party of Indians following
their road, not very far off, but still out of bow and
arrow range. The boys were suddenly able to take
much longer steps than usual and a little more rapidly
too, and swinging round toward the teams as soon as
possible, for they already had some fears that an
arrow might be sticking in their backs in an unpleasantly short space of time, for the Indians were
good travelers. When they came in sight of the
wagons, the Indians vanished as quickly as if they
had gone into a hole, with no sign remaining, except
a small dog which greatly resembled a prairie wolf, and
kept a safe distance away. No one could imagine
where the fellows went so suddenly.

We drove to the west side of this basin and camped
near the foot of a low mountain. The cattle were
driven down into the basin where there was some
grass, but at camp we had only the water in our kegs.

Some of the boys climbed the mountain on the
north but found no springs. Coming down a cañon
they found some rain water in a basin in the rocks
and all took a good drink. Lew West lay down and
swallowed all he could and then told the boys to kill
him for he never would feel so good again. They
finished the pool, it was so small, before they left it.
In going on down the cañon they saw an Indian
dodge behind some big rocks, and searching, they
found him in a cave as still as a dead man. They

pulled him out and made him go with them, and tried
every way to find out from him where they were and
where Owen's Lake was, as they had been told the
lake was on their route.   But he proved to be no
wiser than a man of mud, and they led him along to
camp, put a red flannel shirt on him to cover his
nakedness, and made him sleep between two white
men so he could not get away easily.   In the morning they were more successful, and he showed us a
small ravine four miles away which had water in it,
enough for our   use, and we moved up and camped
there, while the boys and   the Indian started over a
barren, rocky mountain, and when over on the
western slope they were led to a water hole on a steep
rocky cliff where no one but an Indian would ever
think of looking for water.   They took out their cups
and had a good drink all around, then offered the
Indian some, but he disdained the cizilized way, and
laying down his bow and arrows took a long drink
directly out of the pool.   He was so long in getting a
good supply that the boys almost forgot him as they
were gazing over the distant mountain and discussing
prospects, till attracted by a slight noise they looked
and saw Mr. Indian going down over the cliffs after
the fashion of a mountain sheep, and in a few bounds
he was out of sight.   They could not have killed him
if they had tried, the move so sudden and un-
looked for.   They had expected the fellow to show
them the way to Owen's lake, but now their guide
was gone, and left nothing to remember him by except
his bow and arrows.   So they returned to their
wagons not much wiser than before.

All kinds of game was now very scarce, and so
seldon seen that the men got tired of carrying their guns,
and grew fearless of enemies. A heavy rifle was
indeed burdensome over so long a road when there

was no frequent use for it. The party kept rolling
along as fast as possible but the mountains and
valleys grew more barren and water more scarce all
the time. When found, the water would be in hole
at the outlet of some cañon, or in little pools which
had filled up with rain that had fallen on the higher
ground. Not a drop of rain had fallen on us since
we stared on this cut-off, and every night was clear
and warm. The elevated parts of the country seemed
to be isolated buttes, with no running streams between
them but instead, dry lakes with a smooth clay bed,
very light in color and so hard that the track of an
ox could not be seen on its glittering surface. At a
distance those clay beds looked like water shining
in the sun and were generally about three times as
far as any one would judge, the air was so clear. This
mirage, or resemblance to water was so perfect as often
to deceive us, and almost to our ruin on one or two
occasions.

I took Arcane's field glass and took pains to ascend
all the high buttes within a day's walk of the road,
and this enabled me to get a good survey of the
country north and west. I would sometimes be
gone two or three days with no luggage but my canteen and gun. I was very cautious in regard to
Indians, and tried to keep on the safe side of surprises.
I would build a fire about dark and then travel on till
I came to a small washed place and lie down and stay
till morning, so if Mr. Indian did come to my fire he
would not find any one to kill. One day I was going
up a wide ravine leading to the summit, and before I
reached the highest part I saw a smoke curl up before me. I took a side ravine and went cautiously,
bowed down pretty low so no one could see me, and
when near the top of the ridge and about one hundred
yards of the fire I ventured to raise slowly up and

take a look to see how many there were in camp: I
could see but two and as I looked across the ravine
an Indian woman seemed looking at me also, but I
was so low she could only see the top of my head, and
I sank down again out of sight. I crawled further
up so as to get a better view, and when I straightened
up again she got a full view of me. She instantly
caught her infant off its little pallet made of a small
piece of thin wood covered with a rabbit skin, and
putting the baby under one arm, and giving a smart
jerk to a small girl that was crying to the top of her
voice, she bounded off and fairly flew up the gentle
slope toward the summit, the girl following after very
close. The woman's long black hair stood out as she
rushed along, looking over her shoulder every instant
as if she expected to be slain. The mother flying
with her children, untrammeled with any of the arts
of fashion was the best natural picture I ever looked
upon, and wild in the extreme. No living artist
could do justice to the scene as the lady of the desert,
her little daughter and her babe, passed over the
summit out of sight. I followed, but when I reached
the highest summit, no living person could be seen.
I looked the country over with my glass. The region
to the north was black rocky, and very mountainous.
I looked some time and then concluded I had better
not go any further that way, for I might be waylaid
and filled with arrows at some unsuspected moment.
We saw Indian signs almost every day, but as none of
them ever came to our camp it was safe to say they
were not friendly. I now turned back and examined
the Indian woman's camp. She had only fire enough
to make a smoke. Her conical shaped basket left
behind, contained a few poor arrows and some cactus
leaves, from which the spines had been burned, and
there lay the little pallet where the baby was sleeping.
It was a bare looking kitchen for hungry folks.

I now went to the top of a high butte and scanned the country very carefully, especially to the west and north, and found it very barren. There were no trees, no fertile valleys nor anything green. Away to the west some mountains stood out clear and plain, their summits covered white with snow. This I decided was our objective point: Very little snow could be seen elsewhere, and between me and the snowy mountains lay a low, black rocky range, and a wide level plain, that had no signs of water, as I had learned them in our trip thus far across the country. The black range seemed to run nearly north and south, and to the north and northwest the country looked volcanic, black and desolate.

As I looked and thought, I believed that we were much farther from a fertile region then most of our party had any idea of. Such of them as had read Fremont's travels, and most of them going to California had fortified themselves before starting by reading Fremont; said that the mountains were near California and were fertile from their very summits down to the sea, but that to the east of the mountains it was a desert region for hundred of miles. As I explained it to them, and so they soon saw for themselves, they believed that the snowy range ahead of us was the last range to cross before we entered the long-sought California, and it seemed not far off, and prospect quite encouraging.

Our road had been winding around among the buttes which looked like the Indian baskets turned upside down on the great barren plain. What water we found was in small pools in the wash-out places near the foothills at the edge of the valley, probably running down the ravines after some storm. There were dry lake beds scattered around over the plain, but it did not seem as if there had ever been volume

of water enough lately to force itself out so far into
the plain as these lakes were. All the lakes appeared
about the same, the bed white and glistening in the
sun, which made it very hard for the eyes, and so
that a man in passing over it made no visible track.
It looked as if it one time might have been a smooth bed
of plastic mortar, and had hardened in the sun. It
looked as if there must have been water there sometime,
but we had not seen a drop, or a single cloud; every
day was clear and sunny, and very warm, and at night
no stars forgot to shine.

Our oxen began to look bad, for they had poor food.
Grass had been very scarce, and now when we unyoked them and turned them out they did not care to
look around much for something to eat. They moved
slowly and cropped disdainfully the dry scattering
shrubs and bunches of grass from six inches to a foot
high. Spending many nights and days on such dry
food and without water they suffered fearfully, and
though fat and sleek when we started from Salt Lake,
they now looked gaunt and poor, and dragged themselves slowly along, poor faithful servants of mankind.
No one knew how long before we might have
to kill some of them to get food to save our own lives.

We now traveled several days down the bed of a
broad ravine, which led to a southwest direction.
There seemed to be a continuous range of mountains
on the south, but to the north was the level plain
with scattered buttes, and what we had all along
called dry lakes, for up to this time we had seen no
water in any of them. I had carried my rifle with me
every day since we took this route, and though I was
an experienced hunter, a professional one if there be
such a thing, I had killed only one rabbit, and where
no game lived I got as hungry as other folks.

Our line soon brought us in sight of a high butte

which stood apparently about 20 miles south of our
route, and I determined to visit and climb it to get a
better view of things ahead. I walked steadily all
day and reached the summit about dusk. I wandered
around among the big rocks, and found a projecting
cliff where I would be protected from enemies, wind
or storm, and here I made my camp. While the light
lasted I gathered a small stock of fuel, which consisted of a stunted growth of sage and other small
shrubs, dry but not dead, and with this I built a little
fire Indian fashion and sat down close to it. Here
was a good chance for undisturbed meditation and
someway I could not get around doing a little
meditating as I added a new bit of fuel now and then
to the small fire burning at my side. I thought it
looked dark and troublesome before us. I took a
stone for a pillow with my hat on it for a cushion, and
lying down close under the shelving rock I went to
sleep, for I was very tired, I woke soon from being
cold, for the butte was pretty high, and so I busied
myself the remainder of the night in adding little
sticks to the fire, which gave me some warmth, and
thus in solitude I spent the night. I was glad enough
to see the day break over the eastern mountains, and
light up the vast barren country I could see on every
hand around me. When the sun was fairly up I took
a good survey of the situation, and it seemed as if
pretty near all creation was in sight. North and west
was a level plain, fully one hundred miles wide it
seemed, and from anything I could see it would not
afford a traveler a single drink in the whole distance
or give a poor ox many mouthfuls of grass. On the
western edge it was bounded by a low, black and
rocky range extending nearly north and south for a
long distance and no pass though it which I could see,
and beyond this range still another one apparently

parallel to it. In a due west course from me was the high peak we had been looking at for a month, and lowest place was on the north side, which we had named Martin's Pass and had been trying so long to reach. This high peak, covered with snow, glistened to the morning sun, and as the air was clear from clouds or fog, and no dust or haze to obscure the view, it seemed very near.

I had learned by experience that objects a day's walk distant seemed close by in such a light, and that when clear lakes appeared only a little distance in our front, we might search and search and never find them. We had to learn how to look for water in this peculiar way. In my Wisconsin travel I had learned that when I struck a ravine I must go down to look for living water, but here we must invariably travel upward for the water was only found in the high mountains.

Prospects now seemed to me so hopeless, that I heartily wished I was not in duty bound to stand by the women and small children who could never reach a land of bread without assistance. If I was in the position that some of them were who had only themselves to look after, I could pick up my knapsack and gun and go off, feeling I had no dependent ones to leave behind. But as it was I felt I should be morally guilty of murder if I should forsake Mr. Bennett's wife and children, and the family of Mr. Arcane with whom I had been thus far associated. It was a dark line of thought but I always felt better when I got around to the determination, as I always did, to stand by my friends, their wives and children let come what might.

I could see with my glass the train of wagons moving slowly over the plain toward what looked to me like a large lake. I made a guess of the point they

would reach by night, and then took a straight course
for it all day long in steady travel. It was some time
after dark, and I was still a quarter of a mile from the
camp fires, where in the bed of a cañon I stepped into
some mud, which was a sign of water. I poked
around in the dark for a while and soon found a little
pool of it, and having been without a drop of it for
two days I lay down and took a hasty drink. It did
not seem to be very clear or clean, but it was certainly
wet, which was the main thing just then. The next
morning I went to the pond of water, and found the
oxen had been watered there. They stirred up the
mud a good deal and had drank off about all the clean
part, which seemed to refresh them very much. I
found the people in the camp on the edge of the lake
I had seen from the mountain, and fortunately it contained about a quarter of an inch of water. They had
dug some holes here, which filled up, and they were
using this water in the camp.

The ambitious mountain-climbers of our party had
by this, time, abandoned that sort of work, and I was
left alone to look about and try to ascertain the
character of the road they were to follow. It was a
great deal to do to look out for food for the oxen and
for water for the camp, and besides all this it was
plain there were Indians about even if we did not see
them. There were many signs, and I had to be
always on the lookout to outgeneral them. When the
people found I was in camp this night they came
around to our wagons to know what I had seen and
found, and what the prospects were ahead. Above all
they wanted to know how far it was, in my opinion
to the end of our journey. I listened to all their inquiries and told them plainly what I had seen, and
what I thought of the prospect. I did not like telling
the whole truth about it for fear it might dampen

their spirits, but being pressed for an opinion I told them in plain words that it would at least be another month before their journey would be ended. They seemed to think I ought to be pretty good authority, and if I was not mistaken, the oxen would get very poor and provisions very scarce before we could pull through so long. I was up at day break and found Mr. Bennett sitting by the fire. About the first thing he said:—"Lewis, if you please I don't want you here-after to express your views so openly and emphatically as you did last night about our prospects. Last night when I went to bed I found Sarah (his wife) crying and when pressed for the cause, she said she had heard your remarks on the situation, and that if Lewis said so it must be correct, for he knows more about it than all of you. She felt that she and the children must starve."

In the morning Jayhawkers, and others of the train that were not considered strictly of our own party, yoked up and started due west across the level plain which I had predicted as having no water, and I really thought they would never live to get across to the western border. Mr. Culverwell and Mr. Fish stayed with us, making another wagon in our train. We talked about the matter carefully, I did not think it possible to get across that plain in less than four or six days, and I did not believe there was a drop of water on the route. To the south of us was a mountain that now had considerable snow upon its summit, and some small pine trees also. Doubtless we could find plenty of water at the base, but being due south, it was quite off our course. The prospects for reaching water were so much better in that way that we finally decided to go there rather than follow the Jayhawkers on their desolate tramp over the dry plain.

So we turned up a cañon leading toward the mountain and had a pretty heavy up grade and a rough bed for a road. Part way up we came to a high cliff and in its face were niches or cavites as large as a barrel or larger, and in some of them we found balls of a glistening substance looking something like pieces of varigated candy stuck together. The balls were as large as small pumpkins. It was evidently food of some sort, and we found it sweet but sickish, and those who were so hungry as to break up one of the balls and divide it among the others, making a good meal of it, were a little troubled with nausea afterwards. I considered it bad policy to rob the Indians of any of their food, for they must be pretty smart people to live in this desolate country and find enough to keep them alive, and I was pretty sure we might count them as hostiles as they never came near our camp. Like other Indians they were probably revengeful, and might seek to have revenge on us for the injury. We considered it prudent to keep careful watch for them, so they might not surprise us with a volley of arrows.

The second night we camped near the head of the cañon we had been following, but thus far there had been no water, and only some stunted sage brush for the oxen, which they did not like, and only ate it when near the point of starvation. They stood around the camp looking as sorry as oxen can. During the night a stray and crazy looking cloud passed over us and left its moisture on the mountain to the shape of a coat of snow several inches deep. When daylight came the oxen crowded around the wagons, shivering with cold, and licking up the snow to quench their thirst. We took pattern after them and melted snow to get water for ourselves.

By the looks of our cattle it did not seem as if they

could pull much, and light loads were advisable on
this up grade. Mr. Bennett was a carpenter and had
brought along some good tools in his wagon. These
he reluctantly unloaded, and almost everything else
except bedding and provisions, and leaving them
upon the ground, we rolled up the hills slowly, with
loads as light as possible.

Rogers and I went ahead with our guns to look out
the way and find a good camping place. After a
few miles we got out of the snow and out upon an incline, and in the bright clear morning air the foot of
the snowy part of the mountain seemed near by and we
were sure we could reach it before night. From here no
guide was needed and Rogers and I, with our guns
and canteens hurried on as fast as possible, when a
camp was found we were to raise a signal smoke to
tell them where it was. We were here, as before
badly deceived as to the distance, and we marched
steadily and swiftly till nearly night before we reached
the foot of the mountain.

Here was a flat place in a table land and on it a low
brush hut, with a small smoke near by, which we
could plainly see as we were in the shade of the
mountain, and that place lighted up by the nearly
setting sun. We looked carefully and satisfied ourselves there was but one hut, and consequently but
few people could be expected. We approached carefully and cautiously, making a circuit around so as to
get between the hut and the hill in case that the
occupants should retreat in that direction. It was a
long time before we could see any entrance to this
wickiup, but we found it at last and approached
directly in front, very cautiously indeed: We could
see no one, and thought perhaps they were in
ambush for us, but hardly probable, as we had kept
closely out of sight. We consulted a moment and

concluded to make an advance and if possible capture
some one who could tell us about the country, as we
felt we were completely lost. When within thirty
yards a man poked out his head out of a doorway and
drew it back again quick as a flash. We kept out our
guns at full cock and ready for use, and told Rogers
to look out for arrows, for they would come now if
ever. But they did not pull a bow on us, and the red-
man, almost naked came out and beckoned for us to
come on which we did.

We tried to talk with the fellow in the sign language
but he could understand about as much as an oyster.
I made a little basin in the ground and filled it with
water from our canteens to represent a lake, then
pointed in an inquiring way west and north, made
signs of ducks and geese flying and squawking, but I
did no seem to be able to get an idea into his head of
what we wanted. I got thoroughly provoked at him
and may have shown some signs of anger. During
all this time a child or two in the hut squalled
terribly, fearing I suppose they would all be murdered. We might have lost our scalps under some
circumstances, but we appeared to be fully the
strangest party, and had no fear, for the Indian had
no weapon about him and we had both guns and
knives' The poor fellow was shivering with cold, and
with signs of friendship we fired off one of the guns
which waked him up a little and he pointed to the
gun and said "Walker," probably meaning the same
good Chief Walker who had so fortunately stopped us
in our journey down Green River. I understood from
the Indian that he was not friendly to Walker, but to
show that he was all right with us he went into the hut
and brought out a handful of corn for us to eat. By
the aid of a warm spring near by they had raised some
corn here, and the dry stalks were standing around.

As we were about to leave I told him we would come back, next day and bring him some clothes if we could find any to spare, and then we shouldered our guns and went back toward the wagons, looking over our shoulders occasionally to see if we were followed. We walked fast down the hill and reached the camp about dark to find it a most unhappy one indeed. Mrs. Bennett and Mrs. Arcane were in heart-rending distress. The four children were crying for water but there was not a drop to give them, and none could be reached before some time next day. The mothers were nearly crazy, for they expected the children would choke with thirst and die in their arms, and would rather perish themselves than suffer the agony of seeing their little ones gasp and slowly die. They reproached themselves as being the cause of all this trouble. For the love of gold they had left homes where hunger had never come, and often in sleep dreamed of the bounteous tables of their old homes only to be woefully disappointed in the morning. There was great gladness when John Rogers and I appeared in the camp and gave the mothers full canteens of water for themselves and little ones, and there was tears of joy and thankfulness upon their cheeks as they blessed us over and over again.

The oxen fared very hard. The ground was made up of broken stone, and all that grew was a dry and stunted brush not more than six inches high, of which the poor animals took an occasional dainty bite, and seemed hardly able to drag along.

It was only seven or eight miles to the warm spring and all felt better to know for a certainty that we would soon be safe again. We started early, even the women walked, so as to favor the poor oxen all we could. When within two miles of the water some of the oxen lay down and refused to rise again, so we

had to leave them and a wagon, while the rest pushed
on and reached the spring soon after noon. We took
water and went back to the oxen left behind, and gave
them some to drink. They were somewhat rested
and got up, and we tried to drive them in without the
wagons, but they were not inclined to travel without
the yoke, so we put it on them and hitched to the
wagon again. The yoke and the wagon seemed to
brace them up a good deal, and they went along thus
much better than when alone and scattered about,
with nothing to lean upon.

The warm spring was quite large and ran a hundred
yards or more before the water sank down into the
dry and thirsty desert. The dry cornstalks of last
years crop, some small willows, sage brush, weeds and
grass suited our animals very well, and they ate better
than for a long time, and we thought it best to remain
two or three days to give them a chance to get rest.
The Indian we left here the evening before had gone
and left nothing behind but a chunk of crystalized rock
salt. He seemed to be afraid of his friends.

The range we had been traveling nearly paralell
with seemed to come to an end here where this
snow peak stood, and immediately north and south of
this peak there seemed to be a lower pass. The con-
tinous range north was too low to hold snow. In the
morning I concluded to go to the summit of that pass
and with my glass have an extensive view. Two
other boys started with me, and as we moved along
the snow line we saw tracks of our runaway Indian in
the snow, passing over a low ridge. As we went on
up hill our boys began to fall behind, and long before
night I could see nothing of them. The ground was
quite soft, and I saw many tracks of Indians
which put me on my guard. I reached the summit
and as the shade of its mountain began to make it a

little dark, I built a fire of sage brush, ate my grub,
and when it was fairly dark, renewed the fire and
passed on a mile, where in a small ravine with banks
two feet high I lay down sheltered from the wind and
slept till morning. I did this to beat the Indian in
his own cunning.

Next morning I reached the summit about nine
o'clock, and had the grandest view I ever saw. I
could see north and south almost forever. The
surrounding region seemed lower, but much of it black,
mountainous and barren. On the west the snow peak
shut out the view in that direction. To the south the
mountains seemed to descend for more than twenty
miles, and near the base, perhaps ten miles away,
were several smokes, apparently from camp fires, and
as I could see no animals or camp wagons anywhere
I presumed them to be Indians. A few miles to the
north and east of where I stood, and somewhat higher,
was the roughest piece of ground I ever saw. It
stood in sharp peaks and was of many colors, some of
them so red that the mountain looked red hot, I
imagined it to be a true volcanic point, and had never
been so near one before, and the most wonderful
picture of grand desolation one could ever see.

Toward the north I could see the desert the Jayhawkers and their comrades had undertaken to cross,
and if their journey was as troublesome as ours and
very much longer, they might by this time be all
dead of thirst. I remained on this summit an hour or
so bringing my glass to bear on all points within my
view, and scanning closely for everything that might
help us or prove an obstacle to our progress. The
more I looked the more I satisfied myself that we were
yet a long way from California and the serious question
of our ever living to get there presented itself to me
as I tramped along down the grade to camp. I put

down at least another month of heavy weary travel before we could hope to make the land of gold, and our
stock of strength and provisions were both pretty
small for so great a tax upon them. I thought so
little about anything else that the Indians might have
captured me easily, for I jogged along without a
thought of them. I thought of the bounteous stock of
bread and beans upon my father's table, to say nothing
about all the other good things, and here was I, the
oldest son, away out in the center of the Great American
Desert, with an empty stomach and a dry and parched
throat, and clothes fast wearing out with constant
wear. And perhaps I had not yet seen the worst of
it. I might be forced to see men, and the women and
children of our party, choke and die, powerless to
help them. It was a darker, gloomier day than I had
ever known could be, and alone I wept aloud, for I
believed I could see the future, and the results were
bitter to contemplate. I hope no reader of this
history may ever be placed in a position to be thus
tried for I am not ashamed to say that I have a weak
point to show under such circumstances. It is not in
my power to tell how much I suffered in my lonely
trips, lasting sometimes days and nights that I might
give the best advice to those of my party. I believed
that I could escape at any time myself, but all must
be brought through or perish, and with this all I
knew I must not discourage the others. I could tell
them the truth, but I must keep my worst apprehen-
sions to myself lest they loose heart and hope and
faith needlessly.

I reached the camp on the third day where I found the
boys who went part way with me and whom I had
out-walked. I related to the whole camp what I had
seen, and when all was told it appeared that the route
from the mountains westerly was the only route that

could be taken, they told me of a discovery they had made of a pile of squashes probably raised upon the place, and sufficient in number so that every person could have one. I did not approve of this for we had no title to this produce, and might be depriving the rightful owner of the means of life. I told them not only was it wrong to rob them of their food, but they could easily revenge themselves on us by shooting our cattle, or scalp us, by gathering a company of their own people together. They had no experience with red men and were slow to see the results I spoke of as possible.

During my absence an ox had been killed, for some were nearly out of provisions, and flesh was the only means to prevent starvation. The meat was distributed amongst the entire camp, with the understanding that when it became necessary to kill another it should be divided in the same way. Some one of the wagons would have to be left for lack of animals to draw it. Our animals were so poor that one would not last long as food. No fat could be found on the entire carcass, and the marrow of the great bones was a thick liquid, streaked with blood resembling corruption.

Our road led us around the base of the mountain; There were many large rocks in our way, some as large as houses, but we wound around among them in a very crooked way and managed to get along. The feet of the oxen became so sore that we made mocassins for them from the hide of the ox that was killed, and with this protection they got along very well. Our trains now consisted of seven wagons. Bennett had two; Arcane two; Earhart Bros. one. Culverwell, Fish and others one; and there was one other, the owners of which I have forgotton. The second night we had a fair camp with water and pretty fair

grass and brush for the oxen. We were not very far
from the snow line and this had some effect on the
country. When Bennett retired that n¹ght he put on a
camp kettle of the fresh beef and so arranged the fire
that it would cook slowly and be done by daylight for
breakfast. After an hour or so Mr. Bennett went out
to replenish the fire and see how the cooking was
coming on, and when I went to put more water in the
kettle, he found that to his disappointment, the most
of the meat was gone. I was rolled up in my blanket
under his wagon and awoke when he came to the fire
and saw him stand and look around as if to fasten the
crime on the right party if possible, but soon he came
to me, and in a whisper said: "Did you see anyone
around the fire after we went to bed?" I assured
him I did not, and then he told me some one had
taken his meat. "Do you think," said he "that any
one is so near out of food as to be starving?" "I
know the meat is poor, and who ever took it must be
nearly starving. After a whispered conversation we
went to bed, but we both rose at daylight and, as we
sat by the fire, kept watch of those who got up and
came around. We thought we knew the right man,
but were not sure, and could not imagine what might
happen if stealing grub should begin and continue,
It is a sort of unwritten law that in parties such as
ours, he who steals provisions forteits his life. We
knew we must keep watch and if the offense was repeated the guilty one might be compelled to suffer.
Bennett watched closely and for a few days I kept
closely with the wagons for tear there might be
trouble. It was really the most critical point in our
experience. After three or four days all hope of de-
tecting the crimminal had passed, and all danger was
over out of any difficulty.

One night we had a fair camp, as we were close to

the base of the snow butte, and found a hole of clear
or what seemed to be living water. There were a few
minnows in it not much more than an inch long
This was among a big pile of rocks, and around these
the oxen found some grass.

There now appeared to be a pass away to the south
as a sort of outlet to the great plain which lay to the
north of us, but immediately west and across the desert
waste, extending to the foot of a low black range of
mountains, through which there seemed to be no pass,
the distant snowy peak lay still farther on, with
Martin's pass over it still a long way off though we
had been steering toward it for a month. Now as we
were compelled to go west this impassable barrier was
in our way and if no pass could be found in it we
would be compelled to go south and make no progress
in a westerly direction.

Our trail was now descending to the bottom of what
seemed to be the narrowest part of the plain, the same
one the Jayhawkers had started across, further north,
ten days before. When we reached the lowest part of
this valley we came to a running stream, and, as dead
grass could be seen in the bed where the water ran
very slowly, I concluded it only had water in it after
hard rains in the mountains, perhaps a hundred miles,
to the north. This water was not pure; it had a
bitter taste, and no doubt in dry weather was a rank
poison. Those who partook of it were affected about
as if they had taken a big dose of salts.

A short distance above this we found the trail of the
Jayhawkers going west, and thus we knew they had
got safely across the great plain and then turned
southward. I hurried along their trail for several
miles and looked the country over with field glass
becoming fully satisfied we should find no water til
we reached the summit, of the next range, and then

fearing the party had not taken the precaution to bring along some water I went back to them and found they had none. I told them they would not see a drop for the next forty miles, and they unloaded the lightest wagon and drove back with everything they had which would hold water, to get a good supply.

I turned back again on the Jayhawker's road, and followed it so rapidly that well toward night I was pretty near the summit, where a pass through this rocky range had been found and on this mountain not a tree a shrub or spear of grass could be found— desolation beyond conception. I carried my gun along every day, but for the want of a chance to kill any game a single load would remain in my gun for a month. Very seldom a rabbit could be seen, but not a bird of any kind, not even a hawk buzzard or crow made their appearance here.

When near the steep part of the mountain, I found a dead ox the Jayhawers had left, as no camp could be made here for lack of water and grass, the meat could not be saved. I found the body of the animal badly shrunken, but in condition, as far as putrefaction was concerned, as perfect as when alive. A big gash had been cut in the ham clear to the bone and the sun had dried the flesh in this. I was so awful hungry that I took my sheath knife and cut a big steak which I devoured as I walked along, without cooking or salt. Some may say they would starve before eating such meat, but if they have ever experienced hunger till it begins to draw down the life itself, they will find the impulse of self preservation something not to be controlled by mere reason. It is an instinct that takes possession of one in spite of himself.

I went down a narrow, dark cañon high on both sides and perpendicular, and quite so in many places.

In one of the perpendicular portions it seemed to be a varigated clay formation, and a little water seeped down its face. Here the Indians had made a clay bowl and fastened it to the wall so that it would collect and retain about a quart of water, and I had a good drink of water, the first one since leaving the running stream. Near here I staid all night, for fear of Indians who I firmly believe would have taken my scalp had a good opportunity offered. I slept without a fire, and my supply of meat just obtained drove hunger away.

In the morning I started down the cañon which descended rapidly and had a bed of sharp, volcanic, broken rock. I could sometimes see an Indian track, and kept a sharp lookout at every turn, for fear of revenge on account of the store of squashes which had been taken. I felt I was in constant danger, but could do nothing else but go on and keep eyes open trusting to circumstances to get out of any sudden emergency that might arise.

As I recollect this was Christmas day and about dusk I came upon the camp of one man with his wife and family, the Rev. J. W. Brier, Mrs. Brier and two sons. I inquired for others of his party and he told me they were somewhere ahead. When I arrived at his camp I found the reverend gentleman very cooly delivering a lecture to his boys on education. It seemed very strange to me to hear a solemn discourse on the benefits of early education when, it seemed to me, starvation was staring us all in the face, and the barren desolation all around gave small promise of the need of any education higher than the natural impulses of nature. None of us knew exactly where we were, nor when the jonrney would be ended, nor when substantial relief would come. Provisions were wasting away, and some had been reduced to the last alternative of subsisting on the oxen alone. I slept by the fire that night, without a blanket, as I had done on many nights before and after they hitched up and drove on in the morning I searched the camp carefully, finding some bacon rinds they had thrown away. As I chewed these and could taste the rich grease they contained, I thought they were the sweetest morsels I ever tasted.

Here on the north side of the cañon were some rolling hills and some small weak springs, the water of which when gathered together made a small stream which ran a few yards down the cañon before it lost itself in the rocks and sand. On the side there stood what seemed to be one half of a butte, with the perpendicular face toward the cañon. Away on the summit of the butte I saw an Indian, so far away he looked no taller than my finger, and when he went out of sight I knew pretty well he was the very fellow who grew the squashes. I thought it might be he, at any rate.

I now turned back to meet the teams and found them seven or eight miles up the cañon, and although it was a down grade the oxen were barely able to walk slowly with their loads which were light, as wagons were almost empty except the women and children. When night came on it seemed to be cloudy and we could hear the cries of the wild geese passing east. We regarded this as a very good sign and no doubt Owen's Lake, which we expected to pass on this route, was not very far off. Around in those small hills and damp places was some coarse grass and other growths, but those who had gone before devoured the best, so our oxen had a hard time to get anything to eat.

Next morning I shouldered my gun and followed down the cañon keeping the wagon road, and when half a mile down, at the sink of the sickly stream, I

killed a wild goose. This had undoubtedly been attracted here the night before by the light of our camp
fire. When I got near the lower end of the cañon,
there was a cliff on the north or right hand side which
was perpendicuiar or perhaps a little overhanging, and
at the base a cave which had the appearance of being
continuously occupied by Indians. As I wert on
down I saw a very strange looking track upon the
ground. There were hand and foot prints as if
a human being had crawled upon all fours. As this
track reached the valley where the sand had been clean
swept by the wind, the tracks became more plain, and
the sand had been blown into small hills not over
three or four feet high. I followed the track till it
led to the top of one of these small hills where a small
well-like hole had been dug and in this excavation
was a kind of Indian mummy curled up like a dog.
He was not dead for I could see him move as he
breathed, but his skin looked very much like the
surface of a wlle dried venison ham. I should think
by his looks he must be 200 or 300 years old, indeed
he might be Adam's brother and not look any older
than he did. He was evidently crippled. A climate
which would preserve for many days or weeks the
carcass of an ox so that an eatable round stake could
be cut from it, might perhaps preserve a live man for
a longer period than would be believed.

I took a good long look at the wild creature and
during all the time he never moved a muscle, though
he must have known some one was in the well looking
down at him. He was probably practicing on one of
the directions for a successful political career looking
wise and saying nothing. At any rate he was not going
to let his talk get him into any trouble. He probably
had a friend around somewhere who supplied his
wants. I now left him and went farther out into the

lowest part of the valley. I could look to the north for fifty miles and it seemed to rise gradually in that direction. To the south the view was equally extended, and down that way a lake could be seen. The valley was here quite narrow, and the lofty snow-capped peak we had tried so hard to reach for the past two months now stood before me. Its east side was almost perpendicular and seemed to reach the sky, and the snow was drifting over it, while here the day sun was shining uncomfortably hot. I believe this mountain was really miles from its base to its summit, and that nothing could climb it on the eastern side except a bird and the only bird I had seen for two months was the goose I shot. I looked every day for some sort of game but had not seen any.

As I reached the lower part of the valley I walked over what seemed to be boulders of various sizes, and as I stepped from one to another the tops were covered with dirt and they grew larger as I went along. I could see behind them and they looked clear like ice, but on closer inspection proved to be immense blocks of rock salt while the water which stood at their bases was the strongest brine. After this discovery I took my way back to the road made by the Jayhawkers and found it quite level, but sandy. Following this I came to a campfire soon after dark at which E. Doty and mess were camped. As I was better acquainted I camped with them. They said the water there was brackish and I soon found out the same thing for myself. It was a poor camp; no grass, poor water and scattering, bitter sage brush for food for the cattle. It would not do to wait long here, and so they hurried on.

I inquired of them about Martin's Pass, as they were now quite near it, and they said it was no pass at all, only the mountain was a little lower than the one holding the snow. No wagon could get over it, and

the party had made up their minds to go on foot, and
were actually burning their wagons as fuel with which
to dry the meat of some of the oxen which they had
killed. They selected those which were weakest and
least likely to stand the journey, and by drying it the
food was much concentrated. They were to divide
the provisions equally and it was agreed thereafter
every one must lookout for himself and not expect any
help from anyone. If he used up his own provisions,
he had no right to expect anyone else to divide with
him. Rice, tea and coffee were measured out by the
spoonful and the small amount of flour and bacon
which remained was divided out as evenly as possible.
Everything was to be left behind but blankets and
provisions for the men were too weak to carry heavy
packs and the oxen could not be relied on as beasts of
burden and it was thought best not to load them so as
to needlessly break them down.

When these fellows started out they were full of
spirit, and the frolic and fun along the Platte river was
something worth laughing at but now they were very
melancholy and talked in the lowest kind of low spirits.
One fellow said he knew this was the Creator's dump-
ing place where he had left the worthless dregs after
making a world, and the devil had scraped these together a little. Another said this must be the very
place where Lot's wife was turned into a pillar of salt,
and the pillar been broken up and spread around the
country. He said if a man was to die he would never
decay on account of the salt. Thus the talk went on,
and it seemed as if there were not bad words enough
in the language to properly express their contempt
and bad opinion of such a country as this. They
treated me to some of their meat, a little better than
mine, and before daylight in the morning I was
headed back on the trail to report the bad news I had

learned of the Jayhawkers.

About noon I met two of our camp companions with packs on their backs following the wagon trail, and we stopped and had a short talk. They were oldish men perhaps 50 years old, one a Mr. Fish of Indiana and another named Gould. They said they could perhaps do as well on foot as to follow the slow ox teams, but when I told them what those ahead of them were doing, and how they must go, they did not seem to be entirely satisfied, as what they had on their backs would need to be replenished, and no such chance could be expected. They had an idea that the end of the journey was not as far off as I predicted. Mr. Fish had a long nicely made, whiplash wound around his waist, and when I asked him why he carried such a useless thing, which he could not eat, he said perhaps he could trade it off for something to eat. After we had set on a sand hill and talked for awhile, we rose and shook each other by the hand, and bade each other good bye with quivering lips. There was with me a sort of expression I could not repel that I should never see the middle aged men again.

As my road was now out and away from the mountains, and level, I had no fear of being surprised by enemies, so walked on with eyes downcast, thinking over the situation, and wondering what would be the final outcome. If I were alone, with no one to expect me to help them, I would be out before any other man, but with women and children in the party, to go and leave them would be to pile everlasting infamy on my head. The thought almost made me crazy but I thought it would be better to stay and die with them, bravely struggling to escape than to forsake them in their weakness.

It was almost night before I reached our camp, and sitting around our little fire I told, in the most easy way I could the unfavorable news of the party in advance. They seemed to look to me as a guide and adviser, I presume because I took much pains to inform myself on every point and my judgment was accepted with very little opposing opinion, they moved as I thought best. During my absence from camp for the two days the Indians had shot arrows into three of our oxen, and one still had an arrow in his side forward of the hip which was a dangerous place. To be sure and save him for ourselves we killde him. Some were a little afraid to eat the meat thinking perhaps the arrow might be poisoned, but I agreed that they wanted meat themselves and would not do that. I told them if they got a shot themselves it would be very likely to be a poisoned arrow and they must take the most instant measures to cut it out before it went into the blood. So we ventured to dry the meat and take it with us.

Now I said to the whole camp "You can see how you have displeased the red men, taking their little squashes, and when we get into a place that suits them for that purpose, they may meet us with a superior force and massacre us, not only for revenge but to get our oxen and clothing." I told them we must ever be on guard against a surprise, as the chances were greatly against us.

We pulled the arrows out of the other oxen, and they seemed to sustain no great injury from the wounds. This little faint stream where we camped has since been named as Furnace Creek and is still known as such. It was named in 1862 by some prospectors who built what was called an air furnace on a small scale to reduce some ore found near by, which they supposed to contain silver, but I believe it turned out to be lead and too far from transportations to be available.

CHAPTER X.

Bennett and Arcane now concluded not to wait for me to go ahead and explore out a way for them to follow, as I had done for a long time, but to go ahead as it was evidently the best way to turn south and make our own road, and find the water and passes all for ourselves. So they hitched up and rolled down the cañon, and out into the valley and then turned due south. We had not gone long on this course before we saw that we must cross the valley and get over to the west side. To do this we must cross through some water, and for fear the ground might be miry, I went to a sand hill near by and got a mesquite stick about three feet long with which to sound out our way. I rolled up my pants pulled off my moccassins and waded in, having the teams stand still till I could find out whether it was safe for them to follow or not by ascertaining the depth of the water and the character of the bottom.

The water was very clear and the bottom seemed uneven, there being some deep holes. Striking my stick on the bottom it seemed solid as a rock, and breaking off a small projecting point I found it to be solid rock salt. As the teams rolled along they scarcely roiled the water. It looked to me as if the whole valley which might be a hundred miles long might have been a solid bed of rock salt. Before we reached this water there were many solid blocks of salt lying around covered with a little dirt on the top.

The second night we found a good spring of fresh water coming out from the bottom of the snow peak almost over our heads. The small flow from it spread out over the sand and sank in a very short distance and there was some quite good grass growing around.

This was a temporary relief, but brought us face to face with stranger difficulties and a more hopeless outlook.

There was no possible way to cross this high steep range of mountains anywhere to the north and the Jayhawkers had abandoned their wagons and burned them, and we could no longer follow on the trail they made. It seemed that there was no other alternative but for us to keep along the edge of the mountain to the south and search for another pass. Some who had read Fremont's travels said that the range immediately west of us must be the one he described, on the west side of which was a beautiful country, of rich soil and having plenty of cattle, and horses, and containing some settlers, but on the east all was barren, dry, rocky, sandy desert as far as could be seen. We knew this eastern side answered well the description and believed that this was really the range described, or at least it was close by.

We had to look over the matter very carefully and consider all the conditions and circumstances of the case. We could see the mountains were lower to the south, but they held no snow and seemed only barren rocks piled up in lofty peaks, and as we looked it seemed the most God-forsaken country in the world.

We had been in the region long enough to know the higher mountains contained most water, and that the valleys had bad water or none at all, so that while the lower altitudes to the south gave some promise of easier crossing it gave us no promise of water or grass, without which we must certainly perish. In a certain sense we were lost. The clear night and days furnished us with the mean of telling the points of compass as the sun rose and set, but not a sign of life in nature's wide domain had been seen for a month or more.   A vest pocketful of powder and shot would last a good hunter till he starved to death for there was not a living thing to shoot great or small.

We talked over our present position pretty freely, and every one was asked to speak his unbiassed mind, for we knew not who might be right or who might be wrong, and some one might make a suggestion of the utmost value.   We all felt pretty much downhearted. Our civilized provisions were getting so scarce that all must be saved for the women and children, and the men must get along some way on ox meat alone. It was decided not a scrap of anything that would sustain life must go to waste.   The blood, hide and intestines were all prepared in some way for food. This meeting lasted till late at night.   If some of them had lost their minds I should not have been surprised, for hunger swallows all other feelings.   A man in a starving condition is a savage.   He may be as blood-shed and selfish as a wild beast, as docile and gentle as a lamb, or as wild and crazy as a terrified animal, devoid of affection, reason or thought of justice.   We were none of us as bad as this, and yet there was a strange look in the eyes of some of us some-times, as I saw by looking round, and as others no doubt realized for I saw them making mysterious glances even in my direction.

Morning came and all were silent.   The dim pros-pect of the future seemed to   check every tongue. When one left a water hole he went away as if in doubt whether he would ever enjoy the pleasure of another drop.   Every camp was sad beyond descript-ion, and no one can guide the pen to make it tell the tale as it seemed to us.   When our morning meal of soup and meat was finished, Bennett's two teams, and the two of Arcane's concluded their chances of life were better if they could take some provisions and strike out on foot, and so they were given what they could carry, and they arranged their packs and bade us a sorrowful good bye hoping to meet again on the Pacific Coast. There were genuine tears shed at the parting and I believe neither party ever expected to see each other in this life again.

Bennett's two men were named Silas Helmer and S. S. or C. C. Abbott, but I have forgotton the names of Arcane's men. Mr. Abbott was from New York, a harness maker by trade, and he took his circular cutting knife with him, saying it was light to carry and the weapon he should need. One of them had a gun. They took the trail taken by the Jayhawkers. All the provisions they could carry besides their blankets could not last them to exceed 10 days, and I well knew they could hardly get off the desert in that time. Mr. Abbott was a man I loved fondly. He was good company in camp, and happy and sociable. He had shown no despondency at any time untill the night of the last meeting and the morning of the parting. His chances seemed to me to be much poorer than my own, but I hardly think he realized it. When in bed I could not keep my thoughts back from the old home I had left, where good water and a bountiful spread were always ready at the proper hour. I know I dreamed of taking a draft of cool, sweet water from a full pitcher and then woke up with my mouth and throat as dry as dust. The good home I left be·hind was a favorite theme about the campfire, and many a one told of the dream pictures, natural as life, that came to him of the happy Eastern home with comfort and happiness surrounding it, even if wealth was lacking. The home of the poorest man on earth was preferable to this place. Wealth was of value here. A board of twenty dollar gold pieces could now stand before us the whole day long with no temptation to

touch a single coin, for its very weight would drag us
nearer death. We could purchase nothing with it and
we would have cared no more for it as a thing of value
than we did the desert sands. We would have given
much more for some of the snow which we could see
drifting over the peak of the great snow mountains
over our heads like a dusty cloud.

Deeming it best to spare the strength as much as
possible, I threw away everything I could, retaining
only my glass, some ammunition, sheath knife and
tin cup. No unnecessary burden could be put on any
man or beast, lest he lie down under it, never to rise
again. Life and strength were sought to be hus-
banded in every possible way.

Leaving this camp where the water was appreciated
we went over a road for perhaps 8 miles and came to
the mouth of a rocky cañon leading up west to the
summit of the range. This cañon was too rough for
wagons to pass over. Out in the valley near its mouth
was a mound about four feet high and in the top of
this a little well that held about a pailful of water that
was quite strong of sulphur. When stirred it would
look quite black. About the mouth of the well was
a wire grass that seemed to prevent it caving in. It
seems the drifting sand had slowly built this little
mound about the little well of water in a curious way.
We spent the night here and kept a man at the well
all night to keep the water dipped out as fast as it
flowed, in order to get enough for ourselves and cattle.
The oxen drank this water better than they did the
brackish water of the former camp.

The plain was thinly scattered with sage brush, and
up near the base of the mountain some greasewood
grew in little bunches like currant bushes.

The men with wagons decided they would take this
cañon and follow it up to try to get over the range,

and not wait for me to go ahead and explore, as they said it took too much time and the provisions, consisting now of only ox meat were getting more precarious every day. To help them all I could and if possible to be forewarned a little of danger, I shouldered my gun and pushed on ahead as fast as I could. The bottom was of sharp broken rock, which would be very hard for the feet of the oxen, although we had rawhide mocassins for them for some time, and this was the kind of foot-gear I wore myself. I walked on as rapidly as I could, and after a time came to where the cañon spread out into a kind of basin enclosed on all sides but the entrance, with a wall of high, steep rock, possible to ascend on foot but which would apparently bar the further progress of the wagons, and I turned back utterly disappointed. I got on an elevation where I could look over the country east and south, and it looked as if there was not a drop of water in its whole extent, and there was no snow on the dark mountains that stretched away to the southward and it seemed to me as if difficulties beset me on every hand. I hurried back down the cañon, but it was nearly dark before I met the wagons. By a mishap I fell and broke the stock of my gun, over which I was very sorry, for it was an excellent one, the best I ever owned. I carried it in two pieces to the camp and told them the way was barred, at which they could hardly endure their disappointment. They turned in the morning, as the cattle had nothing to eat here and no water, and not much of any food since leaving the spring; they looked terribly bad, and the rough road coming up had nearly finished them. They were yoked up and the wagons turned about for the return. They went better down hill, but it was not long before one of Bennett's oxen lay down, and could not be pursuaded to rise again. This was no place to tarry in the hot sun, so the ox was killed and the carcass distributed among the wagons. So little draft was required that the remaining oxen took the wagon down. When within two or three miles of the water hole one of Arcane's oxen also failed and lay down, so they turned him out and when he had rested a little he came on again for a while, but soon lay down again.

Arcane took a bucket of water back from camp and after drinking it and resting awhile the ox was driven down to the spring.

This night we had another meeting to decide upon our course and determine what to do. At this meeting no one was wiser than another, for no one had explored the country and knew what to expect. The questions that now arose were "How long can we endure this work in this situation?" How long will our oxen be able to endure the great hardship on the small nourishment they receive?" How long can we provide ourselves with food?"

We had a few small pieces of dry bread. This was kept for the children giving them a little now and then. Our only food was in the flesh of the oxen, and when they failed to carry themselves along we must begin to starve. It began to look as if the chances of leaving our bones to bleach upon the desert were the most prominent ones.

One thing was certain we must move somewhere at once. If we stay here we can live as long as the oxen do, and no longer, and if we go on it is uncertain where to go, to get a better place. We had guns and ammunition to be sure, but of late we had seen no living creature in this desert wild. Finally Mr. Bennett spoke and said:—

"Now I will make you a proposition." "I propose that we select two of our youngest, strongest men and

ask them to take some food and go ahead on foot to try
to seek a settlement, and food, and we will go back to
the good spring we have just left and wait for their
return. It will surely not take them more than ten
days for the trip, and when they get back we shall
know all about the road and its character and how
long it will take us to travel it. They can secure
some other kind of food that will make us feel better,
and when the oxen have rested a little at the spring
we can get out with our wagons and animals and be
safe. I think this is the best and safest way.

Now what do you all say?'' After a little discussion
all seemed to agree that this was the best, and now it
remained to find the men to go. No one offered to
accept the position of advance messengers. Finally
Mr. Bennett said he knew one man well enough to
know that he would come back if he lived, and he was
sure he would push his way through. ''I will take
Lewis (myself) if he will consent to go. '' I consented,
though I knew it was a hazardous journey, exposed
to all sorts of things, Indians, climate and probable
lack of water, but I thought I could do it and would
not refuse. John Rogers a large strong Tennessee,
man was then chosen as the other one and he consented also.

Now preparations began, Mr. Arcane killed the ox
which had so nearly failed, and all the men went to
drying and preparing meat. Others made us some
new mocassins out of rawhide, and the women made
us each a knapsack.

Our meat was closely packed, and one can form an
idea how poor our cattle were from the fact that John
and I actually packed seven-eighths of all the flesh
of an ox into our knapsacks and carried it away.
They put in a couple of spoonfulls of rice and about
as much tea. This seemed like robbery to the children,

but the good women said that in case of sickness even
that little bit might save our lives.   I wore no coat or
vest, but took half of a light blanket, while Rogers
wore a thin summer coat and took no blanket.   We
each had a small tin cup and a small camp kettle
holding a quart.   Bennett had me take his seven-
shooter rifle, and Rogers had a good double barreled
shot gun.   We each had a sheath knife, and our hats
were small brimmed, drab affairs fitting close to the
head and not very conspicuous to an enemy as we
might rise up from behind a hill into possible views.
We tried on our packs and fitted the straps a little so
they would carry easy.   They collected all the money
there was in camp and gave it to us.   Mr. Arcane
had about $30 and others threw in small amounts from
forty cents upward.   We received all sorts of advice.
Capt. Culverwell was an old sea faring man and
was going to tell us how to find our way back, but
Mr. Bennett told the captain that he had known
Lewis as a hunter for many years, and that if he went
over a place in the daytime he could find his way
back at night every time.   Others cautioned us about
the Indians and told us how to manage.   Others told
us not to get caught in deep snow which we might
find on the mountains.

This advice we received in all the kindness in which
it was given, and then he bade them all good bye.
Some turned away, too much affected to approach us
and others, shook our hands with deep feeling, grasping them firmly and heartly hoping we would be successful and be able to pilot them out of this dreary
place into a better land.   Every one felt that a little
food to make a change from the poor dried meat would
be acceptable.   Mr. and Mrs. Bennett and J. B.
Arcane and wife were the last to remain when the
others had turned away.   They had most faith in the

plan and felt deeply. Mrs. Bennett was the last, and she asked God to bless us and bring some food to her starving children.

We were so much affected that we could not speak and silently turned away and took our course again up the canyon we had descended the night before.

After a while we looked back and when they saw us turn around, all the hats and bonnets waved us a final parting.

Those left in the camp were Asabel, Bennett and Sarah his wife, with three children, George, Melissa, and Martha; J. B. Arcane and wife with son Charles. The youngest children were not more than two years old. There were also the two Earhart brothers, and a grown son, Capt. Culverwell, and some others I cannot recall; eleven grown people in all, besides a Mr. Wade, his wife and three children who did not mingle with our party, but usually camped a little distance off, followed our trail, but seemed to shun company. We soon passed round a bend of the cañon, and then walked on in silence.

We both of us meditated some over the homes of our fathers, but took new courage in view of the importance of our mission and passed on as fast as we could.

By night we were far up the mountain, near the perpendicular rough peak, and far above us on a slope we could see some bunches of grass and sage brush. We went to this and found some small water holes. No water ran from them they were so small. Here we staid all night. It did not seem very far to the snowy peak to the north of us. Just where we were seemed the lowest pass, for to the south were higher peaks and the rocks looked as if they were too steep to be got over.

Through this gap came a cold breeze, and we had

to look round to get a sheltered place in which to
sleep. We lay down close together, spoon fashion,
and made the little blanket do as cover for the both of
us. In the morning we filled our canteens, which we
had made by binding two powder cans together with
strips of cloth, and started for the summit near by.
From this was the grandest sight we ever beheld.
Looking east we could see the country we had been
crawling over since November 4th. "Just look at
the cursed country we have come over!" said Rogers
as he pointed over it. To the north was the biggest
mountain we ever saw, peaks on peaks and towering
far above our heads, and covered with snow which
was apparently everlasting.

This mountain seemed to have very few trees on it,
and in extent, as it reached away to the north seemed
interminable. South was a nearly level plain, and
to the west I thought I could dimly see a range of
mountains that held a little snow upon their summits,
but on the main range to the south there was
none. It seemed to me the dim snowy mountains
must be as far as 200 miles away, but of course I
could not judge accurately. After looking at this
grand, but worthless landscape long enough to take
in its principal features we asked each other what we
supposed the people we left behind would think to
see mountains so far ahead. We knew that they had
an idea that the coast range was not very far ahead,
but we saw at once to go over all these mountains and
return within the limits of fifteen days which had
been agreed upon between us, would probably be impossible, but we must try as best we could, so down
the rocky steep we clambered and hurried on our way.
In places the way was so steep that we had to help
each other down, and the hard work made us perspire
freely so that the water was a prime necessity.

In one place near here, we found a little water and filled our canteens, besides drinking a good present supply. There were two low, black rocky ranges directly ahead of us which we must cross.

When part way down the mountain a valley or depression opened up in that direction up which it seemed as if we could look a hundred miles. Near by and a short distance north was a lake of water and when we reached the valley we crossed a clear stream of water flowing slowly toward the lake.

Being in need of water, we rushed eagerly to it and prepared to take a big drink, but the tempting fluid was as salt as brine and made our thirst all the more intolerable. Nothing grew on the bank of this stream and the bed was of hard clay, which glistened in the sun.

We now began the ascent of the next ridge, keeping a westernly course, and walked as fast as we could up the rough mountain side. We crossed the head of a cañon near the summit about dark, and here we found a trail, which from indications we knew to be that of the Jayhawkers, who had evidently been forced to the southward of the course they intended to take. They had camped here and had dug holes in the sand in search of water, but had found none.

We staid all night here and dug around in some other places in the bottom of the cañon, in the hope to have better luck than they did, but we got no water anywhere.

We seemed almost perishing for want of water, the hard exercise made us perspire so freely. In the morning we started on, and near the summit we came to the dead body of Mr. Fish, laying in the hot sun, as there was no material near here with which his friends could cover the remains. This Mr. Fish was the man who left camp some two weeks before in company with another and who carried the long whip-lash wound about his body, in hope he could some-where be able to trade it for bread. No doubt in this very place where he breathed his last, his bones still lie.

As we came in sight of the next valley, we could see a lake of water some distance south of our western course.

We had followed the Jayhawkers trail thus far, but as we found no water in small holes in the rocks as we were likely to do when we were the first to pass, we decided to take a new route in the hope to find a little water in this way, for we had no hope of finding it in any other. This valley we now crossed seemed to come to an end about ten miles to the north of us. To the south it widened out, enclosing the lake spoken of. This valley was very sandy and hard to walk over. When about half way across we saw some ox tracks leading toward the lake, and in the hope we might find the water drinkable we turned off at right angles to our course and went that way also. Long before we reached the water of the lake, the bottom became a thin' slimy mud which was very hard on our mocassins. When we reached the water we found it to be of a wine color, and so strongly alkaline as to feel slippery to the touch, and under our feet.

This side trip, had cost us much exertion and made us feel more thirsty than ever.

We turned now west again, making for a cañon, up which we passed in the hope we should at some turn find a little basin of rain water in some rock. We traveled in it miles and miles, and our mouths became so dry we had to put a bullet or a small smooth stone in and chew it and turn it around with the tongue to induce a flow of saliva. If we saw a spear of green grass on the north side of a rock, it was quickly pulled and eaten to obtain the little moisture it contained.

Thus we traveled along for hours, never speaking, for we found it much better for our thirst to keep our mouths closed as much as possible, and prevent the evaporation. The dry air of that region took up water as a sponge does. We passed the summit of this ridge without finding any water, and on our way down the western side we came to a flat place where there was an Indian hut made of small brush. We now thought there surely must be some water near and we began a thorough search. The great snow mountain did not seem far off, but to the south and southwest a level or inclined plain extended for a long distance. Our thirst began to be something terrible to endure, and in the warm weather and hard walking we had secured only two drinks since leaving camp.

We were so sure that there must be water near here that we laid our knapsacks down by the little hut and looked around in every possible place we could think of. Soon it got dark and then we made a little fire as a guide and looked again. Soon the moon arose and helped us some, and we shouted frequently to each other so as not to get lost.

We were so nearly worn out that we tried to eat a little meat, but after chewing a long time, the mouth would not moisten it enough so we could swallow, and we had to reject it. It seemed as if we were going to die with plenty of food in our hand, because we could not eat it.

We tried to sleep but could not, but after a little rest we noticed a bright star two hours above the horizon, and from the course of the moon we saw the star must be pretty truly west of us. We talked a little, and the burden of it was a fear that we could not endure the terrible thirst a while longer. The thought of the women and children waiting for our return made us

feel more desperate than if we were the only ones concerned.   We thought we could fight to the death over
a water hole if we could only secure a little of the
precious fluid.   No one who has ever felt the extreme
of thirst can imagine the distress, the dispair, which
it brings.   I can find no words, no way to express it
so others can understand.

The moon gave us so much light that we decided
we would start on our course, and get as far as we
could before the hot sun came out, and so we went on
slowly and carefully in the partial darkness, the only
hope left to us being that our strength would hold out
till we could get to the shining snow on the great
mountain before us.   We reached the foot of the range
we were descending about sunrise.   There was here
a wide wash from the snow mountain, down which
some water had sometime run after a big storm, and
had divided into little rivulets only reaching out a
little way before they had sunk into the sand.

We had no idea we could now find any water till
we at least got very near the snow, and as the best
way to reach it we turned up the wash although
the course was nearly to the north.   The course was
up a gentle grade and seemed quite sandy and not
easy to travel.   It looked as if there was an all day
walk before us, and it was quite a question if we
could live long enough to make the distance.   There
were quite strong indications that the water had run
here not so very long ago, and we could trace the
course of the little streams round among little sandy
islands.   A little stunted brush grew here but it was
so brittle that the stems would break as easy as an
icicle.

In order to not miss a possible bit of water we
separated and agreed upon a general course, and that
if either one found water he should fire his gun as a

signal. After about a mile or so had been gone
over I heard Roger's gun and went in his direction.
He had found a little ice that had frozen under
the clear sky. It was not thicker than window glass.
After putting a piece in our mouths we gathered all we
could and put it into the little quart camp kettle to
melt. We gathered just a kettle full, besides what
we ate as we were gathering, and kindled a little
fire and melted it.

I can but think how providential it was that we
started in the night for in an hour after the sun had
risen that little sheet of ice would have melted and the
water sank into the sand. Having quenched our
thirst we could now eat, and found that we were nearly
starved also. In making this meal we used up all
our little store of water, but we felt refreshed and our
lives renewed so that we had better courage to go on.

We now took our course west again taking a bee
line for a bluff that lay a little to the south of the
big snow mountain. On and on we walked till the
dark shadow of the great mountain in the setting sun
was thrown about us, and still we did not seem more
than half way to the bluff before us.

All the way had been hill and very tiresome walking. There was considerable small brush scattered
about, here and there, over this steeply inclined plain.

We were still several miles from the base of this
largest of the mountains and we could now see that it
extended west for many miles. The buttes to the
south were low, black and barren, and to the west
as far as we could see there were no mountains with
any snow. As the sun got further down we could
see a small smoke curling up near the base of the
mountain, and we thought it must be some signal
made by the Indians, as we had often seen them
signal in that way, but we stopped and talked the

matter over, and as we were yet a long way from the
bluff which had been our objective point, we concluded we would investigate the smoke signal
a little closer. So we set off toward it in the dusk
and darkness and when within about a mile we found
we were in a tract that had been somewhat beaten.
Feeling with my fingers I was quite sure I could distinguish ox tracks, and then was quite sure that we
had overtaken the Jayhawkers, or at least were on
their trail. And then I thought perhaps they had
fallen among the Indians, who now might be feasting
on their oxen and it became necessary to use great
caution in approaching the little smoke.

We took a circuitous route and soon saw that the
persons were on a little bench above us and we kept
very cautious and quiet, listening for any sounds that
might tell us who they were.

If they were Indians we should probably hear some
of their dogs, but we heard none, and kept creeping
closer and closer, till we were within fifty yards without hearing a sound to give us any idea of who they
were.

We decided to get our guns at full cock and then
hail the camp, feeling that we had a little the advantage
of position. We hailed and were answered in English.
"Don't Shoot" said we and they assured us they had
no idea of such a thing, and asked us to come in.
We found here to our surprise, Ed Doty, Tom Shannon,
L. D. Stevens, and others whom I do not recollect,
the real Jayhawkers. They gave us some fresh meat
for supper, and near the camp were some water holes
that answered well for camp purposes.

Here an ox had given out and they had stopped
long enough to dry the meat, while the others had
gone on a day ahead.

Coming around the mountain from the north was

quite a well defined trail, leading to the west and they
said they were satisfied some one lived at the end of
it, and they were going to follow it if it lead to Mexico
or anywhere else. They said that Mr. Brier and his
family were still on behind, and alone. Every one
mnst look out for himself here, and we could not do
much for another in any way.

We inquired of them about the trail over which
they had come, and where they had found water, and
we told them of our experience in this respect. We
then related how our train could not go over the
mountains with wagons, how they had returned to the
best spring, and that we started to go through to the
settlements to obtain relief while they waited for our
return. We explained to them how they must perish
without assistance, If we failed to get through, they
could probably live as long as the oxen lasted and
would then perish of starvation. We told them how
nearly we came to the point of perishing that very
morning, of thirst, and how we were saved by finding
a little patch of ice in an unexpected place, and were
thus enabled to come on another days travel.

These men were not as cheerful as they used to be
and their situation and prospects constantly occupied
their minds. They said to us that if the present trail
bore away from the mountain and crossed the 1 evel
plain, that there were some of them who could not
possibly get along safely to the other side. Some
were completely discouraged, and some were completely out of provisions and dependent on those who
had either provisions or oxen yet on hand. An ox
was frequently killed, they said, and no part of it was
wasted. At a camp where there was no water, for
stewing, a piece or hide would be prepared for eating
by singeing off the hair and then roasting in the fire.
The small intestines were drawn through the fingers

to clean them, and these when roasted made very fair food.

They said they had been without water for four or five days at a time and came near starving to death, for it was impossible to swallow food when one became so thirsty. They described the pangs of hunger as something terrible and not to be described. They were willing to give us any information we desired and we anxiously received all we could, for on our return we desired to take the best possible route, and we thus had the experience of two parties instead of one. They told us about the death of Mr. Fish and Mr. Isham, and where we would find their bodies if we went over their trail.

In the morning we shouldered our packs again and took the trail leading to the west, and by night we had overtaken the advance party of the Jayhawkers, camped in a cañon where there was a little water, barely sufficient for their use. We inquired why they did not take the trail leading more directly west at the forks, and they said they feared it would lead them into deep snow which would be impasslble. They said they considered the trail they had taken as altogether the safest one.

We met Bennett and Arcane's teamsters, and as we expected they were already out of grub and no way to get anymore. When the party killed an ox they had humbly begged for some of the poorest parts, and thus far were alive. They came to us and very pitifully told us they were entirely out, and although an ox had been killed that day they had not been able to get a mouthful. We divided up our meat and gave them some although we did not know how long it would be before we would ourselves be in the same situation.

Thus far we had not seen anything to shoot, big

or little although we kept a sharp lookout
The whole camp was silent, and all seemed to realize
their situation. Before them was a level plain which
had the appearance of being so broad as to take
five or six days to cross. Judging by the look from the
top of the mountain as we came over, there was little
to hope for in the way of water. We thought it over
very seriously. All the water we could carry would
be our canteens full, perhaps two drinks apiece and the
poor meat had so little nourishment that we were
weak and unable to endure what we once conld.

We were alone, Rogers and I, in interest at any
rate, even if there were other men about. For the
time it really seemed as if there was very little hope
for us and I have often repeated the following lines
as very closely describing my own feelings at that
time.

Oh hands, whose loving, gentle grasp I loosed.
When first this weary journey was begun.
If I could feel your touch as once I could.
How gladly would I wish my work undone.

                                        Harriet Keynon.

During the evening, I had a talk with Capt. Asa
Haines, in which he said he left a good home in Illinois,
where he had everything he could wish to eat, and
every necessary comfort, and even some to spare, and
now he felt so nearly worn out that he had many
doubts whether he could live to reach the mountains,
on the other side. He was so deeply impressed
that he made me promise to let his wife and
family know how I found him and how he died, for
he felt sure he wonld never see the California mines.
I said I might not get through myself, but he thought
we were so young and strong that we would struggle
through. He said if he could only be home once
more he would be content to stay. This was the

general tenor of the conversation. There was no
mirth, no jokes, and every one seemed to feel that he
was very near the end of his life, and such a death
as stood before them, choking, starving in a desert
was the most dreary outlook I ever saw.

This camp of trouble, of forlorn hope, on the edge
of a desert stretching out before us like a small sea,
with no hope for relief except at the end of a struggle
which seemed almost hopeless, is more than any pen
can paint, or at all describe. The writer had tried it
often. Picture to yourself, dear reader the situation
and let your own imagination do the rest. It can
never come up to the reality.

In the morning, as Rogers and I were about to
start, several of the oldest men came to us with their
addresses and wished us to forward them to their
families if we ever got within the the reach of mails.
These men shed tears, and we did also as we parted.
We turned silently away and again took up our march.

As we went down the cañon we came to one
place where it was so narrow, that a man or a poor
ox could barely squeeze through between the rocks,
and in a few miles more reached the open level plain.
When three or four miles out on the trail and not far
from the hills we came to a bunch of quite tall
willows. The center of the bunch had been cut out
and the branches woven in so as to make a sort of
corral. In the center of this was a spring of good
water and some good grass growing around. This
was pretty good evidence that some one had been here
before. We took a good drink and fiilled our canteens
anew, for we did not expect to get another drink for
two or three days at least.

We took the trail again and hurried on as
the good water made us feel quite fresh. After a few
miles we began to find the bones of animals, some

badly decayed and some well preserved. All the heads were those of horses, and it puzzled us to know where they came from. As we passed along we noticed the trail was on a slight up grade and somewhat crooked. If we stepped off from it the foot sank in about two inches in dirt finer than the finest flour. The bones were scattered all along, sometimes the bones of several animals together. Was it the long drive, poison water, or what? It was evident they had not been killed but had dropped along the way.

It was a dreary trail at best, and these evidences of death did not help to brighten it in the least. We wondered often where it led to and what new things would be our experience. After walking fast all day we came to quite an elevation, where we could stand and look in all directions. The low black range where we left the Jayhawkers was in sight, and this spur of the great snowy mountains extended a long way to the south, and seemed to get lower and lower, finally ending in low rocky buttes, a hundred miles away. Some may think this distance very far to see, but those who have ever seen the clear atmosphere of that region will bear me out in these magnificent distances. Generally a mountain or other object seen at a distance would be three or four times as far off as one would judge at first sight, so deceptive are appearances there. The broad south end of the great mountain which we first saw the next morning after we left the wagons, was now plain in sight, and peak after peak extending away to the north, all of them white with snow. Standing thus out in the plain we could see the breadth of the mountain east and west, and it seemed as though it must have been nearly a hundred miles. The south end was very abrupt and sank as one into a great plain in which we stood, twenty miles from the mountain's base.

To the northwest we could see a clay lake, or at
least that was what we called it, and a line of low
hills seemed to be an extension of the mountain in a
direction swinging around to the south to enclose this
thirsty, barren plain before us, which was bounded by
mountains or hills on these sides. To the south this
range seemed to get higher, and we could see some
snow capped mountains to the south of our westerly
course. The low mountains as those seen in the northwest direction is the same place now crossed by the
Southern Pacific Railroad, and known as the Tehachipi
pass, the noted loop, in which the railroad crosses
itself, being on the west slope and Ft. Tejon being
on the same range a little further south where the
Sierra Nevada mountains and the Coast Range join.
The first mountain bearing snow, south of our course
was probably what is know as Wilson's peak, and the
high mountains still farther south, the San Bernardino
mountains. There were no names there known to us
nor did we know anything of the topography of the
country except that we supposed a range of mountains
was all that separated us from California.

We were yet in the desert, and if we kept our due
west course, we must cross some of the snow before
us which if steep gave us some doubts whether we
could get through or not.

We did not know exactly what the people left behind would do if we were gone longer than we intended, but if they started on it was quite plain to us
they would be lost, and as seven days had already
passed we were in serious trouble for fear we could
not complete the trip in the time allotted to us. We
surveyed the plain and mountains to learn its situation
and then started ,on following our trail. As we went
on we seemed to be coming to lower ground, and near
our road stood a tree of a kind we had not seen before.

The trunk was about six or eight inches through and six or eight feet high with arms at the top quite as large as the body, and at the end of the arms a bunch of long, stiff bayonet shaped leaves.

It was a brave little tree to live in such a barren country. As we walked on these trees were more plenty and some were much larger than the first. As we came to the lowest part of the valley there seemed to be little faint water ways running around little clouds of stunted shrubs, but there was no signs that very much water ever run in them. We thought that these were the outlet of the big sandy lake which might get full of water and overflow through these channels after some great storm.

As this low ground was quite wide we lost our trail in crossing it, and we separated as we went along, looking to find it again, till nearly dark when we looked for a camping place. Fortunately we found a little pond of rain water, and some of our strange trees that were dead gave us good material for a fire, so that we were very comfortable indeed, having both drink and fire.

Starting on again our course was now ascending slightly, and we came across more and more of the trees, and larger ones than at first. We saw some that seemed to have broken down with their own weight. The bayonet shaped leaves seemed to fall off when old and the stalk looked so much like an old overgrown cabbage stump that we name them "Cabbage trees," but afterward learned they were a species of Yucca. We were much worned at loosing our trail and felt that it would be quite unsafe to try to cross the mountain without finding it again, so we separated, Rogers going northwest, and I southwest, agreeing to swing round so as to meet again about noon, but when we met, neither of us had found a trail, and we were still about 10 miles from the foot-hills. Rogers said he had heard some of the people say that the trail leading from Salt Lake to Los Angeles crossed such a mountain in a low pass, with very high mountains on each side, and he supposed that the high mountain to the south must be the one where the trail crossed, but as this would take us fully fifty miles south of our course as we supposed it was we hesitated about going there, and concluded we would try the lowest place in the mountain first, and if we failed we could then go and try Roger's route, more to the south.

So we pushed on, still keeping a distance apart to look out for the trail, and before night, in the rolling hills, we saw here and there faint traces of it, which grew plainer as we went along, and about sundown we reached some water holes and from some old skulls of oxen lying around the ground showing that it had at some previous time been a camping ground. We found some good large sage brush which made a pretty good fire, and if we could have had a little fresh meat to roast we thought we were in a good position for supper. But that poor meat was pretty dry food. However it kept us alive, and we curled up together and slept, for the night was cool, and we had to make the little blanket do its best. We thought we ought to find a little game, but we had not seen any to shoot since we started.

In the morning the trail led us toward the snow, and as we went along, a brave old crow surprised us by lighting on a bush near the trail, and we surprised him by killing him with a charge of shot. "Here's your fresh meat," said Rogers as he put it into his knapsack to cook for supper, and marched on. As we approached the summit we could see, on the high mountains south of us, some trees, and

when we came near the highest part of our road there
were some juniper trees near it, which was very encouraging. We crossed over several miles of hard
snow, but it moistened up our moccassins and made
them soft and uncomfortable After we had turned
down the western slope we killed a small hawk.
"Here's your meat" said I, as the poor thin fellow
was stowed away for future grub, to cook with the
crow.

When we got out of the snow we had lost the
trail again but the hills on the sides were covered with
large brush, and on a higher part of the mountain
south, were some big trees, and we began to think the
country would change for the better pretty soon.
We followed down the ravine for many miles, and
when this came out into a larger one, we were
greatly pleased at the prospect, for down the latter
came a beautiful little running brook of clear pure
water, singing as it danced over the stones, a happy
song and telling us to drink and drink again, and you
may be sure we did drink, for it had been months and
months since we had had such water, pure, sweet, free
from the terrible alkali and stagnant taste that had
been in almost every drop we had seen. Rogers
leveled his shot gun at some birds and killed a beautiful one with a top knot on his head, and colors bright all
down his neck. It was a California quail. We said
birds always lived where human beings did, and we
had great hopes born to us of a better land. I told
John that if the folks were only there now I could
kill game enough for them.

We dressed our three birds and got them boiling in
the camp kettle, and while they were cooking talked
over the outlook which was so flattering that our
tongues got loose and we rattled away in strange contrast to the ominous silence of a week ago. While

eating our stew of crow and hawk, we could see willows
alders and big sage brush around and we had noticed
what seemed to be cottonwoods farther down the
cañon, and green trees on the slope of the mountain.
We were sure we were on the edge of the promised
land and were quite light hearted, till we began to tell
of plans to get the good people out who were waiting
for us beside the little spring in the desert. We talked
of going back at once, but our meat was too near
gone, and we must take them something to encourage
them a little and make them strong for the fearful
trip. As to these birds—the quail was as superb a
morsel as ever a man did eat; the hawk was pretty
fair and quite good eating; but that abominable
crow! His flesh was about as black as his feathers
and full of tough and bony sinews. We concluded
we did not want any more of that kind of bird, and
ever since that day, when I have heard people talk of
"eating crow" as a bitter pill, I think I know all
about it from experience.

There seemed to be no other way for us but to push
on in the morning and try to obtain some relief for
the poor women and children and then get back to
them as fast as ever we could, so we shouldered
our packs and went on down the cañon as fast as we
could. We came soon to evergreen oaks and tall
cottonwoods, and the creek bottom widened out to
two hundred yards. There were trees on the south
side and the brush kept getting larger and larger.
There was a trail down this cañon, but as it passed
under fallen trees we knew it could not have been the
same one we had been following on the other side of
the summit, and when we discovered a bear track in a
soft place we knew very well it was not a trail intended for human beings, and we might be ordered
out almost any moment.

On the high bold grassy point about four hundred yards we saw two horses that held their heads aloft and gave a snort, then galloped away out of sight. About 10 o'clock I felt a sudden pain in my left knee, keen and sharp, and as we went along it kept growing worse. I had to stop often to rest, and it was quite plain that if this increased or continued I was sure enough disabled, and would be kept from helping those whom we had left. Nerved with the idea we must get help to them, and that right soon, I hobbled along as well as I could, but soon had to say to Rogers that he had bettter go on ahead and get help and let me come on as best I could, for every moment of delay was a danger of death to our party who trusted us to get them help. Rogers refused to do this, he said he would stay with me and see me out, and that he could not do much alone, and had better wait till I got better. So we worked along through the tangled brush, being many times compelled to wade the stream to get along, and this made our mocassins soft and very uncomfortable to wear. I endured the pain all day, and we must have advanced quite a little distance in spite of my lameness, but I was glad when night came and we camped in the dark brushy cañon, having a big fire which made me quite comfortable all night, though it was quite cold, and we had to keep close together so as to use the blanket. I felt a little better in the morning and after eating some of our poor dried meat, which was about as poor as crow, and I don't know but a little worse, we continued on our way.

The tangle got worse and worse as we descended, and at times we walked in the bed of the stream in order to make more headway, but my lameness increased and we had to go very slow indeed. About enoon we came to what looked like an excavation, a hol

four feet square or more it looked to be, and on the
dirt thrown out some cottonwood trees had grown,
and one of the largest of these had been cut down
sometime before. This was the first sign of white
men we had seen and it was evidently an attempt at
mining, no one knows how long ago. It encouraged
us at any rate, and we pushed on through brush
and briers, tangles of wild rose bushes and bushes of
every sort, till all of a sudden we came out into an
open sandy valley, well covered with sage brush and
perhaps a hundred yards wide; probably more.

The hills on the south side had on them some oak
trees and grassy spots, but the north side was thickly
covered with brush. Our beautiful little brook that
had kept us company soon sank into the dry sand out
of sight, and we moved rather slowly along every
little while we spoke of the chances of wagons ever
getting through the road we had come, and the hope
that my lameness might not continue to retard our
progress in getting back to the place of our starting,
that the poor waiting people might begin to get out of
the terrible country they were in and enjoy as we had
done, the beautiful running stream of this side of the
mountain. If I did not get better the chances were
that they would perish, for they never could come
through alone, as the distance had proved much
greater than we had anticipated, and long dry stretches
of the desert were more than they would be prepared
for. As it was we feared greatly that we had consumed so much time they would get impatient and
start out and be lost.

I continued to hobble along down the barren valley
as well as I could and here and there some tracks of
animals were discovered, but we could not make out
whether they were those of domestic cattle or elk.
Soon, on the side of a hill, rather high up a pack

of prarie wolves were snarling around the carcess of some dead animal, and this was regarded as another sign that more and better meat could be found, for these animals only live where some sort of game can be found, and they knew better than we that it was not for their health to go into the barren desert.

Before us now was a spur from the hills that reached nearly across our little valley and shut out further sight in that direction and when we came to it we climbed up over it to shorten the distance. When the summit was reached a most pleasing sight filled our sick hearts with a most indiscribable joy. I shall never have the ability to adequately describe the beauty of the scene as it appeared to us, and so long as I live that landscape will be impressed upon the canvas of my memory as the most cheering in the world. There before us was a beautiful meadow of a thousand acres, green as a thick carpet of grass could make it, and shaded with oaks, wide branching and symmetrical, equal to those of an old English park, while all over the low mountains that bordered it on the south and over the broad acres of luxuriant grass was a herd of cattle numbering many hundreds if not thousands. They were of all colors shades and sizes. Some were calmly lying down in happy rumination, others rapidly cropping the sweet grass, while the gay calves worked off their superfluous life and spirit in vigorous exercise or drew rich nourishment in the abundant mother's milk. All seemed happy and content, and such a scene of abundance and rich plenty and comfort bursting thus upon our eyes which for months had seen only the desolation and sadness of the desert, was like getting a glimpse of Paradise, and tears of joy ran down our faces. If ever a poor mortal escapes from this world where so many trials come, and joys of a happy Heaven are opened up to

him, the change cannot be much more that this which
was suddenly opened to us on that bright day which
was either one of the very last of December 1849 or
the first of January 1850, I am inclined to think it was
the very day of the new year, but in our troubles, the
accuracy of the calendar was among the least of our
troubles. If it was, as I believe the beginning of the
year, it was certainly a most auspicious one and one
of the most hopeful of my life.

And *now if the others were only here*, was the
burden of our thought, and a serious awakening from
the dream of beauty and rich plenty spread out before
us. This ring-streaked and speckled herd might be
descended directly from Jacob's famous herd, blessed
of the Lord, and while we could not keep our thoughts
from some sad doubts as to the fate of those whom we
had left behind, we tried to be generally hopeful and
courageous and brightened up our steps to prepare
for a relief and return to the hot dry plain beyond the
mountains where they were awaiting us, no doubt
with much tribulation.

I now thought of myself and my failing knee and
we sat down under the shade of an oak to rest, and
after a little, better feeling seemed to come. Down
by a deep gully cut by the rains a yearling steer was
feeding, and I took the rifle and crawled down near
him and put first one ball through him, and then
another, before he fell dead on the other
side of the wash, when we sprang with all the agility
of a deer. We quickly got some good meat and had
it roasted and eaten almost quicker than can be told.
We hardly realized how near starved we were till we
had plenty before us again. We ate till we were
satisfied for once, and for the first time in many long
dreary weeks. We kindled a fire and commenced
drying the meat, one sleeping while the other kept the

fire, and changing off every few hours. What a rest
that was! One who has never been nearly worn out
and starved, down nearly to the point of death can
never know what it is to rest in comfort. No one
can tell. It was like a dream, a sweet, restful dream
where troubles would drown themselves in sleep.
How we felt the strength come back to us with that
food and the long draughts of pure clear water.

The miserable dried meat in our knapsacks
was put away and this splendid jerked beef put in
its place. The wolves came to our camp and howled
in dreadful disappointment at not getting a meal.
Rogers wanted me to shoot the miserable
howlers, but I let them have their concert out, and
thought going without their breakfast must be punishment enough for them. As our mocassins were worn
out we carefully prepared some sinews from the steer
and made new foot gear from the green hide which
placed us in shape for two or three week's walking.

The morning was clear and pleasant. We had our
knapsacks filled with good food we had prepared, and
were enjoying the cool breeze which came up the
valley, when we heard faintly the bark of a dog, or
at least we thought we did. If this were true there
must be some one living not very far away and we felt
better. I was still very lame and as we started along
the walking seemed to make it worse again, so that it
was all I could do to follow John on the trail down
the valley. As we went along a man and woman
passed us some distance on the left, and they did not
seem to notice us, though we were in plain sight.
They were curiously dressed. The woman had no hoops
nor shoes, and a shawl wound about her neck and one
end thrown over her head, was a substitute bonnet.
The man had sandals on his feet, with white cotton
pants, a calico shirt, and a wide rimmed, comical,

snuff-colored hat. We at once put them down as
Spaniards, or then descendants of Mexico, and if
what we had read about them in books was true, we
were in a set of land pirates, and blood thirsty men
whom we might have occasion to be aware of. We
had never heard a word of Spanish spoken, except
perhaps a word or two upon the plains which some
fellow knew, and how we could make ourselves known
and explain who we were was a puzzle to us.

Difficulties began to arise in our minds now we
were in an apparent land of plenty, but in spite of all we
went along as fast as my lame knee would permit me
to do. A house on higher ground soon appeared
in sight. It was low, of one story with a flat roof,
gray in color, and of a different style of architecture
from any we had ever seen before. There was no
fence around it, and no animals or wagons in sight,
nor person to be seen. As we walked up the hill
toward it I told John our mocassins made of green
hide would betray us as having recently killed an
animal, and as these people might be the owners and
detain us by having us arrested for the crime, and
this would be especially bad for us just now. We
determined to face the people, and let the fact of our
close necessities be a sufficient excuse for us, if we
could make them understand our circumstances.

As we came near the house no person was seen, but
a mule tied to a post told us there was some one about,
and a man soon made an appearance, dressed about
same style as the one we had passed a short time
before. As we came near we saluted him, bidding
him good morning, and he in turn touched his hat
politely, saying something in reply which we were
not able to understand. I showed him that I was
lame, and taking out some money pointed to the
mule, but he only shook his head and said something

I could not comprehend. Rogers now began looking around the house, which was built of sun-dried bricks about one by two feet in size, and one end was used as a storehouse. As he looked in, a man came to him and wanted a black, patent leather belt which Rogers wore, having a watch-pocket attached to it. He offered a quart or more of coarse corn meal, and Rogers made the trade.

We tried to inquire where we were or where ought to go, but could get no satisfactory answer from the man, although when we spoke San Francisco he pointed to the north. This was not very satisfactory to us and we seemed as badly lost as ever, and where or which way to go we did not seem very successful in finding out. So we concluded to go on a little way at least, and I hobbled off in the direction he pointed, which was down the hill and past a small, poorly fenced field which was sometimes cultivated, and across the stream which followed down the valley. Passing on a mile or two we stopped on a big patch of sand to rest.

I told Rogers I did not think this course would lead us to any place in a month, and just now a delay was ruinous to us and to those who were waiting for us, and it would not do for us to go off to the north to find a settlement. While I was expressing my opinion on matters and things, Rogers had wet up a part of his meal with water and put it to bake on the cover of his camp kettle. There was a fair sized cake for each of us, and it was the first bread of any kind we had eaten for months, being a very acceptable change from an exclusively meat diet. Looking up the valley we could see a cloud of dust, thick and high, and soon several men on horseback who came at a rushing gallop. I told Rogers they were after us, and believed them to be a murderous set who

might make trouble for us. I hastily buried our
little store of money in the sand, telling him that if
they got us, they would not get our money. Putting
our guns across our laps in an easy position we had
them cocked and ready for business, and our knives
where we could get them handy, and awaited their
arrival.

They came on with a rush until within a short
distance and halted for consultation just across the
creek, after which one of them advanced toward us
and as he came near us we could see he was a white
man, who wished us good evening in our own language.
We answered him rather cooly, still sitting in the
sand and he no doubt saw that we were a little
suspicious of the crowd. He asked us where we were
from, and we told him our circumstances and condition and that we would like to secure some means
of relief for the people we had left in the desert, but
our means were very limited and we wanted to do the
best we could. He said we were about 500 miles
from San Francisco, not far from 100 miles from the
coast and thirty miles from Los Angeles. We were
much afraid we would not be able to get anything
here, but he told us to go across the valley to a large
live oak tree which he pointed out, and said we would
find an American there, and we should wait there till
morning. He said he would go back and stay at the
house we had passed, and would do what he could to
assist us to go to Los Angeles where we could get
some supplies. Then he rode away, and as we talked
it over we saw no way but to follow the directions of
our newfound friend.

It seemed now that my lameness had indeed been a
blessing. If I had been able to walk we would now
have been well on toward the seashore, where we
could have found no such friend as this who had ap-

peared to us. The way seemed clearer to us, but
the time for our return was almost up and there was
no way of getting back in fifteen days as we had agreed
upon, so there was great danger to our people yet.
It seemed very likely to take us twenty four or thirty
days at best, and while they probably had oxen enough
to provide them food for so long a time they might
take a notion to move on, which would be fatal.

At the big live oak tree we found an American
camper, who was on his way to the gold mines. He was
going a new route and said the mines could be
reached much quicker than by going up the coast
by way of San Francisco. A new company with
wagons was soon to start out to break the road, and
when they crossed the east end of the valley he would
follow them. I think this man's name was Springer.
He had come by way of the Santa Fe route, and the
people of Los Angeles had told him this route was
an easy one being often traveled by saddle
horses, and if the company could make it possible for
wagons they could have all the cattle they wanted to
kill along the road as their pay for doing the work.
Our new friend lay down early, and as he saw we
were scant in blankets he brought some to us for our
use, which were most thankfully received.

As soon as we were alone Rogers mixed up some
more of the meal which we baked in our friend's frying pan, and we baked and ate and baked and ate
again, for our appetites were ravenous, and the demand of our stomachs got the better of the judgment
of our brains.

It was hard to find time to sleep, we were so full of
the plans about the way, which we must manage to get
relief for the people. We had many doubts if animals
could ever come over the route we had come over,
from deliberation we decided that by selecting a route

with that idea in our minds, we could get mules and
perhaps horses over the country. We perhaps could
go more to the north and take the Jayhawkers trail,
but this would take us fully a hundred miles farther
and four or five days longer, at the best, ard every
moment of delay was to be carefully avoided as a
moment of danger to our friends.

Thus again, our sleep was troubled from another
cause. Being so long unaccustomed to vegetable food,
and helped on, no doubt, by our poor judgment in
guaging the quantity of our food, we were attacked
by severe pains in the stomach and bowels, from which
we suffered intensely. We arose very early and with
a very light breakfast, for the sickness admonished us,
we started back for the house we had first passed, at
which our friend on horseback, said he would spend
the night and where we were to meet him this morning.
He said he could talk Spanish all right and would do
all he could to help us.

Our suffering and trouble caused us to move very
slowly, so that it was nine or ten o'clock before we
reached the house, and we found they had two horses
all ready for us to go to Los Angeles. There were
no saddles for us, but we thought this would be a good
way to cure my lameness. The people seemed to be
friends to us in every way. We mounted, having
our packs on our backs, and our guns before us, and
with a friendly parting to the people who did not go,
all four of us started on a trip of thirty miles to the
town of Los Angeles.

When we reached the foot of the mountain which was
very steep but not rocky, John and I dismounted and
led our animals to the top, where we could see a long
way west, and south, and it looked supremely beautiful. We could not help comparing it to the long wide,
desert we had crossed, and John and myself said many

times how we wished the folks were here to enjoy the
pleasant sight, the beautiful fertile picture.

There appeared to be one quite large house in
sight, and not far off, which the man told us was the
Mission of San Fernando, a Roman Catholic Church
and residence for priests and followers. The downward slope of the mountain was as steep as the other
side and larger, and John and I did not attempt to
mount till we were well down on the level ground
again, but the other two men rode up and down without any trouble. We would let our leaders get half
a mile or so ahead of us and then mount and put
our horses to a gallop till we overtook them again.
We had walked so long that riding was very tiresome
to us, and for comfort alone we would have preferred
the way on foot, but we could get along a little faster,
and the frequent dismounting kept us from becoming
too lame from riding.

We passed the Mission about noon or a little after,
and a few miles beyond met a man on horseback who
lived up to the north about a hundred miles. His
name was French and he had a cattle range at a place
called Tejon (Tahone). Our friends told him who
we were, and what assistance we needed. Mr. French
said he was well acquainted in Los Angeles and had been
there some time, and that all the travelers who would
take the Coast route had gone, those who had come
by way of Salt Lake had got in from two to four weeks
before, and a small train which had come the Santa Fe
Route was still upon the road. He said Los Angeles
was so clear of emigrants that he did not think we
could get any help there at the present time.

'Now,'' said Mr. French—''You boys can't talk
Spanish and it is not very likely you will be able to
get any help. Now I say, you boys turn back and
go with me and I will give you the best I have, I will

let you have a yoke of gentle oxen, or more if you
need them, and plenty of beans, which are good food
for I live on them; besides this I can give an Indian
guide to help yon back. Will that do? After a
moment we said we doubted if oxen could be got over
the road, and if they were fat now they would soon
get poor, and perhaps not stand it as well as the oxen
which had became used to that kind of life, and of
those they had in camp all they needed. We wanted
to get something for the women and children to ride,
for we knew they must abandon the wagons, and
could not walk so far over that dry, rough country.
"Well," said Mr. French:—"I will stop at the place
you were this morning—I know them well— and they
are good folks, and I am sure when I tell them what
you want they will help you if they possibly can.
This looks to me to be the most sensible course."
After talking an hour our two companions advised us
that the proposition of Mr. French seemed the most
reasonable one that appeared. But for us to go clear
back to his range would take up so much valuable
time that we were almost afraid of the delay which
might mean the destruction of our friends. French
said he had a pack saddle, with him taking it home,
and we could put it on one of our horses, and when
we came back to Los Angeles could leave it at a certain
saloon or place he named and tell them it belonged to
him and to keep it for him. I have forgotten the
name of the man who kept the saloon. We agreed to
this, and bidding our two campanions farewell, we
turned back again with Mr. French.

When night came we were again at the Mission we
had passed on the way down. We were kindly treated
here, for I believe Mr. French told them about us.
They sent an Indian to take our horses, and we sat
down beside the great house. There were many smaller

houses, and quite a large piece of ground fenced in by an adobe wall. The roof of the buildings was like that of our own buildings in having eaves on both sides, but the covering was of semi circular tiles made and burned like brick. Rows of these were placed close together, the hollow sides up, and then another course over the joints, placed with the round side up, which made a roof that was perfectly waterproof, but must have been very heavy. These tiles were about two feet long. All the surroundings, and general make up of the place were new to us and very wonderful. They gave us good dried meat to eat and let us sleep in the big house on the floor, which was as hard as granite, and we turned over a great many times before daylight, and were glad when morning came. We offered to pay them, but they would take nothing from us, and we left leading our horses over the steep mountain, and reaching the house again late in the day. They turned our horses loose and seemed disposed to be very friendly and disposed to do for us what they could.

We were very tired and sat down by the side of the house and rested, wondering how we would come out with our preparations. They were talking together, but we could not understand a word. A dark woman came out and gave each of us a piece of cooked squash. It seemed to have been roasted in the ashes and was very sweet and good. These were all signs of friendship and we were glad of the good feeling. We were given a place to sleep in the house, in a store.room on a floor which was not soft. This was the second house we had slept in since leaving Wisconsin, and it seemed rather pent-up to us.

In the morning we were shown a kind of mill like a coffee mill, and by putting in a handful of wheat from a pile and giving the mill a

few turns we were given to understand we should
grind some flour for ourselves. We went to work
with a will, but found it, hard, slow work.

After a little, our dark woman came and gave us
each a pancake and a piece of meat, also another piece
of roasted sqash, for our breakfast, and this, we thought,
was the best meal we had ever eaten. The lady tried
to talk to us but we could not understand the words,
and I could convey ideas to her better by the sign
language than any other way. She pointed out the
way from which we came and wanted to know how
many day's travel it might be away, and I answered
by putting my hand to my head and closing my eyes,
which was repeated as many times as there had been
nights on our journey, at which she was much surprised that the folks were so far away. She then
place her hand upon her breast and then held it up, to
ask how many women there were, and I answered her
by holding up three fingers, at which she shrugged
her shoulders and shook her head. Then pointing to
a child by her side, four or five years old, and in the
same way asked how many children, I answered by
holding up four fingers, and she almost cried, opening her mouth in great surprise, and turned away.

I said to Rogers that she was a kind, well meaning
woman, and that Mr. French had no doubt told her
something of our story. Aside from her dark complexion her features reminded me of my mother, and
at first sight of her I thought of the best woman on
earth my own far off mother, who little knew the
hardships we had endured. We went to work again
at the mill and after a while the woman came again
and tried to talk and to teach us some words of her
own language She place her finger on me and said
ombre and I took out my little book and wrote down
ombre as meaning man, and in the same way she taught

me that *mujer*, was woman; *trigo*, wheat; *frijoles*,
beans; *carne*, meat; *calazasa*, pumpkin; *caballo*, horse;
vaca, cow; *muchacho*, boy, and several other words
in this way.

I got hold of many words thus to study, so that
if I ever came back I could talk a little and make myself understood as to some of the common objects and
things of necessary use. Such friendly, human acts
shown to us strangers, were evidences of the kindest
disposition. I shall never forget the kindness of
those original Californians. When in Walker's camp
and finding he was friendly to Mormonism we could
claim that we were also Mormons, but the good people
though well known Catholics, did not so much as
mention the fact nor inquire whether we favored that
sect or not. We were human beings in distress and
we represented others who were worse even than
we, and those kind acts and great good will, were
given freely because we were fellow human beings.

The provisions we prepared were, a sack of small
yellow beans; a small sack of wheat, a quantity of
good dried meat, and some of the coarse, unbolted
flour we had made at the mills. They showed us how
to properly pack the horse, which was a kind of work
we had not been use to, and we were soon ready for
a start. I took what money we had and put it on a
block, making signs for them to take what the
things were worth. They took $30, and we were
quite surprised to get two horses, provisions, pack-
saddles and ropes, some of the latter made of rawhide
and some of hair, so cheaply, but we afterward
learned that the mares furnished were not considered
of much value, and we had really paid a good fair
price for everything. To make it easy for us they
had also fixed our knapsacks on the horses.

The good lady with the child, came out with four

oranges and pointed to her own child and then to the East, put them in the pack meaning we should carry them to the children. With a hearty good bye from them, and a polite lifting of our hats to them we started on our return, down toward the gentle decline of the creek bottom, and then up the valley, the way we came. Toward night we came to a wagon road crossing the valley, and as we well knew we could not go up the tangled creek bed with horses we took this road to the north, which took a dry ravine for its direction, and in which there was a pack trail, and this the wagons were following. We kept on the trail for a few miles, and overtook them in their camp, and camped with them over night. We told them we considered our outfit entirely too small for the purpose intended, which was to bring two women and four children out of the desert, but that being the best we could get, we were taking this help to them and hoped to save their lives. Our mission became well known and one man offered to sell us a poor little one-eyed mule, its back all bare of covering from the effect of a great saddle sore that had very recently healed. He had picked it up somewhere in Arizona where it had been turned out to die, but it seemed the beast had enough of the good Santa Ana stock in it to bring it through and it had no notion of dying at the present time, though it was scarcely more than a good fair skeleton, even then. The beast became mine at the price of $15, and the people expressed great sympathy with us and the dear friends we were going to try to save.

Another man offered a little snow-white mare, as fat as butter, for $15, which I paid, though it took the last cent of money I had. This little beauty of a beast was broken to lead at halter, but had not been broken in any other way. Rogers said he would ride

her where he could, and before she got to the wagons
she would be as gentle as a lamb. He got a bridle
and tried her at once, and then there was a scene of
rearing, jumping and kicking that would have made
a good Bufalo Bill circus in these days. No use, the
man could not be thrown off, and the crowd cheered
and shouted to Rogers to—"Hold her level."

After some bucking and backing on the part of the
mare and a good deal of whipping and kicking on the
part of the man, and a good many furious dashes in
lively, but very awkward ways, the little beast
yielded the point, and carried her load without further
trouble.

The people gave us a good supper and breakfast,
and one man came and presented us with 25 pounds
of unbolted wheat flour. They were of great assistance to us in showing us how to pack and sack our
load, which was not heavy and could be easily carried
by our two animals which we had at first. However
we arranged a pack on the mule and this gave me a
horse to ride and a mule to lead, while Rogers rode
his milk-white steed and led the other horse. Thus
we went along and following the trail soon reached
the summit from which we could see off to the East
a wonderful distance, probably 200 miles, of the dry
and barren desert of hill and desolate valley over
which we had come.

The trail bearing still to the north from this point,
we left and turned due east across the country, and
soon came to a beautiful lake of sweet fresh water
situated well up toward the top of the mountain.
This lake is now called Elizabeth Lake. Here we
watered our animals and filled our canteens, then
steered a little south of east among the Cabbage trees,
aiming to strike the rain water hole where we had
camped as we came over. We reached the water hole

about noon and here found the Jayhawkers trail, which we took. They had evidently followed us and passed down the same brushy cañon while we having taken a circuitous route to the north, had gone around there. Getting water here for ourselves and horses, we went back to the trail and pushed on as fast as the animals could walk, and as we now knew where we could get water, we kept on till after dark, one of us walking to keep the trail, and some time in the night reached the Willow corral I have spoken of before. There was good water here, but the Jayhawker's oxen had eaten all the grass that grew in the little moist place around, and our animals were short of feed. One of us agreed to stand guard the fore part of the night and the other later, so that we might not be surprised by Indians and lose our animals. I took the first watch and let the blaze of the fire go out so as not to attract attention and as I sat by the dull coals and hot ashes I fell asleep. Rogers happened to wake and see the situation, and arose and waked me again saying that we must be more careful or the Indians would get our horses. You may be sure I kept awake the rest of my watch.

Next day we passed the water holes at the place where we had so stealthily crawled up to Doty's camp when coming out. These holes held about two pails of water each, but no stream run away from them. Our horses seemed to want water badly for when they drank they put their head in up to their eyes and drank ravenously.

Thirty miles from here to the next water, Doty had told us, and night overtook us before we could reach it, so a dry camp was made. Our horses began now to walk with drooping heads and slow, tired steps, so we divided the load among them all and walked ourselves. The water, when reached

proved so salt the horses would not drink it, and as
Doty had told us the most water was over the mountain
ahead of us, we still followed their trail which went
up a very rocky cañon in which it was hard work for
the horses to travel. The horses were all very gentle
now and needed some urging to make them go.
Roger's fat horse no longer tried to unseat its rider
or its pack, but seemed to be the most downhearted
of the train. The little mule was the liveliest, sharpest
witted animal of the whole. She had probably
traveled on the desert before and knew better how to
get along. She had learned to crop every spear of
grass she came to, and every bit of sage brush that
offered a green leaf was given a nip. She would sometimes leave the trail and go out to one side to get a
little bunch of dry grass, and come back and take her
place again as if she knew her duty. The other
animals never tried to do this. The mule was evidently better versed in the art of getting a living than
the horses.

Above the rough bed of the cañon the bottom was
gravelly and narrow, and the walls on each side nearly
perpendicular. Our horses now poked slowly along
and as we passed the steep wall of the cañon the
white animal left the trail and walked with full force,
head first, against the solid rock. She seemed to be
blind, and though we went quickly to her and took
off the load she carried, she had stopped breathing by
the time we had it done. Not knowing how far it
was to water, nor how soon some of our other horses
might fall, we did not tarry, but pushed on as well
as we could, finding no water. We reached the
summit and turned down a ravine, following the trail,
and about dark came to the water they had told us
about, a faint running stream which came out of a
rocky ravine and sank almost immediately in the dry

sand.   There was water enough for us, but no grass.
It seemed as if the horses were not strong enough to
carry a load, and as we wanted to get them through
if possible, we concluded to bury the wheat and get i
on our return.   We dug a hole and lined it with fine
sticks, then put in the little bag and covered it with
dry brush, and sand making the surface as smooth as
if it had never been touched, then made our bed on it.
The whole work was done after dark so the deposit
could not be seen by the red men and we thought we
had done it pretty carefully.

Next morning the little mule carried all the remaining load, the horses bearing only their saddles, and
seemed hardly strong enough for that.   There was
now seven or eight miles of clean loose sand to go
over, across a little valley which came to an end about
ten miles north of us, and extended south to the lake
where we went for water on our outward journey and
found it red alkali.   Near the Eastern edge of the
valley we turned aside to visit the grave of Mr. Isham,
which they had told us of.   They had covered his remains with their hands as best they could, piling up a
little mound of sand over it. Our next camp was to be on
the summit of the range just before us, and we passed the
dead body of Mr. Fish, we had seen before, and go on
a little to a level sandy spot in the ravine just large
enough to sleep on.   This whole range is a black mass
rocky piece of earth, so barren that not a spear of
grass can grow, and not a drop of water in any place.
We tied our horses to rocks and there they staid all
night, for if turned loose there was not a mouthful of
food for them to get.

In the morning an important question was to be
decided, and that was whether we should continue to
follow the Jayhawker's trail which led far to the north
to cross the mountain, which stood before us, a mass

of piled-up rocks so steep that it seemed as if a dog
could hardly climb it. Our wagons were nearly due
east from this point over the range, and not more than
fifty miles away, while to go around to the north was
fully a hundred miles, and would take us four or five
days to make. As we had already gone so long we expected to meet them any day trying to get out, and
if we went around we might miss them. They might
have all been killed by Indians or they might
have already gone. We had great fears on their account. If they had gone north they might have
perished in the snow.

The range was before us, and we must get to the
other side in some way. We could see the range for
a hundred miles to the north and along the base
some lakes of water that must be salt. To the south
it got some lower, but very barren and ending in black,
dry buttes. The horses must have food and water by
night or we must leave them to die, and all
things considered it seemed to be the quickest way
to camp to try and get up a rough looking cañon
which was nearly opposite us on the other side. So
we loaded the mule and made our way down the
rocky road to the ridge, and then left the Jayhawker's
trail, taking our course more south so as to get
around a salt lake which lay directly before us. On
our way we had to go close to a steep bluff, and cross
a piece of ground that looked like a well dried mortar
bed, hard and smooth as ice, and thus got around the
head of a small stream of clear water, salt as brine.
We now went directly to the mouth of the cañon we
had decided to take, and traveled up its gravelly bed.
The horses now had to be urged along constantly to
keep them moving and they held their heads low down
as they crept along seemingly so discouraged that they
would much rather lie down and rest forever than

take another step. We knew they would do this soon
in spite of all our urging, if we could not get water
for them. The cañon was rough enough where we
entered it, and a heavy up grade too, and this
grew more and more difficult as we advanced, and
the rough yellowish, rocky walls closed in nearer and
nearer together as we ascended.

A perpendicular wall, or rather rise, in the rocks
was approached, and there was a great difficulty to
pursuade the horses to take exertion to get up and
over the small obstruction, but the little mule skipped
over as nimbly as a well-fed goat, and rather seemed
to enjoy a little variety in the proceedings. After
some coaxing and urging the horses took courage to
try the extra step and succeeded all right, when we
all moved on again, over a path that grew more and
more narrow, more and more rocky under foot at every
moment. We wound around among and between the
great rocks, and had not advanced very far before another obstruction, that would have been a fall of about
three feet had water been flowing in the cañon, opposed
our way. A small pile of lone rocks enabled the
mule to go over all right, and she went on looking for
every spear of grass, and smelling eagerly for water,
but all our efforts were not enough to get the horses
along another foot. It was getting nearly night and
every minute without water seemed an age. We had to
leave the horses and go on. We had deemed them
indispensable to us, or rather to the extrication of the
women and children, and yet the hope came to us
that the oxen might help some of them out as a last
resort. We were sure the wagons must be abandoned,
and such a thing as women riding on the backs of
oxen we had never seen, still it occurred to us as not
impossible and although leaving the horses here was
like deciding to abandon all for the feeble ones,

we saw we must do it, and the new hope arose to sustain us for farther effort. We removed the saddles and placed them on a rock, and after a few moments hesitation, moments in which were crowded torrents of wild ideas, and desperate thoughts, that were enough to drive reason from its throne, we left the poor animals to their fate and moved along. Just as we were passing out of sight the poor creatures neighed pitifully after us, and one who has never heard the last despairing, pleading neigh of a horse left to die can form no idea of its almost human appeal. We both burst into tears, but it was no use, to try to save them we must run the danger of sacrificing ourselves, and the little party we were trying so hard to save.

We found the little mule stopped by a still higher precipice or perpendicular rise of fully ten feet. Our hearts sank within us and we said that we should return to our friends as we went away, with our knapsacks on our backs, and the hope grew very small. The little mule was nipping some stray blades of grass and as we came in sight she looked around to us and then up the steep rocks before her with such a knowing, intelligent look of confidence, that it gave us new courage. It was a strange wild place. The north wall of the cañon leaned far over the channel, overhanging considerably, while the south wall sloped back about the same, making the wall nearly parallel, and like a huge crevice descending into the mountain from above in a sloping direction.

We decided to try to get the confident little mule over this obstruction, Gathering all the loose rocks we could we piled them up against the south wall, beginning some distance below, putting up all those in the bed of the stream and throwing down others from narrow shelves above we built a sort of inclined plane along the walls gradually rising till we were nearly as high as the crest of the fall. Here was a narrow shelf scarcely four inches wide and a space of from twelve to fifteen feet to cross to reach the level of the crest. It was all I could do to cross this space, and there was no foundation to enable us to widen it so as to make a path for an animal. It was forlorn hope but we made the most of it. We unpacked the mule and getting all our ropes together, made a leading line of it. Then we loosened and threw down all the projecting points of rocks we could above the narrow shelf, and every piece that was likely to come loose in the shelf itself. We fastened the leading line to her and with one above and one below we thought we could help her to keep her balance, and if she did not make a misstep on that narrow way she might get over safely. Without a moments hesitation the brave animal tried the pass. Carefully and steadily she went along, selecting a place before putting down a foot, and when she came to the narrow ledge leaned gently on the rope, never making a sudden start or jump, but cautiously as a cat moved slowly along. There was now no turning back for her. She must cross this narrow place over which I had to creep on hands and knees, or be dashed down fifty feet to a certain death. When the worst place was reached she stopped and hesitated, looking back as well as she could. I was ahead with the rope, and I called encouragingly to her and talked to her a little. Rogers wanted to get all ready and he said, "holler" at her as loud as he could and frighten her across, but I thought the best way to talk to her gently and let her move steadily.

I tell you, friends, it was a trying moment. It seemed to be weighed down with all the trails and hardships of many months. It seemed to be the time when helpless women and innocent children hung on

the trembling balance between life and death. Our
own lives we could save by going back, and sometimes it seemed as if we would perhaps save ourselves
the additional sorrow of finding them all dead to do so
at once. I was so nearly in despair that I could not
help bursting in tears, and I was not ashamed of the
weakness. Finally Rogers said, "Come Lewis" and
I gently pulled the rope, calling the little animal, to
make a trial. She smelled all around and looked
over every inch of the strong ledge, then took one
careful step, after another over the dangerous place.
Looking back I saw Rogers with a very large stone
in his hand, ready to "holler" and perhaps kill the
poor beast if she stopped. But she crept along trust
ing to the rope to balance, till she was half way across,
then another step or two, when calculating the
distance closely she made a spring and landed on a
smooth bit of sloping rock below, that led up to the
highest crest of the precipice, and safely climbed to the
top, safe and sound above the falls. The mule had
no shoes and it was wonderful how her little hoofs clung
to the smooth rock. We felt relieved. We would
push on and carry food to the people; we would get
them through some way; there could be no more
hopeless moment than the one just past, and we would
save them all.

It was the work of a little while to transfer the load
up the precipice, and pack the mule again, when we
proceeded. Around behind some rocks only a little
distance beyond this place we found a small willow
bush and enough good water for a camp. This was
a strange cañon. The sun never shown down to the
bottom in the fearful place where the little mule
climbed up, and the rocks had a peculiar yellow color.
In getting our provisions up the precipice, Rogers
went below and fastened the rope while I pulled them

up. Rogers wished many times we had the horses
up safely where the mule was, but a dog could hardly
cross the narrow path and there was no hope. Poor
brutes, they had been faithful servants, and we felt
sorrowful enough at their terrible fate.

We had walked two days without water, and we
were wonderfully refreshed as we found it here. The
way up this cañon was very rough and the bed full of
sharp broken rocks in loose pieces which cut through
the bottoms of our mocassins and left us with bare
feet upon the acute points and edges. I took off one of
my buckskin leggins, and gave it to Rogers, and with
the other one for myself we fixed the mocassins with
them as well as we could, which enabled us to go
ahead, but I think if our feet had been shod with steel
those sharp rocks would have cut through.

Starting early we made the summit about noon, and
from here we could see the place where we found a
water hole and camped the first night after we left
the wagons. Down the steep cañon we turned, the
same one in which we had turned back with the
wagons, and over the sharp broken pieces of volcanic
rock that formed our only footing we hobbled along
with sore and tender feet. We had to watch for the
smoothest place for every step, and then moved only
with the greatest difficulty. The Indians could have
caught us easily if they had been around for we must
keep our eyes on the ground constantly and stop if we
looked up and around. But we at last got down and
camped on some spot where we had set out twenty-five
days before to seek the settlements. Here was the
same little water hole in the sand plain, and the same
strong sulphur water which we had to drink the day
we left. The mule was turned loose dragging the
same piece of rawhide she had attached to her when
we purchased her, and she ranged and searched faith-

fully for food finding little except the very scattering bunches of sage brush. She was industrious and walked around rapidly picking here and there, but at dark came into camp and lay down close to us to sleep.

There was no sign that any one had been here during our absence, and if the people had gone to hunt a way out, they must either have followed the Jayhawker's trail or some other one. We were much afraid that they might have fallen victims to the Indians. Remaining in camp so long it was quite likely they had been discovered by them and it was quite likely they had been murdered for the sake of the oxen and camp equipage. It might be that we should find the hostiles waiting for us when we reached the appointed camping place, and it was small show for two against a party. Our mule and her load would be a great capture for them. We talked a great deal and said a great many things at that camp fire for we knew we were in great danger, and we had many doubts about the safety of our people, that would soon be decided, and whether for joy or sorrow we could not tell.

From this place, as we walked along, we had a wagon road to follow, in soft sand, but not a sign of a human footstep could we see, as we marched toward this, the camp of the last hope. We had the greatest fears the people had given up our return and started out for themselves and that we should follow on, only to find them dead or dying. My pen fails me as I try to tell the feelings and thoughts of this trying hour. I can never hope to do so, but if the reader can place himself in my place, his imagination cannot form a picture that shall go beyond reality.

We were some seven or eight miles along the road when I stopped to fix my mocassin while Rogers went slowly along. The little mule went on ahead of both of us, searching all around for little bunches of dry grass, but always came back to the trail again and gave us no trouble. When I had started up again I saw Rogers ahead leaning on his gun and waiting for me, apparently looking at something on the ground. As I came near enough to speak I asked what he had found and he said—"Here is Capt. Culverwell, dead." He did not look much like a dead man. He lay upon his back with arms extended wide, and his little canteen, made of two powder flasks, lying by his side. This looked indeed as if some of our saddest forbodings were coming true. How many more bodies should we find? Or should we find the camp deserted, and never find a trace of the former occupants.

We marched toward camp like two Indians, silent and alert, looking out for dead bodies and live Indians, for really we more expected to find the camp devastated by those rascals than to find that it still contained our friends. To the east we could plainly see what seemed to be a large salt lake with a bed that looked as if of the finest, whitest sand, but really a wonder of salt crystal. We put the dreary steps steadily one forward of another, the little mule the only unconcerned one of the party, ever looking for an odd blade of grass, dried in the hot dry wind, but yet retaining nourishment, which she preferred.

About noon we came in sight of the wagons, still a long way off, but in the clear air we could make them out, and tell what they were, without being able to see anything more. Half a mile was the distance between us and the camp before we could see very plainly, as they were in a little depression. We could see the covers had been taken off, and this was an ominous sort of circumstance to us, for we feared the depredations of the Indians in retaliation for the capture of their squashes. They had shot our oxen before we left and they have slain them this time and the people too.

We surely left seven wagons. Now we could see only four and nowhere the sign of an ox. They must have gone ahead with a small train, and left these four standing, after dismantling them.

No signs of life were anywhere about, and the thought of our hard struggles between life and death to go out and return, with the fruitless results that now seemed apparent was almost more than human heart could bear. When should we know their fate? When should we find their remains, and how learn of their sad history if we ourselves should live to get back again to settlements and life? If ever two men were troubled, Rogers and I surely passed through the furnace.

We kept as low and as much out of sight as possible, trusting very much to the little mule that was ahead, for we felt sure she would detect danger in the air sooner than we, and we watched her closely to see how she acted. She slowly walked along looking out for food, and we followed a little way behind, but still no decisive sign to settle the awful suspense in which we lived and suffered. We became more and more convinced that they had taken the trail of the Jayhawkers, and we had missed them on the road, or they had perished before reaching the place where we turned from their trail.

One hundred yards now to the wagons and still no sign of life, no positive sign of death, though we looked carefully for both. We fear that perhaps there are Indians in ambush, and with nervous irregular breathing we counsel what to do. Finally Rogers suggested that he had two charges in his shot gun and I seven in the Coll's rifle, and that I fire one of mine and await results before we ventured any nearer, and if there are any of the red devils there we can kill some of them before they get to us.   And now both closely watching the wagons I fired the shot.   Still as death and not a move for a moment, and then as if by magic a man came out from under a wagon and stood up looking all around, for he did not see us.   Then he threw up his arms high over his head and shouted —"The boys have come' "The boys have come!" Then other bare heads appeared, and Mr. Bennett and wife and Mr. Arcane came toward us as fast as ever they could.   The great suspense was over and our hearts were first in our mouths, and then the blood all went away and left us almost fainting as we stood and tried to step.   Some were safe perhaps all of those nearest us, and the dark shadow of death that had hovered over us, and cast what seemed a pall upon every thought and action, was lifted and fell away a heavy oppression gone.   Bennett and Arcane caught us in their arms and embraced us with all their strength, and Mrs. Bennett when she came fell down on her knees and clung to me like a maniac in the great emotion that came to her, and not a word was spoken.   If they had been strong enough they would have carried us to camp upon their shoulders.   As it was they stopped two or three times, and turned as if to speak, but there was too much feeling for words, convulsive weeping would choke the voice.

All were a little calmer soon, and Bennett soon found voice to say:—"I know you have found some place, for you have a mule, " and Mrs. Bennett through her tears, looked staringly at us as she could hardly believe our coming back was a reality, and then exclaimed:—Good boys! O, you have saved us all! God bless you forever! Such boys should never die! "It was some time before they could talk without

weeping. Hope almost died within them, and now
when the first bright ray came it almost turned reason
from its throne. A brighter happier look came to
them than we had seen, and then they plied us with
questions the first of which was:—"Where were
you?"

We told them it must be 250 miles yet to any part
of Californa where we could live. Then came the
question;— 'Can we take our wagons?" "You will
have to walk," was our answer, for no wagons could
go over that unbroken road that we had traveled. As
rapidly and carefully as we could we told them of our
journey, and the long distance between the water
holes; that we had lost no time and yet had been twenty
six days on the road; that for a long distance the
country was about as dry and desolate as the region
we had crossed east of this camp. We told them of
the scarcity of grass, and all the reasons that had kept
us so long away from them.

We inquired after the others whom we had left in
camp when we went away, and we were told all
they knew about them. Hardly were we gone before
they began to talk about the state of affairs which
existed. They said that as they had nothing to live
on but their oxen it would be certain death to wait
here and eat them up, and that it would be much
better to move on a little every day and get nearer and
nearer the goal before the food failed. Bennett told
them they would know surely about the way when
the boys returned, and knowing the road would know
how to manage and what to expect and work for, and
could get out successfully. But the general opinion
of all but Mr. Bennett and Mr. Arcane and their
families was, as expressed by one of them:—"If those
boys ever get out of this cussed hole, they are d—d
fools if they ever come back to help anybody."

Some did not stay more than a week after we were gone, but took their oxen and blankets and started on. They could not be content to stay idly in camp with nothing to occupy their minds or bodies. They could see that an ox when killed would feed them only a few days, and that they could not live long on them, and it stood them in hand to get nearer the western shore as the less distance the more hope while the meat lasted. Bennett implored them to stay as he was sure we would come back, and if the most of them deserted him he would be exposed to the danger of the Indians, with no hope of a successful resistance against them.

But the most seemed to think that to stay was to die, and it would be better to die trying to escape than to set idly down to perish. These men seemed to think their first duty was to save themselves, and if fortunate, help others afterward, so they packed their oxen and left in separate parties, the last some two weeks before. They said that Capt. Culverwell went with the last party. I afterward learned that he could not keep up with them and turned to go back to the wagons again, and perished, stretched out upon the sand as we saw him, dying all alone, with no one to transmit his last words to family or friends. Not a morsel to eat, and the little canteen by his side empty. A sad and lonely death indeed!

There was no end to the questions about the road we had to answer, for this was uppermost on their minds, and we tried to tell them and show them how we must get along on our return. We told them of the great snow mountains we had seen all to the north of our road, and how deep the snow appeared to be, and how far west it extended. We told them of the black and desolate ranges and buttes to the south, and of the great dry plains in the same direction. We told

Leaving Death Valley.—The Manly Party On The March After Leaving Their Wagons.

them of the Jayhawkers trail; of Fish's dead body; of the salt lake and slippery alkali water to which we walked, only to turn away in disappointment; of the little sheets of ice which saved our lives; of Doty's camp and what we knew of those gone before; of the discouraged ones who gave us their names to send back to friends; of the hawk and crow diet; of my lameness; of the final coming out into a beautiful valley, in the midst of fat cattle and green meadows, and the trouble to get the help arranged on account of not knowing the language to tell the people what we needed. They were deeply impressed that my lameness had been a blessing in disguise, or we would have gone on to the coast and consumed more time than we did in walking slowly to favor the cripple knee. Our sad adventures and loss of the horses in returning was sorrowfully told and we spoke of the provisions we had been able to bring on the little mule which had clambered over the rocks like a cat; that we had a little flour and beans, and some good dried meat with fat on it which we hoped would help to eke out the poorer fare and get them through at last. They were so full of compliments that we really began to think we had been brought into the world on purpose to assist some one, and the one who could forecast all things had directed us, and all our ways, so that we should save those people and bring them to a better part of God's footstool, where plenty might be enjoyed, and the sorrows of the desert forgotton. It was midnight before we could get them all satisfied with their knowledge of our experience.

It was quite a treat to us to sleep again between good blankets, arranged by a woman's hand, and it was much better resting than the curled up, cramped position we had slept in while away, with only the poor protection of the half blanket for both of us, in nights that were pretty chilly.

We had plenty of water here, and there being no fear of the mule going astray we turned her loose. As the party had seen no Indians during our absence we did not concern ouselves much about them. At breakfast we cautioned them about eating too much bread, remembering, our own experience in that way.

They said they had about given up our coming back a week before, and had set about getting ready to try to move on themselves. Bennett said he was satisfied that they never could have got through alone after what we had told them of the route and its dangers. He said he knew it now that not one of them would have lived if they had undertaken the journey alone without knowledge of the way.

They had taken off the covers of the wagons to make them into houses for the oxen, so they could be used as pack animals. The strong cloth had been cut into narrow strips and well made into breast straps and breeching, for the cattle were so poor and their hide so loose it was almost impossible to keep anything on their backs. They had emptied the feathers out of the beds to get the cloth to use, and had tried to do everything that seemed best to do to get along without wagons. The oxen came up for water, and the mule with them. They looked better than when we left, but were still poor. They had rested for some time and might feel able to go along willingly for a few days at least. I was handy with the needle, and helped them to complete the harness for the oxen, while Bennett and John went to the lake to get a supply of salt to take along, a most necessary article with our fresh meat. I looked around a little at our surroundings, and could see the snow still drifting over the peak of the snowy mountain as we had seen it

farther east, where we were ourselves under the
burning sun. This was now pretty near February
first, or midwinter The eastern side of this great
mountain was too steep to be ascended, and no sign
of a tree could be seen on the the whole eastern slope.
The range of mountains on the east side of this narrow
valley were nearly all the volcanic, barren in the extreme, and the roughest of all the mountains we had
ever seen. I had now looked pretty thoroughly, and
found it to be pretty nearly a hundred miles long, and
this was the only camp I had seen where water could
be had.

When Mrs. Bennet was ready to show me what to
do on the cloth harness, we took a seat under the
wagon, the only shady place and began work.
The great mountain, I have spoken of
as the snow mountain has since been known as
Telescope Peak, reported to be 11,000 feet high. It
is in the range running north and south and has no
other peak so high. Mrs. Bennett questioned me
closely about the trip, and particularly if I had left
anything out which I did not want her to know. She
said she saw her chance to ride was very slim, and
she spoke particularly of the children, and that it
was impossible for them to walk. She said little
Martha had been very sick since we had been gone, and
that for many days they had expected her to die.
They had no medicine to relieve her and the best they
could do was to select the best of the ox meat, and
make a little soup of it and feed her, they had
watched her carefully for many days and nights, ex-
pecting they would have to part with her any time
and bury her little body in the sands. Sometimes it
seemed as if her breath would stop, but they had
never failed in their attentions, and were at last rewarded by seeing her improve slowly, and even to·

relish a little food, so that if no relapse set in they had hopes to bring her through. They brought the little one and showed her to me, and she seemed so different from what she was when we went away. Then she could run about camp climb out and in the wagons, and move about so spry that she reminded one of a quail. Now she was strangely misshapen. Her limbs had lost all the flesh and seemed nothing but skin and bones, while her body had grown corpulent and distended, and her face had a starved pinched and suffering look, with no healthy color in it.

She told me of their sufferings while we were gone, and said she often dreamed she saw us suffering fearfully for water, and lack of food and could only picture to herself as their own fate, that they must leave the children by the trail side, dead, and one by one drop out themselves in the same way. She said she dreamed often of her old home where bread was plenty, and then to awake to find her husband and children starving was a severe trial indeed, and the contrast terrible. She was anxious to get me to express an opinion as to whether I thought we could get the oxen down the falls where we had so much trouble.

I talked to her as encouragingly as I could, but she did not cheer up much and sobbed and wept over her work most all the time. It was not possible to encourage her much, the outlook seemed so dark. Mrs. Arcane sat under another wagon and said nothing, but she probably heard all we had to say, and did not look as if her hopes were any brighter. Bennett and Rogers soon returned with a supply of salt and said the whole shore of the lake was a winrow of it, that could be shoveled up in enormous quantities.

We now in a counsel of the whole, talked over the matter, and the way which seemed most promising.

If we went by the Jayhawkers trail, there was a week of solid travel to get over the range and back south again as far as a point directly opposite our camp, and this had taken us only three days to come over as we had come. The only obstacle in the way was the falls, and when we explained that there was some sand at the bottom of them, Bennett said he thought we could get them over without killing them, and that, as we knew exactly where the water was, this was the best trail to take. Arcane was quite of the same opinion, the saving of a week of hard and tiresome travel being in each case the deciding reason. They then explained to me what they had decided on doing if we had not come back. They had selected two oxen for the women to ride one to carry water and one to carry the four children. There were no saddles but blankets enough to make a soft seat, and they proposed to put a band or belt around the animals for them to hold on by, and the blankets would be retained in place by breast and breeching straps which we had made. They had found out that it was very difficult to keep a load of any kind upon an ox, and had devised all this harness to meet the trouble.

Bennett had one old bridle ox called Old Crump, which had been selected to carry the children, because he was slow and steady. How in the world do you expect it to keep the children on?—said I. "Well" —said Bennett, with a sort of comical air, about the first relief from the sad line of thought that had possessed us all—"We have taken two strong hickory shirts, turned the sleeves inside, sewed up the necks, then sewed the two shirts together by the tail, and when these are placed on the ox they will make two pockets for the youngest children, and we think the two others will be able to cling to his back with the help of a band around the body of the ox to which

they can cling to, with their hands." Now if Old
Crump went steady and did not kick up and scatter
things, he thought this plan would operate first rate.
Now as to the mule they proposed as we knew how
to pack the animal, that we should use her to pack
our provisions so they would go safe.

From a piece of hide yet remaining John and I
made ourselves some new mocassins, and were all
ready to try the trip over our old trail for now the
third time, and the last, we hoped.

Mrs. Bennett and Mrs. Arcane had taken our advice,
and in cooking had not put too much of the flour or
beans into the soup for the children and they had
gotten along nicely, and even began to smile a little
with satisfaction after a full meal. They got along
better than John and I did when we got hold of the
first nutritions after our arrival on the other side.

We must leave everything here we can get along
without. No clothing except that on our backs.
Only a camp kettle in which to make soup, a tin cup
for each one, and some knives and spoons which each
happen to have. Each one had some sort of a
canteen for water, which we must fill up at every
opportunity, and we decided to carry a shovel along,
so we might bury the body of Capt. Culverwell, and
shovel up a pile of sand at the falls to enable us to
get the oxen over. Every ox had a cloth halter on
his head, so he might be led, or tied up at night when
we had a dry camp, and they would most assuredly
wander off if not secured. Old Crump was chosen to
lead the train, and Rogers was to lead him. We had
made an extra halter for this old fellow, and quite a
long strip of bed ticking sewed into a strap to lead
him by.

This packing buiness was a new idea, and a hard
matter to get anything firmly fixed on their backs.

We had made shoulder straps, hip straps, breast straps and breeching as the correct idea for a harness. The only way we could fasten the band around the animals was for one to get on each side and pull it as tight as possible then tie a knot, as we had no buckles or ring in our harness.

The loads of the oxen consisted of blankets and bedding and a small, light tent of their sheeting about four by six feet in size. We rose early and worked hard till about the middle of the forenoon getting all things ready. They had been in a state of masterly inactivity so long in this one camp that they were anxious to leave it now forever. Only in progress was there hope, and this was our last and only chance. We must succeed or perish. We loaded the animals from the wagons, and some of the oxen seemed quite afraid at this new way of carrying loads. Old Crump was pretty steady, and so was the one with the two water kegs one on each side but the other oxen did not seem to think they needed any blankets on these warm days.

Mrs. Arcane was from a city, and had fondly conveyed thus far some articles of finery, of considerable value and much prized. She could not be persuaded to leave them here to deck the red man's wife, and have her go flirting over the mountains with, and as they had little weight she concluded she would wear them and this perhaps would preserve them So she got out her best hat and trimmed it up with extra ribbon leaving some with quite long ends to stream out behind. Arcane brought up his ox Old Brigham, for he had been purchased at Salt Lake and named in honor of the great Mormon Saint.

Mrs. Arcane also dressed her little boy Charlie up in his best suit of clothes, for she thought they might as well wear them out as to throw them away. She

made one think of a fairy in gay and flying apparel.
In the same way all selected their best and most
servicable garments, for it was not considered
prudent to carry any load, and poor clothes were good
enough to leave for Indians. We set it down as a
principle that we must save ourselves all we could, for
it would be a close contested struggle with us and death,
at the very best, and we wanted to get all the advantage
for ourselves we could. As we were making the
preparations the women grew more hopeful, as it
seemed as if something was really going to be
accomplished.

Bennett and Arcane were emphatic in their belief
and expressions that we would succeed. "I know it—
Dont you Sally?" said Bennett very cheerfully, but
after all Mrs. Bennett could not answer quite as
positively, but said "I hope so."—Mrs. Bennett's
maiden name was Sarah Dilley, which I mention
here as I may otherwise forget it afterward. She
realized that hers was no easy place to ride, that they
would have hard fare at best, and that it must be
nearly or quite a month before they could reach a
fertile spot on which to place her feet. One could
easily see that the future looked quite a little dark to
her, on account of her children, as a mother naturally
would.

High overhead was the sun, and very warm indeed
on that day in the fore part of February 1850, when
the two children were put on Old Crump to see if he
would let them ride. The two small children were
placed in the pockets on each side, face outward, and
they could stand or sit as they should choose.
George and Melissa were placed on top and given
hold of the strap that was to steady them in their
place. I now led up Mrs. Bennett's ox and Mr.
Bennett helped his wife to mount the animal, on

whose back as soft a seat as possible had been constructed. Mrs. Arcane in her ribbons was now helped
to her seat on the back of Old Brigham and she carefully adjusted herself to position, and arranged her
dress and ornaments to suit, then took hold of the
strap that served to hold on by as there were no
bridles on these two.

Rogers led the march with his ox; Bennett and I
started the others along, and Arcane followed with
Old Crump and the children. Bennett and Arcane
took off their hats and bade the old camp good bye.
The whole procession moved, and we were once more
going toward our journey's end we hoped. The road
was sandy and soft, the grade practically level, and
everything went well for about four miles, when the
pack on one of the oxen near the lead got loose and
and turned over to one side, which he no sooner saw
thus out of position, then he tried to get away from it
by moving sidewise. Not getting clear of the
objectionable load in this way he tried to kick it off,
and thus really got his foot in it, making matters
worse instead of better. Then he began a regular
waltz and bawled at the top of his voice in terror.
Rogers tried to catch him but his own animal was so
frisky that he could not hold him and do much else,
and the spirit of fear soon began to be communicated
to the others and soon the whole train seemed to be
taken crazy.

They would jump up high and then come down,
sticking their fore feet as far as possible into the sand
after which, with elevated tails, and terrible plunges
would kick and thrash and run till the packs came off,
when they stopped apparently quite satisfied. Mrs.
Bennett slipped off her ox as quick as she could,
grabbed her baby from the pocket on Old Crump, and
shouting to Melissa and George to jump, got her

family into safe position in pretty short order.
Arcane took his Charley from the other pocket and
laid him on the ground, while he devoted his own attention to the animals. Mrs. Arcane's ox followed
suit, and waltzed around in the sand, bawled at every
turn, fully as bad as any of the others, but Mrs.
Arcane proved to be a good rider, and hard to unseat,
clinging desperately to her strap as she was tossed
up and down, and whirled about at a rate enough to
to make any one dizzy. Her many fine ribbons flew
out behind like the streamers from a mast-head, and
the many fancy fixin's she had donned fluttered in the
air in gayest mockery. Eventually she was thrown
however, but without the least injury to herself,
but somewhat disordered in raiment. When I saw
Bennett he was standing half bent over laughing in
almost hysterical convulsion at the entirely impromptu
circus which had so suddenly performed an act not on
the program. Arcane was much pleased and
laughed heartily when he saw no one was hurt. We
did not think the cattle had so much life and so little
sense as to waste their energies so uselessly. The
little mule stepped out one side and looked on in
amazement, with out disarranging any article of her
load.

Mrs. Bennett, carrying her baby and walking
around to keep out of the way, got very much exhausted, and sat down on the sand, her face as red as
if the blood were about to burst through the skin, and
perspiring freely. We carried a blanket and spread
down for her while we gathered in the scattered
baggage. Then the oxen were got together again,
and submitted to being loaded up again as quietly as
if nothing had happened. Myself and the women
had to mend the harness considerably, and Arcane
and his ox went back for some water, while Rogers

and Benn_tt took the shovel and went ahead about a
mile to cover up the body of Capt. Culverwell, for
some of the party feared the cattle might be terrified
at seeing it. All this took so much time that we had
to make a camp of it right here.

We put the camp kettle on two stones, built a fire,
put in some beans and dried meat cut very fine, which
cooke_ till Arcane came with more water, which was
added, and thickened with a little of the unbolted
flour, making a pretty good and nutritious soup
which we all enjoyed. We had to secure the animals,
for there was neither grass nor water for them, and
we thought they might not be in so good spirits another
day.

We had little trouble in packing up again in the
morning, and concluded to take a nearer route to the
summit, so as to more quickly reach the water holes
where Rogers and I camped on our first trip over the
country. This would be a hard rocky road on its course
leading up a small rocky cañon, hard on the feet of
the oxen, so they had to be constantly urged on, as they
seemed very tender footed. They showed no disposition to go on a spree again and so far as keeping
the loads on, behaved very well indeed. The women
did not attempt to ride but followed on, close after
Old Crump and the children who required almost
constant attention, for in their cramped position they
made many cries and complaints. To think of it, two
children cramped up in narrow pockets, in which they
could not turn around, jolted and pitched around over
the rough road, made them objects of great suffering
to themselves and anxiety and labor on the part of the
mothers.

Mrs. Bennett said she would carry her baby if she
could, but her own body was so heavy for her strength
that she could not do it. Bennett, Rogers and

myself hurried the oxen all we could, so that we could reach the water, and let Bennett go back with some to meet the rest and refresh them for the end of the day's march, and he could take poor little Martha from the pocket and carry her in his arms, which would be a great relief to her. Arcane also took his child when he met them, throwing away his double barrel gun, saying:—"I have no use for you."

When the women reached camp we had blankets already spread down for them, on which they cast themselves, so tired as to be nearly dead. They were so tired and discouraged they were ready to die, for they felt they could not endure many days like this.

We told them this was the first day and they were not used to exercise therefore more easily tired than after they became a little used to it. We told them not to be discouraged, for we knew every water hole, and all the road over which we would pilot them safely. They would not consent to try riding again, after their circus experience, and Mrs. Arcane said her limbs ached so much she did not think she could even go on the next day. They had climbed over the rocks all day, and were lame and sore, and truely thought they could not endure such another day .The trail had been more like stairs than a road in its steep ascent, and our camp was at a narrow pass in the range. The sky was clear and cloudless, as it had been for so long for thus far upon this route no rain had fallen, and only once a little snow, that came to us like manna in the desert. For many days we had been obliged to go without water both we and our cattle, and over the route we had come we had not seen any signs of a white man's presence older than our own. I have no doubt we were the first to cross the valley in this location, a visible sink hole in the desert.

The women did not recover sufficient energy to remove their clothing, but slept as they were, and sat
up and looked around with uncombed hair in the
morning, perfect pictures of dejection. We let them
rest as long as we could, for their swollen eyes and
stiffened joints told how sadly unprepared they were
to go forward at once. The sun came out early and
m ade it comfortable, while a cool and tonic breeze,
came down from the great snow mountain the very
thing to brace them up after a thorough rest.

The slope to the east was soon met by a high ridge
ar d between this and the main mountain was a gentle
slope scattered over with sage brush, and a few little
stools of bunch grass here and there between. This
gave our oxen a little food and by dipping out the
water from the holes and letting them fill up again
we managed to get water for camp use and to give
the animals nearly all they wanted.

While waiting for the women Bennett and Arcane
wanted to go out and get a good view of the great
snowy mountain I had told them so much about.
The best point of view was near our camp, perhaps
three or four hundred yards away, and I went with
them. This place where we now stood was lower
than the mountains either north or south, but were
difficult to climb, and gave a good view in almost
every direction, and there, on the back bone of the
ridge we had a grand outlook, but some parts of it
brought back doleful recollections. They said they
had traveled in sight of that mountain for months
and seen many strange formations, but never one like
this, as developed from this point. It looked to be
seventy-five miles to its base, and to the north and
west there was a succession of snowy peaks that
seemed to have no end. Bennett and Arcane said
they never before supposed America contained

mountains so grand with peaks that so nearly seemed
to pierce the sky.   Nothing except a bird could ever
cross such steep ranges as that one.

West and south it seemed level, and low, dark and
barren buttes rose from the plain, but never high
enough to carry snow, even at this season of the year.
I pointed out to them the route we were to follow,
noting the prominent points, and it could be traced
for fully one hundred and twenty-five miles from the
point on which we stood.   This plain, with its barren
ranges and buttes is now known as the Mojave
Desert.   This part of the view they seemed to study
over, as if to fix every point and water hole upon
their memory.   We turned to go to camp, but no
one looked back on the country we had come over
since we first made out the distant snow peak, now
so near us, on November 4th 1849. The only butte
in this direction that carried snow was the one where
we captured the Indian and where the squashes were
found.

The range next east of us across the low valley
was barren to look upon as a naked, single rock.
There were peaks of various heights and colors, yellow,
blue firery red and nearly black.   It looked as if it
might sometime have been the center of a mammoth
furnace.   I believe this range is known as the Coffin's
Mountains.   It would be difficult to find earth enough
in the whole of it to cover a coffin.

Just as we were ready to leave and return to camp
we took off our hats, and then overlooking the scene
of so much trial, suffering and death spoke the
thought uppermost saying:—"*Good bye Death Valley!*"
then faced away and made our steps toward camp.
Even after this in speaking of this long and narrow
valley over which we had crossed into its nearly central
part, and on the edge of which the lone camp was

made, for so many days, it was called Death Valley.

Many accounts have been given to the world as to the origin of the name and by whom it was thus designated but ours were the first visible footsteps, and we the party which named it the saddest and most dreadful name that came to us first from its memories.

CHAPTER XI.

Out of Death Valley we surely were. To Rogers and I, the case seemed hopeful, for we had confidence in the road and believed all would have power to weather difficulties, but the poor women—it is hard to say what compliants and sorrows were not theirs. They seemed to think they stood at death's door, and would about as soon enter, as to take up a farther march over the black, desolate mountains and dry plains before them, which they considered only a dreary vestibule to the dark door after all. They even had an idea that the road was longer than we told them, and they never could live to march so far over the sandy, rocky roads. The first day nearly satisfied them that it was no use to try, Rogers and I counted up the camps we ought to reach each day and in this way could pretty near convince them of time that would be consumed in the trip. We encouraged them in every way we could; told them we had better get along a little every day and make ourselves a little nearer the promised land, and the very exercise would soon make them stronger and able to make a full day's march.

John and I told them we felt in much better spirits now than we did when we set out alone, and now that nothing but the arrows of an Indian could stop us. We said to them. "We are not going to leave you two ladies out here to die for there is not a sign of a grave to put you in,—"and it was a pretty tough place to think of making one. We told told them of the beautiful flowery hillsides over the other side and begged them to go over there to die, as it would be so much better and easier to perform the last sad rites

THE OXEN GET FRISKY.

there instead of here on the top of the dismal
mountain. It seemed quite like a grim joke, but it
produced a reaction that turned the tide of thoughts
and brought more courage. We only laid out the
march for this day as far as the falls and after a little
prepared to move. The cattle seemed to have quit
their foolishness, and they were loaded without
trouble. The children fitted into the pockets better
than usual, and the mothers with full canteens
strapped across their shoulders picked out soft places
on which to place their poor blistered feet at every
step. They walked as if they were troubled with
corns on every toe and on their heels into the bargain,
and each foot was so badly affected, that they did not
know on which one to limp. But still they moved,
and we were once more on our way westward.
They often stopped to rest, and Arcane waited for
them with Old Crump, while they breathed and complained awhile and then passed on again.

The route was first along the foot of the high peak,
over bare rocks and we soon turned south somewhat
so as to enter the cañon leading down to the falls.
The bottom of this was thick with broken rock, and
the oxen limped and picked out soft places about as
bad as the women did. A pair of mocassins would
not last long in such rocks and we hoped to get out
of them very soon. Rogers and I hurried along,
assisting Arcane and his party as much as we could,
while Bennett staid behind and assisted the women as
much as possible, taking their arms, and by this
means they also reached camp an hour behind the
rest.

A kettle of hot steaming soup, and blankets all spread
out on which to rest, was the work Rogers and I
had done to prepare for them, and they sank down on
the beds completely exhausted. The children cried

some but were soon pacified and were contented to lie
still.   A good supper of hot soup made them feel
much better all around.

The first thing Bennett and Arcane did was to look
round and see the situation at the falls, and see if the
obstacle was enough to stop our progress, or if we
must turn back and look for a better way.   They
were in some doubt about it, but concluded to try and
get the animals over rather than to take the time to
seek another pass, which might take a week of time.
We men all went down to the foot of the fall, and
threw out all the large rocks, then piled up all the
sand we could scrape together with the shovel, till
we had quite a pile of material that would tend to break
a fall.   We arranged everything possible for a forced
passage in the morning, and the animals found a few
willows to browse and a few bunches of grass here
and there, which gave them a little food, while the
spring supplied them with enough water to keep them
from suffering with thirst.

Early in the morning we took our soup hastily and
with ropes lowered our luggage over the small precipice,
then the children, and finally all the ropes were
combined to make a single strong one about thirty
feet long.   They urged one of the oxen up to the
edge of the falls, put the rope around his horns, and
threw down the end to me, whom they had stationed
below.   I was told to pull hard when he started so
that he might not light on his head and break his
neck.   We felt this was a desperate undertaking, and
we fully expected to lose some of our animals, but our
case was critical and we must take some chances.
Bennett stood on one side of the ox, and Arcane on the
other, while big Rogers was placed in the rear to give
a regular Tennessee boost when the word was given.
"Now for it," said Bennett, and as I braced out on the

rope those above gave a push and the ox came over,
sprawling, but landed safely, cut only a little by
some angular stones in the sand pile. "Good
enough," said some one and I threw the rope back
for another ox. "We'll get 'em all over safely" said
Arcane, "if Lewis down there, will keep them from
getting their necks broken." Lewis pulled hard every
time, and not a neck was broken. The sand pile was
renewed every time and made as high and soft as
possible, and very soon all our animals were below
the falls. The little mule gave a jump when they
pushed her and lighted squarely on her feet all right.
With the exception of one or two slight cuts, which
bled some, the oxen were all right and we began
loading them at once.

Bennett and Arcane assisted their wives down along
the little narrow ledge which we used in getting up,
keeping their faces toward the rocky wall, and feeling
carefully for every footstep. Thus they worked along
and landed safely by the time we had the animals
ready for a march. We had passed without disaster,
the obstacle we most feared, and started down the
rough cañon, hope revived, and we felt we should get
through. After winding around among the great
boulders for a little while we came to the two
horses we had left behind, both dead and near together.
We pointed to the carcasses, and told them those were
the horses we brought for the women to ride, and that
is the way they were cheated out of their passage.
The bodies of the animals had not been touched by
bird or beast. The cañon was too deep and dark for
either wolves or buzzards to enter, and nothing alive
had been seen by us in the shape of wild game of any
sort. Firearms were useless here except for defence
against Indians, and we expected no real trouble from
them.

From what we could see, it was my opinion that no general rain ever fell in that region. There was some evidence that water had at times flowed down them freely after cloud bursts, or some sudden tempest, but the gravel was so little worn that it gave no evidence of much of a stream.

We hurried on as rapidly as possible so as to get into the Jayhawker's beaten trail which would be a little easier to follow. When we reached the lowest part of the valley we had to turn south to get around a little, slow running stream of salt water, that moved north and emptied into a Salt Lake. No source of the stream could be seen from this point, but when we reached a point where we could cross, we had a smooth, hard clay bed to march over. It seemed to have been, some day, a bed of mortar, but now baked hard, and the hoofs of the oxen dented into it no more than half an inch. On our left hand was a perpendicular cliff, along which we traveled for quite a little way. The range of mountains now before us to cross was black, nothing but rocks, and extremely barren, having no water in it that we knew of, so when we reached the summit we camped, tied all our animals to rocks, where they lay down and did not rise till morning. The women were so tired they were over two hours late, and we had the fire built, the soup cooked and the beds made. As we did not stop at noon all were very hungry, and ate with a relish. The poor animals had to go without either grass or water. When Old Crump and the party came in the men were carrying the babies, and their wives were clinging to their arms, scarcely able to stand. When they reached the beds they fell at full length on them, saying their feet and limbs ached like the tooth ache. It seemed to be best for them to rest a little before eating. Mrs. Bennett said that the

only consolation was that the road was getting shorter
every day, but were it not for the children she would
sooner die than follow the trail any farther. Their
soup was carried to them in the bed, and they were
covered up as they lay, and slept till morning. This
day's walk was the hardest one yet, and probably the
longest one of the whole journey, but there was no
other place where we could find a place large enough
to make a camp and free enough of rocks so that a
bed could be made.

Rogers and I had the kettle boiling early, and put
in the last of the meat, and nearly all that was left of
the flour. At the next camp an ox must be killed.
Just as it was fairly light I went about 200 yards south
where the dead body of Mr. Fish lay, just as he died
more than a month before. The body had not been
disturbed and looked quite natural. He was from
Oscaloosa, Iowa.

The folks arose very reluctantly this morning, and
appeared with swollen eyes and uncombed hair, for
there was no means of making a toilet, without a
drop of water, except what we had used in getting
breakfast. We set the soup kettle near the foot of
the bed so the women could feed the children and
themselves. Now as we loaded the oxen, it was
agreed that Rogers and I should go ahead with all
but Old Crump, and get in camp as soon as possible,
and they were to follow on as best they could. There
was a little water left in the canteens of Bennett and
Arcane, to be given only to the children, who would
cry when thirsty, the very thing to make them feel
the worst.

We were to kill an ox when we reached camp, and
as each of the men had an equal number on the start
each was to furnish one alternately and no disputing
about whose were better or stronger, in any

emergency.

Our road now led down the western slope of the mountain, and loose, hard, broken rocks were harder on the feet of our animals than coming up, and our own mocassins were wearing through. The cattle needed shoes as well as we. Any one who has never tried it can imagine how hard it is to walk with tender feet over broken rock. It was very slow getting along at the best, and the oxen stumbled dreadfully in trying to protect their sore feet. At the foot of the mountain we had several miles of soft and sandy road. The sun shone very hot, and with no water we suffered fearfully. A short way out in the sandy valley we pass again the grave of Mr. Isham, where he had been buried by his friends. He was from Rochester, N. Y. He was a cheerful, pleasant man, and during the forepart of the journey used his fiddle at the evening camps to increase the merriment of his jolly companions. In those days we got no rain, see no living animals of any kind except those of our train, see not a bird nor insect, see nothing green except a very stunted sage, and some dwarf bushes. We now know that the winter of 1849—50 was one of the wettest ever seen in California, but for some reason or other none of the wet clouds ever came to this portion of the State to deposit the most scattering drops of moisture.

Quite a long way from the expected camp the oxen snuffed the moisture, and began to hurry towards it with increased speed. A little while before it did not seem as if they had ambition enough left to make a quick move, but as we approached the water those which had no packs fairly trotted in their haste to get a drink. This stream was a very small one, seeping out from a great pile of rocks, and maintaining itself till it reached the sands, where it disappeared completely.   A few tufts of grass grew along the banks, otherwise everything surrounding was desolate in the extreme.

As soon as we could get the harness off the oxen, we went to look for our little buried sack of wheat, which we were compelled to leave and hide on our way out.   We had hidden it so completely, that it took us quite a little while to strike its bed but after scratching with our hands awhile, we hit the spot, and found it untouched.   Although the sand in which it was buried seemed quite dry, yet the grain had absorbed so much moisture from it, that the sack was nearly bursting.   It was emptied on a blanket, and proved to be still sound and sweet.

Our first work now was to kill an ox and get some meat to cook for those who were coming later.   We got the kettle over boiling with some of the wheat in it, for the beans were all gone.   We killed the ox saving the blood to cook.   Cutting the meat all off the bones, we had it drying over a fire as soon as possible, except what we needed for this meal and the next. Then we made a smooth place in the soft sand on which to spread the blankets, the first good place we had found to sleep since leaving Death Valley.

The next job was to make mocassins for ourselves and for the oxen, for it was plain they could not go on another day barefooted.   We kept busy indeed, attending the fires under the meat and under the kettle, besides our shoemaking, and were getting along nicely about sundown, when Old Christian Crump appeared in sight followed by the women and the rest of the party.   The women were just as tired as ever and dropped down on the blankets the first thing.   "How many such days as this can we endure?"—they said. We had them count the days gone by, and look around to see the roughest part of the road was now behind them. They said that only five days had passed, and that two thirds of the distance still remained untraveled, and they knew they could never endure even another five day's work like the last. We told them to be brave, and be encouraged, for we had been over the road and knew what it was, and that we felt sure of being able to do it nicely. They were fed in bed as usual, and there they lay till morning. We men went to making mocassins from the green hide, and when we had cut out those for the men and women the balance of the hide was used in preparing some also for the oxen, particularly the worst ones, for if I remember correctly there was not enough to go round.

The morning came, bright and pleasant, as all of them were, and just warm enough for comfort in the part of the day. The women were as usual, and their appearance would remind one quite strongly of half-drowned hens which had not been long out of trouble. Hair snarled, eyes red, nose swollen, and out of fix generally. They did not sleep well so much fatigued, for they said they lived over their hard days in dreams at night, and when they would close their eyes and try to go to sleep, the visions would seem to come to them half waking and they could not rest.

There was now before us a particularly bad stretch of the country as it would probably take us four or five days to get over it, and there was only one water hole in the entire distance. This one was quite salt, so much so that on our return trip the horses refused to drink it, and the little white one died next day. Only water for one day's camp could be carried with us, and that was for ourselves alone and not for the animals.

When the mocassins were finished in the morning we began to get our cattle together when it was discovered that Old Brigham was gone, and the general belief was that the Indians had made a quiet raid on us and got away with the old fellow. We circled around till we found his track and then Arcane followed it while we made ready the others. Arcane came in with the stray namesake of the polygamous saint about this time shouting:—"I've got him—No Indians." The ox had got into the wash ravine below camp and passed out of sight behind, in a short time. He had been as easily tracked as if he walked in snow. There was larger sage brush in the wash than elsewhere, and no doubt Brigham had thought this a good place to seek for some extra blades of grass.

Immediately south of this camp now known as Providence Springs, is the salt lake to which Rogers and I went on the first trip and were so sadly disappointed in finding the water unfit to use.

As soon as ready we started up the cañon, following the trail made by the Jayhawkers who had proceeded us, and by night had reached the summit, but passed beyond, a short distance down the western slope, where we camped in a valley that gave us good large sage brush for our fires, and quite a range for the oxen without their getting out of sight. This being at quite a high elevation we could see the foot as well as the top, of the great snow mountain, and had a general good view of the country.

This proved to be the easiest day's march we had experienced, and the women complained less than on any other night since our departure. Their path had been comparatively smooth, and with the new mocassins their feet had been well protected, they had come through pretty nicely. We told them they looked better, and if they would only keep up good courage they would succeed and come out all right to the land where there was plenty of bread a nd water, and when safely out, they might make good re solutions never to get in such a trap again.   Mrs. Bennett said such a trip could never be done over again, and but for the fact that Rogers and I had been over the road, and that she believed all we had said about it; she never would have had the courage to come thus far. Now, for the children's sake, she wished to live, and would put forth any effort to come through all right.

The next day we had a long cañon to go down, and in it passed the dead body of the beautiful white mare Rogers had taken such a fancy to.   The body had not decomposed, nor had it been disturbed by any bird or beast.   Below this point the bed of the cañon was filled with great boulders, over which it was very difficult to get the oxen along.   Some of them had lost their mocassins and had to suffer terribly over the rocks.

Camp was made at the salt water hole, and our wheat and meat boiled in it did not soften and get tender as it did in fresh water.   There was plenty of salt grass above; but the oxen did not eat it any more than the horses did, and wandered around cropping a bite of the bitter brush once in awhile, and looking very sorry.   This was near the place where Rogers and I found the piece of ice which saved our lives.   The women did not seriously complain when we reached this camp, but little Charley Arcane broke out with a bad looking rash all over his body and as he cried most of the time it no doubt smarted and pained him like a mild burn.   Neither his mother nor any one else could do anything for him to give him any relief.   We had no medicines, and if he or any one should die, all we could do would be to roll the body in a blanket and cover it with a light covering of sand.

From this camp to the next water holes at the base of the great snow mountain, it was at least 30 miles, level as to surface, and with a light ascending grade. The Jayhawkers had made a well marked trail, and it it was quite good walking. The next camp was a dry one, both for ourselves and the oxen, nothing but dry brush for them, and a little dried meat for ourselves, but for all this the women did not complain so very much. They were getting use to the work and grew stronger with the exercise. They had followed Old Crump and the children every day with the canteens of water and a little dried meat to give them if they cried too much with hunger, and Arcane had led his ox day after day with a patience that was remarkable, and there was no bad temper shown by any one. This was the way to do, for if there were any differencse, there was no tribunal to settle them by.

In all this desert travel I did not hear any discontent and serious complaint, except in one case, and that was at the Jayhawker's camp, where they burned their wagons at the end of the wagon road, in Death Valley. Some could not say words bad enough to express their contempt, and laid all the trouble of salt water to Lot's wife. Perhaps she was in a better position to stand the cursing than any of the party present.

The next day we reached the water holes at the place where Rogers and I stole up to camp fire in the evening, supposing it to be Indians, but finding there Capt. Doty and his mess, a part of the Jayhawker's band. By dipping carefully from these holes they filled again, and thus, although there was no flow from them we gradually secured what water we needed for the camp, which was a small amount after so long a time without. There was some low brush

here called greasewood, which grew about as high as
currant bushes, and some distance up the mountain
the oxen could find some scattery bunch grass, which,
on the whole, made this camp a pretty good one.
The women, however, were pretty nearly exhausted,
and little Charley Arcane cried bitterly all day and
almost all night.   All began to talk more and feel more
hopeful of getting through.   The women began to
say that every step brought them so much   nearer to
the house we had told them about on the   other side
and often said the work was not so very   hard after
all.   Really it was not so bad travelling as we had at
first.   We were now nine days from the wagons.
"Are we half way?" was the question they began to
ask.   We had to answer them that more than one
half the hard days were over, if one half the distance
had not been traveled, and with the better walking
and getting hardened to the work, they would get
over the last half better than the first.   One thing
was a little hard.   All of our beans and flour had
been used up, and now the wheat was about gone
also.   We had cooked it, and it seemed best, trying
to build up our strength, where it was most needed
for the greatest trials, and now we thought they would
be able to get along on the meat.   We had reached
the base of the great snow mountain.   It seems strange
with the mass of snow resting above, and which must
be continually thawing more or less, no ravines or
large streams of water were produced flowing down
this side.   It seemed dry all around its base, which is
is very singular, with the snow so near.

We had now our barren cañon to go down, and right
here was the big trail coming down from the north,
which we took and followed.   We said all these good
things about the road, and encouraged the people all
we could to keep in good spirits   and   keep moving.

We told them we thought we knew how to manage
to get them safe over the road if they only fully endeavored to do it. We were all quite young, and not
in the decline of life as were most of them who had
perished by the way. No reader can fully realize
how much we had to say and do to keep up courage,
and it is to this more than anything else that we did
which kept up the lagging energies and inspired the
best exertion. I don't know but we painted some
things a little brighter than they were, and tried to
hide some of the most disheartening points of the
prospects ahead, for we found the mind had most to
do with it after all. We have no doubt that if we
had not done all we could to keep up good courage,
the women would have pined away and died before
reaching this far. Whenever we stopped talking
encouragingly, they seemed to get melancholy and
blue.

There was some pretty good management to be exercised still. The oxen were gradually growing
weaker, and we had to kill the weakest one every
time, for if the transportation of our food failed, we
should yet be open to the danger of starvation. As
it was, the meat on their frames was very scarce, and
we had to use the greatest economy to make it last
and waste nothing. We should now have to kill one
of our oxen every few days, as our other means of
subsistance had been so completely used up. The
women contracted a strange dislike to this region and
said they never wanted to see any part of it again.

As the sun showed its face over the great sea of
mountains away to the east of Death Valley, and it
seemed to rise very early for winter season we packed
up and started west on the big trail. Rogers and I
took the oxen and mule and went on, leaving the
others to accompany Old Crump and his little charges.

Arcane had found it best to carry Charley on his back, as it relieved the burning sensation, caused by the eruption on his skin, which was aggravated by the close quarters of the pockets. Thus leaving the pockets unbalanced, Bennett had to carry his baby also. This made it harder for them, but every one tried to be just as accommodating as they could and each one would put himself to trouble to accommodate or relieve others.

Rogers and I made camp when we reached the proper place which was some distance from the mountain, on a perfectly level plain where there was no water, no grass, nothing but sage brush would grow on the dry and worthless soil. We let the oxen go and eat as much of this as they chose, which was very little and only enough to keep them from absolute starvation. The great trail had a branch near here that turned north, and went up a ravine that would seem to reach the snow in a little while. This was believed to be impassable at this time of year. This route is known as Walker's Pass, leading over a comparatively low ridge, and coming out the south fork of the Kern River.

We made our camp here because it was as long a march as the women could make, and, for a dry one, was as good a location as we could find. The cool breeze came down from the snow to the north of us, not so very many miles away, and after a little it became uncomfortably cold. We gathered greasewood bushes and piled them up to make a wind-break for our heads. The oxen, even, would come and stand around the fire, seeming greatly to enjoy the warm smoke, which came from burning the greasewood brush, which by the way, burns about the best of any green wood. When we were ready to lie down we tied the animals to bunches of brush, and they lay contentedly till morning.

To the north of us, a few miles away we could see some standing, columns of rock, much reminding one of the great stone chimney of the boiler house at Stanford Jr., University; not quite so trim and regular in exterior appearance, but something in that order. We reckon the only students in the vicinity would be lizards.

When the women arrived in camp they were very tired, but encouraged themselves that they were much nearer the promised land than they were in the morning. Mrs. Bennett said she was very careful never to take a step backward, and to make every forward one count as much as possible. "That's a good resolution, Sally," said Mr Bennett. "Stick to it and we will come out by and bye."

From near this camp we have a low range of mountains to cross, a sort of spur or offshoot of the great snow mountain that reaches out twenty miles or more to the southeast' and its extremity divides away into what seems from our point of view a level plain. We had attained quite an elevation without realizing it, so gradual had been the ascent, and our course was now down a steep hillside and into a deep cañon. In its very bottom we found a small stream of water only a few yards long, and then it sank into the sands. Not a spear of grass grew there, and if any had grown it had been eaten by the cattle which had gone before. This was the same place, where Rogers and I had overtaken the advance portion of the Jayhawkers when we were on our outward trip in search of relief, and where some of the older men were so discouraged that they gave us their home adresses in Illinois so that we could notify their friends of their precarious situation, and if they were never otherwise heard from they could be pretty sure they had perished from thirst and starvation when almost at their journey's end.

The scenes of this camp on that occasion made so strong an impression on my memory that I can never forget it. There were poor dependent fellows without a morsel to eat except such bits of poor meat as they could beg from those who were fortunate enough to own oxen. Their tearful pleadings would soften a heart of stone. We shared with some of them even when we did not know the little store upon our backs would last us through. Our oxen here had water to drink, but nothing more. It might be a little more comfortable to drink and starve, than both choke and starve, but these are no very pleasant prospects in either one.

Both ours^lves and the oxen were getting barefoot and our feet very tender. The hill we had just come down was very rough and rocky and our progress very slow, every step made in a selected spot. We could not stop here to kill an ox and let the remainder of them starve, but must push on to where the living ones could get a little food. We fastened the oxen and the mule to keep them from wandering, and slept as best we could. The women and children looked worse than for some time, and could not help complaining. One of the women held up her foot and the sole was bare and blistered. She said they ached like toothache. The women had left their combs in the wagons, and their hair was getting seriously tangled. Their dresses were getting worn off pretty nearly to their knees, and showed the contact with the ground that sometimes could not be avoided. They were in a sad condition so far as toilet and raiment were concerned. Life was in the balance, however, and instead of talking over sad things, we talked of the time when we would reach the little babbling brook

PULLING THE OXEN DOWN THE PRECIPICE.

where Rogers and I took such long draughts of clear, sweet water and the waiter at our dinner gave us the choice of *Crow, Hawk* or *Quail*, and where we took a little of all three.

In the morning we were off again down the cañon, limping some as we trod its coarse gravelly bed with our tender feet and stiffened joints, but getting limbered up a little after a bit, and enduring it pretty well. We set out to try to reach the bunch of willows out on the level plain, where the cattle could get some water and grass, but night overtook us at the mouth of the cañon, and we were forced to go into camp. This cañon is now called Red Cañon. This was on an elevated plain, with a lake near by, but as we had been so often deceived by going to the lake for water, and finding them salt in every instance, or poison on account of strong alkali, we did not take the trouble to go and try this one.

Near us was some coarse grass and wet ground where we found water enough for our moderate use, and the oxen, by perseverance, could get something to eat and drink. After supper we were out of meat and we would have to kill an ox to get some food for breakfast. In the night a storm came on, much to our surprise, for we had seen none since the night on the mountain east of Death Valley more than two months before. We tried to fix up a shelter to protect the children and ourselves, but were not very successful. We tried to use our guns for tent poles, but could not keep them in place. We laid down as close as pigs in cold weater, and covered up as best we could, but did not keep dry, and morning found us wet to the skin, cold and shivering. We gathered big sage brush for a fire in the morning, and the tracks of our nearly bare feet could be plainly seen in the snow which lay like a blanket awhile over the ground, about two inches deep. Some lay in bed and we warmed blankets before the fire and put over them to keep them comfortable till the sun should rise and warm the air. We selected an ox and brought him up before the fire where I shot him, and soon there was meat roasting over the fire and blood cooking in the camp kettle. We had nothing to season the blood pudding with but salt, and it was not very good, but answered to sustain life. We ate a hasty meal, then packed our animals and started for the willow patch about four miles away. The snow was about gone.

I staid in camp to keep it till they could get through to the willows and some one to come back with the mule to carry forward the portion of meat that could not be taken at first. We intended to dry it at the willows, and then we could carry it along as daily food over the wide plain we had yet to cross. Having carried the meat forward, we made a rack of willows and dried it over the fire, making up a lot of mocassins for the barefooted ones while we waited. We were over most of the rocky road, we calculated that our shoe-making would last us through. This was a very pleasant camp. The tired ones were taking a rest. No one needed it more than our women and children, who were tired nearly out. They were in much better condition to endure their daily hardships than when they started out, and a little rest would make them feel quite fresh again. They understood that this was almost on the western edge of this desert country and this gave them good hope and courage.

This wonderful spot in the level plain, with a spring of pure water making an oasis of green willows and grass has been previously spoken of as:—"A spring of good water, and a little willow patch in a level desert away from any hill." In all our wander-

ings we had never seen the like before. No
mountaineer would ever think of looking here for
water, much less ever dream of finding a lone spring
away out in the desert, several miles from the
mountain's base. Where the range we just came
through leaves the mother mountain stands a peak,
seemingly alone, and built up of many colored rocks,
in belts, and the whole looks as if tipped with steel.

Arcane's boy Charley still suffered from his bogus
measles or whatever else his disorder might be, and
Bennett's little Martha grew more quiet and improved
considerably in health, though still unable to walk,
and still abdominally corpulent. The other two
children George and Melissa seemed to bear up well
and loved to get off and walk in places where the trail
was smooth and level. Bennett, Arcane and Old
Crump usually traveled with the same party as the
women, and as each of them had a small canteen to
carry water, they could attend to the wants of the
children and keep them from worrying and getting
sick from fretfulness. They often carried the two
younger ones on their backs to relieve and rest them
from their cramped position on the ox.

Arcane used to say he expected the boys—
meaning Rogers and I—would try to surprise the
party by letting them get very near the house before they knew how near they were. "Be patient
Mr. Arcane," said we, we can tell you just how many
camps there must be before we reach it, and we
won't fool you or surprise you in any way. "Well,"
said he. "I was almost in hopes you would, for I
like to be disappointed in that way." "What do you
think the folks will say when we tell them that our
little mule packed most of the meat of an ox four
miles from one camp to another?" "What will they
say when we tell them that the oxen were so poor

that there was no marrow in the great thigh bones?''
Instead of marrow there was a thick dark liquid something like molasses in consistency, but streaked with
different colors which made it look very unwholesome.
Arcane said the whole story was so incredible, that
he never should fight anyone, even if he should tell
him he lied when he related the strange sad truth.
He said he had no doubt many a one would doubt
their story, it was so much beyond what people had
ever seen or heard of before, and they might be accused of very strong romancing in the matter.

They all felt more like talking; for we were thus
far safe and sound, and though there was a desperate
struggle of seventy-five miles or more, from this place
to the next water in the foot-hills. Possibly the
snow storms had left a little in some of the pools, but
we made no calculations on any. The promised
land we had so steadily been approaching, and now
comparatively so near, gave us great hope, which was
better than food and drink to give us strength.

There were surely two camps between this and the
little pond John and I found, among the Cabbage
trees, and not more than six by ten feet square. As
we worked away at our foot-wear we talked more in
an hour than we had in a whole day before. We
were slowly leaving Death Valley behind us with its
sad memories and sufferings. We were leaving
behind the dead bodies of several who had traveled
with us and been just as strong and hopeful as we.
We had left behind us all in our possession in that
terrible spot, and simply with our lives we hoped to
escape, and trust to Providence and humanity on the
other side. Arcane now admitted that they could not
have got along half as well, if we had not gone ahead
and looked out the land. It was such a gain to
know exactly where the next water hole was, so it

could be steered for and struggled toward. He even went so far as to say they would have no chance alone, and that as he now saw the road, he was sure they have would all perished even before reaching as far as this. We had strong hopes of the morrow, when we would be all rested, all were shod, and would make every footstep count in our western progress.

It seems quite a strange occurrence that the only two storms we had had since we turned westward on this route, Nov. 4th, were snow storms, and that both had come while we were asleep, so that all our days were cloudless. Sometimes the sun was uncomfortably warm even in the heart of the winter. One would have naturally expected that the great rainfall all over the California coast in the winter of 1849—50, and the deep snows that came in the Sierra Nevada mountains the same winter, would have extended southerly the few hundred miles that separated the two places. Modern science has shown the tracks of the storms and partially explains the reasors for this dry and barren nature of this region. When rains do come they are so out of the regular order, that they are called cloud-bursts or waterspouts, and the washes in the cañons and their mouths show how great has been the volume of water that sometimes rushed down the slope. If clouds at a warm or moderate temperature float against these snow peaks all the water they contain is suddenly precipitated. The country is an arid one and unless wealth should appear in the shape of mines, the country can never be inhabited. We considered ourselves very fortunate in finding the little pools and holes of water which kept us alive. It was not very good drinking water, but to us thirsty folks it was a blessing and we never passed it by on account of any little stagnent bitter taste. Salt water we could not drink of course, though we sometimes used it to cook with.

We were as well prepared next morning as possible for a move, and the long walk before us, the last one between us and the fertile land. They all talked of how delighted they would be to see once more a running brook, green grass and trees, and such signs of life as they had seen and been used to in the good land they had left behind. The women said they could endure the march of four or five days, if when all over, they could sleep off the terrible fatigue and for once drink all the pure sweet water they could desire. No more forced marches. No more grey road, stretching out its dusty miles as far as the eye could reach. The ladies thought the oxen would be as happy as themselves, and the little mule, the most patient one of the whole train deserved a life of ease for her valuable services. This little black, one-eyed lady wandered here and there at will seeking for grass, but never going astray or getting far enough from the track to alarm us in the least. She seldom drank much water, was always ready, never got foot-sore, and seemed made expressly for such a life and for such a desert.

A good kettleful of soup for breakfast, dried meat fixed in packages, kegs and canteens filled with water, and we were ready for an advance.

There is one less ox to lead, and very little load for those we have, still the load is all such poor weak fellows ought to bear. Old Crump was not thus favored by a gradually lightened load. He bore the same four children every day, faithfully, carefully, with never a stumble nor fall, as though fully aware of the precious nature of his burden.

In this new march John and I took the oxen and pushed on as usual, leaving the families to follow on, at a slower pace, the trail we made. The trail was

slightly inclined. The bushes stunted at the best,
getting smaller as we proceeded, and the horse bones,
new and ancient are now thickly scattered along the
way. The soil is different from that we have had.
We can see the trail, winding gently here and there,
swept clean by the wind, and the surface is hard and
good; but when the mule gets the least bit off of it
she sinks six inches deep into the soft sand, and the
labor of walking is immense. I stepped out to examine
the peculiar soil, and found it finer than superfine
flour. It was evident that a strong wind would lift it
in vast clouds which might even darken the sky, but
we were fortunate in this respect, for during all the
time we were on this peculiar soil, there was no wind
at all, and we escaped a sand-storm, a sort of storm
as peculiar to this region as are blizzards to some of
the states of the great west.

Our first night's camp was out on the barren waterless plain, now known as the Mojave Desert. There
were no shrubs large enough to make a fire of, and
nothing to tie our cattle to, so we fastened all our
animals together to keep them from scattering and
getting lost. We ate a little dry meat and drank
sparingly of the water, for our scanty stock was to last
us another day, when we might reach prospective
water holes. Starting early, John and I took all
but Old Crump and the other travelers, and hurried
on to try and find the water holes as early as possible.
We, as well as the oxen were very dry, for we left
all the water we had with the party, for the children,
for they cannot endure the thirst as the older people
can. We reached the camping place before night.
Quite a time before we reached it, the cattle seemed
to scent the water and quickened their pace, so we
were confident it had not dried up. We got ahead of
the oxen and kept there until we reached the little

pond and then guarded it to keep them from wading
into it, in their eagerness to reach some drink.
They all satisfied their thirst, and then we removed
the harness, built a fire of the dead cabbage trees
which we found round about, laid down the beds and
arranged them neatly, and had all nicely done before
the rear guard came up, in charge of Captain Crump.
The party was eager for water and all secured it.
It was rain water and no doubt did not quench thirst
as readily as water from some living spring or brook.
There was evidence that there had been a recent
shower or snow to fill this depression up for our
benefit. The Jayhawkers had passed not more than
a half mile north of this spot, but no sign appeared
that they had found it, and it was left to sustain the
lives of the women and children.

It often occurs to me that many may read incredul-
ously when I speak of our party eating the entire
flesh of an ox in four or five days. To such I will say
that one cannot form an idea how poor an ox will get
when nearly starved so long. Months had passed
since they had eaten a stomachful of good nutritous
food. The animals walked slowly with heads down
nearly tripping themselves up with their long,
swinging legs. The skin loosely covered the bones,
but all the flesh and muscles had shrunk down to the
smallest space. The meat was tough and stringy as
basswood bark, and tasted strongly of bitter sage
brush the cattle had eaten at almost every camp. At
a dry camp the oxen would lie down and grate their
teeth, but they had no cud to chew. It looked almost
merciless to shoot one down for food, but there was
no alternative. We killed our poor brute servants
o save ourselves. Our cattle found a few bunches
out among the trees at this camp and looked some
better in the morning. They had secured plenty of

water and some grass.

Young Charlie Arcane seemed to grow worse rather than better. His whole body was red as fire, and he screamed with the pain and torment of the severe itching. Nothing could be done to relieve him, and if his strength lasted till we could get better air, water and food he might recover, but his chances were very poor.

Not much rest at this camp for in the morning we aimed to start early and reach the water in the foot-hills. We thought we could do it if we started early, walked rapidly and took no resting spell at noon. Such a poor soil as this we were anxious to get away from, and walk once more on a soil that would grow something besides stunted sage brush. From all appearances the Jayhawkers were here in about the same predicament Rogers and I were when we lost the trail. By their tracks we could see they had scattered wide and there was no road left for us to follow, and they had evidently tried to follow our former tracks. Having no trail to follow we passed on as best we could and came to a wide piece of land on which were growing a great many cabbage trees. The soil was of the finest dust with no grit in it, and not long before a light shower had fallen, making it very soft and hard to get along in with the mocassins. The women had to stop to rest frequently, so our progress was very slow. Rogers and I had feet about as hard as those of the oxen, so we removed our mocassins and went barefoot, finding we could get along much easier in that way, but the others had such tender feet they could not endure the rough contact with the brush and mud. Only a few miles had been made before the women were so completely tired out that we had to stop and eat our little bit of dried meat and wait till morning. The little mule now carried all our stock of

food, and the precious burden lightened every day.
This delay was not expected, but we had to endure it
and bear it patiently, for there was a limit to strength
of the feeble ones of our party. We had therefore to
make another barren camp. Relief seemed so near at
hand we kept good courage and talked freely of the
happy ending which would soon come. If we had
any way to set a good table we would feast and be
merry like the prodigal son, but at any rate we shall
be safe if we can reach the fertile shore.

When the sun went down we tied the mule and
oxen to cabbage trees, and shortly after dusk lay
down ourselves, for we had enjoyed a good fire made
of the trunks of cabbage trees, the first really comfortable one in a long time.. The air was cooler here, for
we were on higher ground, and there was some snow
on the range of mountains before us, which sent these
cool breezes down to us, a change of climate quite
pleasing.

For breakfast in the morning we had only dried
meat roasted before the fire, without water, and
when we started each one put a piece in his or her
pocket to chew on during the day as we walked along.
As we went ahead the ground grew dryer and the
walking much improved. The morning overhead
was perfectly lovely, as away east, across the desert
the sun early showed his face to us. Not a cloud anywhere, not even over the tops of the high peaks where
great white masses sometimes cluster but dissolve as
soon as they float away, and there was not wind
enough to be perceptible. We remarked the same
lack of animal life which we had noticed on our first
passage over this section, seeing not a rabbit, bird,
or living thing we could use for food. Bennett had
the same load in his gun he put there when we left
the wagons, and all the powder I had burned was

that used in killing the oxen we had slain whenever it became necessary to provide for our barren
kitchen.

As we approached the low foot-hills the trail became better travelled and better to walk in, for the
Jayhawkers who had scattered, every one for himself
apparently, in crossing the plain, seemed here to have
drawn together and their path was quite a beaten
one. We saw from this that they followed the tracks
made by Rogers and myself as we made our first trip
westward in search of bread. Quite a little before
the sun went out of sight in the west we reached our
camping place in the lower hills at the eastern slope
of a range we must soon cross. Here was some standing water in several large holes, that proved enough
for our oxen, and they found some large sage brush
and small bushes round about, on which they browsed
and among which they found a few bunches of grass.
Lying about were some old skulls of cattle which
had sometime been killed, or died. These were the
first signs of the sort we had seen along this route.
They might have been killed by Indians who doubtless used this trail.

The next day in crossing the range before us, we
reached the edge of the snow, which the sun had
softened, and we dare not attempt to cross. Early in
the morning, when it was frozen hard the cattle could
travel it very well. The snow belt was five or six
miles wide, and the snow two or three feet deep.
This was a very good camping place except that we
had to melt snow for all our water, but this being
coarse and icy it was not a great job as we found
enough dry juniper trees and twigs to make a very good
fire. Here we also had to kill another ox. This one
in its turn was Arcane's, and left him only two, and
Bennett three, but we think that if we have no

accident we shall get them along with us till we can get other food, as they have very light loads to pack. When the ox is killed and the meat prepared the mule has, for a time, a larger load than all the oxen have, but seems content and nips a bite of food whenever it can see a chance anywhere along the road, giving us no more trouble than a dog. And by the way, I think I have not mentioned our faithful camp dog, a worthy member of our party who stood watch always and gave us a sure alarm if anything unusual happened anywhere about. He was perhaps only one of a hundred that tried to cross the plains and had to be abandoned when they reached the upper Platte, where the alkali dust made their feet so sore they could not travel, and as they could not be hauled on wagons they were left behind. But this dog Cuff did not pro-pose to be left behind to starve, and crippled along after us, we doing all we could for him, and proved as tough as the best of us. Bennett and I had trained him as a hunting dog in the East, and he was very knowing and handy in every particular.

We were out of this camp at daylight. Very little rest for some of us, but we must make the best of the cool morning while the snow is hard, and so move on as soon as we can see the way. As it gets lighter and the sun comes up red and hot out of the desert we have a grand view of the great spread of the country to south and of the great snow mountain to the north and east, the peak standing over the place where we left our wagons nineteen days before, on the edge of Death Valley. The glare of the snow on the sun makes us nearly blind, but we hurry on to try to cross it before it becomes so soft as to slump under our feet. It is two or three feet in the deepest places, and probably has been three times as deep when freshly fallen, but it is now solid and icy. Our raw-

hide mocassins protect our feet from cold, and both
we and the animals got along fairly well, the oxen
breaking through occasionally as the snow softened
up, but generally walking on the top as we did ourselves. The snow field reached much farther down
the western slope than we had hoped, much farther
than on the eastern side. Before we got out of it, we
saw the track of some animal which had crossed our
route, but as it had been made some days before and
now could be seen only as some holes in the surface,
we could not determine what sort of an animal i
was.

A mile or two down the hill we were at last out of
the snow, and a little farther on we came to the little
babbling brook Rogers and I had so long painted in
the most refreshing colors to the tired women, with
water, wood and grass on every hand, the three
greatest blessings of a camper's life. Here was where
Rogers and I had cooked and eaten our meat of crow,
quail and hawk, pretty hard food, but then, the
blessed water!

There it danced and jumped over the rocks singing
the merriest song one ever heard, as it said—Drink,
drink ye thirsty ones your fill—the happiest sweetest
music to the poor starved, thirsty souls, wasted down
almost to haggard skeletons. O! if some poet of
wildest imagination could only place himself in the
position of those poor tired travelers to whom water
in thick muddy pools had been a blessing, who had
eagerly drank the fluid even when so salt and bitter
as to be repulsive, and now to see the clear, pure
liquid, distilled from the crystal snow, abundant,
free, filled with life and health—and write it in
words—the song of that joyous brook and set it to the
music that it made as it echoed in gentle waves from
the rocks and lofty walls, and with the gentle ac-

companiment of rustling trees—a soft singing hush,
telling of rest, and peace, and happpiness.

New life seemed to come to the dear women. "O!
What a beautiful stream!" say they, and they dip in
a tin cup and drink, then watch in dreaming admiration the water as it goes hurrying down; then
dip and drink again, and again watch the jolly rol-
licking brook as if it were the most entertaining thing
in the whole wide earth. "Why can't such a stream
as that run out of the great Snow Mountain in the dry
Death Valley?"! say they—"so we could get water
on the way."

The men have felt as glad as any of them, but have
gathered wood and made a fire, and now a camp
kettle of cut up meat is boiling for our supper. It
was not yet night, but we must camp in so beautiful
a place as this, and though the food was poor, we were
better off than we had been before.

Bennett proposed that I take the mule and go back
to where we saw the track of the animal in the snow
and follow it in hope that we might get some game
for we had an idea it might be an elk or bear or some
large game, good to kill and give us better meat: So
I saddled the mule and took the trail back till I came
to the track, then followed it as best I could, for it
was very dull and gave me no idea what it was. I
traced out of the snow and then in a blind way
through bushes as high as the mule's back—Chaparral
we called it now—among which I made my way with
difficulty. I could now see that the track was made
by an ox or cow—perhaps an elk—I could not tell for
sure it was so faint. This chaparral covered a large
piece of table land, and I made my way through it,
following the track for a mile or two, till I camp to
the top of a steep hill sloping down into a deep cañon
and a creek, on the bank of which grew sycamore and

alder trees, with large willows. I stopped here some
minutes to see if I could see or hear the movement of
of anything Across the oreek I could see a small
piece of perhaps half an acre of natural meadow, and
in it some small bunches of sycamore trees. After a
little I discovered some sort of a horned animal there,
and I reckoned this was good enough game for me to
try and capture, so led the mule out to one side and
down the hill near the creek, then tied her, and crept
along the bank, about four feet high, toward the little
meadow. When about right, as I thought, I climbed
up behind a bunch of sycamores, and when I slowly
and cautiously raised up I was within fifty yards of a
cow or steer of some sort which I could dimly see.
I put a ball square in its forehead and it fell without a
struggle. I loaded again quick as possible, and there
saw two other smaller cattle stepping very high as
though terrified, but not aware of the nature or
location of the danger. I gave a low whistle and one
of them looked toward me long enough for me to put
a ball in it. The third one was now behind a clump of
sycamores, and I soon saw its face through a little
opening not more than three inches wide. I made a
shot, and wounded it, and then rushed up and gave it
a fatal one.

I examined my game and found the first one was a
poor old cow, but the others were yearlings, one of
them very fat and nice, and I soon had the hind
quarters skinned out, and all the fat I could find,
which made a big load for the mule. It was now
almost dark, and the next problem was to get back to
camp again. The brushy hills would be terrible to
cross with a load of meat, and by the way the ground
lay I concluded our camp was on this same creek
farther down.

The only way that seemed at all feasible was to fol-

low the course of the stream if possible, rather than
return the course over which I had come. There
were so many bushes and trees along the bank that I
had to take to the bed and follow in the water, and as
it was rocky and rough, and so dark I could not see
well how to step, I stumbled into holes and pools up
to my waist, wet as a rat. Coming to a small open
place I decided I had better camp for the night and
not attempt further progress in the darkness, and the
decision was hastened by dark clouds, which began to
gather and a few sprinkles of rain began to come. There
was a good patch of grass for the mule, but all was uncomfortable for me, with the prospect for a rainy night,
but as wood was plenty I decided to make a fire and
take the chances. I looked for matches and scratched
one. No go—they were damp, and scratch as careful
and quickly as I could, there was no answering spark
or flame, and darkness reigned supreme. A camp
without a fire in this wet place was not to be thought
of, so I concluded I might as well be slowly working
my way down along the stream, through thick brush
and cold water, as to sit here in the cold and wait.

So the little mule and I started on, wading the creek
in thick darkness, getting only the most dim reflected
light from the sky through now and then an opening
in the trees. I did not know then how easy it was
for a grizzly to capture myself, the mule and meat and
have quite a variety for supper. But the grizzly
stayed at home and we followed on through brambles
and hard brush, through which it was almost impossible to force one's way. As it turned out, I was not in
the track of the storm and did not suffer much from it.
Soon the cañon grew wider, and I could make out on
the right hand a piece of table land covered with brush
that seemed easier to get through than the creek bed.

The hill up to the table land was very steep, but not

more than fifty yards high, and when the mule tried
to get up she got along very well till near the top,
when she slipped in the wet earth and never stopped
till she reached the bottom and lay down. She was
helped up to her feet again and we tried it in another
place, I holding her from slipping when she stopped
to rest, and at last we reached the top. The mule
started on, seeming to follow a trail, but I could not
see whether there was a trail or not, so thick was the
darkness, but there was evidently something of the
kind, for the brush was two or three feet high and very
thick.

After proceeding some distance the mule stopped
and did not seem to wish to go any farther. I was
pretty sure there was something in front of her that
blocked the way, and so worked my way through the
brush and carefully past her. I could partly see and
partly hear something just ahead, and in a moment
found it was our good faithful Cuff, and no frightful
spook at all. The good fellow had discovered our
approach and came out to meet us, and I am sure
the mule was as glad as I was to see him. He crawled
through the brush and smelled at the mule's load
and then went forward in the trail, which we followed.
It was a long time after midnight when we reached
camp. There was a good fire burning, but all were
asleep till I led the mule up to the fire and called
out—"Wake Up," when they were most of them on
their feet in a minute without stopping to dress, for
all had slept a long time without taking off their
clothes.

John took charge of the mule and unloaded it, telling me to get into his warm bed. I took off my wet
clothes and told him to dry them, and then got between the dry, warm blankets in greatest comfort.
Daylight came very quickly, it seemed to me, and be_

befoिe I finally rose, the sun had been up some hours before me. Before I fell asleep I could hear the women say, as they cut off the pieces of meat to roast —"See the fat! Only see how nice it is!" Quickly roasted on the coals they ate the delicate morsels with a relish and, most of all, praised the sweet fat. "We like to have it all fat," said they, showing how their system craved the nourishment the poor starved beef could not give. No one went to bed after I came, but all sat and roasted meat and ate till they were satisfied.

This sporting trip was quite different from deer hunting in Wisconsin, and nothing like looking for game in Death Valley where nothing lived. It was the hardest night's work that ever came to me in many a day, and not the wild sport I generally looked for when on the chase. I felt pretty well when I got up, and a chunk of my last night's prize which had been เoasted for me was eaten with a relish, for it was the best of meat and I, of course, had a first class appetite. I had to tell them my last hunting story, and was much praised as a lucky boy.

We would not be compelled to kill any more of our poor oxen in order to live. So far we had killed six of them, and there were five left. Our present situation was much appreciated, compared with that of a few days ago when we were crawling slowly over the desert, hungry, sore-footed and dry, when to lie was far easier than to take steps forward. We felt like rejoicing at our deliverance and there was no mourning now for us. The surrounding hills and higher mountains seemed more beautiful to us. They were covered with green trees and brush, not a desert place in sight. The clear little singing brook ran merrily on its way, the happiest, brightest stream in all my memory. Wild birds came near us without

fear, and seemed very friendly. All was calm, and
the bright sunshine exactly warm enough so that no
one could complain of heat or cold.

When ready to move it was announced that I had
lost my saddle blanket in my adventure, so they
substituted another one and I took the back track to
the place where the mule slipped down the bank,
and there I found it. I soon overtook them again
just as they were going to camp on Mrs. Bennett's account, as she had been suddenly taken sick with
severe pain and vomiting, something as Rogers and I
had been after eating our first California corn meal.
The rich, fat meat was too strong for her weak
stomach.

Arcane all along had an idea that Rogers and I
meant to surprise them by leading them to believe
the house we had visited was quite a distance off, and
then to so manage it that it should appear upon their
sight suddenly. We assured them it would take two
or more camps before we could get there, and if Mrs.
Bennett did not soon recover, even more than that.
Our camp here was under a great live oak, the ground
deep covered with dry leaves. and near by a beautiful meadow where our cattle and mule ate, drank and
rested, the oxen chewing their cud with such an air of
comfort as had not come to them since leaving their
far-off eastern pastures. They seemed as much
pleased as any one. They would lie down and rest and
eat at the same time in perfectly enjoyable laziness.

Here we all rested and washed such clothes as we
could do without long enough to dry, and washed
our faces and hands over and over again to remove
the dirt which had been burned and sweated in so
completely as not to come off readily. We sat on the
bank of the brook with our feet dangling in the water,
a most refreshing bath, and they too began to look

clean again. We often saw tracks of the grizzly bear
about, but in our ignorance had no fear of them, for
we did not know they were a dangerous animal.
An owl came and hooted in the night, but that was the
only challenge any wild beast or bird gave to our peace-
ful and restful camp. We were out of the dreadful
sands and shadows of Death Valley, its exhausting
phantoms, its salty columns bitter lakes and wild,
dreary sunken desolation. If the waves of the sea
could flow in and cover its barren nakedness, as we
now know they might if a few sandy barriers were
swept away, it would be indeed, a blessing, for in it
there is naught of good, comfort or satisfaction, but
ever in the minds of those who braved its heat and
sands, a thought of a horrid Charnel house, a cornero
the earth so dreary that it requires an exercise of
strongest faith to believe that the great Creator ever
smiled upon it as a portion of his work and pronounced it "Very good." We had crossed the great
North American Continent, from a land of plenty,
over great barren hills and plains, to another mild and
beautiful region, where, though still in winter months,
we were basking in the warmth and luxuriance of
early summer. We thought not of the gold we had
come to win. We were dead almost, and now we
lived. We were parched with thirst, and now the
brightest of crystal streams invited us to stoop and
drink. We were starved so that we had looked at
each other with maniac thoughts, and now we placed
in our mouth the very fat of the land. We had seen
our cattle almost perishing; seen them grow gaunt
and tottering; seen them slowly plod along with
hanging heads and only the supremacy of human will
over animal instinct had kept them from lying down
never to rise again. Now they were in pastures of
sweet grass, chewing the cud of content and satifaction.

Life which had been a burden grew sweet to us, and
though it may be that our words of praise to Him,
whose will was to deliver us out of the jaws of death,
were not set nor formal, yet His all-seeing eye saw
the truth in our hearts, and saw there the fullest expression of our gratitude and thankfulness. Who
shall say the thanks that arose were less acceptable,
because not given on bended knees before gilded
altars?

Though across the desert and evidently in the
long promised land our troubles and trials were not
through by any means, but evidently we were out of
danger. Our lives seemed to be secure, and we were
soon to meet with settlers who would no doubt extend
to us the hand of human sympathy. Many long
miles yet remained between us and the rivers in whose
sands were hidden the tiny grains of gold we came to
seek.

The rest in the lovely camp had answered to cause
Mrs. Bennett to feel quite well again by the next
morning, and we made ready to proceed. We had the
trail of the Jayhawkers to follow, so the vines,
brambles and tangles which had perplexed Rogers
and myself in our first passage were now somewhat
broken down, and we could get along very well without further clearing of the road until the hills came
down so close on both sides that there was no room
except in the very bed of the stream. There was no
other way, so we waded along after the oxen as best
we could. Sometimes the women fell down, for a
rawhide mocassin soaked soft in water was not a very
comfortable or convenient shoe, however it might be
adapted to hot, dry sands. The creek was shaded
and the water quite cool. The trail, such as it was,
crossed the creek often and generally was nothing else
than the stream itself. The constant wading, and

wet, cold clothing caused the women to give out soon and we selected the first dry suitable place which offered food for the oxen, as a place to camp.

Wood was plenty and dry, so a good fire was soon burning, and the poor women, wet to the waist and even higher, were standing before it, turning round and round to get warm and dry. Someone remarked that they resembled geese hanging before the fire to roast, as they slowly revolved, and it was all owing to their fatigue that the suggestor did not receive merited punishment then and there at their hands. As they got a little dry and comfortable they remarked that even an excess of water like this was better than the desert where there was none at all, and as to their looks, there were no society people about to point their fingers at them, and when they reached a settled country they hoped to have a chance to change their clothes, and get two dresses apiece, and that these would be long enough to hide their knees which these poor tatters quite failed to do. One remarked that she was sure she had been down in the brook a dozen times and that she did not consider cold water baths so frequently repeated were good for the health.

Young Charley Arcane had been getting better for some days. No medicine had been given him, and it was no doubt the change of air and water that had begun to effect a cure. Arcane had a hard time of it to keep the brush from pulling George and Melissa off of Old Crump into the water. It was indeed one of the hardest day's work of the whole journey, but no one was low spirited, and all felt very well. The camping place was in a deep cañon, surrounded by thick brush, so that no wind came in to chill us. Everybody was cook and nobody was boss. Not a cent of money among us, nor any chance to use any if we had possessed it. We had nice, sweet, fat meat,

cooked rare or well done as each one perferred, and
no complaints about the waiters.   The conditions were
so favorable, compared with the terrible Death Valley
and its surroundings that every one remarked about it,
and no one felt in the least like finding fault with the
little inconveniencies we were forced to put up with.
It might cure an inveterate fault-finder to take a
course of training in the desert.

The next day we did not wade half as much, and
after a few hours of travel we suddenly emerged from
the brush into a creek bottom which was much wider,
with not a tree to obstruct our way.   The soil was
sandy and covered more or less with sage brush, and
the stream which had been strong and deep enough to
make us very wet now sank entirely out of sight in
the sandy bottom.   The hills were thinly timbered
on the left side but quite brushy on the right, and we
could see the track of cattle in the sand.   No signs
of other animals, but some small birds came near, and
meadow larks whistled their tune, quite familiar to
us, but still sounding slightly different from the song
of the same bird in the East.   High in the air could
be seen a large sailing hawk or buzzard.

We stopped to rest at noon and noticed that the
water ran a little in the creek bed; but, by the time
we were ready to start we found none with which to fill
our canteens.   No doubt this water was poured into
the cañon somewhere near the place where we killed
the three cattle, and we had got out of it before the
flood came down.   It was astonishing to see how the
thirsty sand drank up the quite abundant flow.

The next day we came down to the point of hill
that nearly crossed the valley, and we crossed the low
ridge rather than make a longer trip to get around
by way of the valley.   As we reached the summit
there appeared before us as beautiful a rural picture as

one ever looked upon. A large green meadow, of a thousand acres, more or less; its southwest side bounded by low mountains, at the base of which oak trees were plenty, but no brush or undergrowth. It was like a grand old park, such as we read of in English tales. All over the meadow cattle of all sorts and sizes grazed, the "Ring-streaked and speckled" of old Jacob's breed being very prominent. Some lazily cropped the grass; some still more lazily reclined and chewed their cud; while frisky calves exercised their muscles in swift races and then secured their dinner from anxious mothers. We camped at once and took the loads from all the animals that they might feed in comfort on the sweet grass that lay before them.

We tarried here perhaps two hours, till the cattle stopped eating, and amply enjoyed the scene. Never again would any one of the party go back over that dreary desert, they said,, and everyone wondered why all places could not be as green and beautiful as this one I cannot half tell how we felt and acted, nor what we said in our delight over this picture of plenty. The strong contrasts created strong impressions, and the tongues so long silent in our dry and dreary trouble were loosened to say everything the heart inspired. Think as much as you can; you cannot think it all.

We felt much better after our rest, and the oxen seemed stronger and better able, as well as more willing to carry their loads, so we soon prepared to move on down the valley, toward the house we had spoken of as the goal we were to reach. It was now the 7th day of March 1850, and this date, as well as the 4th day of November 1849 will always remain an important one in memory. On the last named day we left the trail to take the unfortunate cut-off, anp for four long months we had wandered and struggled in terrible hardship. Every point of that terrible journey is indelibly fixed upon my memory and though seventy-three years of age on April 6th 1893 I can locate every camp, and if strong enough could follow that weary trail from Death Valley to Los Angeles with unerring accuracy. The brushy cañon we have just described is now occupied by the Southern Pacific Railroad, and the steep and narrow ridge pierced by a tunnel, through which the trains pass. The beautiful meadow we so much admired has now upon its border a railroad station, Newhall, and at the proper season some portion of it is covered with thousands of trays of golden apricots, grown in the luxuriant orchards just beyond the hills toward the coast, and here drying in the bright summer sun. The cattle in the parti-colored coats are gone, but one who knows the ground can see our picture.

Loaded up again we start down the beautiful grassy valley, the women each with a staff in hand, and everything is new and strange to us. Rogers and I know that we will soon meet people who are strangers to us; who speak a strange language of which we know nothing, and how we, without a dollar, are to proceed to get our food and things we need, are questions we cannot answer nor devise any easy way to overcome. The mines are yet five hundred miles away, and we know not of any work for us to do nearer. Our lives have been given back to us, and now comes the problem of how to sustain them manfully and independently as soon as possible. If worse comes to worst we can walk to San Francisco, probably kill enough game on the way and possibly reach the gold mines at last, but the way was not clear. We must trust much to luck and fortune and the ever faithful Providence which rarely fails those who truly try to help themselves.

We began to think some very independent thoughts. We had a mule to carry our camp kettle and meat; Our cattle were now begining to improve and would soon get fat; these could carry our blankets and odd loads, while Old Crump the christian could still carry the children; Bennett and I knew how to hunt, and had good rifles; so we could still proceed, and we determined that, come what may, *we will be victorious.*

These were some of the plans we talked over at our camps and resting places, and as we walked along. If we could get the two families fixed in some way so they could do without Rogers and I, we could strike for the mines quite rapidly and no doubt soon get ourselves on good footing. We were younger than the rest and could endure more hardship. We decide to remain together till we get to Los Angeles, and then see what is best.

We reached our camping place at the foot of the hill, about a hundred yards from the house we have so long striven to reach. Here we unloaded in the shade of a large willow tree, and scarcely had we removed the harness from the oxen when the good lady of the house and her little child came down to see us. She stood for a moment and looked around her and at the two small children on the blankets, and we could hear her murmur *mucha pobre* (very poor.) She could see our ragged clothes and dirty faces and everything told her of our extreme destitution. After seeing our oxen and mule which were so poor she said to herself "*flaco, flaco*" (so thin.) She then turned to us, Rogers and I, whom she had seen before, and as her lively little youngster clung to her dress, as if in fear of such queer looking people as we were, she took an orange from her pocket and pointing to the children of our party, wanted to know if we had given them

the four oranges she sent to them by us. We made
signs that we had done as she requested, when she
smiled and said *"Buenos Muchuchos"* (good boys.) In
all this talk neither could say a word the other could
understand, and the conversation was carried on by
signs.

Arcane said to her—"Me Catholic" which she
seemed partly to comprehend and seemed more
friendly. About this time two men rode up and took
a look at us. Arcane, who was a mason, gave the
masonic sign, as he told me afterward, but neither of
them recognized it. We used such words of Spanish
as I had taken down in my pass book and committed
to memory and by motions in addition to these made
them understand something of the state of affairs and
that Mr. French who had assisted us before had told
us we could get some meat (*carne*) from them. These
men were finely mounted, wore long leggins made of
hide, dressed with the hair on, which reached to their
hips, stiff hats with a broad rim, and great spurs at their
heels. Each had a coil of braided rawhide rope on
the pommel of the saddle, and all these arrangements
together made a very dashing outfit.

They seemed to understand what we had said to
them, for they rode off with a rush and came back in
a short time, leading a fine, fat two-year-old heifer.
When near our camp the rider who was behind threw
his *riata* and caught both hind feet of the animal when
by a sudden movement of the horses the heifer was
thrown. One of them dismounted, and at the command the horse backed up and kept the rope tight
while the man went up to the protrate beast and cut its
throat. As soon as it had ceased struggling, they
loosened their ropes and coiled them up: they came
to us and pointed to the dead heifer in a way which
said—"Help yourselves."

We were much gratified at the generosity of the people, and at once dressed the animal as it lay, cutting off some good fat pieces which we roasted over the fire and ate with a relish. It seemed as if meat never tasted so good as that did sweet, fragrant, and juicy. If some French cook could only cook a steak that would smell and taste to his customers as that meal tasted to us, his art would be perfect. We separated a hind quarter and hung it to a tree, and when the lady came back we told her that the piece we had selected was enough for our present use, so she caused the remainder with the hide to be taken to the house. Toward night they drove up a lot of cows and calves and other cattle into their cattle yard or corral, as it is called all over California, a stockade of strong oak posts set deep in the ground and close together, enclosing a space of about half an acre. The horsemen now rode in and began to catch the calves with their ropes. It seemed as if they were able to throw a rope over a calf's head or around either leg they desired, with better aim, and at as great a distance as one could shoot a Colt's revolver, and we saw at once that a good raw-hide rope, in the hands of an experienced man and well-trained horse, was a weapon in many respects superior to fire-arms of any kind. A man near the gate loosened the ropes and pushed the calves into a separate corral till they had as many as they pesired.

Rogers watched the circus till it was over and then returned to camp, meeting on the way Bennett and Arcane, with their wives and children, carrying some blankets, for the good lady had invited them to come up to the house and sleep, They said we could go down and keep camp if old dog Cuff was willing, for they had left him guarding the property. He was pleased enongh to have us come and keep him com-

pany, and we slept nicely, disturbed only a little by
the barking of the house dogs and the hooting of an
owl that came to visit our tree.

The people came back to camp in the morning and
had their experience to relate. Their hosts first baked
some kind of slapjacks and divided them among their
guests; then gave them beans seasoned hot with pepper: also great pieces of squash cooked before the fire,
which they said was delicious and sweet–more than
good. Then came a dish of dried meat pounded fine,
mixed with green peppers and well fried in beef tallow.
This seemed to be the favorite dish of the proprietors,
but was a little too hot for our people. They called it
chili cum carne–meat with pepper–and we soon found
this to be one of the best dishes cooked by the Californians. The children were carefully waited on and
given special attention to by these good people, and it
was nearly ten o'clock before the feast was over: then
the household had evening worship by meeting in silence, except a few set words repeated by some in turn,
the ceremony lasting half an hour or more. Then
they came and wished them *buenos noches* in the most
polite manner and left them to arrange their blankets
on the floor and go to sleep.

The unaccustomed shelter of a roof and the restless
worrying of the children, who required much attention,
for the change of diet had about the same effect on them
as on Rogers and myself when we first partook of the
California food, gave them little sleep, but still they
rested and were truly grateful for the most perfect hospitality of these kind hearted people.

In the morning the two horsemen and two Indians
went to the corral, when the riders would catch a cow
with their ropes and draw her head up to a post, binding it fast, while an Indian took a short piece of rope
and closely tied the hind legs together above the gam-

brel joint, making the tail fast also.   They had a large
bucket and several gourds.   The Indians then milked
the cows they had made fast, getting from a pint to two
quarts from each one, milking into a gourd and pouring into the bucket till they had all they desired.   The
calves were separated the night before so they could
secure some milk.   Cows were not trained to stand
and be milked as they were at home.   Setting down
the bucket of milk before us, with some small gourds
for dippers, we were invited to drink all we wished.
This was a regular banquet to us, for our famished
condition and good appetites made food reliss wonderfully.   When we made a sign of wishing to pay them
for their great kindness they shook their heads and
utterly refused.   It was genuine sympathy and hospitality on their part, and none of us ever forgot it; the
sight of a native Californian has always brought out
thoughts of these good people, and respect and thankfulness to the race.   This rancho, at which we were so
kindly entertained was called San Francisquito, or
Little San Francisco Rancho.

This morning Mr. Arcane, with our assistance, made
an arrangement with these people to give them his two
oxen; and they were to take him and his wife and child,
to the sea-shore. at a place called San Pedro, from
which place he hoped, in some way, to get passage to
San Francisco in a sailing vessel.   He had no money,
and no property to sell, except perhaps his spy-glass,
worth about ten dollars.   With this poor prospect before him he started for the sea.   He bade Bennett's
folks good-bye, then came to me and put a light gold
ring on my finger, saying that it and his interest in the
little mule were mine.   Then he gave his silver watch
to Rogers and said it was all he had to give him, but
if he had a million dollars, he would divide, and still
think it a small compensation for the faithful services

we had rendered him. "I can never repay you," said he, "for I owe you a debt that is beyond compensation You have saved our lives, and have done it when you knew you could get nothing for it. I hope we will meet again, and when we do you will be welcome. If you hear of me anywhere, come and see me, for I want to tell my friends who Manly and Rogers are, and how you helped us. Good Bye!" There were tears in his eyes, voice full of emotion, and the firm clasp of his hand told how earnest he was, and that he felt more than he could speak.

He helped Mrs. Arcane on her horse, then gave Charlie to her, and, amid waving hands and many *adios* from our new-found friends, with repeated "good byes" from the old ones, they rode away. Mrs. Arcane could hardly speak when she bade us farewell, she was so much affected. They had about sixty miles to ride to reach the sea, and as she rode on a man's saddle, and was unused to riding, I knew she would be sadly wearied before she reached the coast.

Our little train now seemed much smaller. Three oxen and a mule were all our animals, and the adults must still walk, as they had done on our desert route. But we were comparatively happy, for we had plenty of good meat to eat, plenty of sweet water to drink, and our animals were contented and improving every day; grass and water seemed plenty everywhere. We put our luggage on the oxen and the mule, loaded the children on Old Crump as we had done before, and were ready to move again. Our good friends stood around and smiled good-naturedly at our queer arrangements, and we, not knowing how to say what our hearts would prompt us to, shook their hands and said good bye in answer to their "*adios amigos*" as we moved away, waving hands to each other.

The men then detained me a little while to ask me

more about the road we had come over, how far it was,
and how bad the Indians were, and other particulars.
I told him by signs that we had been twenty-two days
on the road, and that the *Indianos*, as they called them,
had not troubled us, but that there was very little grass
or water in all that land.   He made a sort of map on
the ground and made me understand he would like to
go back and try to bring out the wogons we had left
behind, and he wanted me to go back with him and
help him.   I explained to him by the map he had
made, and one which I made myself, that I considered
it impossible to bring them over.   He seemed much
disappointed, and with a shrug of his shoulders said
"mucho malo" (very bad) and seemed to abandon the
idea of getting a Yankee wagon.   They very much
admired an American wagon, for their own vehicles
were rude affairs, as I shall bye-and-bye describe.   We
bade each other mauy *adios*, and I went on my way,
soon catching np with the little party.   We had been
informed that it was ten leagues, or thirty miles to
Los Angeles, whither we were now headed.

We had now been a whole year on the road between
Wisconsin and California, much of the time with the
ground for a bed, and though our meals had been
sometimes scanty and long between, very few of us
had missed one on account of sickness.   Some, less
stroug than we, had lain down to perish, and had been
left behind, without coffin or grave; bnt we were here,
and so far had found food to nourish us in some degree
with prospects now of game in the future if nothing
better offered.   We still talked of going to the gold
mines on foot, for with good food and rest our courage
had returned, and we wanted to succeed.

Our camp this night was io a nice watering place,
where dry oak wood was plenty and grass abundant.
It was at the foot of the San Fernando Mountain, not

rocky, as we had found our road some time before, but smooth and covered with grass. It was rather steep to climb, but an infant compared with the great mountains so rough and barren, we had climbed on our way from Death Valley. Our present condition and state of mind was an anomalous one. We were happy, encouraged, grateful and quite contented in the plenty which surrounded us, and still there was a sort of puzzling uncertainty as to our future, the way to which seemed very obscure. In the past we had pushed on our very best and a kind Providence had kept us. This we did now, but still revolved the best plans and the most fortunate possibilities in our minds. We talked of the time when we should be able to show hospitality to our friends, and to strangers who might need our open hand as we had needed the favors which strangers had shown us in the last few days.

We ate our supper of good meat, with a dessert of good beans our kind friends had given us, and enjoyed it greatly. As we sat in silence a flock of the prettiest, most graceful birds came marching along, and halted as if to get a better view of our party. We admired them so much that we made not a move, but waited, and they fearlessly walked on again. We could see that there were two which were larger than the rest, and from twelve to twenty smaller ones. The little top-knot on the head and their symmetrical forms made them specially attractive, and Mrs. Bennett and the children were much pleased. The beauty of the California quail is especially striking to one who sees them for the first time.

In the morning we began to climb the hill, getting along very well indeed, for our raw-hide mocassins were now dry and hard and fitted the foot perfectly. We did not try to make great speed, but kept steadily on, and as we were used to climbing, we reached the summit easily. From this elevation we could get a fine view of the big grassy plain that seemed to extend as far as the eye could reach and, not far from us, the buildings and gardens of the San Fernando Mission. If we could shut out the mountains the landscape would remind us of a great Western prairie. We never could get over comparing this country with the desolate Death Valley, for it seemed as if such strange and striking opposites could hardly exist.

We rested here a little while and then wound our way down the hill to the level land. A few miles brought us to the mission houses and the church of San Fernando. There was not much life about them, in fsct they seemed comparatively deserted, for we saw only one man and a few Indians. The man brought some oranges and gave the children one each. After a little rest we moved on over our road which was now quite smooth and gently descending. Night overtook us in a place where there was no water, but we camped and suffered no inconvenience. A stream was passed next day, and a house near by unoccupied. The road now began to enter gently rolling hills covered with big grass and clover, which indicated rich soil, and we never get tired of talking about it.

At the top of these hills we had another beautiful view as far south and west as the eye could reach. Small objects, probably horses and cattle, were scattered about the plain, grazing in the midst of plenty. Our own animals were given frequent opportunities to eat, and again and again we rejoiced over the beauty. Of course it was not such a surprise and wonder as it was when such a view first burst upon our sight, but it pleased and delighted us ever. On the east was a snow-capped peak, and here we were in the midst of green fields of grass and wild flowers, in the softest climate of an early spring. These strong contrasts beat anything we had ever seen. Perhaps the contrast between the great snow mountain and the hot Death Valley was greater in point of temperature, but there the heat brought only barrenness, and of the two the snow seemed the more cheerful. Here the vegetation of all sorts was in full balance with the balmy air, and in comparison the snow seemed a strange neighbor. It was quite a contrast to our cold, windy March in Wisconsin, and we wonder if it is always summer here We were satisfied that even if we could get no further we could live in such a land as this. The broad prairie doubtless belonged to the United States, and we could have our share and own a little piece of it on very easy terms, and raise our own cattle and corn. If the people were all as kind as those we had met we were sure at least of neighborly treatment. I have endeavored to write this just as it seemed to us then and not clothe the impressions with the cover of later experience. The impressions we then daily received and the sights we saw were stranger than the wildest fiction, and if it so strikes you, my friendly reader, do not wonder.

As we came over the hills we could see a village near the southern base and it seemed quite near us. It was a new and strange sight to us as we approached. The houses were only one story high and seemed built of mud of a gray color, the roofs flat, and the streets almost deserted. Occasionly a man could be seen, sometimes a dog, and now and then an Indian, sitting with his back to the house. The whole view indicated a thinly populated place, and the entire absence of wagons or animals was a rather strange circumstance to us. It occurred to us at first that if all the emigrants were gone our reception might be a cool one in this city of mud. One thing was in its favor and that was its buildings were about fire proof for they had earthen floors and flat roofs.

We rested half an hour or so just outside, and then ventured down the hill into the street- We met an American almost the first man, and when we asked about a
suitable camping place, he pointed out the way and we
marched on. Our strange appearance attracted the
attention of the children and they kept coming out of
the houses to see the curious little train with Old
Crump carrying the children and our poor selves following along, dirty and ragged. Mrs, Bennett's dress
hardly reached below her knees, and although her
skirts were fringed about the bottom it was of a kind
that had not been adopted as yet in general circle of
either Spanish-American or good United States society.
The shortness of the dress made the curious raw-hide
mocassins only the more prominent, and the whole
make-up of the party was a curious sight.

We went down the hill a little further to the lower
bottom to camp, while the barefooted, bareheaded ur-
chins followed after to get a further look at the strangers. Before we selected a suitable place, we saw two
tents and some wagons which looked like those of
overland travelers, and we went toward them. When
within fifty yards two men suddenly came to their feet
and looked at our little party approaching as if in
wonder, but at twenty steps they recognized Bennett
and came rushing forward. "My God! It's Bennett"
said they, and they clasped hands in silence while one
greeted Mrs. Bennett warmly. The meeting was so
unexpected they shed tears and quietly led the way
back to camp. This was the camp of R. G. Moody and
H. C. Skinner, with their families. They had traveled
together on the Platte and became well acquainted, the
warmest of friends, and knowing that Bennett had
taken the cut off, they more than suspected he and his
party had been lost, as no sight of them had come to
their eyes. They had been waiting here six weeks in

order to get some reliable news, and now Mr. Bennet answered for himself. Rogers and I, belonging to another party, were of course strangers.

Leaving them to compare notes, Rogers and I took charge of Old Crump, the oxen, and the mule, unpacked them, and arranged camp under a monstrous willow tree. Bennett and his wife were taken into Mr. Moody's tent, and an hour or so later when Mrs. Bennett appeared again, she had her face washed clean, her hair combed, and a new clean dress. It was the first time we had found soap, and the improvement in her looks and feelings was surprising. Bennett looked considerably cleaned up too, and appeared bright and fresh. The children had also been taken in hand and appeared in new clothes selected from the wardrobe of the other children, and the old dirty clothes were put in process of washing as soon as possible.

Supper came, and it was so inviting. There was real bread and it looked so nice we smiled when it was offered to us. Mrs. Bennett broke pieces for the children and cautioned them not to eat too much. It did seem so good to be among friends we could talk with and be understood. After supper was over and the things cleared away we all sat down in a circle and Bennett told the story of where he had been these many days on the cut off that was to shorten the trail. Mr. Moody said he had about given the party up and intended to start up the coast to-morrow. The story was so long that they talked till they were sleepy and then began again after breakfast, keeping it up till they had a good outline of all our travels and tribulations. This Mr. R. G. Moody, his wife and daughter, Mrs. Quinby, and son. Charles, all lived in San Jose and are now dead. H. C. Skinner was a brother-in-law of Moody and also lived a long time in San Jose, but himself, son and one daughter, are now dead.

Rogers and I now took the pack-saddle we had borrowed of Mr. French to use on our trip to Death Valley and return, and carried it to the saloon on the east side of the plaza, where we were to place it if we got back safely, and delivered it to the man in charge, with many thanks to Mr. French for his favors to us, and sent him word that we would always remember him and be ready to do him a similar or equal favor if ever we were able. We considered him a good benevolent man, and such he proved to be when he offered us fat oxen, good beans, and any other thing we needed. He told the people in the house who we were, which no doubt influenced them kindly in our favor when we arrived.

At the saloon there was a large room with tables in it and gambling going on actively. Money changed hands very rapidly, drinks at the bar were frequent, and the whole affair moved forward with the same regularity as any mercantile business. The door stood wide open and any one could come and go at his pleasure. Quite a number of black-eyed, fair-looking women circulated among the crowd, and this, to us, seemed quite out of place, for we had never seen women in saloons before. We watched the game awhile to see some losing and some gaining, the result being quite exciting; but as neither of us had any money, we could not have joined in the game had we been so disposed; so we looked on awhile and then took a seat on the ground outside of the house.

Here we talked over our chances of getting to the mines. All the clothes we had were on our backs and feet and those were the poorest of the poor. We had no money. I had the little black-eyed mule, and Rogers had the watch Arcane had given him. Mr. Moody had said it was 500 miles to San Francisco, and 150 miles further to the mines, so that after the hard

travel of a year we were still a long way off from the
place we started for.

We could not see any way to make a living here.
There was no land cultivated, not a fence, nothing to
require labor of any kind. The valley was rich enough
and produced great crops of grass, and the cattle and
horses we had seen grazing seemed to be about all the
use they put it to. It looked as if the people must live
principally on meat. I thought if we could manage to
get a little provision together, such as flour and beans,
that I could pack there on the mule, and I was pretty
sure I could find game that would be better meat than
we had lived on during the last two months on the
desert.

We looked around to see if we could find something to
do to earn a little for a start, but were not successful.
In our walk about this city of mud we saw many
things that seemed strange to us. There were more
women than men, and more children than grown-up
people, while the dogs were plenty. At the edge of
the town, near the river were some grape vines fenced
in with living willows, interlaced in some places with
dry vines. The Indians moved very moderately around
and no doubt had plenty of beef to eat, with very few
wants to provide for. We noticed some few people
paying for small things at the stores with small money.
The women all dressed much alike. The dress was of
some cheap material, sandals on feet, and a kind of
long shawl worn over the head and thrown over the
shoulder. There seemed to be neither hoops nor cor-
sets in their fashions. The men wore trousers of
white cotton or linen, with a calico shirt, sandals, and
a broad rimmed snuff colored hat. The Indians and
their wives went bareheaded.

Near the end of the street we came to a boarding
house and went in and sat down in the empty room.

Soon a man came in, better dressed than ourselves, and much to our surprise it was one of the old Death Valley travelers, the Rev. J. W. Brier whom I last saw in his lone camp in the desert, discoursing to his young sons on the benefits of an early education. I know the situation struck me very strangely, with death staring them in the face and he preaching!

We had a long talk about the hard journey we had each experienced. As his party had not waited they had come through ahead of us. He said himself and Mr. Granger had started a boarding house when they arrived, and had been doing a good business. He said that as long as the emigrants continued to come he could get along very well. We asked him if there was any chance for ns to work and get money to get some provisions to help us on the way to the mines. He said he could give work to one of us hauling water for the house with oxen and cart, and the one who could manage oxen was the man. I was an ox driver and so told him I would take his team and cart and set out with the work. He said he could pay fifty dollars a month, and I accepted the offer quickly as I saw it was a good chance to build up my exhausted strength and flesh.

I turned the little mule out in the hills near by, and began my work. It was not hard, for the boarders were thinning out. The natives did not patronize this hotel very much, but grub disappeared pretty fast at my corner of the table, for my appetite began to be ravenous. There was not much variety to the food and very few luxuries or delicacies, which were hard to obtain on such a bare market, but all seemed satisfied with the food, and to me it tasted extra good.

Rogers went back to the old camp and helped them there, and I often went over after dark, when my work was done. Moody and Skinner had been active in

trying to get Mr. Bennett ready to go up the coast
with them. Bennett had sold his repeating rifle and
with the proceeds and the help of his friends had got
another ox, making two yoke for him. They fixed
up a wagon for him, and yokes enough could be found
where people had traded off their oxen for horses.
Provisions enough had been gathered by Moody and
Skinner for them all, and Rogers would go along with
the party to help them with the teams.

I was left alone after they started, and it was my
idea to quit when I had worked a month, and if my
mule staid with me, to start for the mines even if I
went alone. The majority of the male inhabitants of
this town had gone to the mines, and this accounted
for the unusual proportion of women. We learned
that they would return in November, and then the
gambling houses would start up in full blast, for these
native Californians seemed to have a great natural desire to indulge in games of chance, and while playing
their favorite game of monte would lay down their last
reale (12½ cents) in the hope of winning the money
in sight before them on the table.

As the boarding house business got dull I was taken
over to a vineyard and set to work, in place of hauling
water. The entire patch was as green as a meadow
with weeds, and I was expected to clean them out. I
inquired of Brier how he came to get hold of this nice
property, and he said that during the war the soldiers
had taken possession of this piece of ground, and had
their camp here, so he considered it was government
land, and therefore had squatted on it and was going
to hold it, and pay for it as regular government land,
and that he already considered it his own, for said he,
"I am an American, and this is a part of the public
domain." "All right," said I, "I will kill weeds for
you, if you wish, when I have time to spare, and you

don't want the oxen worked at any other work ".

I could see every day that I was improving in health and weight and would soon become myself again, able to take the road to the mines. When about two weeks of my time had expired two oldish men came to the house to stop for a few days and reported themselves as from Sacramento, buying up some horses for that market. Thus far they had purchased only six or eight, as they had found the price too high to buy and then drive so far to a market to sell again. They had about decided to go back with what they had and undertake some other kind of business. I thought this would be a pretty good chance for me to go, as I would have company, and so went to Brier and Granger and told them what I would like to do, and that with their permission I would quit and go on with them. They readily consented, for their money was coming in rather slow, and they paid me twenty five dollars for half a month's work. This made me feel pretty rich and I thought this would give me food enough to reach the mines.

Having two or three days to get ready in, I began doing the best I could. I found an old saddle tree which had been thrown away, and managed to fix it up so I could use it. I also found an old gun some traveler had left, and with a little work I fitted the breech of that to my own gun which was broken, and had been roughly tied together with strips of raw-hide. I now had a good sound gun if it was not very handsome. I bought a Spanish blanket, not so wide as ours, but coarse and strong, and having a hole in the center through which to put the head and wear it as a garment in case of storm, or at night. I went to a native store and bought a supply of carné seca (dried beef) and some crackers, put some salt in my pocket and was now provisioned for another trip. I found

my mule in the hills back of town, not far from where
I left her, and the rest and good feed had made her
look better and feel better, as well as myself.

Thedrovers had found two other men who wanted to
go with them and help drive the horses for their board.
I put my blanket on under the saddle, packed my little
sack of meat and crackers on behind, and when I was
in the saddle with my gun before me I considered I
was pretty well fixed and able to make my way against
almost anything. I said to myself that the only way
now to keep me from getting to the gold mines was to
kill me. I felt that there was not a mountain so high
I could not climb, and no desert so wide and dry that
I could not cross it. I had walked and starved and
choked and lived through it, and now I felt so
strong and brave I could do it again — any way to
reach the gold mines and get some of the "dust."

I had not much idea how the gold from the mines
looked. Everybody called it gold dust, and that conveyed an idea to me that it was fine as flour, but how
to catch it I did not know. I knew other people found
a way to get it, and I knew I could learn if any body
could. It was a great longing that came to me to see
some of the yellow dust in its native state, before it
had been through the mint.

At the last meal I took at the house there were only
a few at the table. Among them was a well dressed
Californian who evidently did not greatly fancy American cooking, but got along very well till Mrs. Brier
brought around the dessert, a sort of duff. This the
Californian tasted a few times and then laid down his
spoon saying it was no bueno, and some other words
I did not then understand, but afterward learned that
they meant "too much grease." The fellow left the
table not well pleased with what we generally consider
the best end of a Yankee dinner, the last plate.

While here I had slept in a small store room, where I made my pallet out of old rags and blankets. While I was looking round for material to make my bed I came across a bag partly full of sugar, brought from Chili. It was in very coarse crystals, some as large as corn. There were some other treasures and luxuries there that perhaps I was expected guard. I however had a sweet tooth and a handful or so of the sweet crystals found their way into my pocket.

I bade Mr. Brier and the rest good bye and rode away to join my company.

CHAPTER XII

[Leaving the little party whose wanderings we have followed so closely, safely arrived in Los Angeles, their further history in California will be taken up later on, and this narrative will go back to points when the original party was broken up and trace the little bands in their varied experience. It will be remembered that the author and his friends, after a perilous voyage down Green River, halted at the camp of the Indian chief, Walker, and there separated, the Author and four companions striking for Salt Lake, while Mc Mahon and Field remained behind, fully determined to go on down the river.

The story of these two men is told by Mc Mahon in the following interesting letter.]

Dear Manley:—

    Yours requesting me to give you a synopsis of the history of incidents, experience, and observations of our mutual friend, Richard Field and myself, from the time you, John Rogers, Alfred Walton, and the Hazelrig brothers left us at the camp of the generous old chief Walker on the west bank of the river near the mouth of the "great seven days cañon" is at hand.

You no doubt distinctly, and with pleasure, remember that unbroken friendship which existed among us up to the time of our separation and that we parted warm and tried friends.

Well, after you and your companions had left us we set to work to prepare the canvas for the continuation of the voyage down the river. We drilled holes through the sides of the "Pilot"— you, I have no doubt remember which that was, yours and mine, in which we took so many fearful risks, and "No. 2," so that we might in case of necessity lash the two together. After a day or two Field lost courage and finally determined to go no further down the river. Walker in the meantime had repeated his friendly warnings appertaining to the great danger in going further down the river. You will remember what he had told us about it before you left us.

You know that I was the biggest coward of the whole seven; but I assumed courage and told Field that I would go down the river alone; and, for a time, I thought I would do so; but after some reflection I concluded that, perhaps, discretion was the better part valor, and reluctantly gave it up. We now decided to follow you, or to take some other unknown route and try to make our escape out of this most perilous condition.

We then set about, as you had done, to trade with Walker for a pony or two, and after much dickering Field succeeded in getting the, afterwards famous, big, old, sore-backed mule. You may not remember him, but I do; and, notwithstanding his sore back, he made pretty good beef. I, with pins, needles, thread, a pocket-knife, a handkerchief, etc., succeeded in getting a very nice, round, three-year-old, iron-gray pony.

After making pack-saddles, and getting almost ready to start, we were, through Walker's kindness and persuasiveness, overcome, and consented to go with him, feeling confident that we would not starve to death while with him. We did not now have Manley with his long experience, and his old rusty, but always trusty, rifle as a sure defence against possible hunger and starvation.

The old chief, and, in fact, the whole tribe, seemed pleased when we consented to go with them. Prepar-

ations were now made, and all except the horses and
four head of cattle, was conveyed across the river in
the two canoes which were lashed together, while the
horses and cattle were forced to swim to the other side
where we camped for the night. Next morning the
clever old chief had two good horses fitted up in good
style for Field and I, which we rode all of the nine
days that we remained with the band, while our own
run with the herd. Our baggage was carried on some
of the chief's pack-horses. We were, in fact, his honored guests, as will hereafter appear.

All were soon mounted and off to the buffalo fields,
Walker having informed us that he intended going up
into the buffalo country on the head-waters of Grand
River where he would remain until snow fell, when
he would go to Salt Lake City, or vicinity.

Leaving the river, we set out across a not entirely
barren plain, for there was much sage-brush, and
several varieties of cactus. Towards evening we came
close up to the foot of a range of rugged, rocky mountains, where we found water and camped for the night.
Field and I usually pitched our little muslin tent
somewhere near our friends where we could sleep
without fear of man or beast, for I think some one of
the reds was always on guard.

All went well for four or five days, when we all got
entirely out of food except a few ounces of flour which
we had hidden away for a possible emergency. During the following two days and nights all were entirely
without food except the two little children, whom you
no doubt remember. We gave their mother a little
flour now and then which she mixed with a little milk
which one of the cows afforded, for the little ones.
These Indians did not seem to suffer for want of food;
even when we were starving, they appeared happy
and contented; and one young fellow would sing all

day long while we were starving. During the second day of starvation and hard traveling over hot and barren deserts, the Indians killed a wild-cat and two small rabbits. We got nothing. You will remember that all the arms of the seven men were lost in the river when the canoes were sunk, except your rifle and my double barreled shot-gun and revolver, so that Field and I had only the one gun, and neither of us knew anything about hunting. When we camped, one of the boys brought over to our tent a quarter of the cat, which was more than a fair share of the whole supply. as twenty-two of them had only the two little rabbits and three quarters of the unfortunate cat. we boiled and boiled and boiled that cat's hind leg, but never got it done. We waited as long as we possibly could, gave up in despair and put a little flour into the broth to thicken it,.and drank it. It was not good, but much better the meat of the cat. That cat and the rabbits were all the twenty-four of us had to eat, after fasting two days, until late in the evening of the next day.

My people were religious, and when I was young the family was wont to observe fast days, but never did we have any such long fasts as these were. In the afternoon of the next day the old chief left the caravan and went on ahead of the train toward a chain of mountains, first giving some directions to the band, and taking one son with him. When we arrived in a small cañon in the edge of the momntains we found them with a fine mountain sheep which they had killed and brought down to the dim, little-used trail where we camped; and after we had set up our little tent as usual, a short distance away from our friends, one of the young men brought to us about one fourth of the sheep, while the twenty-two Indians had the rest.

You know that a good-sized mountain sheep would

make a fair supper for twenty-four people, even though
they had been starving three or four days; but this
was a small one, and I think Field and I ate about
half of the quarter. The twenty-two Indians soon devoured the three-fourths and all of the soft viscera,
including the stomach and intestines, after which some
of the boys came to our tent while we were stuffing
our, what had been for several days empty, stomachs.
We offered them part of our bounteous supply of mut-
ton, having much more than we could eat; but no,
they would not touch it until we were filled full, when
they accepted what was left, and soon stowed it away.
All were now pretty well filled up once more.

The next day was spent without food, traveling
over rough mountains. Within a pass, late in the
afternoon, we crossed the fresh trail of some other
band of roving red-skins, and Walker suspected who
they were, and went into camp early. The Indians
had killed nothing that day, but I had killed a small
rabbit which, unfortunately for it, came in my way
during the day. This we offered to the women for
themselves and the little children; but they positively
refused to accept it, insisting that they did not want
it or need it, and that the small supply of milk from
the cow was quite sufficient for the little ones, and
the others spurned the offer to divide so little a thing,
so we had it all to ourselves.

It appeared that these people were accustomed to go
for long periods without food, and with little apparent
inconvenience; but Field and I began to feel as I suppose Dr. Tanner felt after a few days' fasting, and began to wish that the old chief would get hungry and
kill one of his large, fat steers, but he still held them
in reserve.

Early the next morning, now nine days from the
time we had left the river, the old chief took two of

the young men and left camp, as we afterwards
learned, to go in search of the Indians whose trail we
had crossed the evening before. Some time in the
early part of the night, one of the young men returned
and informed us that they had found the wandering
tribe, and that we were to go back to their trail and
follow it to their camp up in a Southeast direction,
Walker and one of the young men having remained
with their new-found friends.

Field and I both felt greatly disappointed in not
being able to proceed north; and in the meantime we
had become very tired of the society of these people,
notwithstanding the fact that they were exceedingly
clever; but we were almost starved to death, and had
about come to the conclusion that we would be obliged
to make some change. We were still on the east side
of, and considerable distance from the river, and probably not more than one hundred, or one hundred and
twenty miles from the place where we parted from
you.

The chief had sent particular instructions for us to
go with the tribe; but, after canvassing the whole situation, we decided to part company with our good
friends, proceed northward, and try to reach Fort
Bridger or some other settlement in the northwest,
and so informed them, and requested the boys to bring
in our mule and horse, which they did after failing to
induce us to go with them.

Bright and early the next morning, they all, even
the polygamous wives and little children, in apparent
sorrow, bade us good-bye, and were off, leaving us
alone with our two poor, lonely, four-footed companions, who were very anxious to follow the band of
horses. After the rather melancholy parting we arranged our packs, and about ten o'clock started out
on what then seemed, and and afterwards proved, to

be a perilous voyage through deserts, and over rough
mountains. To avoid a high range of mountains, our
course was for a time northeast but, after passing that
range we bore to the northwest.

The days were quite warm, but the nights were cold.
During the first day we killed and ate one small rabbit, and this, with a few seed buds gathered from wild
rose bushes, constituted two days' rations. On the
third we did not have even the rabbit or rose seed
buds, but late in the afternoon we found some small
red berries, similar in appearance to what I, in my
childhood, knew and relished as Solomon's seal berries.
I being a natural coward, and fearing that they might
poison me, did not eat any of them, but generously
allowed my good friend to eat them all.

We had now been almost entirely without water for
two days and nights. When night came on we picketed our animals in a grass plot and lay down near
them to see that they did not get tangled in the ropes
and hurt, or that some red skin, not having the fear
of the Lord in his heart, did not come and take them
away. About ten o'clock my companion began to
complain of pain in his stomach and bowels, and was
soon vomiting at a fearful rate; so violently, indeed,
that I was apprehensive that he might die. If I had
had an emetic I would have given it to him to have
assisted nature in pumping those devilish little red
berries out of him, for I felt quite sure that they were
the cause of his illness. Perhaps it was fortunate that
there was no medecine at hand, for if there had been
I might have killed him with it.

He suffered most intensely, and soon became very
thirsty, and, there being no water within many miles
of us, he appealed to me to bleed one of the animals
and let him drink the blood; I refused: he insisted; I
again refused: he commanded; I still refused. He

swore, and called me almost everything except a good
Christian; he even expressed the wish that I, his friend,
might be sent to a certain place where the heat is most
intense, and the fire is never quenched.

At about eleven o'clock, when his pains were most
severe, a dark cloud, the first we had seen for months,
came over us, and a little rain began to fall, when I at
once opened our little camp kettle and turned the lid
upside down, and into both kettle and lid there fell
perhaps two or three teaspoonfuls of pure water, every
drop of which I gave to the sufferer, whereupon he
expressed thanks for another God-send, and at once
apologized for bestowing unmerited abuse on me. He
afterwards often asserted that he believed that the little
rain-cloud was sent by God for his special benefit, and
that the water caught from that cloud was the sweetest and best that he had ever tasted. I did not doubt
the latter half of the above statement, but I did have
some doubt about the truth of the former half when I
called to mind the scene which followed my refusal to
bleed the horse. Whether the small quantity of water
gave him much relief, or not, I do not know, but I do
know that he soon became better and slept some while
I watched. He was quite feeble next morning when
I put him on the old sore-backed mule, where he rode
most of the time for the next four days, while the little horse carried our baggage, and I led the way as
usual, on foot.

For four days from the time Field ate the little red
berries we did not have a drop of water except the two
or three teaspoonfuls which the stingy cloud left to
save the life of the "berry-eater." We were still on
the desert, or in the mountains east of the river, traveling hard during the day, and burning up with fever
n the night. There was plenty of drying grass in
places, but our poor animals could not eat it any longer,

for they, too, weie burning up for want of water. Oh,
how much I did wish that we had some camels from
Arabia, which could have gone so much longer without water, and traveled so much faster.

On the morning of the third day of starvation, we
determined to change our course, and, if possible,
reach the river once more. Bearing to the left over a
high, barren range of rocky mountains, and down into
a plain of sand, sage brush, and cactus. During the
afternoon I shot a small rabbit. not much larger than
a rat, which we carried until night, then broiled and
tried to eat it, not because our apetites craved it, but
hoping that it might strengthen and sustain us, at
least a little while longer. We were, however, so
nearly burned up that there was not a sufficient flow of
saliva to moisten the little bits of broiled meat in the
mouth. Late that afternoon we fancied that our fast
failing brute companions scented water, or that they
instinctively knew that it was not far away. They
would raise their heads, and extend their noses as if
smelling, while their physical force and energy seemed
renewed, and they certainly traveled faster.

That night we ate the little, as before stated, more
as a duty than as a pleasure. There was some green
grass round about where we camped, or, more properly
speaking, where we lay, for we did not erect our little
tent,— but the poor starving animals did not eat a
bite of it, but stood over us as if in sympathy with us
in our deplorable condition. We rose before the sun,
being somewhat rested and refreshed, for the night
had been cool, and took up our line of march, I, as
usual, in the lead, then came the old mule guided by
its precious owner, and lastly, the faithful little horse
with the pack on his still quite round back;— on over
the still dry and barren plain we went, without a
Moses, cloud, or pillar of fire to lead us.

About ten o'clock, through the hot gli nmer of the
down-pouring rays of the sun, we saw what appeared,
and afterwards pi oved, to be a clump of cottonwood
trees. Our hopes and courage were renewed, for we
well knew the cottonwood usually grows near flowing water. There was no beaten pathway, no signs
of animal life, no quails, no manna in that desert; but
on we went, almost without a halt, and at one o'clock
reached the cottonwood grove, immediately on the
bank of the great river down which we had floated in
our canoes more than a month before. On reaching
the bank of the river we recognized objects which we
had seen while on our way down.

We remembered that both men and horses might be
water-foundered, and that self-preservation is said to
be the first law of nature; but it was difficult to prevent the famishing brutes from plunging into the river.
We allowed them to take only a small quantity at
first, and each of us took only a small cupful; then
after a little time all took more, and the thirst was
soon quenched. We were surprised to find how little
water it took to satisfy the raging thirst of four days
of continued fasting. The animals, after taking comparatively small quantities, seemed satisfied, and went
off in search of grass.

We now had an abundance of water, but we well
knew that water alone would not sustain life very
long: therefore our next, and most serious business
was to determine how to prolong our lives. According to our map, our recollections of different objecls,
and present appearances we were now a little above
the mouth of the Uinta river which comes in from the
northwest, all of which proved true. Our little map
pictured Fort Uinta on the Uinta river about one hundred miles from where we were; but whether or not
there were any human beings there, we did not know,

and in order to determine we must cross this great
river and travel a hundred miles, and this seemed a
perilous undertaking for us in our present starving
condition; but after being refreshed by plenty of good
water we determined to undertake it, hoping that good
fortune might attend us.

After a little rest, the animals with grass, we packed
up, and after Field had put on his, once serviceable,
life preserver he mounted the old mule behind the
small pack and started to swim across the river. He
took the lead in this instance for three reasons: first,
we thought that the mule, being much older than the
horse, had probably had more experience and therefore
might be a much better swimmer; then Field had the
advantage in having the life preserver; but the last,
and most potent, reason was my fear of getting
drowned. It was understood that I was to remain on
shore and be ready to assist him if necessary, or until
he had safely landed on the other side.

In he went, and the trusty old mule was swimming
faithfully, and had reached the middle of the river,
when Field, as he afterwards told me, to hurry the
mule, gave a gentle jerk on the bridle, when, to his
utter astonishment, the mule made a complete somer-
set backwards plunging Field, the pack, and himself
entirely under the water, except his heels which appeared above the water as his head went under. In a
moment Field popped up and, after shaking his head
as a swimmer will do after taking a plunge, cast about
to take his bearings, or to determine just where he
was, and began to paddle with his hands, much as he
did when the canoes were upset on the river, or somewhat after the style of a swimming dog. On coming
to the surface, the mule cast a glance at the still living, but unloaded portion of his cargo, then made a
bee line for the shore which he had so recently left.

While Field continued to paddle and float down the river, I dismounted and followed along the bank, trying to encourage him to renewed efforts to float ashore. Finally he passed behind a clump of willows out of sight; but soon I heard him call for help and on going a little further down, found him stuck fast in the mud. I waded waist deep into that mud, and literally dragged him out, almost a mile below his starting point.

As we were struggling in this muddy swamp, Field said he wondered why some of this superfluous water was not distributed over those dry deserts from which we had so recently come. I told him, politely, that I thought that a man of his age, ability, opportunites, and nationality, (you know he was quite proud of being an Englishman) ought to know why the moisture was not so distributed, and that I was too illiterate to enlighten him on that point, but that, when opportunity offered, he might consult some one who knew more of natural science than I did. I informed him that I had an idea that if any considerable portion of the water of that river had been distributed over that desert that we would not have had the experience of the last fifteen days, whereupon he very plainly intimated that I did not have much sense, or, in other words, he called me a d—d fool.

After reaching solid ground and resting for a little while, we returned to the place from which he had started out on his perilous voyage, and where I had hastily left my horse. We found the horse and mule quietly grazing with their packs on their backs. The faithful old mule had the appearance of having been wet, but was now almost dry, yet not so dry, internally, as he had been several days before.

What shall we do now? We are perhaps two hundred or more miles from any white settlement. We do not know thit Fort Uinta is occupied. Shall we make another attempt to cross the river? I asked my brave friend if he was willing to again mount the mule aud make another attempt, when he again exclaimed, "You must be a d—d fool!" I then, pretending to have a little courage, asked him if he would follow provided I would lead, whereupon he declared most emphatically that under no conditions would he again attempt to swim across that river. I had not had his experience, but fear of being drowned was quite sufficient to prevent me from undertaking the perilous task, more especially after witnessing his failure.

Well, what next? We could not depend upon fishing and hunting, for we had no fish-hooks, nor means of catching fish, and not more than a dozen loads of shot, and a little powder; so the matter of slaying one of our animal friends was now seriously debated, and, after thoroughly canvassing the whole situation, it was most reluctantly determined that, however hard, this must be done. No doubt our starving condition at that particular time had some weight in making this decision.

Then the question was, which of the animals shall be sacrificed? The mule was quite thin, and probably tough, while the little horse was young, and, notwithstanding the many days it had, with all of us, starved and traveled without water, was still quite plump and round, and probably tender, or, at the worst, not so tough as the poor old docile mule; so, at length we decided to kill the innocent little creature, jerk his flesh, pack it on the mule, and thereby try to save our own lives, for a time at least, and endeavor to reach some place of safety.

The matter of slaying the horse was determined by casting lots, neither being willing to perform that mel ancholy, but now absolutely necessary, act. It fell to

my lot, and that was one of, if not the most revolting
act in my whole life's experience, for I had, probably,
become as strongly attached to that little horse as man
ever becomes attached to animal.   I most reluctantly
took the bridle in my left hand, my revolver in my
right, stood directly in front of the poor, unsuspecting,
innocent creature with the murderous pistol close to,
and a little above a line extending from eye to eye,
and fired.   When the smoke of the powder had cleared
off a little, I saw at my feet the quivering, dying body.
I staggered off a few steps and sat down, sick at
heart.

Field walked several steps away, and turned his
back upon the scene until after the fatal shot had been
fired; then, after some little time, he entered upon his
share of the enforced duty, and, after having removed
a portion of the skin, cut off some slices of flesh and
brought them to a fire I had started.   We broiled and
ate a little of it, not through desire or relish for it, but
from a sense of duty, knowing that our lives depended
upon it.

It is said that for many years Dr. Franklin refrained
from eating flesh, having an idea that it was wrong to
slay and eat the flesh of other creatures; but that he
changed his mind, and his diet, too, after having seen
large fish devour small ones.   I strongly suspect that
if the doctor had been with us, or in a like condition,
even before his conversion, he would, more than likely
have taken a little flesh, even though it had been a
piece of his own favorite horse.

I said we only ate a little at first: I only ate a little for
two reason; first, I did not relish the food; second, I
had heard of persons being killed by eating too much
after fasting for a long time, and I had no desire to
commit suicide just then.   Field ate too much.   Night
came on, work was suspended, and we retired.   The

poor old lone, and, no doubt, now lonely, mule, having
filled himself with grass, came up near the now terribly
mutilated remains of his late companion, and looked
on as Field continued his bloody work.   Field, with
an expression of sorrow, said, "If that mule could reason and look forward to the time when his body might
be in a like condition as that of this horse, he would,
no doubt, take to his heels, bid us a final farewell, and
seek other society."   But, fortunately for us, he did
not know that he was to be held in reserve for our
future security.   He was securely tied up every night
from that time until the day he was slain for our salvation.

Early in the night following that eventful day, my
companion began to complain much as he had done on
the night after he had eaten the little red berries; but
there was no lack of water now, no need of a special
rain-cloud.   I got up, heated water in our little camp
kettle, applied hot cloths to his aching belly, and did
everything else that either of us could think of for his
relief.   The pain was intense, and we feared that he
would surely die, and earnestly prayed all the rest of
the night that he might be relieved, and get well.
Towards morning most violent vomiting came on,
which continued for thirty hours, or more.   He was
not able to walk for three days, and during that time
I nursed him, finished jerking the meat, and built a
raft of some partly rotten logs, which I found in the
vicinity, on which we floated across the river, on the
fourth day after our arrival here.   I also looked to the
welfare of the mule, and prepared some bags in which
to carry our jerk.   Manley, I am sure that you know
the meaning of the term "jerk" so that a definition of
the word is not at all necessary.

The old logs of which the raft was made were rem-
nants of log cabins, a number of which had been built

and occupied more than half a century before, but by whom I do not know. Field remarked that the finding of these old rotting logs there was another "God send," as we then had neither ax, hammer, nor any tool of iron with which to cut down a tree. I bound these logs together with long strips cut from the hide of the dead horse. Paddles and poles were also provided. The mule was with difficulty driven across the river.

When the raft was landed on the west bank, the mule packed, and all about ready to start, I took the long strip of raw-hide from the raft and tied one end of it around the mule's neck, mounted Field on the mule behind the large pack, which made the whole outfit look quite comical indeed. Before leaving the other side of the river I had discovered that the saddle girth was not very strong, so I cut a wide belt from the hide of the lately slaughtered horse and fitted it to the saddle as a girth, knowing that the pack, now containing all of our goods and a supply of more than a bushel of jerk, would be quite bulky, if not heavy, and more difficult to keep on the back of a mule than it is for the camel to maintain his hump on his back. This girth afterwards made us two or three pretty substantial meals, as did also the long strip of green, wet hide, one end of which I had tied round the mule's neck, allowing it to drag for a long distance through the hot dry sand.

All being ready, I, as usual, took the lead with my shot gun, which I always carried, but with which I seldom killed anything, on my shoulder. The old mule followed with his high, towering pack, and Field almost hidden behind. It was noon, but we did not stop for dinner, but simply reached into one of the great bulging sacks, took out a piece of jerk and ate it as we went marching on; no more trouble now about cook-

ing. Late in the afternoon we reached Uinta river, and,
as my two-legged companion had grown very tired of
the back of the four-legged one, we went into camp
early. Our objective point was Fort Uinta, where we
hoped to find military. We could not risk turning
the mule loose at night, and the long strip of raw-hide
was designed and used to secure him, and yet to afford him liberty to graze while we slept. As you will
see a little further on, both girth and lariat were used
for a purpose not anticipated.

The second, third, fourth, and fifth days came and
went, and we were trudging on, up the Uinta, through
a mostly very barren country, with some little rich
and fertile land. We saw signs of Indians often, but
no Indians. There was much cottonwood, but little
other timber. We saw some fish in the river which
we coveted, but could not get. The main course of
this river is from north-west to south-east. We traveled most of the way to the fort on Indian trails, some
of which were much worn, but mostly at some much
earlier period. Of course we had plenty of good
water, and food, such as it was. Field did not walk
two miles during those five days, but seemed to be
fattening fast. I sometimes thought he might be just
a little lazy, but I never told him so, for I realized that
he had recently had a severe tussel with death.

Early in the morning of the sixth day we arrived
at the abandoned old fort. There were only three log
buildings, and they were in the shape of three sides of
a hollow square, with port-holes on the outer faces of
the buildings, and doors entering each of them from
the hollow square or court. Facing the vacant side of
the court, the port-hole from which I shot the wolf on
the night after we had killed the mule, would be on
right hand side. We were unable to determine
whether this fort had been constructed and occupied

by Americans or Mexicans, but, from its apparent age,
we were inclined to the opinion that it was Mexicans.
It had not been occupied for, probably, three or four
years. Some little farming had been done immediately around the fort. Surrounding the fort is a large
body of fine, fertile land which I have no doubt has
long since been occupied by mormons, or other enterprising people.

Having no means of subsistance here we soon decided to push on towards Fort Bridger, and, after resting a few hours set out following the larger fork of the
river which comes almost directly from the north.
We now believed that we were almost, if not exactly,
due south of Fort Bridger. The river is small, and
very crooked; we crossed it many times within three
days, and, at the end of that time, found ourselves in
the mouth of a rocky cañon, and after struggling for
one whole day, we came to where the steep, high,
stone walls closed the little river in on both sides, ren-
dering it impossible for us to proceed any further.

We were now nearly out of food; the jerk was almost gone. A council was held, and it was decided
that we should return to the fort and take chances of
being rescued, or scalped by some roving band of reds,
or starving to death. We at once set out on our return, full of disappointment and melancholy forebod-
ings.

The next day found us without food: and now came
into use the long, narrow strip of raw-hide which first
bound together the old, rotting logs of which the raft
was made, then to secure the mule of nights. It was
now almost as hard as bone, and nearly round, having been dragged through the hot sand while it was
yet green and wet, closed up like a hollow tube with
sand inside. Two or three yards of it at a time, was
cut into pieces about five inches long, the hair singed

off, the sand scratched out, and these pieces were dropped into our camp kettle and cooked until the whole formed one mass of jelly or gluten which was, to us, quite palatable. When the lasso had all been thus prepared and eaten, the broad girth which had served so well in holding the pack-saddle on the mule's back, was cleaned, cooked, and eaten. These substitutes for jerk sustained us very well till we again arrived at the fort.

Another consultation was now held, and the question was — what shall we do now? We were again, apparently, at the starting point of another long, enforced fast. Our path seemed hedged in. The prospect was, indeed, very gloomy. Our only reasonable hope for even the temporary prolongation of our lives was centered in our ever faithful, and always reliable old mule. We revolted at the idea of killing and eating him, but the last bit of the girth was gone. After canvassing the whole situation over and over, again and again, we finally, but most reluctantly decided to kill the mule, and preserve all the soft parts, even the skin with all of its old scars, and then gather in whatever else we could find, and stay here until spring, or until good fortune might afford us some means escape; till some Moses might come and lead us out of this wilderness, notwithstanding the fact that we had not borrowed any jewelry which we had failed to return.

There were signs of wolves in that vicinity, and it was decided that the mule be slain about ten paces distant and directly in front of one of the port-holes of the fort. with the idea that wolves might smell the blood and come there and subject themselves to being shot, and thereby afford us a chance to increase our stock of winter supplies in the form of wolf steak, or jerk. Accordingly the victim was lead to the spot

indicated, and there slain in the same manner, and
with quite as much reluctance on the part of the slayer,
as on the occasion of the sacrifice of the little horse,
more than three weeks before. The body was skinned,
cut up, and all taken within the building, nothing
being left except the blood which had been spilled on
the ground, and which was intended to attract wolves
or, possibly, bears or other animals.

My now only living associate ridiculed the idea of
killing wolves, and insisted that the flesh could not be
eaten, stating the fact that even hogs would not eat
the dead body of a dog, and insisted that a dog was
only a tamed wolf. I reminded him of a cat which
had been eaten. He finally agreed that, if I killed a
wolf, he would get up and dress it, but said most emphatically that he would not sit up and watch for it;
so he went to bed, that is, rolled himself up in a
blanket on the ground in front of a good fire inside of
the fort, and went to sleep, while I sat with my rather
untrustworthy double barreled shot-gun protruding
through the port-hole in full view of the spot before
indicated. The night was clear, and the moon was
shining in full splendor. It was probably eleven
o'clock; Field had been snoring for a long time, when
I heard something in the tall, dry grass, and soon a
large, brownish-gray wolf came into full view, with
head up, apparently sniffing, or smelling, and cautiously approaching the fatal spot. When he reached
it, and began to lick up the blood which was still on
the surface of the ground, standing with his left side
toward the fort, and in full view, I took deliberate
aim, and fired, and he fell upon the ground without
making any considerable noise.

The tired, sleeping man was aroused by the report
of the gun, and rushed into the room where I was in
great excitement, thinking, perhaps, that some enemy

had appeared, and had just then commenced to bom-
bard the fort; but when I explained to him that I had
simply killed a wolf, he ran out towards it, and, arriving close to it, the wounded creature rose up on its
hind feet and growled quite vigorously, which seemed
to frighten Field as much as did the noise of the gun.
He dashed back to the fort, and, after having time to
recover from his speechless condition, abused me most
fearfully for having told him that I had killed a wolf.
I then went out and put a load of shot into the wolf's
head, and found that my first charge had passed
through and broke both of its fore legs near the body.
Field was so thoroughly frightened that I could not
induce him to approach the dead animal for some time,
and I do believe that that wolf haunted him as long as
I knew him, for he seemed never to forget it.

After dressing it by the light of the moon assisted by
a torch, we retired. On viewing the plump body next
morning Field exclaimed, ''That's another God-send!''
and notwithstanding his opinion that wolf could not
be eaten, he found that wolf to be the best food we
had eaten since we had assisted Walker and his tribe
in eating the mountain sheep.

The French may eat their horses, but I do not want
more horse flesh. The old mule made fair but quite
coarse beef. While out on this little pleasure(?) excursion we ate horse, mule, wolf, wild-cat, mountain
sheep, rose seed buds, raw-hide, a squirrel, fatty matter from the sockets of the mule's eyes and the marrow
from his bones; but that ham of wild-cat was certainly
the most detestable thing that I ever undertook to
eat. The marrow from the mule's bones was a real
luxury.

We now had a pretty good stock of food, such as it
was, but not enough to carry us through the winter on
full rations; therefore we determined to try to add to it

by hunting. One was to go out and hunt while the other would remain at home: we now had undisputed posession of the fort and it was our home. Field took the first day's outing while I occupied my time in drying and smoking meat. Late in the evening he returned, tired and worn out, having seen nothing worth shooting.

Next day came my turn to hunt. I took a lunch, as he had done, consisting of jerked mule. I did not tell him so, but I had determined to make an excursion up the river to a point where we had seen some fresh trails and deer tracks some days before. When I was putting up my lunch my friend intimated that I was taking a very large amount for one lunch, but I told him that I might stay out late and that I did not intend to starve. I went, stayed all day, all night, and part of the next day, and returned as he had done, tired and discouraged, not having seen anything worth bringing in. In the evening of the first day out I found a trail which appeared to have been used daily by deer going to and from the river.

It occurred to me that they might go out early in the morning, so I secreted myself within gun shot of the trail behind an old, moss-covered log where I slept comfortably; and when it was light enough in the morning to see a deer, I leveled my gun across the log in a position commanding the trail and waited and watched until nine o'clock, but nothing came upon that pathway that morning. After getting tired of watching and waiting I went down to the trail where, to my astonishment, I found the fresh tracks of a large bear which must have passed by that way while I was sleeping. As a rule I do not like to be treated discourteously, but in this instance I felt glad that this stranger had passed me by.

On arriving at the fort late in the evening I found

my friend in a terrible state of mental excitement.
He said that he had not slept a minute during the
whole of the night before.   He had filled the door of
his room with rails, and sharpened one end of a long
stick which he intended to use if necessary as a
weapon of defence.   When I arrived he was again filling the door with rails.   I had the gun, pistol ahd big
knife with me so this was his only means of defence.
He said he would not stay alone another night for all
the gold in California.

I was much discouraged by our failures in hunting,
and after a lengthy discussion we decided to make
another attempt to cross tht mountains and escape
from what then seemed to us certain starvation.
This was Thursday night and we set Monday as the
time for starting.   By Saturday night everything was
in readiness for the start and Sunday we devoted to
Bible reading, for we each still had a pocket Bible.
As much of the flesh of the wolf and the lamented mule
as we thought we could carry had been thoroughly
jerked, and finding that we would not be overburdened
by it, we economized by roasting and eating little
scraps of flesh, the marrow from the bones, and even
the head of the mule was roasted, the fragments of
flesh scraped off and eaten, and Field found a rich
fatty substance in behind the eyes, which he ate.

We had a canteen in which our powder was carried,
but the powder was nearly all gone so we emptied it
and used the canteen to carry water in.   Early Monday morning we loaded ourselves, mostly with jerked
mule and wolf, leaving many useful things behind,
bid adieu to Fort Uinta and took up our line of march
rather reluctantly.

My companion was not strong and we soon found it
expedient for me to take on part of his burden.   We
rested often and yet long before night he became so

tired that we had to go into camp.   Most of the day
we had traveled on an old deserted trail.   The nights
being cold we were under the necessity of keeping up
a fire as we had left our blankets at the fort.   The
next morning we made an early start and rested often.
At about noon we found good shade and water, and
the sun being quite hot we stopped and rested in the
shade for more than three hours, then trudged on till
nearly night when we found water, and plenty of old
dry timber for fuel and camped.   Field expressed a
wish that he had his old mule again, and I reminded
him that he had a portion of it left in his knapsack,
and that turn about was fair play: as the mule had
carried him for a long time when he was unable to
walk he should not object to carrying a portion of the
mule now; whereupon he again plainly intimated that
he thought I was a d—d fool.   I kept up the fire and
he slept until morning.

Another day was passed without any unusual occurence; we traveled and ate at the same time as usual.
Another day of pretty hard travel over sandy plains
and rocky hills brought us to the foot of the mountain
where we had plenty of good water and an abundance
of fuel.   A little sprinkle of rain early in the evening
was the first we had seen since the memorable night
after Field had eaten the little red berries.

Early Saturday morning we filled our canteen with
water and started up the mountain.   I had been carrying most of the jerk, but the stock was running down
quite rapidly.   My companions bag now being almost
empty, and as he had little else to carry while I had
the gun and some other things, including his heavy
overcoat, I divided the jerk, putting about half of it
into his sack.   All day long we were climbing the
mountain.   Late in the afternoon I was several rods
ahead of Field when he called to me to stop: I did so

and when he came up he appeared to be a little cross
and insisted that we were not traveling in the direction
formerly agreed upon. I requested him to let me see
the little compass which he had in his pocket, and on
examining it he found that he was mistaken; whereupon he muttered something which I thought was
"swear words," and then we went marching on. In
a little while we were within the old snow limits
where we found large bodies of old icy looking snow
in places shaded by trees and rocks, and a little before
dark went into camp. We gathered some old dry
timber and made a large fire, then some green fir limbs
for a bed. When I began to prepare our bed on one
side of the flaming logs, to my surprise Field began
to prepare one on the other side of the fire. Neither
had spoken since the occurence of the little unpleasantness in the afternoon about the course of travel.
Mutely each took his side of the fire.

We had always slept together except when he was
sick and the night I had left him alone at the fort.
Some time in the night I became thirsty and got up
and procured some snow, put it in our only tin cup
and set it on some live coals to melt and went to
sleep. The snow melted, the water evaporated, the
solder melted and left the tin. While I slept, my
dumb friend woke up thirsty, took the tin cup, filled
it with snow and put it on coals. The snow melted
and the water run out on the coals; his tongue let loose
and he then denounced me as a knave, an ass, a fool,
an unregenerate heathen, and what else I don't want
to remember. I woke up alarmed and did not at first
fully understand what had created the storm, but after
having the bottomless cup dashed at my head I realized the situation, and began to try to apologize and
explain the unavoidable and unfortunate circumstance;
but no explanation would satisfy his now thoroughly

"Johnny Bull" temper. After this little nocturnal disturbance had subsided, I, on my bed of fir branches with my feet towards the fire, soon fell into a sound sleep and knew nothing more of the world until the sun was shining. Whether or not my friend had cooled off I did not inquire; but I do know that there was an unusual coldness between us, for neither spoke to the other until about twelve o'clock and then, as will appear, our conversation was very short.

As we did not rise until late no delay was made, but when each had his bag on his back and a nugget of jerk in his hand we started up the side of the mountain as quiet as two deaf mutes. There was no water to be had; our camp kettle had been left at the fort, and through my stupidity the cup had become useless, therefore we were obliged to eat the icy snow or endure the thirst. No new snow had yet fallen in this high altitude although it was now nearing the end of October. These mountains were then heavily covered with pine and fir but the timber was not large. In some places where the snow had melted away, short green grass was found quite close to great banks of snow.

At about twelve o'clock we reached the summit of the great Uinta range, and I, being a little in advance of my still mute companion, halted to take a survey of the field before me. The top of the range here is bare of timber and there was no snow. When Field came up I broke the silence which had lasted since the little unpleasantness of the night before, by suggesting that we attempt to cross the snow-covered range of mountains which now appeared north of us and probably fifty miles away, through what appeared to be a gap or low place in the great range of mountains. He replied, "You may go that way if you want to, but I am going this way," pointing in another direction

and quickly started off at an angle of about 45 degrees
to the right, or directly north-east. I also started immediately, and when we were a few rods apart I said,
"Good-by;we may not meet again very soon." He
replied "Good-by," and within a few minutes we were
out of sight, and in a very short time beyond hailing
distance.

This was the last I saw or heard of him until after
each of us had undergone many more hardships, so I
will now drop my friend but will hereafter devote a
chapter to him, and give you an account of his experience as he afterwards gave it to me, detailing an account of many most interesting incidents. Fortunately
we had divided the jerk, for nothing was said at this
sudden and unexpected parting about anything which
either had in his possession. I had an idea when I
bade him good-by that he would soon turn about and
follow me.

After the unceremonious parting I immediately began to descend the north side of the mountain which
was very rough, rocky and steep; but down, down,
down I went into a deep, dark cañon where 1 slept on
the leaves under a fir tree, after having taken some
landmarks. When it was light enough to see the objects I had noted to guide me, I set out and spent the
day in crossing over hills and through deep cañons.
In the evening I arrived at the foot of the range of
mountains which I had seen from the point of our parting. The sun disappeared, dark clouds began to float
over the mountains and it was evident that a storm
was approaching.

While it was yet light enough I took some landmarks or guiding points; and it was well I did so, for
on the following morning when I woke I found it
snowing quietly but heavily, and before it was light
enough for me to see my guiding objects there must

have been six or more inches of new snow on the
ground beyond my snug retreat under a sheltering
pine. When it was light enough I rose from my comfortable bed, took my bearings as best I could without
a compass and started up the mountain through the
radidly accumulating bed of snow. The snow continued to fall nearly all day, and before night it was more
than a foot deep.

All day long I struggled through a dense forest.
Some time in the forenoon I crossed the fresh trail of
a large herd of elk which forcibly reminded me that
my sack was almost empty, and I vainly wished that
one of these wild creatures might come in my way,
but I did not dare to follow the herd with the uncertainty of killing one, and the certainty of losing my
way this dark, snowy day.   In order to maintain my
course during such dark days I was under the necessity of looking ahead and observing trees or other objects in my line of travel.

That night I, as usual, slept under a pine tree where
there was no snow.   I saw no sign of fire in either of
these ranges of mountains, nor did I see any signs of
Indians on my trip over these two ranges. The next
day as I approached the top of the mountain I found
the timber much smaller, and mostly pine. There is
much fertile land in some of the valleys between the
two great ranges of mountains.

Early on the following morning I arrived at the bald,
snow-covered summit. On my right and on my left
were high, untimbered, snow-covered peaks. From
this point I could overlook a vast territory extending
over many hills, valleys, and smaller mountains where
there was no snow; in fact, the snow only extended a
few miles down the steep sides of the great range.
As a rule there is more timber on the north than on
the south side of mountains west of the Rockies; but

it was the reverse here, for there was little timber on
the north side of this range.

One more day's tramping brought me down into a
large barren plain where I gathered some dry weeds
for a bed, and slept, without food or water; the last
bit of the mule or wolf, I know not which, I had eaten
during the afternoon. I had had very little jerk for
the last two or three days, and began to wish that I
had another horse, mule, or even a wolf· For many
days I had seen no living thing except when I looked
into a small glass which I carried in my pocket, and
then only saw a familiar shadow.

I spent another day without food, but had plenty
of water; another night on a bed of green brush beside
a good fire. The next day was bright ·and sunny,
quite a contrast to the gloomy days I had spent in the
mountains. For want of food I was becoming quite
weak and was not able to travel as fast as usual.
During the early part of the day I saw some tracks of
an unshod horse, whice renewed my courage and hope
of redemption; and at about two o'clock in the afternoon I saw some dark spots on the plain a long distance away, but almost in the direction I was going.
Hoping that these objects might be living creatures, I
hurried on for a time, then sat down and after having
watched them for a time I found that they changed
positions and that satisfied me to a moral certainty
that they were living creatures, but what I could not
tell. They might be horses, cattle, elk, deer, antelope
or buffalo; but no matter what, I must hurry on and
try to reach them before night.

Late in the evening I determined that they were
horses but could not yet tell whether they belonged to
whites or Indians, or were wild. As I approached
them they stopped grazing and started toward me, but
soon disappeared in a deep gulch between us which I

had not noticed before. On arriving at the edge of
the gulch or narrow valley I saw the horses in the vicinity of about fifteen or twenty wigwams which were
all in a row on the bank of a little creek that ran
through the gulch. Many Indians were sitting outside of their lodges, the weather being warm.

On first sight of the village, being not more than
200 yards away, my heart fluttered just a little, not
knowing whether the savages would scalp me or not;
but, notwithstanding my natural cowardice, I at once
determined to "beard the lion in his den," and walked
as boldly as I could up to the lower end of the row of
wigwams. Within a few feet of the nearest one three
young bucks met me and seemed to be anxious to
know whence I came and whither I was going; whether
right down from Heaven, and if so what was my mission. They seemed as much surprised at my sudden
appearance as I was on coming so suddenly upon
them. My first and most important business was to
determine whether they would give me something to
eat, or eat me.

As the men, women, and children began to gather
around me I heard some one half way up the line of
lodges call out saying something which I did not
understand, but on looking that way saw a man beck-
oning to me, as I thought, when the young men
motioned for me to move on up the line- On arriving
at the place indicated I found myself in the presence
of one whom I then suspected, and afterwards found
to be the chief, who extended to his royal right hand
and greeted me in a most courteous and polite manner,
and then with a graceful wave of his hand and a slight
bow indicated that I should precede him at the low
open door into his Royal Palace where he very politely
introduced me to his wife who proved to be a sensible,
clever, courteous woman. She soon prepared some-

thing for me to eat, and after I had finished my supper an Indian brought in two pistols and wanted me
to take the cap tube from one and put it into the other,
which I soon accomplished. He was much pleased,
went out, and soon returned with ten or more pounds
of elk meat which he tendered to me as compensation
for my work, but the chief objected, and insisted, as I
understood him, that he had plenty and that I was his
guest, but finally consented for me to accept part of
the meat.   I gave him to understand that I wanted to
go to Fort Bridger.

A case of nice new blankets was opened, as it appeared to me, for my especial benefit. The chief, his
lady, two sons almost grown, two or three wolfish
looking dogs which forcibly reminded me of Field's
terrible scare, and myself made up the number of
lodgers in that mansion that night.   Late that night
some warriors who had been out on a campaign came
home, and learning that there was a stranger within
the gates came to the king's palace to see him. and
also to report that they had discovered some white
barbarians in the vicinity who had dared to enter his
domain without a special permit, and that they had
sent a message to his highness informing him that they
had a good assortment of blankets, cutlery, pins, needles, beads, etc., which his people might need or desire,
and also a limited amount of "fire-water," and that
they would be pleased to receive his order for anything
he might desire.

The fact of the presence of these pale-faces in the
vicinity was at once communicated to me, and early
on the following morning I was informed that if it
was my desire to cut short my stay at the palace, the
king would take great pleasure in furnishing me
means of conveyance, a proper escort, and a reliable
guide who would safely conduct me to the camp of the

accomodating merchants or Indian traders, (but, in fact, Indian robbers.) Notwithstanding my reluctance in leaving the society of the noble ruler and his people I most readily accepted his generous offer, and after breakfast, which consisted of elk meat and tobacco root in a combination stew which was very palatable, a fine steed with a good Mexican saddle and bridle was at the door. My escort, consisting of four mounted warriors, was ready, and after bidding my good friends farewell, I with some assistance mounted my charger and we were all off on a full run, up and down hill and across valley, at what seemed to me a fearful rate.

In less than two hours we entered the camp of the traders at full speed, dismounted, and fonnd one man, a long Jake from Illinois, who could speak English. He had two wives, (squaws,) and several children which he claimed, but some of them were quite dark. His name was John Smith; not a very uncommon one. He was a very clever man, about 35 years old, was not a mormon, but had taken the women in order to become popular with the Indians and to improve his opportunities for trade.

After getting something to eat, and learning something, through Smith, of my adventures, my escort made ready to return to their camp. Their trip, as Smith told me, was made solely for my accomodation and now I had nothing with which to compensate tnem; but as they were about to leave I took a large "bandanna," the only one I had left, and tied it around the neck of the chief's son, he being one of the clever escorts. He at first refused to accept it, but when Smith told him that I desired him to take it as a token of regard, he accepted it with an expression of thanks, and after I had bidden them all good-bye, they rode away as rapidly as we had come. I will always hold that chief and his people in kindly remembrance.

All of the other white men with Smith were French, and all had plenty of wives (squaws) and numerous slaves. The wives were not slaves, but they had slaves all around them. The whole tribe traveled about and lived much as other tribes did, only much better, for they lived by trading while the others lived by hunting and fishing. In this camp I ate bread for the first time in many weeks. At the end of three days after my arrival here a caravan was ready to start for Fort Bridger for winter supplies for the traders. I was furnished with a good horse and saddle, and Smith, one of the Frenchmen, five slaves, 20 horses, and myself made up the caravan, and on the evening of the third day we reached the fort where I was very kindly received.

Smith was a large man, had a good head, and some cultivation and apparent refinement, and treated his women and children well. He said he had been to his old home in Illinois since he had entered upon this kind of life, but was not contented there and soon returned to his Indian friends. He and those Frenchmen were as generous and hospitable as old Southern planters, and their kindness to me will not be forgotten while my memory lasts.

I was well treated at the fort which is 116 miles from the point where the seven dug up the little flatboat from its sandy bed on the fifth day of August, just three months before, since which I had undergone many hardships, took many fearful risks, and traveled more than a thousand miles, far enough to have taken me from Green River to San Francisco.

On the morning of the seventh day of November I started with a Government train for Salt Lake City where I arrived on the fifteenth. I soon found a home with a prominent mormon, a Scotchman named Archie Gardner, living in the fifth ward, on Mill Creek, one

of the many small streams coming down from the
mountains east of the city.   Mr. Gardner was a clever
gentleman about 45 years old, had a saw-mill up in
the mountains, and was then building a flour mill
only a few rods from his dwelling.   I assisted him in
completing the little flour mill and in attending it
during the winter.   Mr. Gardner had three wives, all
living in one house, but occupying separate rooms at
night.   I usually attended the little mill until midnight, and Gardner made it part of my duty to go to
his house and call him.   He usually told me where I
could find him, but not always, so at times I was under
the necessity of rapping at more than one door before
I found him.

He had the largest house in the ward, and the religious services were held there by Bishop Johnson
who also acted as Justice of the Peace in that ward.
Gardner's family all ate at the same table over which
the first wife presided.   She was, indeed, mistress of
the house, the other wives treating her with great respect, and all were, to all outward appearance, quite
friendly.   Gardner bestowed much attention on his
first wife, though I always suspected that he was just
a little more fond of the youngest one, and I did not
blame him much for she manifested strong affection
for him even in the presence of the others, and yet
there was no outward manifestation of jealousy.

The second, or the one I will call the second because
she was in age between the others, and was the mother
of the third or youngest, a widowed mother and her
daughter having been sealed to Gardner at the same
time, the first wife having given her consent and standing with them at the triple matrimonial altar, and
then and there joining in the sacred ceremony.   As I
was about to say, the second wife seemed to be pleased
at the manifestation of affection for the common hus-

band by the youngest wife, and No. 1 would in a good-humored way say:—"My, Annie, don't be so demonstrative in the presence of other people," when the husband would laugh and go and kiss No. 1.

Gardner spent most of his leisure time, particularly during the day and evening, in his first wife's apartments with her and her children. He was a very religious man, and always had family prayers before retiring at night, and all persons about the house were expected to join, at least formally, in this service. The use of profane langnage was not allowed in or adout the house.

Many of the higher church officers were entertained at Gardner's house and table, among whom were Brigham Young, George A. Smith, Heber C. Kimble, George Taylor, and Parley P. Pratt, with all of whom I formed some acquaintance. Brigham was a dignified, clever gentleman, not austere but kind and affable. Kimble was also a nice, genteel, genial, red-headed gentleman. Smith was a heavy man with a very large abdomen, dark hair full beard, exceedingly jovial and apparently always happy. Pratt was a small, rather slim, quick and athletic man, rather austere, rofined, active and energetic. Taylor was a large man, hignly intellectual, and rather unsocial. Kimble was my favorite notwithstanding the fact that he had fifteen wives, mostly young and handsome, all in one house, and my impression is that none of them had any children. I think it was conceded that his was the finest harem in Utah. He called me his young Gentile, was very kind and affable, but he never invited me to inspect his harem.

About the first of December, 1849, Field arrived in Salt Lake City, and I will allude to a little matter in which he was concerned, after which I will give you a short account of his trip from the time we parted com-

pany until he arrived in Salt Lake as he afterwards
gave it to me. Soon after he arrived in the City of
the Saints he heard of another who had recently arrived from the south and that he was located in the
fifth ward on Mill creek at the house of one Gardner,
and at which house he soon arrived.

After staying with me for two or three days he
found employment in the family of the Apostle John
Taylor. The family consisted of seven wives living in
seven different houses. How many children there
were I never knew, but there was one wife who did
not have any. She was a fine specimen of English
beauty. Taylor's women were nearly all English.
It was the business of my friend to cut wood, and do
chores generally for the Taylor family living in seven
different places at the same time. Taylor was in
Europe that winter looking after the interest of the
church, and possibly after a few more wives, and consequently could not, in person, attend to all of the
necessities of the seven branches of his family. In
his daily rounds looking after the seven wood-piles
and other little matters appertaining to the comfort of
the family in so many places Field happened to come
in contact with the English beauty, and the result was,
mutual love at first sight, notwithstanding the fact
that this woman had passed, and taken all of the solemn vows of the Lym house with the Apostle and his
six other wives.

I do not think that my English friend had lost one
iota of the fond recollection of his long since dead
English wife, the picture of whom he still carried near
his heart; but, nevertheless, he and this seventh wife
of the noted Apostle fell heels over head in love.
Field, as you know, was a well developed, good-looking, intelligent man of forty. The woman was well
developed, good-looking, and as smart as a steel-trap,

and both being English I was not at all surprised at
their mutual admiration and infatuation, nor did I
blame them much. I was intrusted with many closely
sealed envelopes which I carried from one to the other.
With my feeble assistance they tried to devise some
method by which they might escape from the city before the Apostle should return home; but the Danites
were always on the elert, and they well knew that
detection by the Danites of an attempt to get away
together would lead to certain death to him, and if not
to her she would certainly have been returned to her
polygamous state of bondage. Spring came with little
hope of escape, and they reluctantly parted with the
mutual understanding that, if possible, she would
make her escape and go to Sacramento where he
promised to keep his address. Ten months after the
parting they had not met yet, and if they ever did it
was after I had lost all further knowledge of him.

Mormon morals, exclusive of polygamy, are very
good. I never saw a drunken man in Salt Lake City,
and heard very little profane language there. The
people were industrious and seemed happy. Their
hospitality rivaled that of the old Southern planters,
and their charity was equal to that of other Christ-
ians.

I will now go back to the place where Field and I
separated on the mountain top and give you a short
statement as he gave it to me, and while some things
may border on the miraculous, and seem somewhat
incredible, I do not question the truth of his statements. When we parted so unexpectedly he had
about half of the jerked wolf and mule combined.
I went north while he bore off in a northeasterly direction, and after traveling for three days came to the
river at a point above where we lost our flat-boat.
He struggled on up the river without road or trail, and

nothing to guide him except the little compass which
he still carried in his pocket.

Two days more and his last bit of jerk was gone,
starvation began to stare him in the face once more.
He saw signs of Indians having crossed his pathless
course which gave him renewed courage. Soon after
starting out next morning he was delighted to see a
pony in the distance grazing, and on coming up to it
found one of its front legs broken. This, he said was
another God-send. The poor pony seemed to fear him.
It was probably an Indian pony, had its leg broken
and was left to die. He followed it for some time and
finally got close to it and fired his revolver at its
chest and wounded it, but it then left him with the
blood flowing from its wound. After resting for a
time he followed on and soon found it lying down, but
not dead. He told me how innocent and helpless it
appeared, and looked at him as if pleading with him
not to inflict any more pain; but he felt that his life
was in a balance with its, and after a little meditation
he put the revolver to its forehead and ended its life
and suffering. Then came the usual process of skin-
ning, cutting up and jerking which took the balance
of that day and part of the next.

Eight days more and he was again starving. On
the ninth he arrived at the spot where we had dug up
the little ferry-boat which carried the seven advent-
urers far down the river more than three very long
dreary months before. Snow now covered the entire
country, and all emigrants had long since gone by.
His strength was failing fast but it would not do to
linger there, so he arose and was about to start when
he saw a poor old ox slowly coming towards him, and
when it had come up near to him he discovered a wolf
not far behind which seemed to be following the ox,
but it soon turned and went away. Night was coming

on and he was very hungry. Something must be done.
The last cartridge had been exploded in killing the
poor, broken legged Indian pony, and the revolver
was no longer of use. The ox, though feeble, was
probably yet stronger than the starving man.

Field feared that he was not able to catch the ox by
the horns and hold it until he could cut its throat, so
the next plan was to get hold of the animal's tail with
one hand, and with the big knife in the other cut his
hamstrings so as to disable him, and then cut his
throat. The ox seemed fond of being rubbed and pet-
ted, so after a little time a firm hold on the tail was
secured, and the big knife vigorously applied, but it
was so very dull that he could not sever the tough old
tendons. After sawing with the dull knife and being
literally dragged for some distance, he became so
much exhausted that he was obliged to relinquish his
hold and see the excited old ox disappear.

In almost complete despair Field spent the night
beside a fire under one of those large cottonwoods
which I have no doubt you will remember even though
it is now more than forty years since you saw them.
He rose early next morning and started out on the
well beaten road towards the Golden West, but had
only gone a few hundred yards when he was agreeably
surprised to again behold the old ox approaching him,
but so much exhausted that it could scarcely walk.
The same, or some other, wolf was near by, and had
probably followed the poor old ox all night. When
the ox came close to Field the wolf growled and again
turned away as on the evening before. After the
wolf had left the ox seemed to be relieved.

It then occurred to the starving emigrant that he
had a sharp razor in his "kitt" with which he knew
he could cut those tough tendons, provided he could
get another hold on that tail. Field, as you probably

remember, always kept his face cleanly shaved. Even
while we were starving he would shave almost every
day. The ox was tired and worn out and so was
Field; but he got the razor ready and soon had hold of
that tail again. Off went the ox, the keen razor was
applied, soon the tendons parted and down went the
ox. But only half the victory was won, for the ox
would raise up on his front feet and show fight; but
after resting awhile the would-be victor rushed up,
caught the poor beast by the horns, pushed him over
on his side, held him down and cut his throat.

After a long, much needed rest he cut out a piece of
the poor beef, broiled and ate it, and then spent the
remainder of the day in hunting out the small, lean
muscles that still remained between the skin and bones
of the poor old ox. Tne poor beef was jerked and put
into the sack which on the following morning was
thrown upon the back of its owner, and from which
he fed for the next six days, at the end of which he
arrived at Fort Bridger. From there he soon obtained
a passage for Salt Lake City, arriving there on the
second day of December, seventeen days after I had
reached there, and finding me as before stated.

Some time in the winter we formed an acquaintance
of a gentleman named Jesse Morgan, a Gentile, who
had left Illinois in the spring of 1849 for California,
but for some cause had been delayed and obliged to
winter in the city of the Latter Day Saints. Morgan
had a wife, a little child, a wagon and two yoke of
oxen, but no food nor money. Field and I arranged
to furnish food for all for the trip from there to Sacramento, and assist in camp duties, drive the team, &c.
We made the trip together and arrived in Sacramento
in good condition on the fourth day of July, 1850, and
pitched our tent under a large oak tree where the
State Capitol now stands.

I spent five months with a wholesale grocery and miners supply firm, Elder and Smith, Fourth and J streets, Sacramento, and three months in the mines as a drummer, or solicitor and collector for the same firm. I returned to Sacramento and was almost ready to start home when the Scots River excitement broke out. I then went to the mines on Trinity River and associated myself in mining with Hiram Gould, a young Presbyterian clergyman who had laid aside the "cloth" for the time and engaged in mining. I remained in the mines until July fourth, 1851, exactly one year from the time I entered Sacramento, when I started home by way of Niceragua. In due time, after an interesting trip, I arrived home and again entered upon the study of my chosen profession, graduated from an honorable college, and am now, as you know, practicing my profession on the sea shore.

M. S. McMahon.

CHAPTER XIII.

STORY OF THE JAYHAWKERS.

In the foregoing chapters describing the trip across the deserts and mountains, the author has had occasion many times to refer to the "Jayhawkers." Their history is in many respects no less remarkable and intensely interesting than that of his own party. The author has therefore collected many notes and interviews with prominent members and presents herewith the only written history of their travels.

The little train afterward known by this name was made up in the state of Illinois in 1849, of industrious, enterprising young men who were eager to see and explore the new country then promising gold to those who sought. The young men were from Knoxville, Galesburg and other towns. Not all were influenced by the desire for gold. It was said that California had a milder climate and that pleasant homes could there be made, and the long, cold winter avoided.

They placed some of the best men in position to manage for the whole. The outfit was placed on a steam-boat and transported to Kanesville, on the Missouri River above Council Bluffs. Some of the company went with the goods while others bought teams and wagons in Western Missouri and drove to the appointed place. Kanesville was a small Mormon camp, while Council Bluffs was a trading post of a few log cabins on the river bank, inhabited mostly by Indians. There was no regular ferry at either place, and our party secured a log raft which they used to get their wagons and provisions across, making the oxen swim.

They asked all the questions they could think of
from everyone who pretended to know anything about
the great country to the west of them, for it seemed a
great undertaking to set out into the land they could
see stretching out before them across the river. Other
parties bound the same way, also arrived and joined
them. They chose a guide who claimed to have been
over the road before. When all were gathered together the guide told them that they were about to
enter an Indian country, and that the dusky residents
did not always fancy the idea of strangers richer than
themselves passing through, and sometimes showed
out some of the bad traits the Indians had been said to
possess. It would therefote be better to organize and
travel systematically. He would divide the company
into divisions and have each division choose a captain,
and the whole company unite in adopting some rules
and laws which they would all agree to observe. This
arrangement was satisfactorily accomplished, and they
moved out in a sort of military style. And then they
launched out on the almost endless western prairie,
said then to be a thousand miles wide, containing few
trees, and generally unknown.

These Illinois boys were young and full of mirth
and fun wnich was continually overflowing. They
seemed to think they were to be on a sort of every day
picnic and bound to make life as merry and happy as
it could be. One of the boys was Ed Doty who was a
sort of model traveler in this line. A camp life suited
him; he could drive an ox team, cook a meal of vict-
uals, turn a pan of flap-jacks with a flop, and possessed many other frontier accomplishments. One
day when Doty was engaged in the duty of cooking
flap-jacks another frolicsome fellow came up and took
off the cook's hat and commenced going through the
motions of a barber giving his customer a vigorous

shampoo, saying:—"*I am going to make a Jayhawker out of yon, old boy.*" Now it happened at the election for captain in this division that Ed Doty was chosen captain, and no sooner was the choice declared than the boys took the newly elected captain on their shoulders and carried him around the camp introducing him as the *King Bird of the Jayhawkers.* So their division was afterwards known as The Jayhawkers, but whether the word originated with them, and John Brown forgot to give them credit, or whether it was some old frontier word used in sport on the occasion is more than I will undertake to say; however the boys felt proud of tneir title and the organization has been kept up to this day by the survivors, as will be related further on.

The first few days they got along finely and began to lose all feeling of danger and to become rather careless in their guard duty. When the cattle had eaten enough and lain down, the guards would sometimes come into camp and go to sleep, always finding the stock all right in the mornfng and no enemy or*suspicious persons in sight. But one bright morning no cattle were in sight, which was rather strange as the country was all prairie. They went out to look, making a big circuit and found no traces till they came to the river, when they found tracks upon the bank and saw some camps across the river, a mile or so away. Doty had a small spy glass and by rigging up a tripod of small sticks to hold it steady they scanned the camps pretty closely and decided that there were too many oxen for the wagons in sight.

Some of the smartest of them stripped off their their clothes and started to swim the stream, but landed on the same side they started from. Captain Doty studied the matter a little and then set out himself, being a good swimmer, and by a little shrewd management and swimming up stream when the current was strongest, soon got across to where he could touch bottom and shouted to the others to do the same. Soon all the swimmers were across.

They could now see that there were two trains on that side and that the farther one had already begun to move and was about a mile in advance of the nearest one, Doty said something must be done, and although they only were clothed in undershirts they approached the nearest camp and were handed some overalls for temporary use. The men in this camp on hearing about the missing oxen said the fellows in the forward train went over and got them, for, as they said there were no wagons in sight and they must be strays. He said the forward train was from Tennessee, and that they had some occasion to doubt their honesty and had refused to travel with them any further· They said they were all old Missonrians, and did not want other people's property and if the boys found their cattle with the Tenneseans, and wanted any help to get them back again to call on them, and putting in some good strong swear words for emphasis.

The boys, barefooted and with only overalls and shirts, started after the moving train which they called to a halt when overtaken. The coarse grass was pretty hard to hurry through, clothed as they were. The train men were pretty gruff and wanted to know what was wanted. Capt. Doty very emphatically told them he could see some of his oxen in their train, and others in the herd, and he proposed to have them all back again. The Jayhawker boys were unarmed but were in a fighting mood and determined to have the stock at all hazards, and if not peacably, war might commence. The boys saw that the two trains were of about equal strength, and if worse came to worst they could go back and get their guns and men and come over in full force after their property, and they were assured the Missourians would help them and a combination of forces would give them a majority and they could not be beaten by the Tennessee crowd. There was a good deal of talk, but finally when Doty demanded that their cattle be unyoked and the others seperated from the herd, they yielded and gave them all their stock, some seventy head.

The Missourians had come up and heard the talk, and some of them went back and helped drive the cattle to the river, and deal out some double shotted thunder against the biggest scamps they had come across. It was quite a job to get the cattle across the river. They would go in a little way and then circle round and round like a circus, making no progress. They finally put a rope on one of them and a man led him as far as he could, which was more than half way, and although they landed a good ways down stream, they got them all across safely, left their borrowed overalls in the hands of their friends, with a thousand thanks for valuable assistance, and plunged into the swift running Platte, and swam back again to the northern side. They drove the straggling oxen back to camp with a sense of great satisfaction, and in turn received the praise of their friends who said that Ed Doty was the best Jayhawker of the border.

This was the first unpleasantness and they were afterwards more cautious and stood guard all night, watching closely all the time, both night and day, for for any signs of danger. Thus in time they reached Salt Lake, rather late in the season, but safe and sound, having escaped cholera or other disease, and in good spirits to surmount any further difficulties which might be met.

When the Jayhawkers reached Salt Lake it was

found that it was not safe to try to go the regular
northern route to California, as they were advised by
those who seemed to know, as they might be snowed
in on the Sierra Nevada Mountains and perish. The
Mormons told them that the snow often fell there
twenty feet deep, and some other stories likely to de-
ter them from making the attempt. They also told
them of a route farther south by which they could
come into California at Los Angeles, or they could remain in Salt Lake until May when it would be safe to
try the mountain route again. After listening to the
talk of the mountaineers who claimed to have been
over the route and to know all about it, and camping
some time to rest and learn all they could, they finally
decided on taking the southern route. One Mormon
told them of a place where they could make a cut-off
and save five hundred miles, and, if they would follow
his instructions, they would find the route fully as
good as the one usually traveled which was not much
better than a trail. The cut-off was so instilled into
their minds that they had great confidence in the report and talked very favorably of taking it.

The man Williams made for them a map of the
proposed route and explained it to them and others
who had gathered at Salt Lake, and from the map
they could see how much was to be gained in time and
distance by taking that route. A month or two of
travel was indeed something to gain, and as the roads
seemed similar in quality the reasoning was very plaus-
ible. The map explained all the watering places and
favorable things but said nothing about a desert, and
as there was no one to tell them any unfavorable side
to this plan there were many who quite coucluded to
go this way, and among those who did so were the
Jayhawkers, and the "Williams Short Route" was
freely talked about as a settled thing by them.

They now set about preparing to move. They sold, traded, and bought oxen till they had the best and fattest teams in Salt Lake Valley; selested good provisions, and plenty of them so as to be safe in case of delay, and contended that nothing could stop them in a country where but little snow could be, and water was as plentiful as shown on the map. Tney wanted to reach the gold mines and this was the shortest route and even if it was still considerbly longer than the northern way they said they would rather be moving along and thus gain time than to so long in camp with nothing to do by which they could earn a cent. There were here in Salt Lake ten times as many men as could find employment, and Brigham's saints would be pretty sure to get all of the odd jobs to the exclusion of the heretics.

To bring the matter to a determination a paper was drawn up for those to sign who wanted to go the southern route and it was pretty generally signed. The mormon elder, John Hunt, was consulted, and as he seemed to know the general southern route better than any one else, he was prevailed upon to guide the train through on the old Spanish Trail. This had never been used as a wagon road, but he thought it could be without much difficulty, and he said if they could secure him a fair sized train he would go and conduct them through for ten dollars a wagon. This proposition was accepted after some consideration, and all who wished to do so were given permission to join the train. In a few days there were one hundred and seven wagons enlisted for this route, including seven mormons bound for San Bernardino.

Preparations for the trip now began in good earnest, and the Saints were liberally patronized in purchase of flour and meat which were the principal things they had to sell. As their several wagons were loaded they

moved out in small lots to the south to keep in good
fresh feed for their animals, and to move on slowly till
all were ready, when they would join in one large
body and proceed. The guide was in no special haste
as he said he wanted to wait a little later so the wea-
in the south would be cooler than they would be likely
to find it if they pressed on at once. He said that in
summer it was so hot that no white man could endure
the heat. He said they could work slowly along the
trail, and when the right time came he would move
out himself, and that they might be assured that it
would then be the coolest and best time in which to
travel down there. So the company dallied along,
and it was October before the whole train was made
up at a point about a hundred miles south of Salt
Lake.

The complete organization was divided into seven
divisions, each with its captain, and division No. 1
was to lead the march the first day and then fall to
the rear while No. 2 took the advance, and so continued till all had taken their turn. The leading party
was to guard and care for the cattle and deliver them
in the morning. The regulations were read aloud to
the captains, and this rather large army of men, women and children, with about five hundred head of
stock, moved out very systematically. It would sometimes be fully ten o'clock before the rear division
could make a start, and correspondingly late before
they could get up with the main camp at night. They
got along very well, but cleaned the country of grass
for some distance each side of the trail, as they swept
along.

About the first of November Capt. Smith overtook
us with the pack train, and camped with us at night.
He formed many acquaintances and told them he was
going to take a shorter route and save five hundred

miles, rather than take the long route by way of Los
Angeles. He had a map of his proposed route, and it
was very much like the one we had. He also stated
that it could probably be as easily traveled as the
one by way of Los Angeles, and as a consequence
of his talk, cut-off fever began to rage in camp again.
Some got very enthusiastic in the matter and spoke
publicly in favor of following Capt. Smith when he
should come to the place when his short route turned
away from the other trail. His plan grew so much in
favor that when the place was reached a hundred wagons turned out into the Smith trail, leaving Capt.
Hunt only the seven Mormon wagon bound for San
Bernardino, Hunt stood at the forks of the road as the
wagons went by and said to them;—"Good-bye,
friends. I cannot, according to my agreement go with
you, for I was hired for this road, and no other was
mentioned. I am in duty bound to go even if only
one wagon decides to go."   When the last wagon had
passed him he still stood talking with several who had
chosen the new way and told them they were taking
a big risk, for they did not know very much about
the route, and he had been thinking that they might
find it pretty rough and hard to get over the first
time. He said that if all decided to go that way he
would go and help them, even if they went to h—ll,
but as it was he could not. He wished them luck
and the two trains parted company.

At the end of three days of travel on the Smith
trail they came to the top of a long steep hill. The
trail went down and down, and they see no way of
crossing the terribly deep cañon that was before them.
So they went into camp and sent explorers out to investigate and find a crossing if possible.

On the second day the explorers began to return
with very unfavorable reports, and many who found

their progress thus blocked turned about and started
to follow Hunt. Most of the wagons which remained
had each one or more of their men out exploring and
could not turn back until their return. Several of
the Jayhawkers having once started on this route
were very anxious to get through on it if a way could
be found for them to do it, and therefore searched farther and with greater determination than the others.
When they returned they reported they had found a
way around the head of the cañon and they believed
it to be the right way. The map Williams had given
them did not show this cañon and they believed it to
be correct, and that the real road led around at the
place which they had found, and no further trouble
would be met.

Acting on this report about twenty wagons, including the Jayhawkers, concluded to go ahead. "We
can beat the other fellows a month," said they, and
so they hitched up and pulled out in a northerly direction, feeling in good spirits and hopeful of success.

They named this place Mt. Misery. While camped
here a lone and seemingly friendless man died and
was buried. None seem now to remember his name,
but think he was from Kentucky. He was low with
consumption and not strong enough to endure the
hardships of the journey.

About the third night the Jayhawkers were overtaken by seven more wagons owned by A. Bennett
and friends, J. B. Arcane and family, two men named
Earhart and a son of one of them, and one or two
other wagons.

The Jayhawker's train was made up of men from
many states, but seemed well united and was as complete as when they first started. The Author was
with the party that came up in the rear, which had
started later but traveled faster on account of having

a road broken for them. He visited the leaders in camp when they were discussing the necessity of forming a new travelling compact to help and protect each other on the road. Those who had no families were objecting to being bound to those who had women and children with them. They argued that the road would be hard and difficult and those wagons with women and children would require more assistance than they would be able to render in return. They said they could go back and follow Hunt who was on a better road and they could proceed with more safely.

Among those with this train was Rev. J. W. Brier, his wife and three children. He objected to being turned back and said he did not want to be assisted, but would go with them and do his part and take care of himself. The Author listened to the various speeches without speaking and became satisfied that it would end in every one looking out for himself in case of hard times. He went over to their camp again the next night and wished to ask them why they were steering so nealy due north. He said to them that they were going toward Salt Lake rather than California, and that the Bennet party did not feel inclined to follow them any farther in that direction. They replied that their map told them to go north a day or more and then they would find the ronte as represented. They would then turn west and reach Owen's Lake and from there there would be no more trouble. The Jayhawker crowd seemed to think they could go anywhere and no difficulty could happen which they couldn't overcome. Bennett's little train turned west from this point and the Jayhawkers went on north, but before night they changed their minds and came following on after Bennett whom they overtook and passed, again taking the lead.

Thus far the country had been well watered and
furnished plenty of grass, and most of them talked
and believed that this kind of rolling country would
last all the way through. The men at leisure scattered around over the hills on each side of the route
taken by the train, and in advance of it, hunting camping places and making a regular picnic of it. There
were no hardships, and one man had a fiddle which
he tuned up evenings and gave plenty of fine music.
Joy and happiness seemed the rule, and all of the
train were certainly having a good time of it.

But gradually there came a change as the wagon
wheels rolled westward. The valleys seemed to have
no streams in them, and the mountain ranges grew
more and more broken, and in the lower ground a dry
lake could be found, and water and grass grew scarce--
so much so that both men and oxen suffered. These
dry lake beds deceived them many times. They
seemed as if containing plenty of water, and off the
men would go to explore. They usually found the
distance to them about three times as far as they at
first supposed, and when at last they reached them
they found no water, but a dry, shining bed, smooth
as glass, but just clay, hard as a rock. Most of these
dry lakes showed no outlet, nor any inlet for that matter, though at some period in the past they must have
been full of water. Nothing grew in the shape of
vegetables or plants except a small, stunted, bitter
brush.

Away to the west and north there was much broken
country, the mountain ranges higher and rougher and
more barren, and from almost every sightly elevation
there appeared one or more of these dry lake beds.
One night after about three days of travel the whole
of the train of twenty seven wagons was camped along
the bank of one of these lakes, this one with a very

little water in it not more than one fourth or one half
an inch in depth, and yet spread out to the width of
a mile or more· It was truly providential, for by digging holes along the border the water would run into
them and prove abundant for all, both oxen and men.
If it had proved dry, as so many before had proved,
or if we had been a few days earlier or later we might
not have found a drop. This proved to be the last
time the whole twenty seven wagons were gathered in
one camp together.

The Author came into camp about nine o'clock in
the evening after climbing many peaks and taking a
survey of the surrounding country with a field glass.
Men from nearly every mess came to him to inquire
what he had seen. They asked all sorts of questions
and wanted an opinion as to the advisability of trailing across the prairie directly west, which then seemed
easy. They were told that from what could be seen
from the summit of buttes both north and south of the
camp, ranging a hundred or so miles in almost every
direction, it was believed no water could be found, between the present camp and a range of mountains
which could be seen crossing the route far to the west.
"Well," said Capt. Doty of the Jayhawkers, "I don't
like to hear such discouraging talk from Manley, but I
think we will have to steer straight ahead. The prospect for water seems to be about the same, west or
south, and I cannot see that we would better ourselves
by going north." When morning came Capt. Doty
and his party yoked up and set out straight across the
desert, leaving seven wagons of the Bennett party
still in camp.

For some time all of us had seen in the range a-
head an appearance of a pass, or lower place in the
mountain, and we had got to calling it Martin's Pass,
naming it after Jim Martin. There was a snow-capped

peak just to the south of it and the pass, now apparently exactly west of the lake camp, seemed to the Jayhawkers easy to reach. Their wills were strong enough and they were running over with betermination and energy enough to carry them over any plain, no matter how dry or barren, or over any mountain no matter how rugged and steep.

Five days they traveled, without finding water, and small supply they took along had been consumed. For lack of water they could not eat or sleep. The oxen gathered round the little fire and seemed to beg for water, they had no cud to chew unless it was the cud of disappointment. The range of mountains they had been aiming for still seemed far away and the possible show for reaching it seemed very poor indeed, and the prospect of any water hole between them and the mountains poorer yet. Hope was pretty near gone. Martins mess unyoked their oxen from the wagons, put some small packs on their own backs, and loaded some upon the backs of the oxen, and turned south toward the nearest snowy mountain they could see, the same one towards which the Bennett party steered from the lake camp.

The Doty party kept their courage longer and kept on straight ahead for another day, and then camped, almost without hope. No rest came to them, nor sleep. Towards morning as they stood around the fire a stray cloud appeared and hid the stars, and shortly after began to unload a cargo of snow it carried. They spread out every blanket, and brushed up every bit they could from the smooth places, kindled a little fire of brush under the camp kettles and melted all the snow all of them could gather, besides filling their mouths as fast as ever they could, hoping that it would fall in sufficient quantities to satisfy themselves and the oxen, and quench their dreadful thirst. Slowly

the cloud moved scattering the snowflakes till they
felt relieved. The last time the Author conversed
with a member of this party was in 1892, and it was
conceded that this storm saved the lives of both man
and beast in that little band of Jayhawkers. It was
like manna falling from Heaven, and as surely saved
their lives as did the manna of the Bible save the lives
of the tribes of Israel. They had no reason to expect
a storm of rain or snow, but came to them just as they
were perishing. A little further on they came to a
small stream of water, and as the bed showed only a
recent flow it must also have come from the little local
storm further up the mountain. They used this water
freely, even though it was not very good, and it acted
on them very much like a solution of Glauber Salts.

They decided at first that ihey had better follow the
stream southward, but after a little time, feeling the
sickness caused by the water, they saw it was no advantage and turned west again, bearing to the north
toward a sort of pass they could now see in the mountains in that direction. This stream is now known as
the Amargosa, or bitter, river.

The new direction in which they marched gave
them an up-hill route for thirty or forty miles, rough
and barren, with no water or grass. There was no
road or trail to follow, the oxen were as weak as their
owners from drinking the bitter water, and the road
needed some clearing and breaking in places before
the wagons could pass. They moved quite slowly
and reached the summit on the second night with the
loss of a single ox. The Author would say here that
this was the last ox which was allowed to die without
using the flesh for food, and it was from this same one
he cut a steak to eat on Christmas eve, 1849.

From the summit they took a way down a dark,
deep cañon having a steep slope, and very rocky and

bad, but down which the oxen drew their loads much easier than when they came up, reaching water on the third day, where there were many springs, and a sort of coarse grass for the oxen. The place is now known as Furnace Creek. The Jayhawkers passed on, and here at these very springs was where the Author overtook the Rev. J. W. Brier delivering a lecture to his children on the benefits of an early education, as referred to in his narrative.

As the Jayhawkers drove out of this Furnace Creek Cañon the valley into which they came was very narrow, the high, snow-capped mountain before them seemed steeper and rougher than ever, so steep in fact that it could not be ascended by a man on foot. A short distance below could be seen a lake containing water, and the pass toward which they had been directing their course seemed to the north of them. They therefore turned their course in that direction. The road was sandy, and the brush that grew on it was only a few inches high. On their way they came to an abandoned Indian camp occupied by one poor old blind red man. He would hold his mouth open like a young bird begging for something to eat. One man dropped kernels of parched corn into his mouth, but instead of eating them he quickly spit them out; it seemed that he had been left to die and could not or would not. His hair was white as snow. His skin looked about the color of a smoked ham, and so crippled was he that he crawled about like a beast, on all fours. It was barely possible that he had been left to watch, and that his great infirmities were only pretended, but they seemed genuine enough, and were doubtless true. They left him in peaceable possession of the spot and traveled on.

They approached the base of the mountain in front of what they had all along supposed to be a pass, and found, as they had lately begun to suspect, that there was no pass that their wagons could be taken through, and they must be abandoned. The camp was poor. What little water there was had a salty taste, and they could only find here and there a bunch of the poorest grass. The oxen stood around as if utterly dispirited, and would sometimes make a faint effort to pick up and eat some of the dry brush that grew around the desolate camp. This camp is now known to be in the northern part of Death Valley, but then they knew no names for anything, but if dreariness and absence of life, and threatened danger all around were any indication, they might well have named it Death Valley as was afterwards done by the party with whom the Author traveled.

The party had been brave till now, but when they realized that they must make pack animals of themselves, and trudge on, they knew not where, perhaps to only a lingering death, the keen edge of disappointment cut close, and they realized how desolate they were. They felt much inclined to attribute all their troubles to the advice of the Mormons. Some said that the plan was thus to wipe so many more hated Gentiles out of the way, and wishes were deep and loud that the Mormons might all be buried out of sight in the Great Salt Lake. They thought Lot's wife must have been turned to salt in the neighborhood, everything was so impregnated with saline substances, and the same result might come to them. But the inherent manhood of the little band came to their relief and they determined not to die without a struggle for escape and life.

They killed some of their oxen, and took the wood of their wagons and kindled fires to dry and smoke the flesh so it would be light and easy to carry with them. They scattered all surplus baggage around the

ground, carefully storing and saving the bit of bread
that yet remained and dividing it equally among the
party. They also divided the tea, coffee, rice and
some such things, and each one agreed that he could
not ask aught of his neighbor more. Knapsacks were
improvised from parts of the wagon canvas, and long
strips of canvas were made into a sort of pack harness
for the oxen. It was a sad sight to see the strong and
vigorous young men of a few days ago reduced to
such straits; almost skeletons now, with no hope of
nourishment to invigorate them. They made canteens
by sewing a couple of small powder cans in cloth,
with a band to go over the shoulders·

The Jayhawkers were still making their preparations when the Martin party and Rev. J. W. Brier
and family came up to their camp, having taken a
circuit around farther to the south. The Martin party
was already in marching order and this camp was so
poor that they did not wait, but gave all their oxen
they had left to Mr. Brier and said they could get on
faster without them. They took a straight course
over the hills and up the mountain, saying they
believed they had provisions enough upon their backs
to last them through, and that nothing should check
their progress till they reached the other side, where
they said were fertile valleys and plenty of chance to
live.

The Doty party, or Jayhawkers, when they were
ready started first a northerly course to find a more
favorable place to cross the range and drove their
oxen with them, each with a small pack. They soon
came to some good water, and after refreshing themselves turned westward to cross the great mountain
defore them. Both men and oxen were shod with
mocassins made of raw-hide to protect the feet against
sharp rocks. They could see no trail but merely

picked out the best way to go. While climbing the
steep monntain side they came across a dead ox left
by some party that had gone before them. They cut
out the tongue and some of the best meat and ate it to
eke out their own small stock, and carried some pieces
with them, but soon threw it all away but enongh for
a roast for supper.

When it was getting dark they were almost at the
summit, but there was no good camping place, and
they saw a small fire light at a little distance and
went to it, finding a poor lone camper taking care of
himself. They camped here also. It seemed as if there
were many men from the various parties scattered all
around the country, each one seeking out the path
which seemed to suit best his tender feet or present
fancy, steering west as well as mountains and cañon
would permit, some farther north, some farther south
and generally demoralized, each thinking that as a
last resort he would be able to save his own life. It
seemed to be a question of will and endurance, strong
hearts and keeping the body in motion. The weak
and faint must fail, and the strong said to the weak;—
"Stand up; be a man; don't fall down;" and so the
strong spurred on the weak and kept them up as best
they could.

Down the mountain they went, on the west side and
instead of Los Angeles, which some of them expected
to see, they saw only a salt lake in the midst of a barren desert valley and their route lay directly across it.
They traveled in several directions as they went across.
One went across the valley on a strip of dried mud
between two small lakes. Others followed down along
the east side of the lake near the foot of the mountain,
where they found some good water and an old Indian
camp. They found some mosquite beans, which
they did not know were of much use, but really, if they

had known how to fix them up a little they would
have been good food.

Capt. Doty's mess crossed between the lakes on the
strip of dry mud while others went on where it
was still soft and left marks of their foot-steps. Both
parties turned up a small cañon on the west side and
began the ascent of a black and barren range, containing no water, but in the bed of the ravine near the
summit they found some damp sand and tried to dig
with their hands to find some of the precious fluid.
But no water came, and in the morning one of their
number Mr. Fish died and was left unburied on the
barren rocks. No doubt his bones could be found there
to-day.

Turning west again, they had a down grade over
a most barren and rocky road for many miles The
prospect from this point was any thing but cheering.
To the left a large lake could be seen, and from their
previous experience they concluded it to be salt, and
the valley they were coming to was very sandy, and
the hardest sort of footing for men and animals as
weak as those of the party were. It must be crossed
before there was any possibility of water, and when
across it was quite uncertain whether they could obtain any. One of their number had already died of
thirst and fatigue and all were suffering terribly.

The valley seemed about eight miles across, and before they were half way over Mr. Ischam, one of
their party sat down, perfectly exhausted, and said he
could not take another step. No one was able to assist him or give him a drink of water, and they could
not tarry to see if rest would refresh him. They could
only look sadly at him and and pass on in silence, for
he seemed fast wasting away. The thought came to
everyone that perhaps it would be his turn next to sit
down and see the others pass on. In fact the probab-

ility of any more of them living another day was very
po)r, for they all grew weaker and weaker with every
hour, and no one knew how many hours must pass
before they could hope for water. There was not
moisture enough in their poor bodies to make tears,
and no one dare open his mouth, lest all the moisture
suddenly evaporate and respiration cease.

Those who had no cattle took different courses to
reach the hills and mountains on the west side of this
valley, hoping there to find water and signal to the
others if they were successful. All except the two
men managed to get across, and finding no water the
packs were taken from the oxen and they were driven
to the lake which appeared on the left. Reaching the
lake they found the water red in color and so strong of
alkali that no man or beast could take a single swallow. They drove the cattle back again with sad
hearts, and almost despondent, for in the rough, dry
rocks of the mountains there seemed no signs of water.
But they were saved again. Those who bore farthest
to the right in their course to the mountains, steering
toward a pile of tremendous rocks, found a little
stream of good water which flowed only a short distance and then sank into the sand. This good news
spread rapidly, and all soon gathered at the little
streamlet. It was slow work getting water for them
all, but by being patient they were all filled up. Some
took two canteens of water and hurried back to Mr.
Ischam, whom they found still alive but his mouth
and throat so dry and parched, and his strength so
small that he was unable to swallow a single drop,
and while they waited he breathed his last. With
their hands and feet they dug away the sand for a
shallow grave, placed the body in it, covered it with
his blankets, and then scraped the sand back over
again to make a little mound over their dead comrade.

Perhaps if he could have walked a mile farther he might have lived, and but for the little trickling stream of water from the rocks they might all be dead, so slight were the circumstances that turned the scale to balance toward life or death.

There was so little feed for oxen that they could gain no strength, but were much refreshed by the water and could still travel. One was killed here, and the meat, poor as it was, gave the men new strength. They all guessed it to be at least fifty miles to the base of the great snow mountain before them, and what there was between no one could tell, for there were hills and valleys between. Leaving the little spring their course led first up a small cañon, and when they reached the summit of the ridge a small valley covered with sage brush was before them, the most fertile spot they had seen for a long time. The descent to this valley was through another cañon which was filled with large boulders for much of the way, and over these it seemed almost impossible to get the cattle. They had seen no water since leaving the little stream, and the plain they were now approaching seemed thirty miles wide, with no signs of streams or springs. However just at the foot of the cañon they found a small water hole, but the water was so salt that even the oxen refused to drink it.

They decided to make a push across the plain and endeavor to reach the other side in two days, and they knew there could be no water on its even expanse. The plain seemed quite an up grade from where they were to the base of the mountain.

On the second day they all reached the point they were aiming for except Rev. J. W. Brier and family, and they came in one day behind. Every one looked out for himself and had no time nor strength to spare to help others. Here on a small bench overlooking

the country to the south and east but still a long distance from the snow, they found some holes of water,
and some bunch grass a little farther up the hill.
Here was a large trail coming from the north and
leading from this point westward. There were no
signs of recent use, but there were many indications
that it was quite ancient and had been considerably
traveled in time past. This was quite encouraging to
many of them and they declared they would follow
this trail which would surely lead to some place well
known, in a better country. They cared not whether
it led to California, Mexico, or Texas, only that they
might get out of this country which seemed accursed.
Any place where they could get something to eat and
drink would be better than this.

Mr. and Mrs. Brier had some pretty hard struggles
to get along, and everyone of this party has ever been
loud in praise of the energy and determination of the
brave little woman of the Brier mess. All agreed that
she was by far the best man of the party. She was
the one who put the packs on the oxen in the morning. She it was who took them off at night, built the
fires, cooked the food, helped the children, and did all
sorts of work when the father of the family was too
tired, which was almost all of the time. They all said
that he, like other ministers, had fallen out with any
work but that of the tongue, and seemed perfectly
willing for some one else to do the work. Mrs. Brier
had the sympathy of everyone, and many would have
helped her if they could. She waited on her big husband with untiring zeal, and still had time to care for
the children with all of a mother's love. It seemed
almost impossible that one little woman could do so
much. It was entirely to her untiring devotion that
her husband and children lived. Mr. Brier had but
ittle sympathy or help from any one but her. Some

were quite sarcastic in their remarks about the invalid preacher who never earned his bread by the sweat of his brow, and by their actions showed that they did not care very much whether he ever got through or not. They thought he ought to have asserted his manliness and taken the burden on himself, and not lean upon his delicate and trusting wife as he seemed to do. All are sure that it is to his faithful wife the Rev. J. W. Brier owed his succor from the sands of that desert.

Looking back on the scenes of that day, the way the selfish dispositions of people were made manifest is almost incredible. Every one seemed to think only of saving his own life, and every spark of human sympathy and kindness seemed extinguished. A man would drink the last cup of water even if his neighbor choked.

This camp was the same one which the Author mentions in his narrative, to which Rogers and himself crept so silently and carefully at night to ascertain whether the occupants were friends or foes. They were much pleased to find it was Capt. Doty of the Jayhawkers and his mess who had remained behind to dry the flesh of an ox they had killed when it could travel no longer. The others had gone on ahead, following the trail, leaving these to follow. They staid here two days, and it was while waiting here that the Rev. J. W. Brier came up as before related, and they all went on together when they moved.

Nearly every man had carried a gun in the early days of the expedition, hoping to kill game, and to be well armed in case of attack by Indians or enemies, but they began to find that they were useless incumbrances, and first one and then another would throw away his fire-arms as a burden too great for a weary man to bear. There was no game, and the poor weak

men hardly deemed their own lives worth defending
against an enemy when a day or two of lack of water
would end the matter of life at any rate.

As they slept they dreamed the most tantalizing
dreams of clear, rippling brooks of water; of wading
knee deep in rhe most beautiful of ponds; of hoisting
the old moss-covered bucket from some deep old well;
of breaking and eating great white loaves of bread;
of surrounding the home table with its load of steaming beans and bacon, fragrant coffee and delicious
fried cakes. With such dreams of comfort, they awoke
to realize more more fully the terrors of their dry and
swollen throats, the discomfort of empty stomachs.
Water and food were the great riches of life to them
then. Had piles of twenty-dollars pieces been on the
one hand and a bucket of cold water on the other there
is no doubt of the choice that would have been made.

Seven or eight miles from this place were two branches to the trail. One led into the mountains toward
the snow, and the other still bore southerly. They
could see that some other party who had no oxen
to drive had taken the more northerly route, which
seemed to lead more directly in the direction of the
mines of California. Those who came later, with
animals thought it would be folly to try to cross the
deep snow they could see on the mountains before them
and concluded that it would be safer to the south of the
snow line, braving the danger of scarcity of water,
rather than to perish in the snow. Capt. Doty was
willing to attempt the northern branch of the trail if
the others so decided, but the general feeling was in
favor of the more plain and open trail which led away
from the snows. It is known that this Northern
branch led over what is known as Walker's Pass, coming out at the Kern River.

Taking then the southern branch, the party passed

through a range of low mountains, and then the country before them seemed quite level for a hundred miles.
They expected they would find much difficulty on
account of water, as their experience had taught
them that it was very scarce in such locations,
but this trail when they came to follow it led them for
eight or ten miles over a level piece of high land that
looked as if it might have slid down from the high
mountain at some day long past, and this easily traveled road brought them at last to the top of a steep
hill, down which they went and found near the bottom,
a small weak stream of water, but no grass, and but
little fuel of any kind. (This was the same camp at
which Rogers and the Author overtook the advance
party.) Here they killed an ox, which made a good
meal for all, and not much remained over, for many
had no oxen and were getting out of all sorts of provisions. They depended much on the generosity of
their fellow travelers. Many of them stood back,
and waited till those who owned the food were satisfied, and were very grateful when they were invited
to take even the poorest morsels.

They could count the oxen and make a pretty close
guess of how many days they could live in this way,
even with the best probable fortune favoring them,
and to the best of them there was but little hope, and
to those who were dependent it seemed as if the fate of
Fish and Ischam might be theirs almost any day.
When the Author conversed with them at this camp
he found them the first really heart-broken men he had
ever seen Some were men of middle age who had left
good farms that gave them every need, and these they
had left to seek a yellow phantom, and now there
were yellow phantoms of a different sort rearing their
dreadful forms all about them. They called themselves foolish gold hunters to forsake a land of plenty

for a chance to leave their bones in a hot desert.
More eyes than one filled with tears, and hopes in
more than one breast vanished to almost nothing.
More than one would gladly have placed himself back
where he could have been assured of the poorest fare
he ever saw upon his farm, for bread and water would
have been an assurance of life, of which there seemed
to be really but little expectation here.

When they left this camp in the cañon the trail was
between two high rocks, rising like walls on each side.
In one place they were so near together that an ox could
hardly squeeze through. In a very short time they
came to a bunch of willows growing out in the open
ground. The little bunch or grove was forty or fifty
feet in diameter, and in the center was a spring of
water. The center of the clump had been cleared out,
making a sort of corral of bushes, enclosing the spring.
On the outside there was quite a little growth of grass,
which was a fortunate thing for their poor beasts.

Away in the distance, rising up a little against the
western sky they could see mountains with snow on
them, and it seemed as if it were a journey of five or
six days to reach them, but the good water and the
grass bolstered up their spirits wonderfully for there
was present relief and rather better prospects ahead.
They were pretty sure that the wide plain held no
water. Everything that would hold the precious
drink was filled, and the best preparations made for
what they believed was to be the final struggle for
life. They rested one day and prepared for the very
worst that might before them. Early in the morning
when they could see plainest, they looked across the expanse before them and really it did not seem quite so
barren, hot and desolate as the region they had passed,
and they talked and hoped that this would be the last
desert they must cross and that Los Angeles lay just

beyond the sunny ridge they could dimly see ahead.
There were some tears that more than one would not
live to answer roll call on the other side, but it was
the last hope, and worth an earnest, active trial.

Early in the morning, much refreshed, they started
on again with rather sober faces. That night one man
insisted on sleeping with his clothes and boots all on,
for he said if he died he wanted to die in full dress.
Another day and some thought they could see trees on
the mountains ahead of them, and this renewed their
courage greatly. In the middle of the day they suffered greatly with the heat and the dry air seemed to
drink up every bit of moisture from everybody. When
they killed an ox they saved the blood and ate it.
The intestines, cleaned with the fingers, made food
when roasted on the fire, and pieces of hide, singed
and roasted, helped to sustain life. The water was
nearly all gone. Only power of will and strength
of body had kept any. Capt. Asa Haines sat down
one day and said he could go no farther, but his comrade, L. D. Stephens, who had kept a little rice, a little tea, and a dry crust of bread for time of need, took
a little water in a cup and made some soup which he
forced his friend to eat and soon he revived and was
able to move on again. That was true friendship.

The next night Stevens himself awoke and seemed
perishing with thirst. He crawled over to Doty's bed
and begged for just one sup of water, Doty in the
goodness of his heart, took his canteen from under his
head divided the last few drops with him and the death
which threatened him was held off. Capt. Doty found
it necessary to talk very seriously to those who
mourned and talked of failing He never gave up in
the least. He encouraged all to make every step they
could and know no such word as fail. When they
said that death would be easier than life, he told them

so, but that life was possible if they only willed it,
and a better life than had been theirs. And so he
kept them encouraged and kept them putting one foot
before the other, pointing out the ever lessening distance to the mountain before them. He appealed to
their manhood. "Be men," said he, "Be brave and
courageous, and you have more strength than you
believe." Thus by example and words he proved to
be a true captain to his little band.

Their water was all gone, every drop, and still the
foot-hills seemed far away. The supply of meat ran
out. Tom Shannon killed an ox, and when those who
had cattle had taken some, the others who had none
were told to divide the rest. There was no water to
dress or cook it, but it helped to sustain life. Entrails,
bones, sinews, bits of hide and everything was used.
One man was seen with an ox horn, burning the end
in the fire and gnawing away at the softened portion.
It was something terrible to see human beings eating
what the dogs would cast aside. One man saw some
moist looking earth on the shady side of a bunch of
brush and he dug down and got a handful of it, from
which he tried to suck the moisture. He failed, and
the bad taste of the earth made him suffer more than
before. Many bones of horses and cattle now appeared
along the trail. They seemed to have been there a
long time, and some were partly decayed. On this
waterless stretch one of their number, a Frenchman,
wandered off, searching for water in little hollows or
puddles, and never came back to camp. He was supposed to be dead, but ten years afterward some sur-
veyors found him in a Digger Indian camp.

An idea how selfish men will get under such circumstances may be gained by relating that on one occasion when an ox was killed the liver was carried to
the brave little Mrs. Brier for herself and children,

and she laid it aside for a few moments till she could attend to some other duties before cooking it. Darkness coming on meanwhile, some unprincipled, ungallant thief stole it, and only bits of offal and almost uneatable pieces were left to sustain their lives. That any one could steal the last morsel from a woman and her children surpasses belief, but yet it was plain that there was at least one man in the party who could do it. No one can fully understand or describe such scenes as this unless he has looked into just such hungry looking, haggard eyes and faces, a mixture of determination and despair, the human expression almost vanishing, and the face of a starving wolf or jackal taking its place. There are no words to paint such a state of things to him who has never seen and known.

But there were true men, true, charitable hearts in that little band. Though death stared them in the face they never forgot their fellow men. As they slowly crawled along many would wander here and there beside the trail and fall behind, especially the weaker ones, and many were the predictions that such and such a one would never come up again, or reach the camp. Then it was that these noble souls, tired almost beyond recovery themselves, would take water and go back to seek the wandering ones and give them drink and help them on. More than one would thus have perished in the sands but for the little canteen of water carried back by some friend. Only a swallow or two would often revive their failing strength and courage, and with slow step they would move on again. How much good a crust of bread would have done such a poor creature. Bread there was none — nothing but the flesh of their poor oxen, wasted and consumed by days of travel and lack of food till it had no goodness in it. Even the poor oxen, every night seemed to be the end of their walking; every morning it was feared that that would be the last time they would be able to rise upon their feet.

Already five or six days had passed since they left the camp at the willows where they had their last supply of water, and still they were on the desert. The journey was longer than they had expected, partly owing to the slow progress they had made for there were frequent stops to rest or they could not move at all. The mountains seemed nearer every day, and the trees were outlined more plainly each morning as they started out. Capt. Doty used every circumstance to encourage them. He would remark upon the favorable signs of water in the hills before them, and the hope that there might be some game to provide better meat than that of starving oxen. Thus he renewed their hope and kept alive their courage. He must have had a great deal of fortitude to hide his own sad feelings, for they must as surely have come to him as to any one, and to keep up always an air of hope, courage, and determination to succeed. If he had been a man of less spirit and good judgment it is very probable that many more would have been left by the wayside to die.

About this point the trail which had been growing fainter and fainter, seemed to vanish entirely. One could move in almost any direction to right or left as he chose, and because of this, previous travel had doubtless scattered and thus left no trail. It was thought best that this company should spread out and approach the mountains in as broad a front as possible so as to multiply the chances of finding water, and so they started out in pairs, some to the right and some to the left, each selecting the point where water seemed most probable.

Tom Shannon and a companion were one of these

pairs. Tom was one of the few who still stuck to his
gun, for he felt that it might save his life sometime.
He and his companion separated about a mile, each
looking at all points that showed the least sign of
water. Suddenly a jack rabbit started from a bush,
the first game Shannon had seen for more than a
month. He pulled the rifle on him as he was making
some big bound and had the good luck to nearly split
his head open. Rushing up to his game he put his
mouth to the wound and sucked the warm blood as it
flowed, for it was the first liquid he had seen; but instead of allaying his fearful thirst it seemed to make it
worse and he seemed delirious. A little way up the
gulch he saw a rock and a green bush and steered for
it, but found no water. He sat down with his back
to the rock, his rifle leaning up near by, pulled his
old worn hat over his eyes, and suffered an agony of
sickness. He realized that life was leaving his body,
and there he sat with no power to move and no desire
to make an effort. It seemed as if he could see plain
before him all the trail from where he sat, back over
all the deserts, mountains and rivers to the old place
in Illinois. He entirely forgot the present, and seemed
unconscious of everything but the pictures of the past.
The mind seemed growing freer from its attachment
to the body and at liberty to take in his whole past life,
and bright scenes that had gone before. How long
he sat thus he knows not. His companion was fortunate in finding water, and when he had refreshed
himself he set out to find poor Tom of whom he could
see nothing. Going toward where he heard the shot
he followed on till he saw him at the rock, almost
doubled up, with his face concealed by his hat. "O!
Tom!" said he, but there came no answering motion,
and going nearer he called again and still no answer
and no sign. Poor Tom had surely passed on to the

better land, thought he, and salvation was so near.
He approached and lifted the hat rim. There was a
movement of the eyes, a quivering of the muscles of
the face, and a sort of semi-unconscious stare such as
precedes approaching dissolution.

Quickly holding back his head he poured water between his lips from his canteen and it was swallowed.
Then a little more, and then some more, and life
seemed coming back again into a troublesome world,
bringing pain with it, and the consciousness of a suffering body. After a time he felt better and was
helped to his feet, and together they went to the water
hole where they made a fire and cooked the rabbit
which was the first savory meat they had tasted for a
long time. Tom felt better and told his companion
how he felt after tasting the warm rabbit's blood, and
how he had nearly gone off into the sleep of death.

"If you had been a little longer finding me," said
Tom, "I should soon have been out of this sad world."
They fired a signal gun, looked down at the bones of
the rabbit, drank more water, and gradually felt new
life coming to them. The mountains seemed more
fertile, and there was brush and grass near by, timber farther up, and still higher a cap of snow extending far along the range, both north and south. Towards night on this eventful day the scattered travelers
began to come slowly into camp attracted by the guns
and the smoke of the fire made by those who first
found the water. Some were nearly as far gone as
Tom Shannon was, and great caution had to used in
giving them water on their empty stomach. One man
named Robinson became so weak before he got near
camp that his companions placed him on the back of
one of the animals and a man walked on either side to
catch him if he fell off. When they got within a mile
of the water he insisted that he was strong enough to

take care of himself and not be watched every minute,
and they relaxed their vigilance. He soon fell off,
and when they went to him he refused to be put back
on the animal again or to walk any farther. "Just
spread my blankets down," said he, "and I will lie
down and rest a little and after a while I will come
along into camp." So they left him and pushed on to
water, and when they were a little refreshed went
back to him with water, and to help him to come in,
but when they came to him they found him dead.
He did not seem to have moved after he had lain down.
He did not seem so bad off as Shannon was when he
lay down, and probably a few swallows of water at
that time would have saved his life. It seemed sad
indeed, after so much suffering and striving to get
along, that he should die within a mile of water that
would have saved his life. If he had posessed a little
more strength so that the spark of life could have remained a little longer, the cooling moisture from the
canteen would have revived it, and a little rest would
have placed him on his feet again. They had no tools
to dig a grave, not even a knife for they had left every
weight in camp, so they covered him closely in his
blankets and sadly returned to their friends. They
had all along hoped that the Frenchman who had wandered away would come in, but he never came. There
were several water holes scattered around at this point
which seemed to be a sort of sunken place in the hills,
and quite large brush could be obtained for fire, and
grass for the oxen Those who had been good hunters
and had thrown away their rifles as useless burdens,
now began to look at hills before them and think that
game might be found in them, as well as water.
There were only one or two guns in the whole party,
They thought that this must surely be the edge of the
great desert they had crossed, and only the snow

range before them could be the obstacle that separated
them from Los Angeles.

One day from here would bring them to the edge of
the snow, and they debated as to the best course to
pursue. Some of them were fearful they could not
cross the snow with the oxen, for it seemed to be quite
deep. The best place to cross seemed directly west
of them. South was a higher peak, and to the north
it was surely impassible. There seemed to be a faint
sign of a trail from this point towards the lowest point
in the snow mountains. There were some bones of
cattle around the springs which they thought was an
indication that in years gone by there had been some
traveling on this trail. There surely would be water
in the snow which could be got by melting it, and on
the whole it seemed best to make the attempt to cross
at the lowest place. There were no signs of travel
except the trail which had not been used in years, nor
signs of civilization except the bones.

Starting from the water holes which showed no signs
of having been used for several years, their next camp
was, as they had calculated, on the edge of the snow
where they found plenty of dry juniper trees for fire,
and of course plenty of water. Here they killed an ox
and fed the hungry so that they were pretty well refreshed. This was an elevated place and they could
look back over the trail across the desert for, what
seemed to them, a hundred miles, and the great dangers of their journey were discussed. Said one of
them to Tom Shannon:— ''Tom, you killed the first
game we have come across in two months. Even the
buzzards and coyotes knew better than to go out into
the country where the cursed Mormon saint sent us
numbskulls.'' Another said that while they had been
seeking a heaven on earth they had passed through
purgatory, or perhaps a worse place still nearer the

one from which sulphurous fumes arise, and now they
hoped that there might be a somewhat more heavenly
place beyond the snow. One who had been silent
seemed awakened by inspiration and spoke in impromptu lines somewhat as follows, as he pointed out
to the dim distance:—

> "Yonder in mountains' gray beauty,
> Wealth and fame decay.
> Yonder, the sands of the desert,
> Yonder, the salt of the sea,
> Yonder, a fiery furnace,
> Yonder, the bones of our friends,
> Yonder the old and the young
> Lie scattered along the way."

Some even confessed the desperate thoughts that
had come to their minds when they were choking and
starving. We have mentioned four of the train who
had perished beside the trail and it will be remembered that one party of eleven started out on foot before the wagons were abandoned by the rest of the party.
Nothing was heard of these for seven years, but long
afterward nine skeletons were found at the remains of
a camp, and the other two were afterward seen in the
gold fields. When spoken to about this party, they
burst into tears and could not talk of it. So it is known
that at least thirteen men perished in the country
which has well been named Death Valley.

People who have always been well fed, and have
never suffered from thirst till every drop of moisture
seemed gone from the body, so they dare not open
their mouth lest they dry up and cease to breathe, can
never understand, nor is there language to convey the
horrors of such a situation. The story of these parties
may seem like fairy fables, but to those who experienced it all, the strongest statements come far short
of the reality. No one could believe how some men,

when they are starving take on the wild aspect of savage beasts, and that one could never feel safe in their presence. Some proved true and kind and charitable even with death staring them in the face, and never forgot their fellow men. Some that seemed weakest proved strongest in the final struggle for existance.

Early next morning before the sun rose they started to cross the snow, leaving their comrade Robinson behind, rolled up in his blankets, taking his everlasting sleep so far as the troubles of this world are concerned. What the day would bring forth very few could have any idea. Go on they must, and this direction seemed most promising. If the snow should prove hard enough to hold up the oxen they could probably cross before night, but if compelled to camp in the snow it was a doubtful case for them.

The snow held them as they advanced on it, but grew a little softer as the sun got higher. The tracks of both men and animals were stained with blood from their worn-out feet. When they turned the summit they found more timber and the ravine they followed was so shaded that the force of the sun was broken, and they really did not suffer very much from slumping through the snow, and so got safely over. Not far below the snow they found a running brook of clear, sweet water, with willows along the banks and trees on the hills, the first really good water for a month or two. This is the same camp where Rogers and his companion ate their meal of quail, hawk and crow a few days before, and these travelers knew by the remains of the little camp fire that they were following on the trail of the two men who had gone before.

This place was so great an improvement on the camps of the past that all hands began to talk and act more rational as hope dawned more brightly on them.

Those who had guns branched off to search for game,
but found they were too weak for that kind of work,
and had to sit down very often to rest. When they
tried to run they stumbled down and made very poor
progress.

Capt. Doty, Tom Shannon and Bill Rude sat down
to rest on a bold point above the creek. While there
three wild horses came along within easy range, and
thinking they would form better meat than the oxen
each man picked his animal and all fired simultane-
ously, bringing them all to the ground. This seemed
a piece of glorious luck, and all rushed in like wolves
after a wounded animal. It was not very long before
each had a chunk of meat in his hand, and many a one
did not stop from eating because it was not cooked.
Such declared they never ate anything so delicious in
all their lives before, and wondered why horses were
not used as food instead of hogs and cattle. As they
satisfied their ravenous apetites they ate more like
beasts than like men, so nearly were they starved, and
so nearly had their starving condition made them fall
from their lofty estate.

As they passed on down this cañon they found it
very brushy and on the dry leaves under the wide-
spreading trees they saw signs of bear and perhaps
other animals. There were some swampy places
where it was grassy, and into these the cattle rushed
with great eagerness for the food they had so long suffered for. Some of Mr. Brier's cattle went in, and
in tramping around for food sank deep into the mud
and could not be coaxed out again. Mrs. Brier threw
clubs at them but they did not seem inclined to pay
much attention to her attacks so she was forced to go
in after them herself, and in so doing also sank into
the mud and could not get out without assistance.
All this time her reverend husband sat outside on the

hard ground at a safe distance, but did not offer any
help. Probably if an extended and learned lecture on
the effects of gravitation would have done any good
he would have been ready with prompt and extended
service to one whom he had promised to love and cher-
ish.

About this time L. D. Stevens came along and seeing the condition of the unfortunate woman, at once
went to her assistance and helped her to dry land.
Brier himself never made a move nor said a word.
Stevens looked terribly cross at him and remarked to
his companions that if the preacher himself had been
the one stuck in the mud he would have been quite
inclined to leave him there for all of helping him.

The cañon grew narrow as they descended, and the
brush thicker, so that to follow the bed of the stream
was the only way to get along. The cattle seemed to
scent a bear and stampeded in terror through the brush
in various directions, all except one which was being
led by a rope. They tried to follow the animals in a
desperate effort to recover them and a few blankets
they had upon their backs, but could only make slow
progress. Tom Shannon and two others found a fresh
bear track and determined to follow it awhile in the
hope of having revenge on the cause of their mishap
with the oxen. They took their blankets and kept
the trail till night when they camped, but were at so
great an elevation that a snowstorm came with six inches of snow so they could no longer follow the track.

They were very hungry and on the way back came
across some wild cherries which had dried perfectly
dry as they hung on the bushes. These they picked
and ate, cracking the seeds with their teeth, and declaring them to be the best of fruit. Good appetites
made almost anything taste good then. They got
back to the creek next day pretty nearly starved, and

with neither a bear nor runaway oxen to reward them
for their two days' hard work.

Wood and water were plenty, but grass was scarce
and their ox had to live on brush and leaves, but this
was infinitely better than the stunted and bitter shrubs
of the desert. They came out of the brush at last into
the open bottom land where the brook sank out of
sight in the sand, and sage brush appeared all about.
From this on, over the elevated point which projected
out nearly across the valley, their experience and
emotions in coming in sight of vast herds of cattle
feeding on rolling grassy hills, or reclining under
great oak trees scattered over the more level lands,
were much the same as came to the Author and his
party when the same scene was suddenly opened to
them. Signs of civilization and of plenty so suddenly
appearing after so many weeks of suffering·and desolation was almost enough to turn their heads, and
more than one of the stout-hearted pioneers shed tears
of joy. Only a few days before and they could scarcely
have believed it possible to find a spot so lovely.

But to hungry, more than half starved men, points
of artistic beauty and sober reflections over the terrors
of the past found little place, and their first thought
was to satisfy the cravings of hunger which were assuredly none the less when they beheld the numerous
fat cattle all around them. There was no one to ask
or to buy from and to kill and eat without permission
might be wrong and might get them into difficulty,
but one might as well ask a starving wolf to get permission to slay and eat when a fat lamb came across
his path as to expect these men to take very much
time to hunt up owners. When life or death are the
questions that present themselves men are not so apt
to discuss the right or wrong of any matter.

Tom Shannon and a couple of others did not wait

long at any rate, but crawled down the creek bed till
they were opposite a few fine animals and then crept
up the bank very near to them. Two or three shots
rang out and as many fine cattle were brought down.
The live cattle ran away and the hungry men soon
had the field to themselves. Much quicker than can
be told the men had fat pieces of meat in their hands
which they devoured without cooking. The men
acted like crazy creatures at a barbacue—each one cut
for himself with very little respect for anyone. The
boldest got in first and the more retiring came in later,
but all had enough and gradually resumed more human actions and appearance.

They had hardly finished their bloody feast when
they saw a small squad of men on horseback advanc-
ing toward them, and as they came near it was quite
plain that they were all armed in some way. All had
lassoes at their saddles, some had old-fashioned blun-
derbusses, and nearly every one had a *macheta* or long
bladed Spanish knife. As the horsemen drew near
they formed into something like military order and
advanced slowly and carefully. It was pretty evident
they thought they were about to encounter a band of
thieving Indians, but as they came closer they recognized the strangers as Americans and passed the compliments with them in a rather friendly manner.

Some of the Jayhawkers had been in the Mexican
War and understood a few words of Spanish, and by
a liberal use of signs were able to communicate with
the armed party and tell them who they were, where
they were going, and the unfortunate condition in
which they found themselves. The men did not seem
angry at losing so few of their cattle, and doubtless
considered themselves fortunate in not suffering to the
extent of some hundreds as they did sometimes by Indian raids, and invited the whole party down to the

ranch house of the San Francisquito Rancho of which this was a part. Arrived at the house the ranch men brought in a good fat steer which they killed and told the poor Americans to help themselves and be welcome. This was on the fourth day of February, 1850.

The whole party remained here to rest themselves and their oxen for several days, and were royally entertained by the people at the ranch. They talked over the plans for the future, and considered the best course to pursue. They thought it would be wise to keep their oxen for these would now improve in flesh, and as they had no money with which to buy food they might still rely on them in further travels. The best oxen had survived, for the failing ones were selected to be killed when they were forced to have food. The weaker of their comrades had perished in the desert, and the remainder of the train consisted of the strongest men and the strongest oxen, and there seemed to be no question but that they could all live in this country where grass and water were both abundant, and every sign of more or less wild game.

Those of the company who had no cattle made their way directly to Los Angeles, and from thence to the coast from which most of them reached San Francisco by sailing vessel. Those who had no money were given a passage on credit, and it is believed that all such debts were afterwards honestly paid.

Capt. Doty made a proposition to buy out the oxen of some who had only one or two, giving his note for them payable in San Francisco or anywhere up north they might chance to meet, and many of them accepted and went to the coast. In this way Doty secured oxen enough to supply one for each of those who decided to go with him. They decided to use them for pack animals to carry their blankets, and to proceed slowly toward the mines, killing game, if possible, and permitting their animals to graze and improve in condition as they moved.

There must have been from twenty-five to forty people gathered at the ranch. Among them was the Rev. J. W. Brier who seemed to want to impress it on the new California friends that he was the man of all others to be honored. The ranchman was a good Catholic, and Brier tried to make him understand that he, also, was very devout. He said, and repeated to him very often—"Me preacher," but he did not succeed very well in impressing the good Californian with the dignity of his profession, for he could talk no Spanish and was not highly gifted in sign language.

When they went away they had no way to reward their good friends who had been friends indeed to them. They could only look their thanks and express themselves in a very few words of Spanish. "*Adios Amigos,*" said they to the scantily clothed travelers as they set out on their way to the mines.

They followed down the course of the river that flowed through the valley, the Santa Clara River, and knew that it would take them to the sea at last. Before they reached the mission of San Buena Ventura, near the sea, they ran out of meat again, for they had failed to find game as they had expected, and Capt. Asa Haynes took the chances of killing a Spanish cow that looked nice and fat. They camped around the carcass and ate, and smoked the meat that was left. While thus engaged two horsemen approached, and after taking a good look at the proceedings, galloped off again. When the party arrived at the Mission they were arrested and taken before the alcalde to give an account of their misdeeds. They realized that they were now in a bad fix, and either horn of the dilemma was bad enough. They could not talk Spanish; they had no money; they had killed somebody's cow; they

were very hungry; they might be willing to pay, but
had no way of doing it; they did not want to languish
in jail, and how to get out of it they could not understand. Luck came to them, however, in the shape of
a man who could speak both English and Spanish, to
whom they told their story and who repeated it to the
alcalde, telling him of their misfortunes and unfortunate condition, and when that officer found out all the
circumstances he promptly released them as he did not
consider them as criminals. The cow was probably
worth no more than ten dollars.

At Santa Barbara they found a chance to trade off
some of their oxen for mares, which were not considered worth much, and managed the barter so well that
they came out with a horse apiece and a few dollars.
besides, with which to buy grub along the road. They
depended mostly on their guns for supplying them
with food. They supposed they were about three
hundred miles from San Francisco, and expected to
meet with but few people except at the Missions, of
which they had learned there were a few along the
road. At these there was not much to be had except
dried beef. However, they managed to use the guns.
with fair success, and at last arrived safely at Stockton
where they sold some of their horses for more than
double what they cost, and with a small number of
horses they packed on to the gold mines.

Those of the party who went to Los Angeles managed in one way or another to get through on schoon-
ers, and many of them, after a year or two of hard
work, made some money and returned to their homes.
in Illinois. It is hardly necessary to add that they did.
not return via Death Valley.

Some years afterward the members of this party who
had returned to their Eastern homes formed themselves into an organization which they called the Jay-

hawkers' Union, appointed a chairman and secretary, and each year every one whose name and residence could be obtained was notified to be present at some designated place on the fourth day of February which was the date on which they considered they passed from impending death into a richly promising life. They always had as good a dinner as Illinois could produce, cooked by the wives and daughters of the pioneers, and the old tales were told over again.

One part of the program was the calling of the roll, and such reports and letters as had come to hand. The following is a list of the members of the party so far as can be ascertained, as gathered from recollec-ions and from the reports of the meetings of the re-unions.

LIST OF JAYHAWKERS.

The following named were living, so far as known, in 1893:— John B. Colton and Alonzo C. Clay, of Galesburg, Ill., Luther A. Richards, of Woodhull, Ill., Chas. B. Mecum, of Ripley, Iowa, John W. Plummer, of Tulon, Ill., Edward Bartholomew, Urban P. David-son, John Crosscup and L. Dow Stephens, of San Jose, California, Harrison Frans and Thomas Shannon, of Los Gatos, Cal., J. W. Biier and wife, Lodi, Cal., three children of Mr. Brier.

The following are supposed to be dead:— Asa Haines, Knoxvilie, Ill., Sidney P. Edgerton, formerly of Blair, Nebraska, Thomas McGrew, John Cole, Wm. B. Rude, Wm. Robinson and Alex. Palmer, of Knox-ville, Ill., Marshall B. Edgerton, late of Galesburg, Ill. Wm. Ischam, of Rochester, N. Y., Mr. —--- Fish, of Oskaloosa, Iowa, John L. West, Aaron Larkin, Capt. Edwin Doty and Brien Byram, of Knoxville, Ill., Mr. —— Carter, of Wisconsin, Geo. Allen, Lean-der Woolsey and Chas. Clark, of Henderson, Ill., Mr.

—— Gretzinger, of Oskaloosa, Iowa, and a Frenchman
whose name is unknown.

There were some others connected more or less with
the party at some part of the trip, but not coming in
with the Jayhawker organization. So far as learned,
their names are as follows:— John Galler, Jim Woods
and Jim Martin of Miss., Ed Croker of N. Y., David
Funk, Mr. Town, Henry Wade, wife and three children, Nat Ward, John D. Martin, of Texas, Old Francis, a Frenchman, Fred Carr and Negro "Joe," from
Miss.

There were a great many reports about finding rich
mines about this time, and these stories have been
magnified and told in all sorts of ways since then, and
parties have returned to try to find the great riches.

Among the Jayhawkers were two Germans who
could speak but little English and probably for this
reason, kept apart from the remainder of the party.

One day, after the wagons were abandoned
these German fellows were marching along alone with
their packs on their backs in the warm sun, suffering
very much for want of water and food, when one of
them sat down on a hill-side in pretty nearly absolute
despair, while the other man went down into a ravine
hoping to find a puddle of water in the rocky bottom
somewhere, though it was almost a forlorn hope. All
at once he called out to his partner on the hill—"John,
come down here and get some of this gold. There is
a lot of it." To this poor John Galler only replied:—
"No, I won't come. I don't want any gold, but I
would like very much to have some water and some
bread." And so they left the valuable find and slowly
walked on, pulling through at last with the rest of
them, and reaching Los Angeles.

The man who found the gold went to the Mission
of San Luis Rey and started a small clothing store,

and some time afterward was killed. John Galler settled in Los Angeles and established a wagon shop in which he did a successful business. He was an honest, industrious man and the people had great confidence in him. He often told them about what his partner had said about finding the gold in the desert, and the people gave him an outfit on two or three occasions to go back and re-locate the find, but he did not seem to have much idea of location, and when he got back into the desert again things looked so different to him that he was not able to identify the place, or to be really certain they were on the same trail where his companion found the gold.

The Author saw him in 1862 and heard what he had to say about it, and is convinced that it was not gold at all which they saw. I told him that I more than suspected that what he saw was mica instead of gold and that both he and his partner had been deceived, for more than one man not used to gold had been deceived before now. "No sir!" said he, " I saw lots of gold in Germany, and when I saw that I knew what it was." The Author went back over that trail in 1862 and sought out the German on purpose to get information about the gold. He could not give the name of a single man who was in the party at that time, but insisted that it was gold he saw and that he knew the trail.

The Author was able to identify with reasonable certainty the trails followed by the different parties, but found no signs of gold formation except some barren quartz, and this after an experience of several years in both placer and quartz mines. So honest John Galler's famous placer mine still remains in the great list of lost mines, like the Gunsight Lead and other noted mines for which men have since prospected in vain.

CHAPTER XIV.

Alexander Combs Erkson was one of the pioneers of 1849, having left the state of Iowa in the month of May, when he assisted in organizing a company known as the "Badger Company" at Kanesville, the object being mutual assistance and protection. This company joined the Bennett party mentioned so prominently in this history, at the Missouri, and traveled with them or near them to the rendezvous near Salt Lake where the new company was organized for the southern trip taken by the Death Valley party, the Jayhawkers and others. As the experience of Mr. Erkson was in some respects different to that of the parties mentioned, he having taken a different route for a part of the way, it was thought best to embody it in this history. The following was dictated to the editor of this book, and as Mr. Erkson died before the written account could be revised by him, it is the best that can possibly be obtained.

MR. ERKSON'S STATEMENT.

"We arrived at the Mormon camp near Salt Lake, Salt Lake City, in the month of August. Several of us went to work getting out lumber for Brigham Yonng while we were waiting and resting. The mormons all advised us not to undertake to go on by the northern route, and as the travelers gathered at this point they canvassed the situation. We used our teams when we were at work for Brigham and assisted in building a dam across a cañon where he intended to build a woolen mill. I earned about a hundred dollars by my work, which was paid to me in ten-dollar pieces of a gold coin made by the Mormons. They were not like the U. S. coins. I remember one side had an eye and the words—"Holiness to the Lord."

We entered into an agreement with Capt. Hunt, a Mormon, to pilot us through, and turned all our gold into that company, thus bringing none of the Mormon gold with us. We went on with the company as has been related in the foregoing pages, till we arrived at Mt. Misery, so named by us, when we took the back track, while Mr. Manley and the others went on as they have related. We had meetings by the light of a greenwood fire, and the matter was talked up in little knots of people, and then some one would get up and speak. One J. W. Brier, a preacher, was the principal blower. 'You are going wrong!' said he, We should go west, and in six weeks we will be loaded with gold!'

Hunt got a little confused at a place called Beaver Meadows, or Mountain Meadows, and thought perhaps he could find a new road. Several men were sent out to look, and some of us in camp played ball for amusement while we were waiting. Hunt's men came back and said there were no prospects of a new road, and he said he knew the southern route and believed it would be safe to go that way.

He told us that we must decide the next day. When we came to the road where we were to separate he filed off on his road and the others filed off on their road and then came back with their whips in their hands. I had filed in after Hunt, and they tried to convince me that I was very wrong. A Mr. Norton of Adrian, Mich., promised Mrs. Erkson a horse to ride if she would go, and so I left Hunt and turned in on the other road, the hindmost wagon. This is going back a little with the history and bringing it up to Mt. Misery. On my way back from Mt. Misery I climbed up on a big rock and inscribed the date—Nov. 10, 1849.

In our journey we came to what is called 'The rim
of the Basin,' and traveled along on that a distance till
we came to the Santa Clara River and saw where the
Indians had raised corn and melons. We followed on
down that stream and found our teams gradually failing. Noting this we decided to overhaul our loads and
reject a lot of things not strictly necessary to preserve
life. I know I threw out a good many valuable and
pretty things by the roadside. I remember six vol-
umes of Rollin's Ancient History, nicely bound, with
my name on the back, that were piled up and left.
We followed along near the Santa Clara River till it
emptied into the Virgin River. It was somewhere
along here that we first saw some Yucca trees. The
boys often set fire to them to see them burn.

The Virgin River was a small stream running on
about the course we wanted to travel, and we followed
this course for thirty or forty miles. We found plenty
of wood and water and mesquite. After awhile the
river turned off to the left, while we wanted to keep
to the right, so we parted company there. We heard
of a river beyond which they called the 'Big Muddy'
and we went up a little arroyo, then over a divide to
some table land that led us down to the Big Muddy.
We made our wagons as light as possible, taking off
all the boards and stakes we could possibly get along
without. Wm. Philipps and others were placed on
short allowance. They had an idea that I had more
provisions in my wagon than I ought to have, but I
told them that it was clothing that we used to sleep
on. I divided among them once or twice. When we
reached the Muddy we stopped two or three days for
there was plenty of feed. It was a narrow stream
that seemed as if it must come from springs. It was
narrow between banks, but ran pretty deep, and a
streak of fog marked its course in the morning. We

understood it was not very far from where we left the
Virgin River to the Colorado, some said not more than
fourteen miles and that the Colorado turned sharply
to the south at that point.   Mr. Rhynierson and wife
had a child born to them on the Virgin River, and it
was named Virginia.

It was a gloomy trip the whole time on the Muddy.
I lost three or four head of cattle, all within a day and
a night.   Mrs. Erkson walked to lighten the load, and
would pick all the bunches of grass she saw and put
them on the wagon to feed the oxen when we stopped.
I let them pass me and stopped and fed the cattle, and
slept ourselves.   It was said that we ran great risks
from Indians, but we did not see any.   I had at this
time only two yoke of oxen left.

We overtook the party next morning at nine o'clock,
having met some of them who were coming back after
us.   All were rejoiced that we had come on safely.
Here I met Elisha Bennett and told him my story.
He said he could sell me a yoke of oxen.   He had a
yoke in J. A. Phllipps' team and was going to take
them out.   He said nothing in particular as to price.
I said that I wanted to see Mr. Philipps and talk with
him about the matter, for he had said Bennett should
not have the cattle.   I went over to see him and spoke
to him about Bennett's cattle and he told me they had
quarreled and I could have them, and so we made a
bargain.   I gave twenty dollars for the cattle, the last
money I had, and as much provisions as he could
carry on his back.   They were making up a party to
reach the settlements at the Williams ranch, and I
made arrangements for them to send back provisions
for us.   About thirty started that way—young men
and men with no families with them.

I got along very well with my new team after that.
It was about forty miles from water to water, and I

think we camped three times. At one place we found
that provisions had been left, with a notice that the
material was for us, but the red-skins got the provisions. We struck a spring called ——, a small spring
of water, and a child of some of the party died there
and was buried.

We then went more nearly south to find the Mojave
River, for we hoped to find water there. It was very
scarce with us then, We had one pretty cold day, but
generally fine weather, and to get along we traveled
at night and a party struck the Mojave. Here there
was some grass, and the mustard was beginning to
start up and some elder bushes to put forth leaves. I
picked some of the mustard and chewed it to try to
get back my natural taste. Here the party divided, a
part going to the left to San Bernardino and the remainder to the right to Cucamunga. I was with the
latter party and we got there before night.

Rhynierson said to one of the party—'Charlie, you
had better hurry on ahead and try to get some meat
before the crowd comes up.' Charlie went on ahead
and we drove along at the regular gait which was not
very fast about these times. We saw nothing of
Charlie and so I went to the house to look for him
and found him dead drunk on wine. He had not said
a word to them about provisions. That wine wrecked
us all. All had a little touch of scurvy, and it seemed to be just what we craved. I bought a big tum-
bler of it for two bits and carried it to my wife. She
tasted it at first rather gingerly, then took a little larger sup of it, and then put it to her lips and never
stopped drinking till the last drop was gone. I looked
a little bit surprised and she looked at me and inno-
cently asked—'Why! Haven't you had any?' I was
afraid she would be the next one to be dead drunk,
but it never affected her in that way at all. We

bought a cow here to kill, and used the meat either
fresh or dried, and then went on to the Wiliiams, or
Chino ranch. Col. Williams was glad to see us, and
said we could have everything we wanted. We
wanted to get wheat, for we had lived so long on meat
that we craved such food. He told us about the journey before us and where we would find places to camp.
Here we found one of the Gruwells. We camped here
a week, meeting many emigrants who came by way
of Santa Fe.

We went on from here to San Gabriel where we
staid six weeks to rest and recuperate the cattle. In
the good grass we found here they all became about
as fat as ever in a little while. Here the party all
broke up and no sort of an organization was kept up
beyond here. Some went to Los Angeles, some went
on north, trading off their cattle for horses, and some
went directly to the coast. We went to the Mission
of San Fernando where we got some oranges which
were very good for us. There is a long, tedious hill
there to get over. We made up ten wagons. By the
time we reached the San Francisquito Ranch I had
lost my cattle. I went down to this ranch and there
met Mr, and Mrs. Arcane getting ready to go to San
Pedro. We came north by way of Tejon pass and
the Kern River, not far from quite a large lake, and
reached the mines at last. I remember we killed a
very fat bear and tried out the grease, and with this
grease and some flour and dried apples Mrs. Erkson
made some pretty good pies which the miners were
glad to get at a dollar and even two dollars apiece.''

Mr. Erkson followed mining for about a year and
then went into other business until he came to Santa
Clara Valley and began farming near Alviso. He has.
been a highly respected citizen and progressive man.
He died in San Jose in the spring of 1893.

THE EXPERIENCE OF EDWARD COKER.

Edward Coker was one of a party of twenty-one men who left their wagons, being impatient of the slow progress made by the ox train, and organized a pack train in which they were themselves the burden carriers. They discarded everything not absolutely necessary to sustain life, packed all their provisions into knapsacks, bravely shouldered them and started off on foot from the desert to reach California by the shortest way.

Among those whom Mr. Coker can recollect are Capt. Nat. Ward, Jim Woods, Jim Martin of Missouri, John D. Martin of Texas, ''Old Francis,'' a French Canadian, Fred Carr, Negro ''Joe'' and some others from Coffeeville, Miss., with others from other states.

Mr. Coker related his experience to the Author somewhat as follows:—

One other of the party was a colored man who joined us at the camp when we left the families, he being the only remaining member of a small party who had followed our wagon tracks after we had tried to proceed south. This party was made up of a Mr. Culverwell who had formerly been a writer in a Government office at Washington, D. C , a man named Fish claiming to be a relative of Hamilton. Fish of New York, and another man whose name I never knew. He, poor fellow, arrived at our camp in a starving condition and died before our departure. The other two unfortunates ones died on the desert, and the colored man reported that he simply covered their remains with their blankets.

I well remember that last night in camp before we started with our knapsacks and left the families, for it was plain the women and children must go very slow, and we felt we could go over rougher and shorter roads on foot and get through sooner by going straight across the Sierra Nevada Mountains. Our condition was certainly appalling. We were without water, all on the verge of starvation, and the three poor cattle which yet remained alive were objects of pity. It seemed almost a crime to kill the poor beasts, so little real food was there left on their skeleton frames. They had been so faithful and had plodded along when there seemed no hope for them. They might still serve to keep the party from starvation.

It was at this camp that Mr. Ischam died. The night before our departure he came wandering into camp and presented such an awful appearance, simply a living skeleton of a once grand and powerful man. He must have suffered untold agony as he struggled on to overtake the party, starving and alone, with the knowledge that two of his companions had perished miserably of starvation in that unknown wilderness of rocks and alkali.

Our journey on foot through the mountains was full of adventure and suffering. On our arrival at the shores of Owen's Lake not a man of the party had a mouthful of food left in his pack, and to add to our difficultes we had several encounters with the hostile Indians. There was a fearful snow storm falling at Owen's Lake on the evening that we arrived there, and we could make no fire. The Indians gathered around us and we did not know exactly what to make of them, nor could we determine whether their intentions were good or bad. We examined the lake and determined to try to ford it, and thus set out by the light of the moon that occasionally peeped out from behind the clouds, while the red devils stood howling on the shore.

The following morning we found what was then known as the Fremont Trail, and by the advice of some friendly Indians who came into our camp, we kept the "big trail" for three days and came to Walker's Pass. While on this trail we were followed at night by a number of wild Indians, but we prudently avoided any collisions with them and kept moving on. Going on through the pass we followed the right hand branch of the trail, the left hand branch leading more to the south and across a wide plain. We soon came to a fair-sized stream, now known to be the south fork of the Kern River, which we followed until we came to its junction with a larger river, the two making the Kern River. Here we were taken across by some friendly Indians who left the Missions farther west during the Mexican war and took to their own village located at the foot of the Sierra Nevada Mountains. At this village we were on exhibition for several hours with an audience of five hundred people or more, of the red men, and on the following morning we commenced the ascent of the mountains again, the Indians furnishing us with a guide in the person of an old Pi-Ute. He brought us over the range, through the snow and over the bleak ridges, in the month of December, 1849, and we made our first camp at an Indian village in Tulare Valley, a few miles south of where Porterville now stands.

From this Indian village we walked on until we arrived at the present site of Millerton on the south bank of the San Joaquin River. Our sufferings were terrible from hunger, cold, and wet, for the rains were almost continual at this elevation, and we had been forced several times to swim. The sudden change from the dried-up desert to a rainy region was pretty severe on us. On our arrival at the San Joaquin River we found a camp of wealthy Mexicans who gave us a small amount of food, and seemed to want us to pass on that they might be rid of us. I can well believe that a company of twenty-one starving men was the cause of some disquietude to them. They gave us some hides taken from some of the cattle they had recently slain, and from these we constructed a boat and ferry rope in which we crossed the river, and then continued our journey to the mining camp on Aqua Frio, in Mariposa county.

It is very strange to think that since that time I have never met a single man of that party of twenty-one. I had kept quite full notes of the whole trip from the state of New York to the mines, and including my early mining experience up to the year 1851. Unfortunately this manuscript was burned at the Russ House fire in Fresno, where I also lost many personal effects."

In the year 1892 Mr. Coker was living in Fresno, or near that city, in fairly comfortable health, and it is to be hoped that the evening of his days, to which all the old pioneers are rapidly approaching, may be to him all that his brightest hopes pictured.

CHAPTER XV.

Having followed the various little parties into which the great train had resolved itself when it began to feel the pressure of suffering and trouble which came with contact with the desert, followed them in their various ways till they came through to the Pacific Slope, the travels and experiences of the Author are again resumed.

It will be remembered that he had rested at Los Angeles, working for Mr. Brier who had temporarily turned boarding house keeper, and finally made arrangements with some drovers to assist in taking a small stock of horses noith to the mines. His story is thus continued:—

We followed the wagon road which the companies that had gone on before had made, and got along very well. At night I acted independently—staked out my mule and ate my meal of dried meat and crackers—then joined the others around a large fire, and all seemed to enjoy the company. After a few days the two men who owned the horses proposed to me to let my mule carry the provisions, and they wanted me to ride one of their horses that was not carrying a pack, as they said it would keep it more gentle to ride it.

To please the old gentleman from Sacramento I agreed to the proposition, for I thought perhaps by being accomodating I could get along more pleasantly.

Thus we traveled on, over rolling hills covered with grass and wild flowers, and I was much pleased with all that I could see. For the first two days we did not pass a house, which shows how thinly settled the country was. Cattle were often seen, and sometimes horses, but people were very scarce. In time we went

down a long, steep hill, then across a wide valley that
supported a rank growth of vegetation, and came to a
Mission called San Buena Ventura (good luck.)
Here the men seemed scarce, but Indians and dogs
plenty. The houses were of the same sort as at Los
Angeles, except the church, all made of dried mud,
and never more than one story high.

As we journeyed along we came to the sea shore,
the grandest sight in the world to me, for I had never
before seen the ocean. What a wide piece of water it
was! Far out I could see small waves coming toward
the shore, and the nearer they came the faster they
seemed to rush and at last turned into great rollers
and breakers which dashed upon the rocks or washed
far up the sandy shore with a force that made the
ground tremble. There was no wind and I could not
see what it could be that so strangely agitated the
water. Here the waves kept coming, one after another, with as much regularity as the slow strokes of
a clock. This was the first puzzle the great sea pro-
pounded to me, and there under the clear blue sky
and soft air I studied over the ceaseless, restless motion and the great power that was always beating on
the shore. I tasted the water and found it exceedingly salt, and I did not see how anything could live
in it and not become in the condition of pickled pork
or fish. Where was the salt to make this mighty
brine pond, and why did it keep so when the great
rivers kept pouring in their torrents of fresh waters?
I did not understand, and these are some of the
thoughts that came to the boy who had been raised
upon the prairie, and to whom the great ocean was
indeed an unknown sea.

We followed along the road and in time came to
another village and Mission called Santa Barbara.
The village was near the shore, and the church farther

back upon an elevated piece of ground near the foot of
the mountain, overlooking the town and sea and much
of the country to the south, west and east. The
mountain was high and rough, and a point ran out
into the sea making a sort of harbor. This town was
built much as the others had been except perhaps the
Mission which seemed better. The roofs were as flat
as the floors and were covered with a sort of tar which
made them water-proof. The material of the houses
was sun-dried bricks, two feet long by one foot wide
and four to six inches thick. There was no lime in
the mortar of this mason work, and the openings in
the walls had iron bars across them instead of sash and
glass. Dried hides were spread upon the floors, and
there was a large earthen jar for water, but not a table,
bedstead or chair could be seen in the rooms we saw.
A man came along, rode right in at the door, turned
around and rode out again. The floor was so hard
that the horse's feet made no impression on it. Very
few men, quite a number of Indians, more women, and
a still larger quantity of dogs made up the inhabitants.

Leaving here the road led back from the sea shore
and over quite a level table land, covered with a big
growth of grass and some timber, and then down to
the sandy shore again where the mountain comes so
close that we were crowded down to the very water's
edge. Here the never-tiring waves were still following each other to the shore and dashing themselves to
pieces with such a noise that I felt awed to silence.
What a strange difference in two parts of the earth so
little distance from each other! Here was a waste of
waters, there was a waste of sands that may some time
have been the bottom of just such a dashing, rolling
sea as this. And here, between the two, was a fertile
region covered with trees, grass and flowers, and watered with brooks of fresh, sweet water. Paradise and

Desolation! They surely were not far apart. Here I saw some of the queer things that wash on shore, for we camped close to the beach.

It was a circumstance of great interest to me to see the sun slowly go down into the great ocean. Slowly and steadily it went, getting redder and redder as it went down, then it just touched the distant water and the waves dashed over more and more of its face till all was covered. Were it not for the strong, bright rays that still shot up across the sky one might think it was drowned forever, but in the morning it came up over the mountain top, having apparently made half the circuit of the globe.

Soon after this the road left the shore and turned into the mountains. Another Mission was on this road, Santa Ynez, situated in a beautiful place but apparently in decay, for the men had gone to the mines, leaving the Indians, women, and dogs as in other places. San Luis Obispo was another Mission similarly inhabited, but the surroundings did not seem so pleasant as those we had seen before, although it bore signs that considerable had been done. From here our road bore still more north and we had a long mountain to work over, very rocky, and in some places barren.

San Miguel was a Mission situated on the bank of a dry stream that evidently had seen plenty of water earlier in the season. The surrounding country was covered with scattering timber. Soledad was another place where there were some improvements, located on a small river, but nearly deserted like the other places. Prospects at the gold mines were so favorable that every man felt an irresistable desire to enrich himself, and so they left their families at the Missions and in the towns and rushed off to the mines. Nearly all of them expected to return by winter.

I think I must stop right here and tell about the
California carriages of which I had seen several at Los
Angeles and at the Missions along our road. The
first time I saw one it was a great curiousity, I assure
you. The wheels were cut off the end of a sycamore
log a little over two feet in diameter and each section
about a foot long. The axle was a piece of wood
eight inches square with a tongue fastened to it long
enough to be used with a yoke of oxen, and the ends
of the axle were roughly rounded, leaving something
of a shoulder. The wheels were retained in place by
a big lynch-pin. On the axle and tongue was a strong
frame of square hewed timbers answering for bed
pieces, and the bottom was of raw-hide tightly stretched, which covered the whole frame. Tall stakes at
each corner of the frame held up an awning in hot
weather. The yoke was fastened to the horns of the
oxen by strong, narrow strips of raw-hide, and the
tongue was fastened to the yoke in the same way.
The driver was generally an Indian, armed with a
small pole six or eight feet long, who marched on before, the oxen following after. I saw many a wagon
like this, the platform well filled up with women and
children, and a pack of dogs following along behind,
slowly rolling over the country, and this is the way
they traveled when they went visiting friends who
lived a few miles in the country. Sometimes the
wheels gave perfectly agonizing shrieks as they revolved, and when they made so much noise that their
strong Spanish nerves could stand it no longer, if
there was any green grass to be found the drivers
would crowd in a quantity around the axle, and there
was generally room for a good lot of it, to answer for
a lubricator.

We passed on from Soledad and shortly rose into the
table land we had seen for some time before us. From

here we could look north for a long way with no hill
or mountain in sight; but our road led along on the
east side of this treeless plain, so thickly covered with
grass that we recalled some of the old tales of the
grassy plains.   We passed a landholder's house on the
road, then crossed a range of low mountains and came
to the Mission of San Juan (St. John) situated near
the foot-hills, overlooking a level, rich appearing extent of valley land with a big vegetable growth all
over it; in some places wild mustard which stood
thickly and was from four to ten feet high.   I thought
what a splendid place it would be for the Yankees who
are fond of greens.

This was the first place since we left Los Angeles
where we could buy any kind of breadstuff, and we
were here enabled to get a change of diet, including
greens.   This seemed to be one end or side of another
valley, and as we went along it seemed to widen away
to the east; but our course was to the north, and we
followed the road.   The architecture of all the buildings except the churches was all the same, being built
of the sun dried adobes or bricks made by mixing up
a clay mud with tough grass and letting it get dry and
hard.   We saw the same kind of roof material as before, a sort of mineral tar which I supposed they must
find somewhere about.

I could imagine why the houses were built in this
way, for when the Jesuit missionaries first came in
they found the country occupied by Indians who used
their arrows to good effect, as they were jealous of all
outside occupation.   The early settlers evidently made
the walls of their dwellings thick and strong enough
to resist all kinds of weapons used by Indians.   They
could not set fire to them for they were fire proof and
arrow proof, and the hostile Indian could dance on the
roof without being able to get in or do any injury.

Thus the poor Indian was fairly beat and eventually became a better Indian.

The Indians of what is now Nevada and Arizona used to come over into these rich valleys and clandestinely capture a band of a hundred or more head of cattle or horses and make their escape. They were often followed by the herders, but if they did not overtake the thieves before they got into the deep cañons of the mountains, they would usually turn back and let them go rather than be led into ambush in some strange narrow place where escape would be impossible and they might be filled with arrows. No doubt the trail we had followed across the plains, where there were so many horses' bones, was one of these trails along which the thieving Indians took their booty which died upon the trip.

Our road from here was near the foot-hills on the west side of a level, grassy, thinly timbered valley, and as we advanced we noticed that the timber grew more plentiful and the trees larger, without much underbrush. We also noticed that the vegetation was ranker and no doubt the soil was very rich. We then came to a point where the mountain reaches out almost across the valley to meet the mountain on the east side. Here we found a gravelly creek with but little water, but as soon as we passed this point we saw the valley suddenly widening out, and beautiful groves of live oak trees scattered all around. The vegetation here was very rank, the mustard ten feet high in places, making it difficult to see out of the road. This was perhaps the strongest contrast to the arid desert that we had seen.

As we went on down the valley the hills seemed to stand farther and farther back as if to make more room for those who would soon settle in this fertile place, and we soon came in sight of the village or pueblo of

San Jose (St. Joseph) where we camped. Here we
learned that the two owners of the horses intended to
go to San Francisco instead of Sacramento, and as we
considered the former place a very poor one for a penniless person to go we concluded to break up the company camp and each do the best he could for himself,
for our objective point was the gold mines, and the
sooner we reached them the better.

The drovers who had been anxious to have us go
with them and help them now began to talk about a
settlement with us, as if they had done us great favors,
and called on the other fellows to help pay for their
board upon the way. When they came to me they
said my share would be an ounce. This struck me
hard, but they said I had ridden their horse all the
way and the charge was very low. I told them I had
fnrnished the most of the provisions I had eaten, and
my mule had packed a good load all the way, which
I considered worth as much as the use of the horse.
But they refused to allow me anything for the use of
the mule and became very urgent in their demand for
money.

These men were evidently of the tribe of Skinflint,
who had no souls, or they would not have attempted
to rob an almost penniless emigrant in this way of the
last few dollars he had, and all the hope he had of
reaching the mines. I did not desire to give up to
such narrow principles as this and hesitated, but they
were bound to have the money or make a quarrel, and
talked pretty loud of the way they collected debts in
Sacramento, so that to avoid trouble and get out of
the clutches of such mean scoundrels as these I counted out sixteen dollars, almost every cent I had, and
reluctantly gave them to my enemy. I immediately
mounted my mule, and without stopping to say good-
bye rode off. I may have quoted a part of the speech

Capt. Hunt made when the party wanted to leave the
trail and take the cut-off, especially that part where
he alluded to their going to h—l. I very much fear
the little piety my mother taught me was badly strain-
ed on that occasion, and I thought of a good many
swear words if I did not say them, which I suppose is
about as bad. I could see how cunningly they had
managed to get me to ride their horse that it might
serve as the foundation for a claim on me for about all
the money I had in the world.

I hitched my mule in the edge of the town and went
in to look at the place. The houses were situated
very much as in other places we had come through—
scattered around over much ground and built low, but
had a different style of roof, a peaked or sloping one,
and covered with half round tile two feet or more long
and an inch thick. One course of these would be laid
with the hollow side up, and then a course with the
hollow side down, covering the joints of the lower
course. This allowed the air to circulate freely and
was proof against rain. I saw no flat roofs such as I
had seen down along the coast. I saw one gambling
house and about all the men in town were gathered
there, and some women, too. This was the busi-
est place in town and situated near the plaza. This
was the largest town I had yet been in. There seemed to be plenty of women and lots of dogs, but the
men were as scarce as they had been in any of the
towns—gone to the gold mines to make a stake. I
took in the sights pretty well, and there were a great
many new things for me to see, and when pretty well
satisfied concluded I would go back to my mule and
camp in some place just out of town for the night.

Before I reached my animal whom should I meet
but my old traveling companion John Rogers whom I
thought to be a hundred miles away by this time.

We shook hands heartily and he told me that Bennett, Moody and Skinner were camped not far off, and he was still with them.   He wore a pair of blue overalls, a blue woolen shirt and the same little narrow rimmed hat he had worn so long.   I observed, too, that he was barefoot, and told him I had a dollar or two which he could take and get some shoes.   He said it was no use for there was not a pair of shoes in the town to buy, and he had not found any material of which he could make himself a pair of mocassins.   I told him how I had been swindled coming up, and he was about as angry as I had been.   I think if I had known that my friend John Rogers had been so near I should have bidden the rascals an unceremonious good-bye and we would have been able to hold our own on a claim for the services of myself and mule.

We went up to the place where our people were camped, perhaps a mile above town on the bank of a river, nearly dry, but where plenty of wood, water and grass were at hand; such a place as we had looked for in vain for many a weary day upon the desert. This was as far above Death Valley as a king above a pauper, and we hoped never to see such a country again.

In camp we talked about moving on to the mines. Rogers said he was going to start next day, and in answer to exclamations of surprise that he should start off alone, he said that some fellows camped a little way down the river were going to start and he had made arrangements to go with them, as the Bennett party would not go yet for a week.   In the morning he shook hands and bade us good-bye and good luck, and started off down the river bank, lost to us, as it proved, for many years.

The next day as we were all sitting on the ground I felt a sort of moving of the earth under me and heard

a rumbling sound that seemed very queer. It seemed
there was a motion also to the trees around us. We
all started and looked a little frightened, and Skinner
said he believed it was an earthquake, for he said he
could see the motion in a sort of wave. It was gone
in half a minute. Moody said:—"How do you like
California now?" I said I thought this part of it was
a pretty good place for there was plenty of wood water
and grass, and that was better than we had seen in
some places.

He then went on to say that he had heard Mr. Bennett's story of their sufferings and narrow escape from
death, and it was the most wonderful story he had
ever heard. He said the idea of Mrs. Bennett walking over such a country for twenty-two days was almost beyond belief, for he would not have thought
her able to walk one-third the distance. He never
knew before how much women could do when they
were called to do it, and they proved in emergencies
to be as tough as any body. He said if he ever got
back home he should move to give them all the rights
and privileges of men for sure.

One day I mounted my mule for a ride to the eastern foothills, and sat down on a little incline and overlooked the valley, a beautiful landscape, while my
mule cropped the rich grasses in a circle described by
the rope which confined him. I was always a great
admirer of nature, and as I sat there alone I could see
miles on miles of mammoth mustard waving in the
strong breeze which came down over the San Francisco Bay just visible to the northward, and on the
mountain summits to the west could see tall timber
reaching up into the deep blue of the sky. It was a
real contented comfort to be thus in the midst of luxuriance and beauty, and I enjoyed it, coming as it did
at the end of the long and dreary road I had been trav-

eling for the past twelve months. Up the Platte; across the Rockies; down the Green River cañons in my canoe; across the mountains to Salt Lake; out over the "Rim of the Basin," and across the desert, guided only by the fact that we knew the Pacific Ocean was to the west of us, and choosing our road as best we could in view of the lofty, snow-clad, impassible mountains; seeing thirteen of our comrades lie down never to rise again, and, when hope and strength were almost gone, to suddenly come out into a fertile region on the seventh of March, 1850. How I wished the fellows who slept in Death Valley could have seen this view. The change from all that barrenness and desolation to this beautiful, fertile country, covered with wild flowers and luxuriant live oaks, was as strong a contrast as one could imagine a sudden coming from purgatory to paradise in the space of a single hour.

I waked up from my dreamy thoughts, mounted my mule and rode to camp. As I rode along the nimble ground squirrel, with his keen black eye, would climb to the top of the high mustard stalks to get a better view and, suspicious of an enemy within his almost undisputed territory, disappear in a wink to his safe underground fortress. Fat cattle and horses would appear before me a moment, and then, with a wild look and high heads, dash through the tall mustard out of sight.

Next day my trip was toward the western hills, and before I came to them was confronted with an extensive stretch of chaparral brush, absolutely impenetrable, which I must go around or stop my progress in this direction. These thickets were a regular paradise for grizzly bears, for within the protection of this matted and thorny growth he is as safe as is the soldier in the rocky fort of Gibralter. I soon found a

way around the brush and rose high enough so that a
backward look over the valley was charming, quite as
much so as the eastern side. I wandered over the
grassy hills covered with great scattering oaks, and
came to a grove of mammoth trees, six feet or more
in diameter, with tops reaching two hundred or three
hundred feet toward the blue sky. They seemed to
me to be a kind of cedar, and were far larger and taller
than any trees I had ever seen in the forests of Vermont, Michigan or Wisconsin, and in my long journey from the East the route had been principally
through a country devoid of good timber. A stranger
in a strange land, everything was new and wonderful.
After satisfying my inquiring mind I returned to camp
again, and soon learned that my newly discovered
trees were the famous redwoods, so greatly prized for
their valuable qualities.

Taking the most direct course to camp I came, when
within two or three miles of San Jose, to a large extent of willows so thick, and so thickly woven together with wild blackberry vines, wild roses and
other thorny plants, that it appeared at first as if I
never could get through. But I found a winding trail
made by the cattle through the bushes and mustard,
and this I followed, being nearly scared occasionally
by some wild steers as they rushed off through the
thickets. I got through safely, though it would have
been difficult to escape a wild, enraged steer, or a
grizzly had I met him face to face even with a rifle in
hand. I could see nowhere but by looking straight
up, for the willows were in places fifty feet high and a
foot in diameter. The willows where I came from
were mere bushes, and these astonished me. This
bit of brush is still locally known as "The Willows,"
but the trees are all gone. and the ground thickly covered with orchards and fine residences, the land sell-

ing at from one thousand to two thousand dollars per acre.

The sun rose without a cloud, and a little later the sea breeze from the bay blew gently over the valley, making the climate perfectly delightful in its temperate coolness, a true paradise on earth it seemed to me, if I was able to judge or set a value upon so beautiful a spot; and surely I had seen all sorts, good and poor, desert and valley, mountain and plain.

But I was poor in purse, and resolved I would seek first the gold mines and secure gold enough to buy a piece of this valley afterward.

When I had seen what was to be seen about San Jose I had a talk with my friends and found that Mr. Bennett favored going on to the mines at once and that Moody and Skinner thought they would remain a little while at least.

I went along in company with Bennett, and when we got a little way from San Jose, on the road to the Mission, the road seemed walled in on both sides with growing mustard ten or twelve feet high and all in blossom. How so much mustard could grow, and grow so large, I could not understand. I had seen a few plants in the gardens or fields which people used for greens, and here seemed to be enough to feed the nation, if they liked mustard greens.

The second day out we passed the big church at Mission San Jose and soon left the valley and turned into the mountains and when part way over we came to a stream which we followed up and came out into Livermore valley, where we found a road to follow. Houses were scarce, and we camped a mile or so before we got to the Livermore ranch buildings. There was very little sign of life about the place, and we soon went out of the valley and into the mountains again.

The first sign of settlement we saw when part way

through the mountains was a stone corral, but no house or other improvements. The next place was a small house made of willow poles set in the ground and plastered over with mud. This rejoiced in the name of "Mountain House." This wayside inn looked like a horse thief's glory; only one or two men, a quarter of an elk hanging on a pole, and no accmodations for man or beast. There was very little water, nothing to sell as well as nothing wanted. On the summits of the mountains as we passed through we saw, standing like guards, many large buck elks.

It was now fifteen miles to the San Joaquin river, and a level plain lay before us. When our road turned into the river bottom we found the water too deep to get through safely, so we concluded to go on and try to find some place where we could cross. On our way droves of antelopes could be seen frolicking over the broad plains, while in the distance were herds of elk winding their way from the mountains towards the river for water. When far away their horns were the first things visible, and they much resembled the dry tops of dead pine trees, but a nearer view showed them to us as the proud monarchs of the plain.

When we came up opposite the mouth of the Merced river we concluded to try again to cross. The river here, as below, was out of its banks, and the overflowed part was quite wide which we had to pass through before we could reach the river proper.

I waded in ahead of the team and sounded the depth of the river so as not to get in too deep water, and avoid if possible such accidents as might otherwise occur. Sometimes the water was up to the wagon bed and it looked a little doubtful of our getting through in safety, but we made it at last.

We found a narrow strip of dry land along the river bank. A town was on the east side of the San Joaquin

river, just below where the Merced river came in.   I
think this place was called Merced City.   This so-
called city contained but one residence, a tent occupied by the ferryman.   We crossed the sluggish stream
and for the privilege paid the ferryman ten dollars for
toll.   The road was not much used and the ferry business seemed lonesome.

Here we camped for the night.   The mosquitoes
soon found us, and they were all very hungry and
had good teeth.   They annoyed me so that I moved
my lodgings to the ferryboat, but here they quickly
found me and troubled me all night.   These insects
were the first I had seen since I left the lower Platte
river, and I thought them as bad as on the Mississippi.

From here the road led up the Merced river near
the bottom, and as we came near groves of willows,
big, stately elk would start out and trot off proudly
into the open plains to avoid danger.   These proud,
big-horned monarchs of the plains could be seen in
bunches scattered over the broad meadows, as well as
an equal amount of antelope.   They all seemed to fear
us, which was wise on their part, and kept out of rifle
shot.   As were not starving as we were once, I did
not follow them out on the open plain, for I thought I
could get meat when we were more in need.

We followed up the river bottom and saw not a single house until we reached the road leading from
Stockton to the Mariposa mines, where we found a
ferry and a small store.   Here we learned that some
men were mining a few miles up the river, so we drove
on until we found a little work being done in a dry
gulch near the river bank.   We made our camp at this
spot and had plenty of wood, water and grass.   We
found there was something to be learned in the art of
gold mining.   We had no tools nor money, and had
never seen a speck of native gold and did not know

how to separate it from the dirt nor where to search
for it. We were poor, ignorant emigrants. There
were two or three men camped here. One of them
was more social than the rest and we soon got acquainted. His name was Williams, from Missouri.
He came down to the river with a pan of dirt, and
seeing me in my ignorance trying to wash some as
well, he took the pan from me and very kindly showed
me how to work so as to let the dirt go and save the
gold. When he had the pan finished a few small,
bright scales remained. These to me were curious
little follows and I examined them closely and concluded there was a vast difference between gold and lead
mining. Williams became more friendly and we told
him something about our journey across the plains,
and he seemed to think that we deserved a good claim.
He went to a dry gulch where a Spaniard was working and told him that all of California, now that the
war was over, belonged to Americans and he must
leave. Williams had his gun in his hand and war
might follow, so Mr. Spaniard left and his claim was
presented to Bennett and myself.

Williams had been twice to Santa Fe from Missouri
and had learned the Spanish language and could swear
at them by note if necessary. We now began work
almost without tools, but our ground we had to work
was quite shallow and Williams helped us out by loan-
ing us some of his tools at times. We soon succeeded
in scratching together some of the yellow stuff and I
went down to the store and bought a pan for five dollars, a shovel for ten dollars, and a poor pick cost me
ten dollars more. This took about two ounces of my
money.

We now worked harder than ever for about three
weeks, but we could not save much and pay such
high prices as were charged. Our gulch claim was

soon worked out, and as the river had fallen some we tried the bar, but we could only make four or five dollars a day, and the gold was very fine and hard to save. We bought a hind quarter of an elk and hung it up in a tree and it kept fresh till all of it was eaten.

Some others came and took up claims on the bar, and as the prospects were not as good as was wished, three of us concluded to go and try to find a better place. The next day was Sunday and all lay in bed late. Before I rose I felt something crawling on my breast, and when I looked I found it to be an insect, slow in motion, resembling a louse, but larger. He was a new emigrant to me and I wondered what he was. I now took off my pants and found many of his kind in the seams. I murdered all I could find, and when I got up I told Williams what I had found. He said they hurt nobody and were called *piojos*, more commonly known as body lice.

We started on our prospecting tour and went northeast to a place now called Big Oak Flat. This was at the head of a small stream and there were several small gulches that emptied into it that paid well. This flat was all taken up and a ditch was cut through to drain it. A ship load of gold was expected to be found when it was worked. A small town of tents had been pitched on both sides of the flat. One side was occupied by gamblers, and many games were constantly carried on and were well patronized. On the opposite side of the flat were many small tents, and around on the hillside some mules and jacks were feeding. One of the little long-eared donkeys came down among the tents and went in one and commenced eating flour from the sack. The owner of the flour ran to the tent, took his shot gun and fired a load of buck-shot into the donkey's hams. The animal reeled and seemed shot fatally. I now looked for

a battle to commence, but the parties were more reasonable.   The price of the animal was fully paid, and
no blood shed as I expected there surely would be.

We now prospected further east, but nothing good
enough was found.   The place we looked over was
where the town of Garota now stands.   We concluded
to go back, have a council, and go somewhere else.
On our way back we stopped to get dinner.   While I
was around the fire, barefooted, I felt something crawl
up my instep, and it proved to be another of those
piojos of Williams'.   I now thought these torments
must be all over this country.

Gold dust was used to transact all business; all the
coin was in the hands of the gentlemen gamblers.
Most miners found it necessary to have a small pair
of scales in the breast pocket to weigh the dust so as
not to have to trust some one who carried lead weights
and often got more than his just dues.   Gold dust was
valued at sixteen dollars an ounce.

We now thought it would be best for two of us to
take our mules and go down in the small hills and try
to get some elk meat to take with us, as our route
would be mostly through the unsettled part of the
country, and no provisions could likely be procured,
so Mr. Bradford of New Orleans and myself took our
mules and went down where the hills were low and
the game plenty.   We camped in a low ravine, staked
out our mules and staid all night without a fire, believing that when we woke in the early morning some of
the many herd of elk then in sight would be near us
at daylight, and we could easily kill all we wanted
without leaving camp; but we were disappointed.
Hundreds of the big-horned fellows were in sight, but
none in rifle shot, and there was no chance for us to
get any nearer to them.   We got near a couple of antelope and Mr. Bradford, who was a brag shot and

had the best gun, proposed to kill them as we stood.
The larger of the two was on his side and much nearer
than the smaller one, but we fired together just as we
stood.   Bradford's antelope ran off unhurt: mine fell
dead in its tracks.   Bradford bragged no more about
his fine gun and superior marksmanship.

We went back to camp with the little we had killed
and soon got ready to start north.   Bennett was to go
with his team to Sacramento and wait there until he
heard from us.

Four of us, mounted on mules, now started on our
journey along the foothills without a road.   We struck
the Tuolumne river at a ferry.   The stream was high
and rapid and could not be forded, so we had to patronize the ferryman, and give him half an ounce apiece.
We thought such charges on poor and almost penniless emigrants were unjust.

The point we were seeking to reach was a new discovery called Gold Lake on Feather River, where
many rich gulches that emptied into it had been
worked, and the lake was believed to have at least a
ship load of gold in it.   It was located high in the
mountains and could be easily drained and a fortune
soon obtained if we got there in time and said nothing
to anyone we might meet on the road.   We might
succeed in getting a claim before they were all taken
up.   We followed along the foothills without a road,
and when we came to the Stanislaus River we had to
patronize a ferry and pay half an ounce each again.
We thought their scale weights were rather heavy
and their ferrymen well paid.

We continued along the foothills without any trail
until we struck the road from Sacramento to Hang-
town.   This sounded like a bad name for a good village, but we found it was fittingly named after some
ugly devils who were hanged there.   The first house

that we came to on this road was the Mormon Tavern.
Here were some men playing cards for money, and
two boys, twelve or fourteen years old, playing poker
for the same and trying in every way to ape the older
gamblers and bet their money as freely and swear as
loud as the old sports. All I saw was new and strange
to me and became indelibly fixed on my mind. I had
never before seen such wicked boys, and the men paid
no attention to these fast American boys. I began to
wonder if all the people in California were like these,
bad and wicked.

Here we learned that Gold Lake was not as rich as
reported, so we concluded to take the road and go to
Coloma, the place where gold was first found on the
American River.

We camped at Coloma all night. Mr. Bradford got
his mule shod and paid sixteen dollars, or in the mining phrase, an ounce of gold dust. I visited the small
town and found that the only lively business place in
it was a large gambling house, and I saw money (gold
dust) liberally used—sometimes hundreds of dollars
bet on a single card. When a few hundred or thous-
and were lost more would be brought on. The purse
would be set in the center of the table and the owners
would take perhaps twenty silver dollars or checks,
and when they were lost the deposited purse would
be handed to the barkeeper, the amount weighed out
and the purse returned. When the purse was empty
a friend of the better would bring another, and so the
game went on almost in silence. The game called
Monte seemed to be the favorite. How long these
sacks of gold lasted or who eventually got the whole
I never knew. This was a new country with new
people, and many seemed to be engaged in a business
that was new, strange and hazardous. The final result of all this was what puzzled me.

We now followed the road up the mountain to
Georgetown. Here was a small village on the summit of the ridge and it seemed to be in a prosperous
mining section. After some inquiry about a good
place to work we concluded to go down a couple of
miles northeast of town on Cañon creek and go to
work if vacant ground could be found. There was a
piece of creek bottom here that had not been much
worked. Georgia Flat above had been worked and
paid well, and the Illinois and Oregon cañons that
emptied into the bottom here were rich, so we concluded to locate in the bottom. Claims here in the flat
were only fifteen feet square. I located one and my
notice told others that I would go to work on it as
soon my partner came from Sacramento. I sent my
partner, Mr. Bennett a note telling him to come up.

While waiting for Mr. Bennett I took my pan and
butcher knife and went into a dry gulch out of sight
of the other campers and began work. As the ground
was mostly bare bed rock by scratching around I succeeded in getting three or four pans of dirt a day.
The few days I had to wait for Bennett I made eight
dollars a day until my claim was worked out.

I then went to Georgetown to meet Bennett and
family, and soon after my arrival they came well and
safe. All of them, even to the faithful camp dog, Cuff,
were glad to see me. Old Cuff followed me all around
town, but when we got ready to start for camp the
dog was gone and could not be found. Some one had
hidden him away knowing he could not be gotten any
other way, for six ounces would not have bought him.
We had raised him in Wisconsin, made him a good
deer dog, and with us he had crossed the dry and
sandy deserts. He had been a great protection to
Bennett's children on the plains, and company for us
all.

We now located claims on the creek bottom. The channel of the creek was claimed by Holman of Alabama and the Helms brothers of Missouri. They had turned the stream into a ditch in order to work the bed of the stream, believing that their claims had all the gold in them. Our claims joined theirs.

Mr. W. M. Stockton, who left his family in Los Angeles, came with Mr. Bennett and went to work with us. As everything here was very high we concluded to let Mr. Stockton take the team and go to Sacramento for provisions for our own use. Flour and meat were each fifty cents a pound, potatoes twenty-five cents a pound and onions one dollar and twenty-five cents each. Onions and potatoes eaten raw were considered very necessary to prevent and cure scurvy, which was quite a common complaint. Whiskey, if not watered, cost one dollar a drink.

Our claims were about ten feet deep. The bottom was wet and a pump needed, so we went to a whip saw-mill and got four narrow strips one by three and one by five and twelve feet long, paying for them by weight, the price being twelve cents a pound. Out of these strips we made a good pump by fixing a valve at the end and nailing a piece of green rawhide on a pole, which answered for a plunger, and with the pump set at forty-five degrees it worked easily and well. One man could easily keep the water out and we made fair wages.

In the creek bottom Mr. Bush of Missouri had a saloon. The building was made mainly of brush, with a split piece for a counter, and another one for a shelf for his whiskey keg, a box of cigars, a few decks of cards and half a dozen glasses, which made up the entire stock of trade for the shop. In front was a table made of two puncheons with a blanket thrown over all, and a few rough seats around. There was no roof except the brush, and through the dry season none was needed except for shade.

There was also at this place five brothers by the name of Helms, also from Missouri. Their names were Jim, Davenport, Wade, Chet and Daunt. These men, with Mr. Holman, owned the bed of the stream, and their ground proved to be quite wet and disagreeable to work. Mr. Holman could not well stand to work in the cold water, so he asked the privilege of putting in a hired man in his place, which was agreed to. He then took up a claim for himself outside of the other claims, and this proved to be on higher bed rock and dry, and paid even better than the low claims where the Helms brothers were at work. This was not what the Helms boys considered exactly fair, as Holman seemed to be getting rich the fastest, and as there was no law to govern them they held a free country court of their own, and decided the case to suit themselves; so they ordered Holman to come back and do his own work. No fault was found with the hired man but what he did his work well enough, but they were jealous and would not be bound by their agreement.

But this decision did not satisfy all parties, and it was agreed to submit the case to three men, and I was chosen one of them. We held Court on the ground and heard both sides of the story, after which we retired to the shade of a bunch of willows to hold council over the matter with the result that we soon came to a decision in favor of Mr. Holman. About this time one of the Helms boys began to quarrel with Holman and grew terribly mad, swearing all kinds of vengeance, and making the cañon ring with the loudest kind of Missouri oaths. Finally he picked up a rock to kill Holman, but the latter was quick with his pistol, a single shot duelling piece, and as they were

not more than ten feet apart Helms would have had a
hole in him large enough for daylight to shine through
if the pistol had not missed fire. We stopped the
quarrel and made known our decision, whereupon
Helms went off muttering vengeance.

We now went back to our work again at our claims,
mine being between Helms' cabin and the saloon.
Holman stopped to talk a little while on my claim,
while I was down below at work, and soon Helms
came back again in a terrible rage, stopping on the
opposite side of the hole from Holman, swearing long
and loud, and flourishing a big pistol with which he
threatened to blow Holman into purgatory. He was
so much enraged that he fairly frothed at the mouth
like a rabid dog. The men were about twenty feet
apart, and I at the bottom of the hole ten feet below,
but exactly between them. It seemed to me that I
was in some little danger for Helms had his big pistol
at full cock, and as it pointed at me quite as often as
it did at anybody, I expect I dodged around a little to
keep out of range. Helms was terribly nervous, and
trembled as he cursed, but Holman was cool and drew
his weapon deliberately, daring Helms to raise his
hand or he would kill him on the instant. Helms
now began to back off, but carefully kept his eye on
Holman and continued his abuse as he went on to the
saloon to get something to replenish his courage.
Holman, during the whole affair, talked very calmly
and put considerable emphasis into his words when he
dared Helms to make a hostile motion. He was a true
Alabamian and could be neither scared nor driven.
He soon sold out, however, and went to a more con-
genial camp for he said these people were cowardly
enough to waylay and kill him unawares.

Soon after this unpleasantness a man and wife who
lived in Georgetown came into notice, and while the

man made some money mining his wife did a good stroke of business washing for the boys who paid her a dollar a shirt as laundry fees. As she began to make considerable money the bigger, if not better, half of this couple began to feel quite rich and went off on a drunk, and when his own money was spent he went to his wife for more, but she refused him, and he, in his drunken rage, picked up a gun near by and shot her dead.

All of a sudden the Helms boys and others gathered at the saloon, took drinks all around, and did a good deal of swearing, which was the biggest portion of the proceedings of the meeting; and then they all started off toward town, swearing and yelling as they struggled up the steep mountain side—a pack of reckless, back-woods Missourians who seemed to smell something bloody.

It was near night when they all came back and gathered around the saloon again. They were all in unusual good humor as they related the adventures of the afternoon, and bragged of their bravery and skill in performing the little job they had just completed, which consisted in taking the murderer out to the first convenient oak tree, and with the assistance of some sailors in handling the ropes, hoisting the fellow from the ground with a noose around his neck, and to the "Heave, yo heave" of the sailor boys, pulling the rope that had been passed over an elevated limb. They watched the suspended body till the last spark of life went out, and then went back to town leaving the corpse hanging for somebody else to cut down and bury. They whooped and yelled at the top of their voices as they came down along the mountain trail, and at the saloon they related to the crowd that had gathered there how they had helped to hang the——— ———who had killed his wife. They said justice must

be done if there was no law, and that no man could
kill a woman and live in California. They imagined
they were very important individuals, and veritable
lords of Creation.

These miners, many of them, were inveterate gamblers and played every night till near day-light, with
no roof over them, and their only clothes a woolen
shirt and overalls which must have been a little scanty
in the cool nights which settled down over the mouht-
ain camp; but they bore it all in their great desire for
card playing.

Near by there were three men who worked and
slept together, every night dividing the dust which
each put into a purse at the head of his bed. One day
the news came to the saloon that one of the purses
had been stolen. The Helms boys talked it over and
concluded that as one of the men had gone to town, he
might know something about the lost dust; so they
went to town and there, after a little search, found
their man in a gambling house. After a little while
they invited him to return to camp with them, and all
started together down the mountain; but when about
half way down they halted suddenly under an oak
tree and accused their man of knowing where his partner's money was. This he strongly denied, and was
very positive in his denial till he felt the surprise of a
rope around his neck, with the end over a limb, and
beginning to haul pretty taut in a direction that would
soon elevate his body from the ground, when he weak-
ened at their earnestness and asked them to hold on a
minute. As the rope slackened he owned up he had
the dust and would give it up if they would not send
the news to his folks in Missouri. This was agreed
to and the thief was advised to leave at once for some
distant camp, or they might yet expose him. He was
not seen afterward.

The boys bragged a good deal of their detective ability after this, and said that a little hanging would make a — thief tell the truth even if it did not make an honest man of him, and that a thief would be lucky if he got through with them and saved his life. Their law was "Hanging for stealing."

The Helms brothers were said to be from western Missouri, and in early days were somewhat of the border ruffian order, and of course preferred to live on the frontier rather than in any well regulated society. As the country became settled and improved around them they moved on. A school house was an indication that the country was getting too far advanced for them.

They crossed the plains in 1849 and began mining operations near Georgetown in Placer county. It was well known that they were foremost in all gambling, and in taking a hand in any excitement that came up, and as a better class of miners came in they moved on, keeping ahead with the prospectors, and just out of reach of law and order. If anyone else committed a crime they were always quite eager to be on the vigilance committee, and were remarkably happy when punishing a wrong-doer. When any of their number was suspected it was generally the case that they moved quickly on and so escaped. It was reported, however, that one of their number was in the hands of the vigilance committee and hanged in Montana.

After a time, it is said, they went down to southern California and settled on the border of the Colorado desert, about seventy-five miles east of San Diego, in a mountainous and desert region. Here they found a small tribe of Indians, and by each marrying a squaw they secured rights equal to any of them in the occupation of the land. This was considered pretty sharp practice, but it suited them and they became big chiefs and midecine men, and numerous dusky descendants grew up around them.

It is said that their property consists of extensive pasture lands on which they raise cattle, and that they always go well armed with pistol, rifle and riata. It is said that some of the Indians undertook to claim that the Helms brothers were intruders, but that in some mysterious way accidents happened to most of them and they were left without any serious opposition.

They are very hospitable and entertaining to people who visit them, provided they do not know too much about the men or their former deeds or history. In this case ignorance is bliss and it is folly, if not dangerous, to be too wise. They have made no improvements, but live in about the same style as the Indians and about on a level with them morally and intellectually.

There may be those who know them well, but the writer only knows them by hearsay and introduces them as a certain type of character found in the early days.

As I was now about barefoot I went to town to look for boots or shoes. There were no shoes, and a pair of the cheapest boots I found hanging at the door were priced to me at two ounces. This seemed a wonderful sum for a pair of coarse cow-hide boots that would sell in the state for two dollars and fifty cents; but I had to buy them at the price or go barefoot.

While rambling around town I went into a round tent used as a gambling saloon. The occupants were mostly men, and one or two nice appearing ladies, but perhaps of doubtful reputation. The men were of all classes—lawyer, doctors, preachers and such others as wanted to make money without work. The miners, especially sailors, were eager to try to beat the games.

While I was here the table was only occupied by a sailor lying upon it and covered with a green blanket. All at once the fellow noticed a large *piojo* walking slowly across the table, and drawing his sheath knife made a desperate stab at him, saying "You kind of a deck hand can't play at this game."

Our claims, by this time, were nearly worked out, and I thought that I had upward of two thousand dollars in gold, and the pile looked pretty big to me. It seemed to me that these mines were very shallow and would soon be worked out, at least in a year or two. I could not see that the land would be good for much for farming when no irrigation could be easily got, and the Spanish people seemed to own all the best land as well as the water; so that a poor fellow like myself would never get rich at farming here.

Seeing the matter in this light I thought it would be best to take my money and go back to Wisconsin where government land was good and plenty, and with even my little pile I could soon be master of a good farm in a healthy country, and I would there be rich enough. Thus reasoning I decided to return to Wisconsin, for I could not see how a man could ever be a successful farmer in a country where there were only two seasons, one wet and the other long and dry.

I went out and hunted up my mule which I had turned out to pasture for herself, and found her entirely alone. After a little coaxing I caught her and brought her with me to camp, where I offered her for sale. She was sleek and fat and looked so well that Helms said that if I could beat him shooting he would buy both mule and gun; so three or four of us tried our skill. My opponents boasted a good deal of their superior marksmanship, but on the trial, which began at short range, I beat them all pretty badly. Helms was as good as his word and offered me twelve ounces

for my gun and mule, which I took. I thought a
great deal of my fat little one-eyed mule, and I thought
then, as I think now, how well she did her part on
the fearful road to and from Death Valley.

Helms was now going to the valley to have a winter's hunt, for here the snow would fall four feet deep
and no mining work could be done till spring, when
he would return and work his claim again.

I now had all in my pocket, and when I got ready
to go Mrs. Bennett was much affected at knowing that
I would now leave them, perhaps never to return to
them again. She clasped me in her arms, embraced
me as she would her own son, and said "Good luck
to you—God bless you, for I know that you saved all
our lives. I don't suppose you will ever come back,
but we may come back to Wisconsin sometime and
we will try to find a better road than the one we came
over. Give my best regards to all who inquire after
us." She shook my hand again and again with earnest
pressure, and cried and sobbed bitterly. As I climbed
the mountain she stood and watched me so long
as I was in sight, and with her handkerchief waved a
final adieu. I was myself much affected at this parting, for with Mr. and Mrs. Bennett had been really a
home to me; she had been to me as a mother, and it
was like leaving a home fireside to go away from
them. I was now starting out among strangers, and
those I should meet might be the same good friends as
those whom I had left behind. Mr. Bennett and I
had for many years been hunting companions; I had
lived at his house in the East, and we never disagreed
but had always been good friends. I had now a traveling companion whose home was in Iowa Co., Wis.,
where I had lived for several years, and we went
along together by way of Greenwood where there was
a small mining town built of tents, many of which

were used as gambling places. These places were occupied by gentlemen, some of whom wore white shirts to distinguish them, I presume, from the common herd of miners from whom they won their dust.

We crossed the American River at Salmon Falls, and walked thence on to Sacramento City, which was the largest town we had seen on the coast. The houses were all small wooden ones, but business seemed to be brisk, and whiskey shops and gambling houses plenty. One game played with three cards, called three card Monte, was played openly on the streets, with goods boxes for tables. Every one who came along was urged to bet by the dealer who would lay out his cards face up so all could see them, then turn them over and shuffle them and say "I'll bet six ounces that no one can put his finger on the queen." I watched this a while and saw that the dealer won much oftener than he lost, and it seemed to be a simple and easy way to make a living when money was plenty.

We strolled around town looking at the sights, and the different business places, the most lively of which had plenty of music inside, lots of tables with plenty of money on them, and many questionable lady occupants. These business places were liberally patronized and every department flourishing, especially the bar. Oaths and vulgar language were the favorite style of speech, and very many of the people had all the whiskey down them that they could conveniently carry.

We got through the town safely and at the river we found a steamboat bound for San Francisco and the fare was two ounces. The runners were calling loudly for passengers, and we were told we could never make the trip any cheaper for they had received a telegram from below saying that no boat would come up again

for two days. I said to him "I can't see your telegram. Where is it?" At this he turned and left us.
He had thought, no doubt, that miners were green
enough to believe anything. In the course of an hour
the smoke of a steamer was seen down the river, and
this beat out the runners who now offered passage for
half an ounce.

At this time there was no telegraph and the delay
was a lucky one for us. We took passage and went
to San Francisco that night, where we put up at a
cheap tavern near where the Custom House now
stands.

Here we learned that we would have to wait two
days before a ship would sail for Panama, and during
this time we surveyed the town from the hill-tops and
walked all over the principal streets. It was really a
small, poorly built, dirty looking place, with few
wharves, poor, cheap hotels, and very rough inhabitants. There were lots of gambling houses full of tables holding money, and the rooms filled with pretty
rough looking people, except the card dealers, most of
whom wore white shirts, and a few sported plug hats.
There was also a "right smart sprinkling" of ladies
present who were well dressed and adorned with rich
jewelry, and their position seemed to be that of paying teller at the gambling tables.

The buildings seemed to be rather cheap, although
material was very expensive, as well as labor, mechan-
ics of all sorts getting as much as ten or twelve dollars
per day for work. Coin seemed to be scarce, and a
great deal of the money needed on the gambling tables
was represented by iron washers, each of which represented an ounce of gold.

I noticed some places in the streets where it was
muddy and a narrow walk had been made out of boxes
of tobacco, and sometimes even bacon was used for

the same purpose. Transportation from the city to
the mines was very slow and made by schooner. Ship
loads of merchandise had arrived and been unloaded,
and the sailors having run away to the mines, everything except whiskey and cards was neglected. Whiskey sold at this place for fifty cents a drink.

A man at the tavern where we stopped tried hard to
sell me a fifty-vara lot there in the edge of the mud
(near where the Custom House now stands) for six
hundred dollars. I thought this a pretty high price
and besides such a lot was no use to me, for I had
never lived in town and could not so easily see the
uses to which such property could be put. It seemed
very doubtful to me that this place would ever be
much larger or amount to much, for it evidently depended on the mines for a support, and these were so
shallow that it looked as if they would be worked out
in a short time and the country and town both be deserted. And I was not alone in thinking that the
country would soon be deserted, for accustomed as we
all had been to a showery summer, these dry seasons
would seem entirely to prevent extensive farming.
Some cursed the country and said they were on their
way to "good old Missouri, God's own country."
Hearing so much I concluded it would be wise not to
invest, but to get me back to Wisconsin again.

The steamer we took passage in was the Northener,
advertised to sail on the twenty-ninth day of November, 1850. The cabin room was all engaged, and they
charged us nine ounces for steerage passage; but I did
not care as much about their good rooms and clean
sheets as I would have done at one time, for I had
been a long time without either and did not care to
pay the difference. When we were at the ship's office
we had to take our turns to get tickets. One man
weighed out the dust, and another filled out certifi-

cates.   When the callers began to get a little scarce I
looked under the counter where I saw a whole panful
of dust to which they added mine to make the pile a
little higher.   They gave out no berths with these
tickets, but such little things as that did not trouble
us in the least.   It was far better fare than we used
to have in and about Death Valley, and we thought
we could live through anything that promised better
than the desert.

The passenger list footed up four hundred and forty,
and when all got on board, at about ten o'clock in the
morning, there was hardly room for all to stand up
comfortably.   It seemed to me to be a very much
over-crowded boat in which to put to sea, but we
floated out into the current, with all the faces toward
the shore, and hats and handkerchiefs waving good-
bye to those who had come down to see the home-goers
safely off.

As we passed out through the wonderful Golden
Gate and the out going current met the solid sea, each
seemed wrestling for the mastery, and the waves beat
and dashed themselves into foam all around us, while
the spray came over the bows quite lively, frightening
some who did not expect such treatment.   When we
had passed this scene of watery commotion and got
out into the deeper water, the sea smoothed down a
great deal; but sea-sickness began to claim its victims,
at first a few, then more and more, till the greater
part were quite badly affected.   I had a touch of it
myself, but managed to keep my feet by bracing out
pretty wide, and hugging everything I could get hold
of that seemed to offer a steady support, and I did not
lie down until after I had thrown my breakfast overboard.

By the time dark came nearly every one was on his
back, mostly on deck, and no one asleep.   All were

retching and moaning bitterly. Some who had a few
hours before cursed California now cursed the sea, and
declared that if they could induce the Captain to turn
about and put them back on shore again, they would
rather creep on their hands and knees clear back to
old Missouri over rocks and sand, than to ride any
further on such a miserable old boat as this one was.

Next morning the decks looked pretty filthy, and
about all the food the passengers had eaten was now
spread about the decks in a half digested condition.
Most of the passengers were very sick. With the
early daylight the sailors coupled the hose to the big
steam pump, and began the work of washing and
scrubbing off the decks, and though many begged
hard to be left alone as they were, with all the filth, a
good flood of salt water was the only answer they received to their pleading, and they were compelled to
move, for the sailors said they could not change their
orders without the Captain, and he would not be out
of bed till ten o'clock or later. So the cursing and
swearing went for naught, and the decks were clean
again. There were no deaths to report, but there
were very few to do duty at the tables in eating the
food prepared for them. After a few days the tables
filled up again, and now it took them so long to eat
that there had to be an order for only two meals a day
or there would not have been a chance for all to get
something. They were terribly hungry now, and
every one seemed to try his best to take in provisions
enough to last him for at least twelve hours.

As the fellows began to get their sea legs on, they
began to talk as if they were still in California, and
could easily manage any little boat like this, and could
run things as they did when they crossed the plains,
where no sheriff, court or judge had anything to say
about matters, and all law was left behind. They be-

gan to act as if they were lords over all they could see,
and as many of them were from the Southern states,
they seemed to take an especial pride in boasting of
how they did as they pleased, about like the Helms
brothers. They talked as if they could run the world,
or the universe even, themselves without assistance.

One morning at breakfast, when the table was full
and the waiters scarce, some of these fellows swore
and talked pretty rough, and as a waiter was passing
a blue-blood from New Orleans rose in his seat and
called for sugar, holding the empty bowl in his hand,
but the waiter passed on and paid no attention, and
when a mulatto waiter came along behind him the
angry man damned him the worst he could, ordering
him to bring a bowl of sugar, quick. This waiter did
not stop and the Louisiana man threw the bowl at the
waiter's head, but missed it, and the bowl went crash-
ing against the side of the ship. I expected surely
the Captain and his men would come and put the un-
ruly fellow in irons, and there might be a fight or a
riot, so I cut my meal short and went on deck about
as soon as I could do so, thinking that would be a
safer place. But the Captain seemed to know about
how to manage such fellows, and never left his state-
room, which I think was a wise move. The darky
did not make his appearance at table afterwards, and
the man who threw the bowl said that colored folks
had to mind a gentleman when he spoke to them, or
fare worse.

The Captain now got out his passenger list, and we
all had to pass through a narrow space near the wheel-
house and every one answer to his name and show his
ticket. This made work for about one day. Some
stowaways were found and put down into the hole to
heave coal. One day the Captain and mate were out
taking an observation on the sun when a young Mis-

sourian stepped up to see what was being done, and
said to the Captain:—"Captain, don't you think I
could learn how to do that kind of business?" The
Captain took the young man's hand and looked at his
nails which were very rough and dirty and said:—
"No, my lad; boys with such finger nails can't learn
navigation." This made a big laugh at the brave
lubber's expense.

Many of the sea-sick ones did not get up so soon,
and some died of that, or something else, and their
bodies were sewed up in blankets with a bushel of
coal at their feet to sink them, and thrown overboard.
The bodies were laid out on a plank at the ship's side,
the Captain would read a very brief service, and the
sailors would, at the appropriate time, raise the end
of the plank so that the body slid off and went down
out of sight in a moment.

In due time we went into the harbor of Acapulco
for water and coal. Here nearly every one went on
shore, and as there was no wharf for the vessel to lie
to, the native canoes had many passengers at a dollar
apiece for passage money. Out back of town there
was a small stream of clear water which was warm
and nice to bathe in, and some places three or four
feet deep, so that a great many stripped off for a good
wash which was said to be very healthful in this climate. Many native women were on hand with soap
and towels ready to give any one a good scrubbing
for *dos reales*, (twenty-five cents) and those who employed them said they did a good, satisfactory job.

As I returned to town the streets seemed to be deserted, and I saw one man come out on an adjoining
street, and after running a few steps, fall down on his
face. Hearing the report of a gun at the same time, I
hurried on to get out of danger, but I afterward learned that the man was a travelling gambler who had

come across the country from Mexico, and that he was killed as he fell. No one seemed to care for him.

Near the beach were some large trees, and under them dancing was going on to the music of the guitar. There were plenty of pretty Spanish girls for partners, and these and our boys made up an interesting party. The girls did not seem at all bashful or afraid of the boys, and though they could not talk together very much they got along with the sign language, and the ladies seemed very fond of the *Americauos*.

There was a fort here, a regular moss-backed old concern, and the soldiers were bare footed and did not need much clothing.

The cattle that were taken on board here were made to swim out to the ship, and then, with a rope around their horns, hoisted on deck, a distance of perhaps forty feet above the water. The maddened brutes were put into a secure stall ready for the ship's butcher. The small boys came around the ship in canoes, and begged the passengers to throw them out a dime, and when the coin struck the water they would dive for it, never losing a single one. One man dropped a bright bullet and the boy who dove for it was so enraged that he called him a d—d Gringo (Englishman.) None of these boys wore any clothes.

This town, like all Spanish towns, was composed of one-story houses, with dry mud, fire-proof walls. The country around looked very mountainous and barren, and comfortably warm.

After two days we were called on board, and soon set sail for sea again; and now, as we approached the equator, it became uncomfortably warm and an awning was put over the upper deck. All heavy clothing was laid aside, and anyone who had any amount of money on his person was unable to conceal it; but no one seemed to have any fear of theft, for a thief could

not conceal anything he should steal, and no one re
ported anything lost. There was occasionally a dead
body to be consigned to a watery grave.

A few days out from here and we were again mustered as before to show our tickets, which were carefully examined.

It seemed strange to me that the water was the
poorest fare we had. It was sickish tasting stuff, and
so warm it would do very well for dish-water.

There were many interesting things to see. Sometimes it would be spouting whales; sometimes great
black masses rolling on the water, looking like a ship
bottom upward, which some said were black-fish.
Some fish seemed to be at play, and would jump ten
feet or more out of the water. The flying fish would
skim over the waves as the ship's wheels seemed to
frighten them; and we went through a hundred acres
of porpoises, all going the same way. The ship plowed right through them, but none seemed to get hurt
by the wheels. Perhaps they were emigrants like
ourselves in search of a better place.

It now became terribly hot, and the sun was nearly
overhead at noon. Sometimes a shark could be seen
along-side, and though he seemed to make no effort,
easily kept up with the moving ship. Occasionally
we saw a sea snake navigating the ocean all by himself. I did not understand how these fellows went to
sea and lived so far from land. The flying fish seemed
to be more plentiful as we went along, and would
leave the water and scud along before us.

We had evening concerts on the forecastle, managed
by the sailors. Their songs were not sacred songs by
any means, and many of them hardly fit to be heard
by delicate ears. We again had to run the gauntlet
of the narrow passage and have our tickets looked
over, and this time a new stowaway was found, and

he straightway made application for a job. "Go below, sir" was all the Captain said. Several died and
had their sea burial, and some who had been so sick
all the way as not to get out of bed, proved tough
enough to stand the climate pretty well.

As we were nearing Panama the doctor posted a
notice to the mast cautioning us against eating much
fruit while on shore, as it was very dangerous when
eaten to excess. We anchored some little distance
from the shore and had to land in small boats managed
by the natives. I went in one, and when the boat
grounded at the beach the boatman took me on his
back and set me on shore, demanding two dollars for
the job, which I paid, and he served the whole crowd
in the same way. The water here was blood warm,
and they told me the tide ran very high.

This was a strange old town to me, walled in on
all sides, a small plaza in the center with a Catholic
church on one side, and the other houses were mostly
two story. On the side next to the beach was a high,
thick wall which contained cells that were used for a
jail, and on top were some dismounted cannon, long
and old fashioned.

The soldiers were poor, lazy fellows, barefooted, and
had very poor looking guns. Going out and in all
had to pass through a large gateway, but they asked
no questions. The streets were very narrow and dirty
and the sleeping rooms in the second story of the
houses seemed to be inhabited by cats. For bed
clothes was needed only a single sheet. On the roofs
all around sat turkey buzzards, and anything that fell
in the streets that was possible for them to eat, was
gobbled up very quickly. They were as tame as
chickens, and walked around as fearless and lordly as
tame turkeys. In consideration of their cleaning up
the streets without pay, they were protected by law.

Ono of the passengers could not resist the temptation
to shoot one, and a small squad of soldiers were soon
after him, and came into a room where there were
fifty of us, but could not find their man. He would
have been sent to jail if he had been caught. We had
to pay one dollar a night for beds in these rooms, and
they counted money at the rate of eight dimes to the
dollar.

The old town of Panama lies a little south in the
edge of the sea, and was destroyed by an earthquake
long ago I was told. To me, raised in the north,
everything was very new and strange in way of living,
style of building and kind of produce. There were
donkeys, parrots and all kinds of monkeys in plenty.
Most of the women were of very dark complexion,
and not dressed very stylishly, while the younger population did not have even a fig leaf, or anything to
take its place. The adults dressed very economically,
for the days are summer days all the year round, and
the clothing is scanty and cheap for either sex.

The cattle were small, pale red creatures, and not
inclined to be very fat, and the birds mostly of the
parrot kind. The market plaza is outside the walls,
and a small stream runs through it, with the banks
pretty thickly occupied by washerwomen. All the
washing was done without the aid of a fire.

On the plaza there were plenty of donkeys loaded
with truck of all sorts, from wood, green grass, cocoa-
nuts and sugar-cane to parrots, monkeys and all kinds
of tropical fruits. Outside the walls the houses were
made of stakes interwoven with palm leaves, and
everything was green as well as the grass and trees.
Very little of the ground seemed to be cultivated, and
the people were lazy and idle, for they could live so
easily on the wild products of the country. A white
man here would soon sweat out all his ambition and

enterprise, and would be almost certain to catch the Panama yellow fever. The common class of the people here, I should say, were Spanish and negro mixed, and they seem to get along pretty well; but the country is not suitable for white people. It seems to have been made on purpose for donkeys, parrots and long-heeled negroes.

The cabin passengers engaged all the horses and mules the country afforded on which to ride across the Chagres River, so it fell to the lot of myself and companion to transfer ourselves on foot, which was pretty hard work in the hot and sultry weather. My gold dust began to grow pretty heavy as I went along, and though I had only about two thousand dollars, weighing about ten pounds, it seemed to me that it weighed fifty pounds by the way that it bore down upon my shoulders and wore sore places on them. It really was burdensome. I had worn it on my person night and day ever since leaving the mines, and I had some little fear of being robbed when off the ship.

Our road had been some day paved with cobble stones. At the outskirts of the town we met a native coming in with a big green lizard, about two feet long, which he was hauling and driving along with a string around its neck. I wondered if this was not a Panama butcher bringing in a fresh supply of meat.

When we reached the hills on our way from Panama, the paved road ended and we had only a mule trail to follow. The whole country was so densely timbered that no man could go very far without a cleared road. In some places we passed over hills of solid rock, but it was of a soft nature so that the trail was worn down very deep, and we had to take the same regular steps that the mules did, for their tracks were worn down a foot or more. On the road we would occasionally meet a native with a heavy pack

on his back, a long staff in each hand, and a solid
half-length sword by his side. He, like the burro,
grunted every step he took. They seemed to carry
unreasonably heavy loads on their backs, such as
boxes and trunks, but there was no other way of getting either freight or baggage across the isthmus at
that time.

It looked to me as if this trail might be just such a
one as one would expect robbers to frequent, for it
would of course be expected that Californians would
carry considerable money with them, and we might
reasonably look out for this sort of gentry at any turn
of the trail. We were generally without weapons,
and we should have to deliver on demand, and if any
one was killed the body could easily be concealed in
the thick brush on either side of the trail, and no
special search for anyone missing would occur.

About noon one day we came to a native hut, and
saw growing on a tree near by something that looked
like oranges, and we made very straight tracks with
the idea of picking some and having a feast, but some
of the people in the shanty called out to us and made
motions for us not to pick them for they were no good;
so we missed our treat of oranges and contented ourselves with a big drink of water and walked on.

After a little more travel we came to another shanty
made of poles and palm leaves, occupied by an American. He was a tall, raw-boned, cadaverous looking
way-side renegade who looked as if the blood had all
been pumped out of his veins, and he claimed to be
sick. He said he was one of the Texas royal sons.
We applied for some dinner and he lazily told us there
were flour, tea and bacon and that we could help ourselves. I wet up some flour and baked some cakes,
made some poor tea, and fried some bacon. We all
got a sort of dinner out of his pantry stuff, and left

him a dollar apiece for the accomodation. As we walked on my companion gave out and could carry his bundle no longer, so I took it, along with my own, and we got on as fast as we could, but darkness came on us before we reached the Chagres River and we had to stay all night at a native hut. We had some supper consisting of some very poor coffee, crackers, and a couple of eggs apiece, and had to sleep out under a tree where we knew we might find lizards, snakes, and other poisonous reptiles, and perhaps a thieving monkey might pick our pockets while we slept.

Before it was entirely dark many who rode horses came along, many of them ladies, and following the custom of the country, they all rode astride. Among this crowd was one middle-aged and somewhat corpulent old fellow, by profession a sea-captain, who put on many airs. The old fellow put on his cool white coat—in fact, a white suit throughout—and in this tropical climate he looked very comfortable, indeed, thus attired. He filled his breast pocket with fine cigars, and put in the other pocket a flask with some medicine in it which was good for snake bites, and also tending to produce courage in case the man, not used to horse-back riding, should find his natural spirits failing. The rest of his luggage was placed on pack animals, and in fact the only way luggage was carried in those days was either on the backs of donkeys or men.

All was ready for a start, and the captain in his snow-white suit was mounted on a mule so small that his feet nearly touched the ground. The little animal had a mind of his own, and at first did not seem inclined to start out readily, but after a bit concluded to follow his fellow animals, and all went well. The rider was much amused at what he saw; some-

times a very lively monkey, sometimes a flock of par-
oquets or a high-colored lizard—and so he rode along
with a very happy air, holding his head up, and smoking a fragrant Havana with much grace. The road
was rough and rocky, with a mud-hole now and then
of rather uncertain depth. At every one of these
mud-holes the Captain's mule would stop, put down
his head, blow his nose and look wise, and then carefully sound the miniature sea with his fore-feet, being
altogether too cautious to suit his rider who had never
been accustomed to a craft that was afraid of water.

At one of these performances the mule evidently
concluded the sea before him was not safe, for when
the captain tried to persuade him to cross his persua-
sions had no effect. Then he coaxed him with voice
gentle, soft and low, with the result that the little animal took a few very short steps and then came to anchor again. Then the captain began to get slightly
roiled in temper, and the voice was not so gentle,
sweet and low, but it had no greater effect upon his
craft. He began to get anxious, for the others had
gone on, and he thought perhaps he might be left.

Now, this sea-faring man had armed his heels with
the large Spanish spurs so common in the country,
and bringing them in contact with the force due to
considerable impatience, Mr. Mule was quite suddenly
and painfully aware of the result. This was harsher
treatment than he could peaceably submit to, and at
the second application of the spurs a pair of small
hoofs were very high in the air and the captain very
low on his back in the mud and water, having been
blown from the hurricane deck of his craft in a very
sudden and lively style. The philosophical mule stood
very still and looked on while the white coat and
pantaloons were changing to a dirty brown, and
watched the captain as he waded out, to the accom-

paniment of some very vigorous swear words.

Both the man and beast looked very doubtful of each other's future actions, but the man shook the water off and bestowed some lively kicks on his mule-ship which made him bounce into and through the mud-hole, and the captain, still holding the bridle, followed after. Once across the pool the captain set his marine eye on the only craft that had been too much for his navigation and said "Vengeance should be mine," and in this doubtful state of mind he cautiously mounted his beast again and fully resolved to stick to the deck, hereafter, at all hazards, he hurried on and soon overtook the train again, looking quite like a half drowned rooster. The others laughed at him and told him they could find better water a little way ahead, at the river, and they would see him safely in. The captain was over his pet, and made as much fun as any of them, declaring that he could not navigate such a bloody craft as that in such limited sea room, for it was dangerous even when there was no gale to speak of.

The ladies did not blush at the new and convenient costumes which they saw in this country, and laughed a good deal over the way of traveling they had to adopt. Any who were sick were carried in a kind of chair strapped to the back of a native. Passengers were strung along the road for miles, going and coming. We would occasionally sit down awhile and let the sweat run off while a party of them passed us. Some were mounted on horses, some on mules, and some on donkeys, and they had to pay twelve dollars for the use of an animal for the trip.

Our night at this wayside deadfall was not much better than some of the nights about Death Valley, but as I was used to lowfare, I did not complain as some did. This seemed a wonderful country to a

northern raised boy. The trail was lined on both
sides with all kinds of palms and various other kinds
of trees and shrubs, and they were woven together in
a compact mass with trailing and running vines. The
trees were not tall, and the bark was as smooth as a
young hickory. The roots would start out of the tree
three feet above the ground and stand out at an angle,
and looked like big planks placed edgewise.

It seemed as if there were too many plants for the
ground to support, and so they grew on the big limbs
of the trees all around, the same as the mistletoe on
the oak, only there were ever so many different kinds.

The weather was very clear, and the sun so hot that
many of the travelers began to wilt and sit down by
the roadside to rest. Many walked along very slowly
and wore long faces. The road from Panama to Cru-
cez, on the Chagres River, was eighteen miles long,
and all were glad when they were on the last end of
it. The climate here seems to take all the starch and
energy out of a man's body, and in this condition he
must be very cautious or some disease will overtake
him and he will be left to die without burial for his
body if he has no personal friends with him.

We started on the next morning, and on our way
stepped over a large ship anchor that lay across the
trail. I suppose the natives had undertaken to pack
it across the isthmus and found it too heavy for them.
Perhaps it was for Capt. Kidd, the great pirate, for it
is said that he often visited Panama in the course of
his cruising about in search of treasures.

Passing along a sandy place in the trail, a snake
crossed and left his track, big as a stovepipe it seemed
to be, and after this we kept a sharp watch for big
snakes that might be in waiting to waylay us for
game.

There were plenty of monkeys and parrots climbing

and chattering around in the trees. The forest is here
so dense that the wind never blows, and consequently
it never gets cool. The sun, ever since we got down
near the equator, was nearly overhead, and the moon
seemed to be even north of us.

When we reached the Chagres River we hired a
boat of an Irishman for the trip down. I wondered if
there was a place on earth so desolate that the "Paddy"
would not find it. The boat for the journey cost two
hundred dollars, and would hold passengers enough
so that it would cost us ten dollars each, at any rate,
and perhaps a little more. Two natives had charge of
the boat and did the navigating. There were two
ladies among the passengers, and when the two natives, who I suppose were the captain and mate of the
craft, came on board, clad very coolly in Panama hats,
the ladies looked at them a little out of the corners of
their eyes and made the best of it. Our two navigat-
ors took the oars and pulled slowly down the stream.

Nothing but water and evergreen trees could we see,
for the shore on either hand was completely hidden
by the dense growth that hung over and touched the
water. On a mud bar that we passed a huge alligator
lay, taking a sun bath, and though many shots were
fired at him he moved away very leisurely. No one
could get on shore without first clearing a road
through the thick brushes and vines along the bank.
On the way one of our boatmen lost his hat, his only
garment, into the river, and overboard he went, like
a dog, and soon had it and climbed on board again.
I wondered why some of the big alligators did not
make a snap at him.

The water in the run looked very roily and dirty,
and no doubt had fever in it. The only animals we
saw were monkeys and alligators, and there were parrots in the trees. The farther we went down the stream

the wider it became, and the current slacker so that
we moved more slowly with the same amount of row-
ing. At a place called Dos Hermanos (two brothers)
we could see a little cleared spot near the bank, which
seemed to be three or four feet above the water. There
were no mountains nor hills in sight, and the whole
country seemed to be an extensive swamp. It was
near night that we came to a small native village of
palm huts, and here our boatmen landed and hid themselves, and not being able to find them we were compelled to stay all night, for we dare not go on alone.
The place looked like a regular robbers' roost, and being forced to sleep outside the huts, we considered it
safest to sleep with one eye open. We would have
gone on with the boat only that we were afraid the
river might have more than one outlet, and if we
should take the wrong one we might be too late for
the steamer, which even now we were afraid would
not wait for us, and getting left would be a very serious matter in this country.

We had very little to eat, and all we could buy was
sugar cane, bananas, monkeys and parrots. We kept
a sharp eye out for robbers, keeping together as much
as we could, for we knew that all returning Californians would be suspected of having money. Most all
of them were ready for war except myself who had no
weapon of any kind. All of these people had a bad
name, and every one of them carried a long bladed
knife called a Macheta, with which they could kill a
man at a single blow. But with all our fears we got
through the night safely, and in the morning found
our boatmen who had hidden away. We waited not
for breakfast, but sailed away as soon as we could, and
reached Chagres, near the mouth of the river, before
night.

The river banks here are not more than three feet

high, and farther back the land fell off again into a
wet swamp of timber and dense vegetable growth.
The town was small and poorly built, on the immediate bank, and the houses were little brush and palm
affairs except the boarding house which was "T"
shaped, the front two stories high, with a long dining
room running back, having holes for windows, but no
glass in them.

Before the bell rung for meals a long string of hungry men would form in line, and at the first tap would
make a rush for the table like a flock of sheep. After
all were seated a waiter came around and collected a
dollar from each one, and we thought this paid pretty
well for the very poor grub they served afterwards.

No ship had as yet been in sight to take us away
from this lowest, dirtiest, most unhealthful place on
earth, and the prospect of remaining here had nothing
very charming about it. The river was full of alligators, so the bathing was dangerous, and the whole
country was about fit for its inhabitants, which were
snakes, alligators, monkeys, parrots and lazy negroes.
It could not have been more filthy if the dregs of the
whole earth had been dumped here, and cholera and
yellow fever were easy for a decent man to catch.

My companion and I went out on the beach a mile
or two to get the salt water breeze, and leave the
stinking malaria for those who chose to stay in the
hot, suffocating village, and here we would stay until
nearly night. Across a small neck of water was what
was called a fort. It could hardly be seen it was so
covered with moss and vines, but near the top could
be seen something that looked like old walls. There
was no sign of life about it, and I should judge it was
built at some very early day. Surely there was nothing here to protect, for the whole country did not seem
able to support even a few barefooted soldiers.

Some men who wandered along up the river bank, following a path, said they had seen some dead human bodies thrown into the swamp and left, probably because it was easier than putting them under ground.

For a bedroom I hired a little platform which a store keeper had placed before his store, where I slept, and paid a dollar for the privilege. Some one walked around near me all night, and I dared not close more than one eye at a time for fear of losing a little bag of gold dust. This little bag of gold was getting to be a great burden to me in this sickly climate, and the vigilant guard I had to keep over so small a treasure was very tiresome.

The second night no steamer came, but on the third morning the steamer was riding at anchor three or four miles out, and soon after a ship came in from the Atlantic end of the Nicaragua route with one thousand passengers, there being no steamer there for them to take a passage home on, and so they had to come here for a start. This filled the little town to overflowing, but as the ship that had arrived was the Georga, one of the largest afloat, all could go if they only could endure the fare.

We now had to go in small boats from the shore to the ship, and the trip cost two dollars and a half. I waited till I had seen some of the boats make a trip or two, and then choosing one that had a sober skipper, I made the venture. It was said that one drunken boatman allowed his boat to drift into some breakers and all were lost.

I tell you I was over anxious to get out of this country, for I well knew that if I stayed very long I should stay forever, for one like myself raised in a healthful climate, could not remain long without taking some of the fatal diseases the country was full of.

We made the trip to the vessel safely, and as our

boat lay under the ship's quarter, the men holding
the ropes, I looked up, and when I saw the swinging
rope ladder on which I was expected to climb up to
the ship's deck, it seemed a pretty dangerous job; but
I mustered up courage and made the attempt. The
sea was pretty rough out here for the small boats, and
the ship rolled some, so that when persons tried to get
hold of the ladder they were thrown down and sometimes hurt a little. A man held on to the lower end
of the ladder so that the one who was climbing might
not get banged against the side of the ship and have
his breath knocked out of him. I mounted the ladder
safely and climbed away like a monkey, reaching the
deck all right. Ladies and weak people were hauled
up in a sort of chair with a block and rope.

It took the most of two days to get the people on
board, and when they were counted up there were
one thousand four hundred and forty, all told. This
steamer had a very long upper deck and a comparatively short keel. and rolled very badly; and as for me,
I had swallowed so much of the deadly malaria of the
isthmus that I soon got very seasick, and the first day
or two were very unpleasant. I went to the bar and
paid two bits for a glass of wine to help my appetite,
but it staid with me no longer than time enough to
reach the ship's side. When night came the decks
were covered with sleepy men, and if the weather had
been rough and all sick, as was the case when we left
San Francisco, we should have had more filthy decks
than we had even on that occasion.

Approaching the harbor at Havana, Cuba, we
seemed to be going head foremost against a wall of
solid rock, but when within speaking distance an officer came in sight on the fort right before us, and
shouted through his speaking trumpet, saying:—
"Why don't you salute us?" Our officer said, "You

know us well enough without.'' Our ship had a small cannon on the forecastle, but did not choose to use it, and I suppose the Cuban officer felt slighted. We now turned short to the right and entered the beautiful harbor, which is perfectly landlocked and as still as a pond. The city is all on the right side of the bay and our coal yard was on the left at a short wharf at which we landed.

A lot of armed soldiers were placed a short distance back on the high ground and no one was allowed to go beyond them. We now had a port officer on board who had entire charge of the ship, and if anyone wanted to go to the city, across the bay two or three miles, he had to pay a dollar for a pass. This pass business made the blue bloods terribly angry, and they swore long and loud, and the longer they talked the madder they got, and more bitter in their feelings, so that they were ready to fight (not with sugar-bowls this time.)

The weather here was very warm and the heat powerful, and as these fellows saw there was only one course to be pursued if they wanted to get on shore, they slowly took passes good for all day and paid their dollar for them, and also another dollar each to the canoe men to take them to the city. Myself and companion also took passes and went over.

Arriving at the city we walked a short distance and came to the plaza, which is not a very large one. Here was a single grave nicely fenced in, and across the plaza were some large two-story houses in front of which was stationed a squad of cavalry standing as motionless as if every man of them was a marble statue. We kept on the opposite side of the street, and chancing to meet a man whom we rightly supposed to be an Englishman, we inquired about the grave on the plaza and were informed that it was that of Christopher Columbus, the discoverer of America. Just then we noticed the cavalry moving up the street at a slow gallop, and so formed that a close carriage was in the center of the squad. As they rushed by and we gazed at them with purely American curiousity, our new English friend raised our hats for us and held them till the cavalcade had passed, merely remarking that the Governor General was within the carriage. We spoke perhaps a bit unpleasantly when we asked him why he was so ungentlemanly in his treatment of us as to remove our hats, but he said:— "My friends, if I had not taken off your hats for you as a friend, some of those other fellows would have knocked them off, so I did for you an act of greatest kindness, for every one removes his hat when the Governor General passes." He also informed us that the special occasion for this rather pompous parade was the execution of some criminals at a park or prison not far away, and that this was done by beheading them.

Our friend proposed that we also walk out in that direction, and we went with him to the edge of the city, but when he turned into a by.path that did not seem much frequented, we declined to follow farther, and turned back along the open road. The path looked to us a sort of robber's route, and not exactly safe for unarmed men like us in a strange country.

The man followed us back and took us into a large, airy saloon, in the center of which a big fountain was playing, and the great basin in which the water fell was filled with beautiful fish. Our friend called for an iced drink for each of us, and as we sat at the table we tasted it and found it rather intoxicating. For this they charged us one dollar each, but we noticed that our friend paid nothing, and we set him down as a sort of capper, after the style we had seen at the

gold mines.   We sat a few minutes and then so coolly
bade our friend good-bye that he had not the face to
follow us further, and continued our walk about the
streets which seemed to us very narrow, and the
houses generally two stories high.

A chaise passed us, containing two young ladies
with complexions white and fair, and eyes and hair
black, in striking contrast. The carriage was drawn
by two horses tandem, the horse in the shafts being
mounted by a big negro of very dignified appearance,
dressed in livery and having top boots that came to
his knees.   This was the only vehicle of the kind we
saw on the streets.

We did not dare to go very far alone, for with our
ignorance of the Spanish language we might go astray
and not get back to the ship within the lifetime of our
passes, and not knowing how much trouble that
might cause us, we were naturally a little timid; so
we took a boat back to the ship, and when on board
again we felt safe.   We had only about four dollars
cash left.

A big gang of darkies were coaling the ship.   Each
one carried a large tub full of coal upon his head and
poured it down into the ship's hold.   All the clothes
these fellows wore was a strip of cloth about their
middle.   When they were let off for dinner they skim-
med off all they could get from the ship's slop barrel
which stood on the wharf alongside, to help out their
very scanty food.   The overseer stood by them all the
time with a big whip and made them hurry up as fast
as possible, talking Spanish pretty vigorously, and
though we could not understand, we made up our
minds that a good part of it was swearing.

The next morning the steamship Prometheus came
in and tied up near us, and soon word was brought
that she would take the New Orleans passengers on

board and sail immediately for that port. It now occurred to me that I could get nearer home by going
up the Mississippi River than by way of New York,
so I went on board the Prometheus, and we soon
sailed out of the harbor, passing under the gate of the
fortress called, I think, San Juan de Ulloa.

Nothing special occurred during our passage till we
were near the mouth of the Mississippi River, when,
in the absence of a pilot boat or tug, our Captain
thought he would try to get in alone, and as a consequence we were soon fast in the mud. The Captain
now made all the passengers go aft, and worked the
engine hard but could not move her at all. The tide
was now low, and there was a prospect that we should
have to wait full six hours to get away. We worked
on, however, and after a few hours a tug came to our
assistance and pulled us out of the mud and towed us
into the right channel, up which we steamed on our
way to New Orleans, one-hundred-twenty miles away.

The country on both sides of us was an immense
marsh—no hills in sight, no timber, nothing but the
same level marsh or prairie. When we were nearer
the Crescent City some houses came in sight; then we
passed General Jackson's battle-field, and in due time
reached the city.

On board this ship I became acquainted with Dick
Evans who lived in the same county that I used to in
Wisconsin, near Mineral Point, so the three of us now
concluded to travel together.

New Orleans seemed to be a very large city. Near
the levee a large government building was in course
of construction for a Custom House. It was all of
stone, and the walls were up about two stories. We
put up at a private boarding house, and the first business was to try and sell our gold dust. So we went
to the mint and were told we would have to wait ten

days to run it through the mill, and we did not like
to wait so long. We were shown all through the
mint and saw all the wonders of coin making. Every
thing seemed perfect here. Beautiful machinery was
in operation making all sizes of gold coins, from a
twenty dollar piece down. Strips of gold bands about
six feet long and of the proper thickness for twenty
dollar pieces are run through a machine which cuts
out the pieces, and when these are cut they can stamp
out the pieces as fast as one can count.

This was the most ingenious work I ever saw, and
very wonderful and astonishing to a backwoodsman
like myself, for I supposed that money was run in
moulds like bullets.

As we could not wait we went to a bank and sold
our dust, getting only sixteen dollars per ounce, the
same price they paid in Calfornia. We now took the
cars and rode out to Lake Ponchantrain—most of the
way over a trestle work. We found a wharf and
warehouse at the lake, and a steamer lay there all
ready to go across to the other side. The country all
about looked low, with no hills in sight.

When we returned to the city we looked all about,
and in the course of our travels came to a slave market. Here there were all sorts of black folks for sale;
big and little, old and young and all sorts. They all
seemed good-natured, and were clean, and seemed to
think they were worth a good deal of money. Looking at them a few minutes sent my mind back to St.
Joseph, Missouri, where I saw a black sold at auction.
From my standpoint of education I did not approve
of this way of trading in colored people.

We continued our stroll about the city, coming to
a cemetery, where I looked into a newly dug grave
to find it half full of water. On one side were many
brick vaults above ground. The ground here is very

low and wet, and seemed to be all swamp. The drainage was in surface gutters, and in them the water stood nearly still. It seemed to me such water must have yellow fever in it.

For a long way along the levee the steamboats lay thick and close together, unloading cotton, hemp, sugar, hoop poles, bacon and other products, mostly the product of negro labor.

Here our friend Evans was taken sick, and as he got no better after a day or two, we called a doctor to examine him. He pronounced it a mild case of yellow fever. His skin was yellow in places, and he looked very badly. The doctor advised us to go on up the river, saying it was very dangerous staying here with him. Evans gave me most of his money and all of his gold specimens to take to his wife, and when he got well he would follow us. We bade him good-bye, and with many wishes for his speedy recovery, we took passage on a steamer for St. Louis. This steamer, the Atlantic, proved to be a real floating palace in all respects. The table was supplied with everything the country afforded. and polite and well-dressed darkies were numerous as table waiters. This was the most pleasant trip I had ever taken, and I could not help comparing the luxuriance of my coming home to the hardships of the outward journey across the plains, and our starvation fare.

Our boat was rather large for the stage of water this time of year, and we proceeded rather slowly, but I cared little for speed as bed and board were extra good, and a first cabin passage in the company of friends, many of whom were going to the same part of Wisconsin as myself, was not a tedious affair by any means.

At night gambling was carried on very extensively, and money changed hands freely as the result of sundry games of poker, which was the popular game. We reached St. Louis in time, and here was the end of our boat's run. The river had some ice floating on its surface, and this plainly told us that we were likely to meet more ice and colder weather as we went north. We concluded to take the Illinois River boat from here to Peoria, and paid our passage and stepped on board. We were no more than half way through this trip when the ice began to form on the surface of the water, and soon became so thick and strong that the boat finally came to a perfect standstill, frozen in solid.

We now engaged a farm wagon to take us to Peoria, from which place we took regular stages for Galena. Our driver was inclined to be very merciful to his horses, so we were two days in reaching that town, but perhaps it was best, for the roads were icy and slippery, and the weather of the real winter sort. From here we hired a team to take four of us to Platt-ville, and then an eighteen-mile walk brought me to Mineral Point, the place from which I started with my Winnebago pony in 1849. I had now finished my circle and brought both ends of the long belt together.

I now went to a drug store and weighed Mr. Evans' specimens, wrapping each in a separate piece of paper, with the value marked on each, and took them to his wife, to whom I told the news about her husband. In two week's time he came home sound and well.

I was quite disappointed in regard to the looks and business appearance of the country. It looked thinly settled, people scarce, and business dull. I could not get a day's work to do, and I could not go much far ther on foot, for the snow was eight or ten inches deep, and I was still several hundred miles from my parents in Michigan. So my journey farther east was delayed until spring. The hunting season was over, and when I came into Mineral Point without a gun, and wore good clothes, making a better appearance than I used to, they seemed to think I must be rich and showed me marked attention, and made many inquiries about their neighbors who started for California about the same time I did. The young ladies smiled pleasantly when near me, and put on their best white aprons, looking very tidy and bright, far superior to any of the ladies I had seen in my crooked route from San Francisco through Acapulco, Panama, the West Indies and along the Mississippi.

After a few days in town I went out into the neighborhood where I used to live and stopped with Mr. E. A. Hall, who used to be a neighbor of Mr. Bennett, as he had invited me to stay with himself and wife, who were the only occupants of a good house, and all was pleasant. But notwithstanding all the comfort in which I was placed, I grew lonesome, for the enforced idleness, on account of the stormy weather, was a new feature in my life, and grew terribly monotonous.

After some delay I concluded to write to my parents in Michigan and give them a long letter with something of a history of my travels, and to refresh my memory I got out my memorandum I had kept through all my journey.

As my letter was liable to be quite lengthy I bought a quantity of foolscap paper and begun. I took my diary as my guide, and filled out the ideas suggested in it so they would understand them. I soon ran through with my paper and bought more, and kept on writing. The weather was cold and stormy, and I found it the best occupation I could have to prevent my being lonesome; so I worked away, day after day, for about a month, and I was really quite tired of this sort of work before I had all the facts recorded which I found noted down in my diary. My notes began in

March, 1849, in Wisconsin, and ended in February, 1852, on my return to Mineral Point. I found, as the result of my elaboration, over three hundred pages of closely written foolscap paper, and I felt very mucn relieved when it was done. By the aid of my notes I could very easily remember everything that had taken place during my absence, and it was recorded in regular form, with day and date, not an incident of any importance left out, and every word as true as gospel. I had neither exaggerated nor detracted from any event so far as I could recollect.

I now loaned Mr. Hall, with whom I lived, six hundred dollars to enable him to cross the plains to California and try to make his fortune. To secure this I took a mortgage on his eighty-acre farm, and he set out to make the journey. I had another eighty acres of land near here which I bought at government price before going to California, but I could not now sell it for what it cost me. When I went away I had left my chest and contents with my friend Samuel Zollinger, and he had kept it safely, so I now made him my lawful agent. I placed my narrative and some other papers in the ehest and gave the key into his charge, while I went north, across the Wisconsin River, to visit my old hunting and trapping friend, Robert Mc Cloud. Here I made a very pleasant visit of perhaps a week, and the common prospects of the country were freely talked over. It seemed to us as if the good times were still far off; every day was like Sunday so far as anything going on; no money in circulation, many places abandoned, and, like myself, many had gone to California to seek gold instead of lead. (The mines at Mineral Point are mostly of lead, with some copper.)

Looking at matters in this light it did not need a great deal of McCloud's persuasion to induce me to go back with him to California, all the more so as my little pile seemed to look smaller every day, while three or four years ago it would have seemed quite large. Deciding to go, I wrote to Mr. Zollinger to send the account I had written to my parents in Michigan, reading it first himself, and admonishing him not to lend it. I also wrote to my parents telling them what they might look for in the mails, and cautioning them never to have it printed, for the writing was so ungrammatical and the spelling so incorrect that it would be no credit to me.

I afterward learned that in time they received the bundle of paper and read it through and through, and circulated it around the neighborhood till it was badly worn, and laid it away for future perusal when their minds should incline that way. But the farm house soon after took fire and burned, my labor going up in smoke.

When the news of this reached me I resolved to try to forget all the trials, troubles and hardships I had gone through, and which I had almost lived over again as I wrote them down, and I said to myself that I would not talk about them more than I could help, the sooner to have them vanish, and never write them down again, but a few years ago an accident befell me so that I could not work, and I back-slid from my determination when I was persuaded so earnestly by many friends to write the account which appeared a few years ago in the Santa Clara Valley now the Pacific Tree and Vine, edited by H. A. Brainard, at San Jose, Calfornia. The diary was lost, and from memory alone the facts have been rehearsed, and it is but fair to tell the reader that the hardest and worst of it has never been told nor will it ever be.

CHAPTER XVI.

McCloud and I now took his skiff, and for two days floated down the Wisconsin River till we reached the Mississippi, boarded the first steamboat we could hail, and let our own little craft adrift. In due time we reached St. Louis and boarded another steamer for New Orleans.

At a wood-yard, about dark, a lot of negroes, little and big, came on board to sell brooms. The boat's clerk seemed to know negro character pretty well, so he got out his violin and played for them. For a while the young colored gentry listened in silence, but pretty soon he struck a tune that suited them, and they began to dance in their own wild style.

In seven days from St. Louis we landed in New Orleans, and found the government steamer, Falcon, advertised to sail in two days. We went together to one of the slave warehouses. Outside and in all was neat and clean, and any day you could see men, women and children standing under the shed as a sign of what they had within, and the painted signs "For Sale" displayed conspicuously. We were very civilly treated, and invited to examine the goods offered for sale. There were those of all ages and all colors, for some were nearly white and some intensely black, with all the shades between. All were to be sold, separately, or in families, or in groups as buyers might desire. All were made to keep themselves clean and neatly dressed, and to behave well, with a smile to all the visitors whether they felt like smiling or not. Some seemed really anxious to get a good master, and when a kind, pleasant looking man came along they would do their utmost to be agreeable to him and inquire if he did not want to buy them. We talked it over some between ourselves, and when we thought of the market and the human chattels for sale there, McCloud spoke up and said:—"I am almost persuaded to be an abolitionist."

I now went on board the steamer Falcon, in command of a government officer, to try to learn something about the family of Capt. Culverwell who perished alone in Death Valley. He told me he had once belonged to the Navy and had his life insured, and as I was an important witness for his family I wanted to learn where they lived. The Captain looked over a list of officers, but Culverwell's name was not there. I then wrote a letter to Washington stating the facts of his death, and my own address in Sacramento, California. I also stated that I would assist the widow if I could, but I never received an answer.

We soon started down the river, having on board about one hundred passengers, men going to work on the Panama Railroad. At Chagres we found a small stern wheeled river steamer and took passage on it for Gorgona, as far as the steamer could well go up the river. While going up we met a similar boat coming down, and being near a short bend they crashed together, breaking down our guards severely, but fortunately with no damage to our wheel. A few miles above this a dark passing cloud gave us rain in streams, and we had to drift in near shore to wait for the storm to pass. I never before saw water fall so fast, and yet in half an hour the sun was out and burning hot.

Before we reached Gorgona we got acquainted with a man named John Briggs from Wisconsin, and Lyman Ross from Rhode Island, and concluded to travel in company. Our fare thus far was ten dollars, and two horses to Panama for which we paid twelve dollars

each. We now rode and walked turn about, and
when we inquired about the road we were told that
being once in it we could not possibly get out except
at the other end, and would need no guide, and at the
end of a very disagreeable day's work we reached the
big gate at Panama and entered the ancient city.

We waited but little here before taking the steamer
Southerner, bound for San Francisco. Three days
after we sailed away one of our passengers went overboard, a corpse, and three or four more died and were
buried alongside before we reached Acapulco.

Here we took on water and coal and were soon at
sea again. McCloud soon had to take his place in the
sick ward, and I attended him most of the time, but
was not allowed to give him anything without a permit from the doctor, and the long delays between the
administrations of medicine made the sickness hard to
endure. The sick could see the dead sewed up in
blankets with a bucket of coal for a weight; then resting on a plank with sailors on each side, the mate
would read the brief services appropriate to a burial
at sea, the plank was tilted, and the lifeless body slid
down into the depths. Such scenes were no benefit
to the suffering, for each might think his turn was
next, when a bright hope and prospect would be better for his recovery.

One forenoon the fire gong rang out sharply, and
all was in confusion, supposing the ship to be on fire,
but nothing could be seen but a dense fog. except as a
gentle wind lifted it a little and there, dead ahead, was
a rocky island, against which it seemed we must dash
to destruction, for there was no beach and very little
chance for any one to be saved. Ten minutes more
in this direction and we were lost, but the officers
quickly changed the course, and we passed the pile of
rocks scarcely a rifle shot away. Whose fault it was,

thjs danger so miraculously avoided, we did not know, the captain's or the imperfect chart, and opinions were freely given both ways.

About those days the air felt cooler the fog less dense, and the foggy rain-bows we had seen so much when the sun tried to shine, were scarce, while a more northern wind created a coolness that made sick folks feel refreshed and hopeful. It gave me a chance to cheer up my sick friend who was still in bed, and tell him it would continue to be cooler as we went.

On the Fourth of July the officers produced the ship's full supply of flags, and the sailors climbed high and low, fastening them to every rope till we had a very gay Independence day appearance. In this gay dress we steamed into San Diego harbor to leave the mail for a few soldiers stationed there, and get their letters in return.

I could see no town in San Diego, but a beautiful harbor, and some poor looking mustard wigwams some way off seemed to contain the good people of that place.

A boat with a small crew pulled out and came alongside to get the mail and deliver theirs, and then we turned to sea again. The country all around this beautiful little harbor looked mountainous and extremely barren, and no one wanted to go on shore.

About dark we had made sufficient offing and turned northward, plowing through large fields of kelp. The next morning the forward watch announced land ahead, which could dimly be seen as the fog rose. The officers rushed on deck and could see not far ahead a sandy beach, and a moment more showed that we were headed directly for it, and that it was not more than a quarter of a mile away. Quickly the helmsman was given orders to steer almost west instead of the north course he had been following. He

was asked why he kept on his north course when he
saw danger ahead, and answered:—"It is my business
to steer according to orders, even if the ship goes
ashore, and I can not change course unless ordered
to." The Captain now examined his chart and decided he was in San Pedro harbor, off Los Angeles.

The sun came out bright and clear a little later, and
I got McCloud out of his bed and gave him a seat at
the ship's side where he could see the green grassy
hills near the beach, and larger hills and mountains
farther back. We could see cattle feeding in the nearest pastures, and the whole scene was a pleasant one;
and as we sat on the eastern side of the ship and
snuffed the cool breeze which came from the north,
we thought we were comparatively happy people, and
hoped that, if no accident befell, we would soon be at
the end of our voyage.

On the seventh day of July, 1851, we entered the
Golden Gate, this being my second arrival in California. On our trip from Panama seven or more had
died and been buried at sea, but the remainder of us
were quite safe and sound. We found the heart of
the city still smoking, for a fire had broken out on
July fourth and burned extensively, and these broad,
blackened ruins were the result. Some said the work
had been done by the Sidney "ducks" and their numerous helpers, who were really the rulers of the city.
The place now looked much worse than it did when I
left in November before. These Sidney "ducks" were
English convicts from Australia, and other thieves and
robbers joined them as agreeable companion, making
a large class that seemed to glory in destruction and a
chance for booty.

I walked around over the hills where I could see the
burned district and the destruction of so much valuable property, and when I thought the civil law was

not strong enough to govern, it seemed to me it would
be a good place for such men as the Helms brothers of
Georgetown to come down and do a little hanging
business, for they could here find plenty to do, and
they could carry out their plan of letting no guilty
man escape.

About four o'clock one afternoon we went aboard
the Sacramento steamer, Antelope, paying our passage
with half an ounce apiece, and were soon on our way
past the islands and up the bay. When we were beyond Benicia, where the river banks were close, Mc
Cloud sat watching the shore, and remarked that the
boat ran like a greyhound, and it seemed to him, beat
the old ocean steamer pretty bad.

He seemed to be nearly well again, and compli-
mented me as the best doctor he ever saw. Since
he had been sick I had paid him all the attention I
could, and he gave me all the praise I deserved, now
that he was getting to feel himself again.

At Sacramento we changed to another boat bound
for Marysville, which place we reached without special incident. Here we invested in a four-ounce donkey, that is, we paid four ounces of gold for him, just
an ounce apiece for four of us—W. L. Manley, Robert
McCloud, Lyman Ross and John Briggs. We piled
our blankets in a pack upon the gentle, four-ounce
donkey, and added a little tea and coffee, dried beef
and bread, then started for the Yuba River, ourselves
on foot. We crossed the river at Park's Bar, then
went up the ridge by way of Nigger Tent, came down
to the river again at Goodyear Bar, then up the stream
to Downieville. This town was named after John
Downie, a worthless drunkard. I remember that he
once reformed, but again back-slid and died a drunkard's death.

We found this a lively mining town about sixty

miles above Marysville, on the north fork of the Yuba
River, and only reached by a pack trail, but everything was flush here, even four aces. The location
was a veritable Hole-in-the-Ground, for the mountains
around were very high, and some of them wore their
caps of snow all summer, particularly those on the
east. The gold dust we found here was coarser than
it was where I worked before, down south on the Merced River. Before I came to California I always supposed that gold dust was really dust, and about as fine
as flour.

We went up the North Fork about a mile or two
above town and camped on Wisconsin Flat to begin
our mining operations. Our luck was poor at first,
and all except myself were out of money, and more or
less in debt to me. We made expenses, however, and
a little more, and as soon as Mr. Ross got his small
debt paid he said he was discouraged mining, and with
blankets on his shoulders started up the trail towards
Galloway's ranch, on the summit south of town. Mr.
Ross said the work was too hard for him, for he was
not strong enough to handle pick and shovel, and he
believed he could go down to Sacramento and make
more by his wits than he could here. I went with
him to town and saw him start off with a fair load on
his back, and watched him as he toiled up the steep
mountain trail for about two miles, when he went out
of sight.

The rest of us kept on mining. Our luck was not
very good, but we persevered, for there was nothing
to be gained by fainting by the way. I went into an
old abandoned shaft about ten feet deep and found the
bottom filled with a big quartz boulder, and as I had
been a lead miner in Wisconsin, I began drifting, and
soon found bed rock, when I picked up a piece of pure
gold that weighed four ounces. This was what I

called a pretty big find, and not exactly what I called gold dust. It was quite a surprise to me, for the gravel on the bed rock was only about three or four inches thick.

We kept on drifting for some time, sometimes making good wages, and on the whole so satisfactory that we concluded to stay. We now located some claims back in the flat where the ground would be thirty feet deep, and would have to be drifted. These we managed to hold until winter, and in the meantime we worked along the river and could make something all the time.

We put in a flume between two falls on the Middle Fork, but made only wages, and I got my arm nearly broken, and had to work with one hand for nearly a month.

One afternoon I went crevicing up the river, and found a crevice at the water's edge about half an inch wide, and the next day we worked it out getting forty ounces, and many of the pieces were about an inch long and as large around as a pipe-stem.

Winter was now near by, and we set to work to build a cabin and lay in a stock of grub, which cost quite a good deal, for the self-raising flour which we bought was worth twenty cents a pound, and all kinds of hog meat fifty cents, with other supplies in proportion. Our new claims now paid very well. Snow came down to the depth of about four feet around our cabin, but as our work was under ground, we had a comfortable place all winter.

In the spring McCloud and I went to Sacramento and sold our chunks of gold (it was all very coarse) to Page, Bacon & Co. who were themselves surprised at the coarseness of the whole lot. When our savings were weighed up we found we had made half an ounce ҽ day, clear of all expenses, for the entire year.

We now took a little run down to San Francisco, also to Santa Clara where we staid a night or two with Mr. McCloud's friend, Mr. Otterson, and then went back to our claims again. In taking care of our money we had to be our own bankers, and the usual way was to put the slugs we received for pay into a gallon pickle jar, and bury this in some place known only to our particular selves, and these vaults we considered perfectly safe. The slugs were fifty dollar pieces, coined for convenience, and were eight-sided, heavy pieces. In the western counties the people called them "Adobies," but among the miners they were universally known as "Slugs."

The winter proved a little lonesome, the miners mostly staid at home and worked. During the year we had been here I had not seen a respectable woman in this mining country. There were few females here, and they were said to be of very doubtful character. As a general thing people were very patient with their wickedness, but not always.

Twice only in the history of California were women made the victims of mob violence, once at Los Angeles and once at Downieville. The affair at the last-named place occurred in 1851, and the victim was a pretty little Spanish woman named Juanita. She and her husband, like many another couple at that time, kept a monte game for the delectation of the miners who had more money than sense, but beyond this fact absolutely nothing was said against her character.

There was an English miner named Cannon living in town, who was very popular among a large number of gamblers and others. He got drunk one night and about midnight went to the house occupied by the Spanish woman and her husband and kicked the door down. Early the following morning he told his com rades that he was going to apologize to the woman for what he had done.   He went alone to the house, and, while talking with the husband and wife, the woman suddenly drew a knife and stabbed Cannon to the heart.   What had been said that provoked the deed was never known, further than that Juanita claimed she had been grossly insulted.

She was given a mock trial, but the facts of the case were not brought out, as the men who were with Cannon were too drunk to remember what had happened the previous night.   It was a foregone conclusion that the poor woman was to be hanged, and the leaders of the mob would brook no interference.   A physician examined Juanita and announced to the mob that she was in a condition that demanded the highest sympathy of every man, but he was forced to flee from town to save his life.   A prominent citizen made an appeal for mercy, but he was driven down the main street and across the river by a mob with drawn revolvers, and with threats of instant death.   The well-known John B. Weller was in town at the time, and was asked to reason with the mob, but refused to do so.

The execution was promptly carried out.   A plank was put across the supports of the bridge over the Yuba, and a rope fastened to a beam overhead.   Juanita went calmly to her death   She wore a Panama hat, and after mounting the platform she removed it, tossed it to a friend in the crowd, whose nickname was "Oregon," with the remark, "Adios amigo." Then she adjusted the noose to her own neck, raising her long, loose tresses carefully in order to fix the rope firmly in its place, and then, with a smile and wave of her hand to the bloodthirsty crowd present, she stepped calmly from the plank into eternity.   Singular enough, her body rests side by side, in the cemetery on the hill, with that of the man whose life she had taken.

On Sundays Downieville was full of men, none very old, and none very young, but almost every one of middle age. Nearly every man was coarsely dressed, with beard unshaved and many with long hair, but on any occasion of excitement it was not at all strange to see the coarsest, roughest looking one of all the party mount a stump and deliver as eloquent an address as one could wish to hear. On Sunday it was not at all unusual for some preacher to address the moving crowd, while a few feet behind him would be a saloon in full blast, and drinking, gambling, swearing and vulgar language could be plainly seen and heard at the same time, and this class of people seemed to respect the Sunday preacher very little. The big saloon was owned by John Craycroft, formerly a mate on a Mississippi River steamboat, who gained most of his money by marrying a Spanish woman and making her a silent partner.

One enterprising man who was anxious to make money easily, took a notion to try his luck in trade, so, as rats and mice were troublesome in shops and stores, he went down to the valley and brought up a cargo of cats which he disposed of at prices varying from fifty to one hundred dollars each, according to the buyer's fancy.

During the summer Kelley the fiddler came up in the mines to make a raise, and Craycroft made him a pulpit about ten feet above the floor in his saloon, having him to play nights and Sundays at twenty dollars per day. He was a big uneducated Irishman, who could neither read nor write, but he played and sang and talked the rich Irish brogue, all of which brought many customers to the bar. In the saloon could be seen all sorts of people dealing different games, and some were said to be preachers. Kelley staid here as long as he could live on his salary, and left town much

in debt, for whiskey and cards got all his money.
One of the grocers kept out a sign, "CHEAP JOHN,
THE PACKER," and kept a mule to deliver goods,
which no other merchant did, and in this way gained
many friends, and many now may praise the enterprise
of Cheap John, the Packer. Prices were pretty high
in those days. Sharpening picks cost fifty cents, a
drink of whiskey one dollar, and all kinds of pork,
fifty cents per pound. You could get meals at the
McNutty house for one dollar. The faro and monte
banks absorbed so much of the small change that on
one occasion I had to pay five dollars for a two dollar
pair of pants in order to get a fifty dollar slug changed.

No white shirts were worn by honest men, and if
any man appeared in such a garment he was at once
set down as a gambler, and with very little chance of
a mistake. One Langdon had the only express office,
and brought letters and packages from Sacramento.
I paid one dollar simply to get my name on his letter
list, and when a letter came I had to pay one dollar
for bringing it up, as there was no Post Office at
Downieville.

Newspapers were eagerly sought for, such was the
hunger for reading. The Western folks bought the
St. Louis papers, while Eastern people found the New
York Tribune a favorite. One dollar each for such
papers was the regular price. It may seem strange,
but aside from the news we got from an occasional
newspaper, I did not hear a word from the East during the two years I remained on Yuba river. Our
evenings were spent in playing cards for amusement,
for no reading could be got. The snow between
Marysville and Downieville was deep and impassable
in winter, but we could work our drifting claims very
comfortably, having laid in a stock of provisions early
in the season, before snowfall. The nights seemed

tediously long and lonesome, for when the snow was deep no one came to visit us, and we could go nowhere, being completely hemmed in. All the miners who did not have claims they could work underground, went down below the winter snow-line to find work, and when the snow went off came back again and took posession of the old claims they had left.

After the snow went off three German sailors came up and took a river claim a short distance above us on a north fork of the north fork of the stream, where one side of the cañon was perpendicular and the other sloped back only slightly. Here they put logs across the river, laid stringers on these, and covered the bottom with fir boughs. Then they put stakes at the sides and rigged a canvas flume over their bridge through which they turned the whole current of the river, leaving a nearly dry bed beneath. This we called pretty good engineering and management on the part of the sailor boys, for no lumber was to be had, and they had made themselves masters of the situation with the material on hand.

They went to work under their log aqueduct, and found the claim very rich in coarse gold. They went to town every Saturday night with good big bags of dust, and as they were open-hearted fellows, believing that a sailor always has the best of luck, they played cards freely, always betting on the Jack and Queen, and spent their money more easily than they earned it. They were quite partial to the ladies, and patronizing the bar and card tables as liberally as they did, usually returned to camp on Monday or Tuesday with a mule load of grub and whiskey as all the visible proceeds of a week's successful mining; but when Saturday night came around again we were pretty sure to see the jolly sailors going past with heavy bags of gold. They left one nearly pure piece of gold at Langdon's Express

office that weighed five pounds, and another as large
as a man's hand, of the shape of a prickly pear leaf.
They worked their claim with good success until
the snow water came down and forced them out. I
went one day to see them, and they took a pan of dirt
from behind a big rock and washed it out, getting as
much as two teacupfuls of nuggets, worth perhaps a
thousand dollars. When they went away they said
they would go to Germany to see their poor relatives
and friends, and one of them really went home, but
the other two had spent all their money before they
were ready to leave San Francisco. These men were,
without doubt, the inventors of the canvas flume
which was afterward used so successfully in various
places.

While I was still here the now famous Downieville
Butte quartz mine was discovered, but there was no
way then of working quartz successfully, and just at
that time very little was done with it, but afterward,
when it was learned how to work it, and the proper
machinery introduced, it yielded large sums of bullion.

The miners had a queer way of calling every man
by some nickname or other instead of his true name,
and no one seemed offended at it, but answered to his
new name as readily as to any.

It was nearly fall when we found we had worked
our claims out, and there were no new ones we could
locate here, so we concluded to go prospecting for a
new locality. I bought a donkey in town of a Mr.
Hawley, a merchant, for which I paid sixty dollars,
and gave the little fellow his old master's name. We
now had two animals, and we packed on them our
worldly goods, and started south up the mountain
trail by way of the city of six, where some half dozen
men had located claims, but the ground was dry and
deep, so we went on.

We still went south, down toward the middle Yuba
River, and when about half way down the mountain
side came to a sort of level bench where some miners
were at work, but hardly any water could be had·
They called this Minnesota. We stayed here a day
or two, but as there seemed to be no possible further
development of water, concluded to go on further.
Across the river we could see a little flat, very similar
to the one we were on, and a little prospecting seemed
to have been done on the side of the mountain. We
had a terribly steep cañon to cross, and a river also,
with no trail to follow, but our donkeys were as good
climbers as any of us, so we started down the mountain in the morning, and arrived at the river about
noon. Here we rested an hour or two and then began
climbing the brushy mountain side. The hill was
very steep, and the sun beat down on us with all his
heat, so that with our hard labor and the absence of
any wind we found it a pretty hot place.

It was pretty risky traveling in some places, and
we had to help the donkeys to keep them from rolling
down the hill, pack and all. It took us four hours to
make a mile and a half or two miles in that dense
brush, and we were nearly choked when we reached
the little flat. Here we found some water, but no one
lived here. From here we could see a large flat across
a deep cañon to the west, and made up our minds to
try to go to it. We went around the head of the
cañon, and worked through the brush and fallen timber, reaching our objective point just as night was
coming on. This flat, like the one we had left, was
quite level, and contained, perhaps, nearly one hundred acres. Here we found two men at work with a
"long tom"—a Mr. Fernay and a Mr. Bloat. They
had brought the water of a small spring to their claim
and were making five or six dollars per day. We

now prospected around the edge of this flat, and getting pretty fair prospects concluded we would locate here if we could get water.

We then began our search for water and found a spring about three quarters of a mile away, to which we laid claim, and with a triangle level began to survey out a route for our ditch. The survey was satisfactory, and we found we could bring the water out high on the flat, so we set to work digging at it, and turned the water in. The ground was so very dry that all the water soaked up within two hundred yards of the spring.

By this time we were out of grub, and some one must go for a new supply, and as we knew the trail to Downieville was terribly rough, I was chosen as the one to try to find Nevada City, which we thought would be nearer and more easily reached. So I started south with the donkeys, up the mountain toward the ridge which lies between the middle and south Yuba Rivers, and when I got well on the ridge I found a trail used some by wagons, which I followed till I came to a place where the ridge was only wide enough for a wagon, and at the west end a faint trail turned off south into the rolling hills. I thought this went about the course I wanted to go, so I followed it, and after two or three miles came to the south Yuba river. This seemed to be an Indian trail, no other signs on it. I climbed the mountain here, and when I reached the top I found a large tent made of blue drilling, and here I found I was four or five miles from Nevada City with a good trail to follow. The rolling hills I then passed through are now called North Bloomfield, and at one time were known as "Humbug."

I started along the trail and soon reached the city where I drove my donkeys up to a store which had out the sign "Davis & Co.." I entered and inquiring

the prices of various sorts of provisions such as flour,
bacon, beans, butter, etc., soon had selected enough
for two donkey loads. They assisted me in putting
them in pack, and when it was ready I asked the
amount of my bill, which was one hundred and fifty
dollars. This I paid at once, and they gave me some
crackers and dried beef for lunch on the way. Davis
said—"That is the quickest sale I ever made, and here
the man is ready to go. I defy any one to ·beat it."
Before sun down I was two or three miles on my way
back where I found some grass and camped for the
night, picketed the animals, ate some of Mr. Davis'
grub for supper, and arranged a bed of saddle blankets. I arrived at camp the next day about sun down.

Next day I went on up the divide and found a house
on the trail leading farther east, where two men lived,
but they seemed to be doing nothing. There were no
mines and miners near there, and there seemed to be
very little travel on the trail. The fellows looked
rough, and I suspected they might be bad characters.
The stream they lived near was afterward called
Bloody Run, and there were stories current that blood
had been shed there.

Here was a section of comparatively level land, for
the mountain divide, and a fine spring of good cold
water, all surrounded by several hundred acres of the
most magnificent sugar pines California ever raised,
very large, straight as a candle, and one hundred feet
or more to the lowest limbs. This place was afterward called Snow Tent, and S. W. Churchill built a
sawmill at the spring, and had all this fine timber at
the mercy of his ax and saw, without anyone to dis-
pute his right. He furnished lumber to the miners at
fifty dollars or more per thousand feet. Bloody Run
no doubt well deserves its name, for there was much
talk of killing done there.

I, however, went up and talked to the men and told them I wished to hire a cross cut saw for a few days to get out stuff for a cabin, and agreed to pay two dollars a day for the use of it till it came back.

We cut down a large sugar pine, cut off four six feet cuts, one twelve feet, and one sixteen feet cut, and from these we split out a lot of boards which we used to make a V-shaped flume which we placed in our ditch, and thus got the water through. We split the longer cuts into two inch plank for sluice boxes, and made a small reservoir, so that we succeeded in working the ground. We paid wages to the two men who worked, and two other men who were with us went and built a cabin.

I now went and got another load of provisions, and as the snow could be seen on the high mountains to the east, I thought the deer must be crowded down to our country, so I went out hunting and killed a big fat buck, and the next day three more, so fresh meat was plenty.

About this time a man came down the mountain with his oxen and wagon, wife and three or four children, the eldest a young lady of fifteen years. The man's name was H. M. Moore. We had posted notices, according to custom, to make mining laws, and had quite a discussion about a name for the place. Some of the fellows wanted to name it after the young lady, "Minda's Flat," but we finally chose "Moore's Flat" instead, which I believe is the name it still goes by. Our laws were soon completed, and a recorder chosen to record claims. We gave Mr. Moore the honor of having a prospecting town named after him because he was the first man to be on hand with a wife.

I became satisfied after a little that this place would be a very snowy place, and that from all appearances

it would fall from two to four feet deep, and not a
very pleasant place to winter in. An honest acquaintance of mine came along, Samuel Tyler and to him
iI let my claim to work on shares and made McCloud
my agent, verbally, while I took my blankets and
started for the valley.

The first town I passed through was a newly discovered mining town called French Corral. Here I
found an old Wisconsin friend Wm. Sublet, the foster
father of the accomplishen wife of Mayor S. W. Boring
of San Jose. From here I went to Marysville. The
storm had been raging high in the mountains for some
days, and the Yuba river rising fast, overflowing its
banks as I walked into town, and the next day the
merchants were very busy piling their goods above
high water mark. I went to a hotel and called for a
bed. "Yes," says the landlord, "Is your name John
or Peter?" I told him William, which he set down in
his book and we went up stairs to the best room
which was fitted up with berths three tiers high on
each side, and only one or two empty ones. He looked around for covers, but none could be found unoccupied, but one fellow who was sound asleep and
snoring awfully, so he took the blanket off from him
saying: "He wont know a thing about it till morning, be jabers, so don't say a word."

Next morning the river was booming, its surface
covered with all sorts of mining outfit such as flume
timber, rockers, various qualities of lumber, pieces of
trees as well as whole ones, water wheels and other
traps. The river between Downieville and here must
have been swept clean of all material that would float,
including "long Toms." The water continued to rise
till it covered the Plaza, and in two days a steamer
came up and sailed across the public square. This
looked like a wet season to me, and when the boat

was ready to go down the river I went on board,
bound for Sacramento. Here it was also getting terrible wet and muddy, and the rain kept pouring down.
In the morning I worked my way up J street and saw
a six·mule team wading up the streets the driver on
foot, tramping through the sloppy mud, occasionally
stepping in a hole and falling his whole length in the
mud. On the street where so much trouble was met
by the teamsters, a lot of idlers stood on the sidewalk,
and when a driver would fall and go nearly out of
sight, they would, like a set of loafers, laugh at him
and blackguard him with much noise, and as they
were numerous they feared nothing.

Suddenly a miner, who had lately arrived from the
mountains, raised his room window in the second
story of a house, put out one leg and then his body,
as far as he could, and having nothing on but his
night clothes, shouted to the noisy crowd below:—
"Say, can't you d—d farmers plow now?" At this he
dodged back quickly into his window as if he expected something might be thrown at him. The rain continued, and the water rose gradually till it began to
run slowly through the streets, and all the business
stopped except gambling and drinking whisky. which
were freely carried on in the saloons day and night.

While here in Sacramento I was sufficiently promp-
ted by curiosity to go around to the place on J street
where the Legislature was in session. I stood sometime outside the enclosure listening to the members
who were in earnest debate over a question concerning the size of mining claims. They wanted them
uniform in size all over the state, but there was some
opposition, and the debate on this occasion was between the members from the mining counties on one
side and the "cow" counties on the other. The
miners took the ground that the claims were of differ-

ent richness in the different mining localities and that
the miners themselves were the best judges of the
proper size of claims, and were abundantly able to
make their own laws as they had done under the present mining customs, and their laws had always been
respected, making any further legislative action unnecessary.

While this wrangle was going on.   Capt. Hunt, of
San Bernardino (our guide from Salt Lake in 1849,
came along and stopped where I stood, shaking me
heartily by the hand, inquiring where I was from, and
when I told him I was from the mines he said he
thought the cow county fellows were trying to make
the miners some trouble.   I told him the present mining regulations suited us very well, and after he had
talked with me a little he went inside and whispered
to some of the silent members that the miners wanted
no change, for he had just consulted a miner to that
effect.   When occasion offered he called for a vote
which resulted in the defeat of the cow counties and a
postponement of the measure indefinitely.

My next move was to try to find a dryer place so I
took a boat for Benicia, then for Stockton, where I
found a sea of mud, so that a man needed stilts or a
boat to cross the street.

Here in a livery stable I found my old Platte River
boss, Chas. Dallas, for whom I drove in 1849, but he
did not seem to know me and took no notice of me,
but talked "horse" and horse-racing to the bystanders
very loudly.   I suppose that Dallas had made money
and did not care for a poor ox driver, and on my part
I did not care very much for his friendship, so I walked away and left him without a word.

Every way I looked was a sea of black, sticky mud;
dogs mired in the streets and died, and teams and
animals had forsaken the usual route of travel.   The

gambling houses and saloons were crowded, gum
boots in demand, and the only way to get out of town
was by water. I took this way out, and on the same
boat by which I came, going to San Francisco. This
was high and dry enough to be above the highest floods
of Yuba, Sacramento or San Joaquin, but all business
except the saloons was dull. Fronting on Portsmouth
Square was the Hall of Corruption. Inside was a
magnificently furnished bar, more than one keeper and
various gambling tables, most of them with soiled
doves in attendance. The room was thronged with
players and spectators, and coin and dust were plenty.
The dealers drew off their cards carefully, and seemed
to have the largest pile of coin on their side.

I climbed Russian Hill and to take a look over the
city. It seemed poorly built, but the portion that had
been burned in July 1852, had been built up again.
The business part was near the beach and north of
Market street.

I had never lived in a town and did not know its
ways, so I strolled around alone, for without acquaintance I did not know where to go nor what to look for.
I therefore thought I would see some other part of the
country. I found that a schooner was about to sail
for San Pedro, near Los Angeles. I took hold of a
rope to help myself on board, when it gave way and I
found myself floundering in the water. They helped
me out and the Captain gave me a dry suit to put on,
I was profoundly grateful for the favor, and found him
a generous man.

We sailed away and stopped at Monterey for 24 hours
which gave me a good chance for a good look at the
old Capitol houses, which were of adobe, and to find
that this city was also liberally supplied with gambling, card and billiard tables. The majority of the
people were Spanish and fond of gaming, and the gen_

eral appearance of the place was old and without good
improvements, though there were more two story
houses than in most places in California.

Some houses were of stone, but more of adobe, and
there seemed to be no fertile country round, and the
hills about had small pines on them.

Some of the sailors went out and gathered a large
bag of mussels and clams, from which they made a
liberal allowance of chowder for the table. After
seven or eight days we arrived in San Pedro, and
found the town to consist of one long adobe house.
The beach was low and sandy, and we were wet somewhat in wading through a light surf to get on shore.
We had on board a Mr. Baylis, who we afterward
learned came down with Capt. Lackey on a big speculation which was to capture all the wild goats they
could on Catalina Island, and take them to San Francisco for slaughtering.

The goats were easily captured and taken on board
the schooner, and thence to shore but many were
drowned in the transit, and when driven to San Francisco the dead were scattered all along the route. Although wild they seemed to lack the vitality that tame
goats possess. The speculation proved a disappointment to the projectors.

At the adobe house, kept by a Spainard we had
breakfast, then shouldered our packs for the march of
ten leagues to Los Angeles for there was no chance to
ride. It was night before we reached the City of
Angels, and here I staid a day to take a look at the
first city I saw in California in March 1850.

I inquired for my mining companion, W. M. Stockton who worked with Bennett and myself near Georgetown in 1850, and found he lived near the old mission
of San Gabriel nine miles away, whither I walked and
found him and family well and glad to see me. He

had jumped an old pear orchard which was not claimed by the Mission Fathers, although it was only three-fourths of a mile away. The trees were all seedlings and very large, probably 50 or more years old. Some of the Mission buildings were falling down since they had been abandoned, and the Americans would go to these houses and remove the tile flooring from the porches and from the pillars that supported them. These tiles were of hard burned clay, in pieces about a foot square, and were very convenient to make fire places and pavements before the doors of their new houses. Out-side the enclosed orange and fig orchard at this place were some large olive and fig trees, apparently as old as the mission, being a foot or more in diameter and about 50 feet high. I had never seen olives, and when I saw these trees covered with plenty of fruit about the size of damson plums I took the liberty of tasting it and found it very disagreeable, and wondered of what use such fruit could be.

Mr. Stockton fenced his orchard by setting posts and tying sycamore poles to them to keep the stock away, built an adobe house on the claim and called the property his. I went to work for him at once, pruning the trees, which improved their appearance, and then turned on a little stream of water which ran through the place, and on down to the mission. With this treatment the trees did well without cultivation.

I bought one half the stock consisting of some Spanish cows, one yoke of oxen and some horses, worked enough to pay my board, watched the stock and still had plenty of time to ride around over the adjoining country.

When the pears were ripe the Spanish men, women and children eagerly bought them at 25 cents per dozen and some Sundays the receipts for fruit sold would be as high as $100. That taken to town would bring

from $5. to $8. per box, the boxes being a little larger
than those in present use.   An Indian woman, widow
of a Mr. Reed, claimed a vineyard near the orchard,
and laid claim to the whole property, so Stockton gave
her $1000 for a quit claim deed.

Near by was a small artificial lake made by a dam
of cobble stones, laid in cement across a ravine, which
was built perhaps 50 years before, and yet the tracks of
a child who had walked across before the cement was
dry, were plainly seen.

Stockton and I visited Mr. Roland, an old settler
who lived south of San Gabriel river, and staid all
night with him, finding him very sociable and hospitable.   All his work was done by Indians who lived
near by, and had been there as long as he.   He had a
small vineyard, and raised corn, squashes, melons and
all that are necessary for his table, having also a small
mill near by for grinding corn and wheat without bolt-
ing.   The Indians made his wine by tramping the
grapes with their feet in a rawhide vat hung between
four poles set in the ground.   The workmen were
paid off every Saturday night, and during Sunday he
would generally sell them wine enough to get about
all the money back again.   This had been his practice
for many years, and no doubt suited Mr. Roland as
well as the red men.

Roland was an old Rocky Mountain trapper who
came to California long before gold was discovered,
and during the evening the talk naturally ran to the
subject of early days.

Mr. Roland related that while his party were in
camp in the upper Colorado they were visited by a
small band of Indians who professed friendship and
seated themselves around the fire.   Suddenly they
made an attack and each trapper had an Indian to con-
tend with, except Mr. Roland who was left to be dis-

patched afterwards. But as he ran, a squaw among
them followed him, and after a while overtook him
and showed friendship. He had neither gun or knife
and so concluded to put faith in the woman who
safely guided him in a long tramp across the desert
where they both came near starving, but finally reached Los Angeles Valley, when the brave squaw min-
gled with her own people and he lost sight of her forever.

No white man could alone have traversed that desert
waste and found food enough to last him half the
journey.

He gradually learned to speak Spanish, and was
granted the piece of land he applied for, and where
he then lived; married a Spanish girl, with whom he
had a happy home and raised a large family, and grew
rich, for they were both industrious and economical.
The first wife died, and he was persuaded to marry a
Texas widow, and now had to buy the first carriage
he ever owned, and furnish a fine turn-out and driver
for the lady, who wore much jewelry and fine clothes,
and spent money freely. Roland was not a society
man, his thoughts and habits were different from his
wife, and he staid at home, better contented there.

There were many other pioneers in the neighborhood, Dan Sexton, Col. Williams, of Chino ranch,
Workman, B. D. Wilson, Abel Stearns, Temple,
Wolfskill and many others, Scott and Granger were
lawers. Granger was the same man who read the
preamble and resolutions that were to govern our big
train as we were about to start from Utah Lake.

Scott was quite a noted member of the bar, and
when Gen. Winfield Scott ran for President, some
wide awake politicians caused the uneducated Spaniards to vote for their favorite lawyer instead of the
redoubtable general, and they did this with a good

will for they thought the famous avacado was the best man, and thus the manipulators lost many votes to the real candidate. Scott was afterward retained by many of the Spaniards to present their claims for their land to the U. S. Goverment and was considered a very able man.

Mr. Stockton related that when he left his family here to go to the mines he rented one half a house of Michael Blanco who had a Spanish wife and children, and these and his own were of course constant play-mates. When he returned in the fall he found his children had learned to speak Spanish and nearly for-gotten English, so that he had to coax them a great deal to get them to talk to him at all, and he could not understand a word they said.

I now tried to learn the language myself. I had money to loan, and the borrowers were Spanish who gave good security and paid from 5 to 25 per cent in-terest per month, on short time. Mrs. Stockton as-sisted me very much as an interpreter.

I bought young steers for $8. each and gradually added to my herd. I got along well until next spring when the beef eating population began to steal my fat cattle, and seemed determined I should get no richer. The country was over-stocked with desperate and law-less renegades in Los Angeles and from one to four dead men was about the number picked up in the streets each morning. They were of low class, and there was no investigation, simply a burial at public expense.

The permanent Spanish population seemed honest and benevolent, but there were many bad ones from Chili, Sonora, Mexico, Texas, Utah and Europe, who seemed always on an errand of mischief a murder, thieving or robbery.

Three or four suspicious looking men came on horse-

back and made their camp near the Mission under an
oak tree, where they staid sometime. They always
left someone in camp while the others went away every
day on their horses, and acted so strangely that the report soon became current that they were stealing
horses and running them off to some safe place in the
mountains till a quantity could be accumulated to take
to the mines to sell. On this information the Vigilance
Committee arrested the man in camp and brought him
to a private room, where he was tried by twelve men,
who found him guilty of horse stealing, and sentenced
to be hung at once, for horse stealing was a capital
offence in those days.

To carry out the sentence they procured a cart, put
a box on it for a seat, and with a rope around his neck
and seated on the box, the condemned man was drag-
ed off by hand to an oak tree not far away, whither he
was followed by all the men, women and children of
the place, who where nearly all natives. While preparations were being made under the tree some one
called out that men were riding rapidly from the direction of Los Angeles, and from the dust they raised
seemed to be more than usually in haste. So it was
proposed to wait till they came up. It was soon
known that an Indian had been sent to Los Angeles
to give news to the man's friends there, and they had
come with all the speed of their horses to try to save
his life. They talked and inquired around a little and
then proposed the question whether to hang him or to
turn him over to the lawful authorities for regular
trial. This was put to a vote and it was decided to
spare him now. So the rope was taken off his neck,
and he was turned over to Mr. Mallard the Mission
Justice of the Peace, much to the relief of the fellow
who saw death staring him in the face.

The Santa Anita ranch, now owned by E. J. Baldwin, was owned by Henry Dalton, an Englishman, who came with a stock of goods worth $75,000, years before, but now had only the ranch left. The Azuza, a short distance south was occupied by his brother.

I became well acquainted with many of these old California natives, and found them honest in their dealings, good to the needy and in all my travels never found more willing hands to bestow upon relatives, friends or strangers ready relief than I saw among these simple natives. Their kindness to our party when we came starving on the desert in 1850, can never be praised enough, and as long as I shall live my best wishes shall go with them.

I was one day riding with Vincent Duarte down toward Anaheim when he suddenly dismounted to kill a large tarantula by pelting him with stones. It was the first one I had seen, and seemed an over-grown spider. I asked him if the thing was harmful, and he replied with considerable warmth, ''Mucho malo por Christianos'' and I wondered if the insect knew saints from sinners.

This spring we concluded to go to the Mormon settlement at San Bernardino and secure some American bulls to improve our stock, and starting late one day I rode as far as the Azuza Rancho where I staid all night with Mr. Dalton, reaching the holy city, a branch of Brigham Young's harem next day. Here I found a town of log houses in a circle, enclosing a plaza. There was a passage between the houses. I stopped at the principal hotel kept by a vigorous and enthusiastic Mormon woman, who delighted to preach the doctrine.

Walking around on the outside of the fortifications I came across Capt. Hunt, the man who was hired in the fall of 1849 to bring the big train from Salt Lake to San Bernardino.

I told him who I was, and what I wanted, and he
seemed to know me, inviting me in the most friendly
and social manner to take supper with him, which I
did. He sat at the head of the table and introduced
me to his three wives. The furnishing of the house
was cheap and common, but the table was fairly provided for. He said he would help me to find the animals I wanted, and in the morning showed me two
which he had, that were young and suitable, and a
larger one which he said I could have if I could drive
him.

l soon found out that I had better move or sell my
cattle, for with all my watching I could do they gradually disappeared, and hungry thieves who could live
on beef alone, visited my little band of cattle too often
and took what they wanted, and I could not detect
them. I soon sold to four buyers from the north, L.
D. Stevens, David Grant, Sam Craig and Mr. Wilson,
and hired out with my two horses to help them drive
the band north, at a salary of $100 per month.

Disposing most of my money with Palmer, Cook &
Co., I went to see my mine at Moore's Flat. There
were two boats leaving at about the same time, one for
Stockton, and one for Sacramento, the latter of which
I took, and Rogers the other. Both landed at Benecia,
and when we swung away from that wharf Rogers and
I saluted each other with raised and swinging hats,
shouted a good bye, and I have never seen him since.

At Moore's Flat I found my mine well and profitably worked by Mr. Tyler and as his lease was not out
I returned to San Jose, as I had learned from Rogers
that Mr. A. Bennett was at Watsonville, and Mr.
Arcane at Santa Cruz, and I desired to visit them. I
rode back across the country and found Mr. Bennett
and family at the point where the Salinas river enters
Monterey Bay. They were all well, and were glad to

see me for they did not know I was in California.
Mrs. Bennett was greatly affected at our meeting and
shed tears of joy as she shook hands.

Bennett had a nice Whitehall boat and we had a
genuine happy time hunting, fishing and gathering
clams, and also in social visits amoung the neighbors
and old acquaintances, among them one Jacob Rhode-
house of Wisconsin.

While here I rode my horse around to Monterey and
to Carmel Mission, where I staid two or three days
with Mr. Gourley, a brother of Mrs. William M. Stockton, who was here engaged in raising potatoes. I
walked along the beach near some rocky islands near
the shore, and on these rocks were more sea lions and
seals than I supposed the whole ocean contained—the
most wonderful show of sea life on the California coast.
Returning I staid all night at the crossing of the Salinas
with a colored family who gave me good accommo-
dations for self and horse. I heard afterward that this
family was attacked by robbers and all but one murdered.

Mrs. Bennett's father D. J. Dilley lived near here
also, and I had not seen him since the time in Wisconsin, when he hauled my canoe over to the river in 1849.
One day while fishing on the beach we found the body
of a man, which we carried above the tide and buried
in the sand.

I gave one of my horses to Geo. Bennett, and went
over to Santa Cruz, where I found Mr. and Mrs. J. B.
Arcane and son Charles in a comfortable home, well
situated, and overjoyed to see me.

He knew everyone in town, and as we went about he
never missed to introduce me to every one we met, as
the man who helped himself and family out of Death
Valley, and saved their lives. Arcane was a very po-
ite Frenchman and knew how to manage such things.

very gracefully, but with all his grace and heartiness
it made me feel quite a little embarrassed to be made
so much of publicly and among strangers. He took
me in his buggy and we drove along the beach, and to
the lime-kiln of Cowel & Jordan, also to the court
house when court was in session.

Upon the hill I met Judge Watson, the father of
Watsonville, and a Mr. Graham, an old settler and
land owner, and on this occasion he pulled a sheet of
ancient, smoky looking paper from beneath his arm,
pointed to a dozen or so of written lines in Spanish
and then with a flourish of the precious document in
Watson's face dared him to beat that, or get him off
his land. I must say that never in my life was I better entertained than here.

From Santa Cruz I crossed the mountain on a lonely
and romantic trail to San Jose again, finding very few
houses on the road. Here I went to work for R. G.
Moody building a gristmill on the banks of the Coyote
Creek, to be run by water from artesian wells. When
the mill was done I went for my horse, and on my return I ran very unexpectedly upon Davenport Helms,
to whom I had sold my little black mule in 1850. Our
talk was short but he told me he had killed a man in
Georgetown, and the sheriff was looking for him. He
was now venturing to town for tobacco, and would
hurry back to the hills again where he was herding
cattle.

He said he kept them off at one time by getting in
a piece of chaparral and presenting his gun to them
when they came near, they dare not advance on him.
Then he laughed and said—"And all the time my gun
was empty, for I did not have a d—d thing to put into
it." "I tell you they don't catch old Davenport. Now
don't you tell on me. Good-bye." I saw him no
more after that.

The town of San Jose was now more of a town than it was a few years before. The "Forty Thieves," and others, commenced building a city hall of brick on the top of old adobe walls, and this was the principal improvement, except the Moody mill near the Sutter house, one street north of Julian.

After finishing work on the mill I drew my money from the bank in San Francisco and started for the mines on horseback. Near French Camp, on the east side of the San Joaquin Valley, many cattle were feeding on the plains, and among them, much to my surprise I found "Old Crump," the ox that brought Bennett's and Arcane's children safe through from Death Valley in February, 1850. He was now fat and sleek and as kind and gentle as when so poor upon the terrible journey. I got off my horse and went up to him, and patted my old friend. I was glad to find him so contented and happy, and I doubt not that he too was glad. I met a man near by and asked him about the ox, and he said that the owner would not sell him nor allow him to be worked, for he knew of the faithful part he performed in the world, and respected him for it.

At Sacramento I deposited my money with Page, Bacon & Co., a branch of the St. Louis firm of the same name, considered the safest bank in the United States. Their bills were taken in payment of Government land. Some rascals had some counterfeit bills on their bank, and traded them off for gold with the Missourians who were going home, and the poor fellows found themselves poor on arrival.

Going to my mine, where I left only a cabin or two, I found quite a village with two hotels and a post office.

News soon came that the banks had closed their door, and Page and Bacon also, so I concluded that I was broke. The "Pikers" said Page and Bacon could not, nor would not fail, but news was against them.

The boys now tried to persuade me to go to Sacramento, and try to get my money and if I succeeded, to bring up a good stock of goods and they would buy of me in preference to any one else. On this showing I went down, and finding my old friend Lyman Ross (well known in San Jose) who was keeping a fruit store. I told him my business and he took me to L. A. Booth, Carrol & Co., and I stated to him the facts about my money in the bank and the doors closed. I told him if he would assist me I would buy $2000 worth of his goods, and send them to Moore's Flat. I endorsed the certificate over to him, and in half an hour he came back with the coin. How he got it I never knew, but he did me a great favor, and we have been good friends ever since. I was no merchant, nor had I any mercantile education, so I took lessons from Mr. Booth, and allowed him to make out for me a bill of goods such as he well knew I needed. With these we loaded up two 6 mule teams, and started for the mountain.

I had about $700 left besides paying for the goods, but I felt a very little troubled as to my prospect for success, for it was a new business to me. Mr. Booth in a business way was a true father to me, and the much needed points in trade which he gave me were stored away for the use I knew I would make of them. Of all those whom I bear in grateful remembrance none stand higher than this worthy man.

I went first direct to Nevada City to take out a license that I might best protect myself against oppositions and from there I had a walk of 18 miles over a rough mountain trail to my selected place of business. Climbing the great hill of the S. Yuba river I often tired and sat down to rest, and I used this time to study my bill of goods, and add the freight and profit to the cost, so as to be well posted, and able to answer

all questions readily when I unloaded the stock. The
new trade seemed quite a task to learn, but I felt that
I was compelled to succeed, and I worked manfully at it.

When I reached Moore's Flat I found that the boys
had rented a store for me, and their welcome was very
hearty when they found how lucky I had been in securing my money and starting out as their "grub sup-
plier."

Four of us now located some mining claims, and began a tunnel both to drain the ground, and to work
through the bed-rock. This we named The Paradise,
and we expected that three or four months would
elapse before we made it pay, but there was in truth
two years of solid rock-work before we got under the
ground, but it paid well in the end.

The largest nugget of gold ever found before this
time was a quartz boulder from the Buckeye sluice,
about 8 by 10 inches in size, and when cleaned up at
tne San Francisco mint the value was about $10,000.

Two of my partners in the work, L. J. Hanchett,
and Jas. Clark ran out of funds at the end of the first
year, and I took as much of the expense as I could upon my own shoulders.

About this time learning by a letter from her father
that Mrs. Bennett was lying at the point of death at
Mr. L. C. Bostic's in San Jose, I left H. Hanchett in
charge of my business, and in four days I stood beside
the bedside of my friend, endeared through the trials
when death by thirst, starvation and the desert sands,
stared us in the face with all its ghastliness.

She reached out her arms and drew me down to her,
and embraced me and said in a faint whisper—"God
bless you:—you saved us all till now, and I hope you
will always be happy and live long." She would
have said more, but her voice was so weak she could
not be heard. She was very low with consumption,

and easily exhausted. I sat with her much of the
time at her request and though for her sake I would
have kept back the tears I could not always do it.
Two doctors came, one of them Dr. Spencer, and as I
sat with my face partly turned away I over heard Dr.
S. say to his assistant—"He is a manly man."

This presence and the circumstances brought back
the trying Death Valley struggles, when this woman
and her companions, and the poor children, so nearly
starved they could not stand alone, were only prevented from sitting down to die in sheer despair by the
encouraging words of Rogers and myself who had
passed over the road, and used every way to sustain
their courage.

She died the following day; with Mr. Bennett, I
followed her remains to Oak Hill cemetery, where she
was buried near the foot of the hill, and a board marked in large letters, "S. B." (Sarah Bennett) placed to
mark the mound. The grave cannot now be found,
and no records being then kept it is probably lost.

I went home with Mr. Bennett to his home near
Watsonville, and spent several days, meeting several
of our old Death Valley party, and Mr. D. J. Dilley,
Mrs. Bennett's father. Mrs. Bennett left surviving
her a young babe.

I returned to Moore's Flat, and soon sold out my
store, taking up the business of purchasing gold dust
direct from the miners, which I followed for about two
years, and in the fall of 1859 sold out the business to
Marks & Powers. I looked about through Napa and
Sonoma Counties, and finally came to San Jose, where
I purchased the farm I now own, near Hillsdale, of
Bodley & McCabe, for which I paid $4,000.

In the fall of the same year my old friend W. M.
Stockton of Los Angeles Co. persuaded me to come
down and pay him a visit. His wife had died and he

felt very lonely. I had been there but a few days
when my old friend A. Bennett and his children also
came to Stockton's. The children had grown so much
I hardly knew them, but I was glad indeed to meet
them.

I found Mr. Bennett to be a poor man. He had
been persuaded to go to Utah, being told that a fortune awaited his coming there, or could be accumulated
in a short time. He gave away the little babe left by
his wife to Mrs. Scott, of Scott's Valley, in Santa Cruz
Co. and sold his farm near the mouth of the Salinas
River. With what money he had accumulated he
loaded two 4 mule teams with dry goods, put his four
children into his wagon, and went to Cedar City, Utah.

He gave a thrilling account of passing through
Mountain Meadows, where he saw, here and there
little groups of skeletons of the unhappy victims of the
great massacre at that place of men, women and children, by J. D. Lee, and his Mormon followers and
told me the terrible story, which I here omit.

Smarting under the terrible taxation of one tenth of
everything, Bennett grew poorer and poorer and at
last resolved that he must go away, but his wife could
not leave her own people, and so he set off with his
children, somewhat afraid he might be shot down, but
he reached Los Angeles Co. in safety. One daughter
married a lawyer in San Bernardino, and died a few
years afterwards. The other married a Capt. Johnson
of Wilmington, and Bennett and two sons went to
Idaho.

A few years ago in passing from San Jose to the
Coast, my wife and I spent Sunday at Scott's Valley.
Mrs. Scott invited us to visit them in the evening at
the house when all would be at home. Mrs. Scott
was the lady to whom Bennett gave his girl baby
when he started away for Utah, and I felt very anxious

to see her now she was grown up.   Mrs. Scott introduced us, and I sat and looked at the little woman
quite a long time, but could not see that she resembled either father or mother.   My mind ran back over
the terrible road we came and I pictured to myself the
woman as she then appeared.

I studied over our early trials, crossing the plains
over the deserts and our trying scenes out of Death
Valley and turned all over in my mind for some time
and finally all came to me like a flash and I could
clearly see that the little lady was a true picture of
her mother; I now began to ask questions about her
folks, she said her father lived near Belmont, Nevada,
and her grand-father died at the Monte, Los Angeles
county Cal..   Our visit now became very interesting
and we kept a late hour.

CHAPTER XVII.

Since writing the connected story which has thus
far appeared, I turn back to give some incidents of
life in the mines, and some description of those pioneer
gold days.

I have spoken of Moore's Flat, Orleans Flat and
Woolsey's Flat, all similarly situated on different
points of the mountain, on the north side of the
ridge between the South and Middle Yuba River, and
all at about the same altitude. A very deep cañon
lies between each of them, but a good mountain road
was built around the head of each cañon, connecting
the towns. When the snow got to be three or four
feet deep the roads must be broken out and commu-
nication opened, and the boys used to turn out *en masse*
and each one would take his turn in leading the army
of road breakers. When the leader got tired out some
one would take his place, for it was terrible hard work
to wade through snow up to one's hips, and the progress very slow. But the boys went at it as if they
were going to a picnic, and a sort of picnic it was when
they reached the next town, for whisky was free and
grub plenty to such a party, and jollity and fun the
uppermost thoughts. On one such occasion when the
crowd came through Orleans Flat to Moore's Flat, Sid
Hunt, the butcher, was in the lead as they came in
sight of the latter place, and both he and his followers
talked pretty loud and rough to the Moore's Flat fellows calling them "lazy pups" for not getting their
road clear. Hunt's helper was a big stout, loud talking young man named Williams, and he shouted to
the leader—"Sid Hunt, toot your horn if you don't
sell a clam." This seemed to put both sides in good

humor, and the Orleans fellows joined in a plenty to eat and drink. rested and went home. Next day, both camps joined forces and broke the road over to Woolsey's Flat, and the third day crowded on toward Nevada City, and when out and across Bloody Run, a stream called thus because some dead men had been found at the head of the stream by the early settlers, and it was suspected the guilty murderers lived not far off, they turned down into Humbug, a town now called Bloomfield, and as they went down the snow was not so deep. They soon met Sam Henry, the express man, working through with letters and papers, and all turned home again.

A young doctor came to Moore's Flat and soon became quite popular, and after a little while purchased a small drug store at Orleans Flat. In this town there lived a man and his family and among them a little curly headed girl perhaps one or two years old. She was sick and died and buried while the ground was covered thick with snow. A little time after, it was discovered that the grave had been disturbed, and on examination no body was found in the grave.

Then it was a searching party was organized, and threats of vengence made against the grave robber if he should be caught. No tracks were found leading out of town so they began to look about inside, and there began to be some talk about this Dr. Kittridge as the culprit. He was the very man, and he went to his drug store and told his clerk to get a saddle horse and take the dead child's body in a sack to his cabin at Moore's Flat, and conceal it in a back room. The clerk obeyed, and with the little corpse before him on the horse started from the back door and rode furiously to Moore's Flat, and concealed the body as he had been directed.

Some noticed that he had ridden unusually fast, and

having a suspicion that all was not right, told their
belief to the Orleans Flat people, who visited the Doctor at his store and accused him of the crime, and talked about hanging him on the spot without a trial. At
this the Doctor began to be greatly frightened and
begged piteously for them to spare his life, confessing
to the deed, but pleading in extenuation that it was
for the purpose of confirming a question in his profession, and wholly in the interest of science that he did
it, and really to spare the feelings of the parents that
he did it secretly. He argued that no real harm had
been done, and some of his friends sided with him in
this view. But the controversy grew warmer, and
the house filled up with poeple. Some were bloodthirsty and needed no urging to proceed to buy a rope
and use it. Others argued, and finally the Doctor
said that the body had not been dissected, and if they
would allow him, and appoint a committee to go with
him, he would produce the body, and they could decently bury it again and there it might remain forever.
This he promised to do, and all agreed to it, and he
kept his word, thus ending the matter satisfactorily
and the Doctor was released. But the feeling never
died out. The Doctor's friends deserted him, and no
one seemed to like to converse with him. At the saloon he would sit like a perfect stranger, no one notic-
ing him, and he soon left for new fields.

The first tunnel run at Moore's Flat was called the
Paradise, and had to be started low on the side of the
mountain in order to drain the ground, and had to be
blasted through the bed rock for about 200 feet.

Four of us secured ground enough by purchase so we
could afford to undertake this expensive job and we
worked on it day and night. Jerry Clark and Len
Redfield worked the day shifts, and Sam King and
Wm. Quirk the night shift. When the tunnel was

completed about 100 feet, the night shift had driven
forward the top of the tunnel as a heading, leaving
the bottom, which was about a foot thick, or more, to
be taken out by the day shift. They drilled a hole
about two feet horizontally to blast out this bench.
King would sit and hold the drill between his feet,
while Quirk would strike with a heavy sledge. When
the hole was loaded they tramped down the charge
very hard so as to be sure it would not blow out, but
lift the whole bench.   One day when they were loading a hole, King told Quirk to come down pretty
heavy on the tamping, so as to make all sure, and
after a few blows given as directed, there was an ex-
plosion, and Quirk was forced some distance out of the
tunnel, his eyes nearly put out with dirt blown into
them, and his face and body cut with flying pieces of
rock.   He was at first completely stunned, but after
awhile recovered so as to crawl out, and was slowly
making his way up the hill on hands and knees when
he was discovered and helped to his cabin where his
wounds were washed and dressed.

   Then a party with lighted candles entered the tunnel to learn the fate of King, and they found him lying on the mass of rock the blast had lifted, dead.
On a piece of board they bore the body to his cabin.
There was hardly a whole bone remaining. A cut
diagonally across his face, made by a sharp stone, had
nearly cut his head in two. He had been thrown so
violently against the roof of the tunnel, about 6 feet
high, that he was completely mashed.

   He had a wife in Mass. and as I had often heard
him talk of her, and of sending her money, I bought
a $100 check and sent it in the same letter which bore
the melancholy news. King had a claim at Chip's
Flat which he believed would be very rich in time, so
I kept his interest up in it till it amounted to $500 and

then abandoned the claim and pocketed the loss.

We made a pine box, and putting his body in it, laid it away with respect. I had often heard him say that if he suffered an accident, he wished to be killed outright and not be left a cripple, and his wish came true.

After this accident the blacksmith working for the Paradise Co., was making some repairs about the surface of the air shaft, and among his tools was a bar of steel an inch square, and 8 or 10 feet long, which was thrown across the shaft, and while working at the whim wheel he slipped and struck this bar which fell to the bottom of the shaft, 100 feet deep and the blacksmith followed. When the other workmen went down to his assistance they found that the bar of steel had stuck upright in the bottom of the shaft, and when the man came down it pierced his body from hip to neck, killing him instantly. He was a young man, and I have forgotten his name.

Those who came to California these later years will not many of them see the old apparatus and appliances which were used in saving the gold in those primitive days. Among them was the old "Rocker." This had a bottom about 5 feet long and 16 inches wide, with the sides about 8 inches high for half the lenght, and then sloped off to two inches at the end. There was a bar about an inch high across the end to serve as a riffle, and on the higher end of this box is a stationary box 14 inches square, with sides 4 inches high and having a sheet iron bottom perforated with half inch holes. On the bottom of the box are fastened two rockers like those on the baby cradle, and the whole had a piece of board or other solid foundation to stand on, the whole being set at an angle to allow the gravel to work off at the lower end with the water. A cleat was fastened across the bottom to catch the

gold, and this was frequently examined to see how the
work was paying, and taking out such coarse pieces
as could be readily seen. To work the rocker a pan
of dirt would be placed in the square screen box, and
then with one hand the miner would rock the cradle
while he poured water with the other from a dipper to
wash the earth. After he had poured on enough water
and shaken the box sufficiently to pass all the small
stuff through he would stir over what remained in the
screen box, examining carefully for a nugget too large
to pass through the half inch holes. If the miner found
that the dirt did not pay he took his rocker on his back
and went on in search of a better claim.

Another way to work the dirt was to get a small
head of water running in a ditch, and then run the
water and gravel through a series of boxes a foot
square and twelve feet long, using from one to ten
boxes as circumstances seemed to indicate. At the
lower end of these boxes was placed the "Long Tom"
which was about two feet wide at the lower end, and
having sides six inches high at the same point. The
side pieces extend out about 3 feet longer than the
wooden bottom, and are turned up to a point, some
like a sled runner, and this turned up part has a bottom of sheet iron punched full of holes, the size of the
sheet iron being about 3 feet by 16 inches.

The miners shovel dirt into the upper end of the
boxes slowly, and regulate the water so that it dissol-
ves the lumps and chunks very thoroughly before it
reaches the long tom where a man stands and stirs the
gravel over, and if nothing yellow is seen throws the
washed gravel away, and lets the rest go through the
screen. Immediately below this screen was placed
what was called a "riffle box," 2 by 4 feet in size with
bars 4 inches high across the bottom and sides, and
this box is set at the proper angle. Now when the

water comes through the screen it falls perpendicularly in this box with force enough to keep the contents continually in motion, and as the gold is much heavier than any other mineral likely to be found in the dirt, it settles to the bottom, and all the lighter stuff is carried away by the water. The gold would be found behind the bars in the riffle box.

These methods of working were very crude, and we gradually became aware that the finest dust was not saved, and many improvements were brought into use. In my own mine the tailings that we let go down the mountain side would lodge in large piles in different places, and after lying a year, more gold could be washed out of it than was first obtained, and some of it coarser, so that it was plainly seen that a better way of working would be more profitable. There was plenty of ground called poor ground that had much gold in it but could not be profitably worked with the rocker and long tom. The bed rock was nearly level and as the land had a gradual rise, the banks kept getting higher and higher as they dug farther in. Now it was really good ground only down close to the bed rock, but all the dirt had some gold in it, and if a way could be invented to work it fast enough, such ground would pay. So the plan of hydraulic mining was experimented upon.

The water was brought in a ditch or flume to the top of a high bank, and then terminated in a tight box. To this box was attached a large hose made by hand out of canvas, and a pipe and nozzle attached to the lower end of the hose. Now as the bank was often 100 feet or more high the water at this head, when directed through the nozzle against the bank, fairly melted it away into liquid mud. Imagine us located a mile above the river on the side of a mountain. We dug at first sluices in the rock to carry off the mud

and water, and after it had flowed in these a little way
a sluice box was put in to pass it through. These
were made on a slope of one in twelve, and the bottom paved with blocks, 3 inches thick, so laid as to
make a cavity or pocket at the corner of the blocks.
After passing the first sluice box the water and gravel
would be run in a bed rock sluice again, and then into
another sluice box and so on for a mile, passing
through several sluice boxes on the way. Quicksilver
was placed in the upper sluice boxes, and when the
particles of gold were polished up by tumbling about
in the gravel, they combined with the quicksilver
making an amalgam.

The most gold would be left in the first sluice boxes
but some would go on down to the very last, where
the water and dirt was run off into the river. They
cleaned up the first sluices every week, a little farther
down every month, while the lower ones would only
be cleaned up at the end of the season.

In cleaning up, the blocks would be taken out of
the boxes, and every little crevice or pocket in the
whole length of the sluice cleaned out, from the bottom to the top, using little hooks and iron spoons
made for the purpose.

The amalgam thus collected was heated in a retort
which expelled the quicksilver in vapor, which was
condensed and used again.

When they first tried hydraulic work a tinsmith
made a nozzle out of sheet iron, but when put in practice, instead of throwing a solid stream, it scattered
like an shotgun, and up at Moore's Flat they called
the claims where they used it the "shotgun" claims.

From that time great improvements were made in
hydraulic apparatns until the work done by them was
really wonderful.

In 1850 there lived at Orleans Flat and Moore's

Flat, in Nevada County a few young, energetic and
very stirring pioneers in the persons of lads from 10 to
15 years of age, always on the search for a few dimes
to spend, or add to an already hoarded store, and the
mountain air, with the wild surroundings, seemed to
inspire them always with lively vigor, and especially
when there was a prospect of a two-bit piece not far
ahead.

In winter when the deep snow cut off all communi-
cation with the valley, our busy tinner ran short of
solder, and seeing a limited supply in the tin cans
that lay thick about, he engaged the boys to gather in
a supply and showed them how they could be melted
down to secure the solder with which they had been
fastened, and thus provide for his immediate wants.
So the boys ransacked every spot where they had been
thrown, under the saloon and houses, and in old dump
holes everywhere, till they had gathered a pretty large
pile which they fired as he had told them, and then
panned out the ashes to secure the drops of metal
which had melted down and cooled in small drops and
bits below.   This was re-melted and cast into a mould
made in a pine block, and the solder made into regular
form.   About one-third was made up thus in good and
honest shape.

But the boys soon developed a shrewdness that if
more fully expanded might make them millionaires,
but in the present small way they hoped to put to account in getting a few extra dimes.   They put a big
chunk of iron in the mould and poured in the melted
solder which enclosed it completely, so that when they
presented the bright silvery bar to the old tinker he
paid the price agreed upon and they divided the money
between them, and then, in a secure place, they laughed till their sides ached at the good joke on the tinman.

In due time the man found out the iron core in his

bar of solder, and thought the joke such a good one that he told of it in the saloon, and had to spend at least $5 in drinks to ease off the laugh they had on him as the victim of the young California pioneers. And these young fellows—some have paddled their own canoe successfully into quiet waters and are now in the fullness of life, happy in their possessions, while some have been swamped on the great rushing stream of business, and dwell in memory on the happy times gone by.

The older pioneers in these mining towns were, in many respects a peculiar class of men. Most of them were sober and industrious, fearless and venturesome, jolly and happy when good luck came to them, and in misfortune stood up with brave, strong, manly hearts, without a tear or murmur. They let the world roll merrily by, were ever ready with joke, mirth and fun to make their surroundings cheerful.

Fortunes came and went; they made money easily, and spent it just as freely, and in their generosity and kindly charity the old expression—"He has a heart like an ox" fitted well the character of most of them.

When luck turned against them they worked the harder, for the next turn might fill their big pockets with a fortune, and then the dream of capturing a wife and building up a home could be realized, and they would move out into the world on a wave of happiness and plenty. This kind of talk was freely carried on around the camp fire in the long evenings, and who knows how many of these royal good fellows realized those bright hopes and glorious anticipations? Who knows?

The names come back in memory of some of them, and others have been forgotten. I recall Washington Work, H. J. Kingman, A. J. Henderson, L. J. Hanchett, Jack Hays, Seth Bishop, Burr Blakeslee, Jim

Tyler, who was the loudest laugher in the town, and as he lived at the Clifton House he was called "The Clifton House Calf." These and many others might be mentioned as typical good fellows of the mining days. The biggest kind of practical joke would be settled amicably at the saloon after the usual style.

One day Jack Hays bought a pair of new boots, set them down in the store and went to turn off the miners supply of water. When he returned he found his boots well filled with refuse crackers and water. This he discovered when he took them up to go to dinner, and as he poured out the contents at the door, a half dozen boys across the street raised a big laugh at him, and hooted at his discomfiture. Jack scowled an awful scowl, and if he called them "pukes" with a few swear words added, it was a mild way of pouring out his anger. But after dinner the boys surrounded him and fairly laughed him into a good humor, so that he set up drinks for the crowd.

Foot races were a great Sunday sport, and dog fights were not uncommon. One dog in our camp was champion of the ridge, and though other camps brought in their pet canines to eat him up, he was always the top dog at the end of the scrimmage, and he had a winning grip on the fore foot of his antagonist.

A big "husky" who answered to the name of Cherokee Bob came our way and stopped awhile. He announced himself a foot racer, and a contest was soon arranged with Soda Bill of Nevada City, and each went into a course of training at his own camp. Bob found some way to get the best time that Bill could make, and comparing it with his own, said he could beat in that race. So when it came off our boys gathered up their money, and loaded down the stage, inside and out, departing with swinging hats and flying colors, and screaming in wild delight at the sure pros-

pect of doubling their dust. In a few days they all
came back after the style of half drowned roosters.

Bob had 'thrown' the race and skipped with his
money before they could catch him. Had he been
found he would have been ungently hoisted to the
first projecting limb, but he was never seen again.
The boys were sad and silent for a day or two, but a
look of cheerful resignation soon came upon their
faces as they handled pick and shovel, and the world
rolled on as before.

One fall we had a county election, and among the
candidates for office was our townsman, H. M. Moore,
from whom Moore's Flat secured its name. He was
the Democratic nominee for County Judge, and on the
other side was David Belden, he whom Santa Clara
County felt proud to honor as its Superior Judge, and
when death claimed him, never was man more sin-
cerely mourned by every citizen.

The votes were counted, and Belden was one ahead.
Moore claimed another count, and this time a mistake
was discovered in the former count, but unfortunately
it gave Belden a larger majority than before, and his
adversary was forced to abandon the political fight.

In the fifties I traveled from the North Yuba River
to San Bernardino on different roads, and made many
acquaintances and friends. I can truly say that I
found many of these early comers who were the most
noble men and women of the earth. They were brave
else they had never taken the journey through unknown deserts, and through lands where wild Indians
had their homes. They were just and true to friends,
and to real enemies, terribly bitter and uncompromis-
ing. Money was borrowed and loaned without a note
or written obligation, and there was no mention made
of statute laws as a rule of action. When a real murderer or horsethief was caught no lawyers were needed

nor employed, but if the community was satisfied as to the guilt and identity of the prisoner, the punishment was speedily meted out, and the nearest tree was soon ornamented (?) with his swinging carcass.

Many of these worthy men broke the trail on the rough way that led to the Pacific Coast, drove away all dangers, and made it safer for those who dared not at first risk life and fortune in the journey, but, encouraged by the success of the earliest pioneers, ventured later on the eventful trip to the new gold fields. I cannot praise these noble men too much; they deserve all I can say, and much more, too; and if a word I can say shall teach our new citizens to regard with reverent respect the early pioneers who laid the foundations of the glory, prosperity and beauty of the California of to-day, I shall have done all I hope to, and the historian of another half century may do them justice, and give to them their full meed of praise.

As long as I have lived in California I have never carried a weapon of defense, and never could see much danger. I tried to follow the right trail so as to shun bad men, and never found much difficulty in doing so. We hear much of the Vigilance Committee of early days. It was an actual necessity of former times. The gold fields not only attracted the good and brave, but also the worst and most lawless desperadoes of the world at large. England's banished convicts came here from the penal colonies of Australia and Van Diemen's Land. They had wonderful ideas of freedom. In their own land the stern laws and numerous constabulary had not been able to keep them from crime. A colony of criminals did not improve in moral tone, and when the most reckless and daring of all these were turned loose in a country like California, where the machinery of laws and officers to execute them was not yet in order, these lawless "Sidney

Ducks,'' as they were called, felt free to rob and murder, and human life or blood was not allowed to stand
between them and their desires.   Others of the same
general stripe came from Mexico and Chili, and Texas
and Western Missouri furnished another class almost
as bad.

The Vigilance Committee of San Francisco was composed of the best men in the world.   They endured
all that was heaped upon them by these lawless men,
and the law of self protection forced them to organize
for the swift apprehension and punishment of crime,
and the preservation of their property and lives.   No
one was punished unjustly, but there was no delay,
and the evil-doer met his fate swiftly and surely.
Justice was strict, and the circumstances were generally unfavorable to thoughts of mercy.   I was in San
Francisco the day after Casey and Cory were hung
by the Vigilance Committee.   Things looked quite
military.   Fort Gunny-bags seemed well protected,
and no innocent man in any danger.   I was then a
customer of G. W. Badger and Lindenberger, clothiers,
and was present one day in their store when some of
the clerks came in from general duty, and their comrades shouldered the same guns and took their places
on guard.   The Committee was so truly vigilant that
these fire-bugs, robbers and cut-throats had to hide
for safety.

Those who came early to this coast were, mostly,
brave, venturesome, enduring fellows, who felt they
could outlive any hardship and overcome all difficulties; they were of no ordinary type of character or habits.   They thought they saw success before them, and
were determined to win it at almost any cost.   They
had pictured in their minds the size of the ''pile'' that
would satisfy them, and brought their buckskin bags
with them, in various sizes, to hold the snug sum they

hoped to win in the wonderful gold fields of the then
unknown California.

These California pioneers were restless fellows, but
those who came by the overland trail were not without education and refinement; they were, indeed,
many of them, the very cream of Americans. The
new scenes and associations, the escape from the influ-
ence of home and friends, of wife and children, led
some off the dim track, and their restlessness could
not well be put down. Reasonable men could not expect all persons under these circumstances to be mod-
els of virtue. Then the Missouri River seemed to be
the western boundary of all civilization, and as these
gold hunters launched out on the almost trackless
prairies that lay westward of that mighty stream,
many considered themselves as entering a country of
peculiar freedom, and it was often said that "Law and
morality never crossed the Missouri River." Passing this great stream was like the crossing of the Rub-
icon in earlier history, a step that could not be retraced,
a launching to victory or death. Under this state of
feeling many showed the cloven foot, and tried to
make trouble, but in any emergency good and honest
men seemed always in the majority, and those who
had thoughts or desires of evil were compelled to submit to honorable and just conclusions.

There were some strange developments of character
among these travelers. Some who had in long attendance at school and church, listened all their lives to
teachings of morality and justice, and at home seemed
to be fairly wedded to ideas of even rights between
man and man, seemed to experience a change of character as they neared the Pacific Coast. Amiable dispositions became soured, moral ideas sadly blunted,
and their whole make-up seemed changed, while others
who at home seemed to be of rougher mould, devel-

oped principles of justice and humanity, affection almost unbounded, and were true men in every trial and in all places. A majority of all were thus fairminded and true.

Men from every state from New Hampshire to Texas gathered on the banks of the Missouri to set out together across the plains. These men reared in different climates, amid different ways and customs, taught by different teachers in schools of religion and politics, made up a strange mass when thus thrown together; but the good and true came to the surface, and the turbulent and bad were always in a hopeless minority. Laws seemed to grow out of the very circumstances, and though not in print, flagrant violations would be surely punished.

Some left civilization with all the luxuries money could buy—fine, well-equipped trains of their own, and riding a fat and prancing steed, which they guided with gloved hands, and seemed to think that water and grass and pleasant camping places would always be found wherever they wished to stop for rest, and that the great El Dorado would be a grand pleasure excursion, ending in a pile of gold large enough to fill their big leather purse. But the sleek, fat horse grew poor; the gloves with embroidered gauntlet wrists were cast aside; the trains grew small, and the luxuries vanished, and perhaps the plucky owner made the last few hundred miles on foot, with blistered soles and scanty pack, almost alone. Many of these gay trains never reached California, and many a pioneer who started with high hopes died upon the way, some rudely buried, some left where they fell upon the sands or rocks.

Those who got through found a splendid climate and promising prospects before them of filling empty stomachs and empty pockets, and were soon searching

eagerly for yellow treasure. When fortunate they
recovered rapidly their exhausted bodies to health
and strength, and gained new energy as they saw
prosperity.

Prospectors wandered through the mountains in
search of new and suitable gold diggings, and when
they came to a miner's cabin the door was always
open, and whether the owner was present or absent
they could go in, and if hungry, help themselves to
anything they found in shape of food, and go away
again without fear of offense. for under such circumstances the unwritten law said that grub was free.

By the same unwritten law, stealing and robbery, as
well as murder, were capital offences, and lawless
characters were put down. Favors were freely
granted, and written obligations were never asked or
given, and business was governed by the rules of
strictest honor. The great majority of these pioneers
were tne bone and sinew of the nation, and possessed
a fair share of the brains. In a personal experience
with them extending from early days to the present
time I have found them always just and honorable,
and I regret that it is not within my ability to give
the praise they deserve. When a stranger and hungry I was never turned away without food, and my
entertainment was free, and given without thought of
compensation or reward.

In the chambers of my mind are stored up the most
pleasant recollections of these noble men whose good
deeds in days gone by have earned for them the right
to a crown of glory of greatest splendor.

These noble souls who came here 40 years ago are
fast passing away across the Mystic River, and those
who trod on foot the hot and dusty trail are giving
way to those who come in swiftly rolling palace cars,
and who hardly seem to give a thought to the differ-

ence between then and now.   Those who came early
cleared the way and started the great stream of gold
that has made America one of the richest nations of
the world.

I have a suggestion to make to the descendants of
these noble pioneers, that to perpetuate the memory
of their fathers, and do reverence to their good
and noble deeds in the early history of this grand
State, there should be erected upon the highest
mountain top a memorial building wherein may be
inscribed the names and histories of the brave pioneers, so they may never be blotted out.

THE JAYHAWKERS.

The most perfect organization of the pioneers who
participated more or less in the scenes depicted in this
volume, is that of the Jayhawkers, and, strange to
say, this organization is in the East, and has its annual meetings there, although the living members are
about equally divided between the East and the
Pacific Coast.   As related elsewhere, February 4th is
the day of the annual meeting, for on that day they
reached the Santa Clara Valley.

It is greatly regretted that a more direct and complete account of the Death Valley experience of the
Jayhawkers could not have been obtained for this
work.   To be sure it was from the lips of a living
witness told in many conversations, but no doubt
many striking incidents were left out.   It is, however,
a settled thing that these, and other individuals with
whom he was immediately connected, were more in-
timately connected with the horrors of the sunken
valley which was given its name by them, than were
any other persons who ever crossed that desert region.

It will be considered that this was the most favorable time of year possible, and that during the spring or
summer not one would have lived to tell the tale.

The Author, to his best, has done his duty to all, and concludes with the hope that this mite may authenticate one of the saddest chapters in the history of the Golden State.

CONCLUSION.

This story is not meant to be sensational, but a plain, unvarnished tale of truth—some parts hard and very sad. It is a narrative of my personal experience, and being in no sense a literary man or making any pretense as a writer, I hope the errors may be overlooked, for it has been to me a difficult story to tell, arousing as it did sad recollections of the past. I have told it in the plainest, briefest way, with nothing exaggerated or overdone. Those who traveled over the same or similar routes are capable of passing a just opinion of the story.

Looking back over more than 40 years, I was then a great lover of liberty, as well as health and happiness, and I possessed a great desire to see a new country never yet trod by civilized man, so that I easily caught the gold fever of 1849, and naught but a trip to that land of fabled wealth could cure me.

Geography has wonderfully changed since then. Where Omaha now stands there was not a house in 1849. Six hundred miles of treeless prairie without a house brought us to the adobe dwellings at Fort Laramie, and 400, more or less, were the long miles to Mormondom, still more than 700 miles from the Pacific Coast. Passing over this wilderness was like going to sea without a compass.

Hence it will be seen that when we crossed a stream that was said to flow to the Pacific Ocean, myself and comrades were ready to adopt floating down its current as an easier road than the heated trail, and for three weeks, over rocks and rapids, we floated and tumbled down the deep cañon of Green River till we

emerged into an open plain and were compelled to
come on shore by the Indians there encamped. We
had believed the Indians to be a war-like and cruel
people, but when we made them understand where
we wanted to go, they warned us of the great impassable Colorado Cañon only two days ahead of us, and
pointed out the road to "Mormonie" with their advice
to take it. This was Chief Walker, a good, well
meaning red man, and to him we owed our lives.

Out of this trouble we were once again on the safe
road from Salt Lake to Los Angeles, and again made
error in taking a cut-off route, and striking across a
trackless country because it seemed to promise a
shorter distance, and where thirteen of our party lie
unburied on the sands of the terribly dry valley.
Those who lived were saved by the little puddles of
rain water that had fallen from the small rain clouds
that had been forced over the great Sierra Nevada
Mountains in one of the wettest winters ever known.
In an ordinary year we should have all died of
thirst, so that we were lucky in our misfortune.

When we came out to the fertile coast near Los
Angeles, we found good friends in the native Californians who, like good Samaritans, gave us food and
took us in, poor, nearly starved creatures that we
were, without money or property from which they
could expect to be rewarded. Their deeds stand out
whiter in our memories than all the rest, notwithstanding their skins were dark. It seems to me such
people do not live in this age of the world which we
are pleased to call advanced. I was much with these
old Californians, and found them honest and truthful,
willing to divide the last bit of food with a needy
stranger or a friend. Their good deeds have never
been praised enough, and I feel it in my heart to do
them ample justice while I live.

The work that was laid out for me to do, to tell when and where I went, is done. Perhaps in days to come it may be of even more interest than now, and I shall be glad I have turned over the scenes in my memory and recorded them, and on some rolling stone you may inscribe the name of WILLIAM LEWIS MANLEY, born near St. Albans, Vermont, April 20th, 1820, who went to Michigan while yet it was a territory, as an early pioneer; then onward to Wisconsin before it became a state, and for twelve long, weary months traveled across the wild western prairies, the lofty mountains and sunken deserts of Death Valley, to this land which is now so pleasant and so fair, wherein, after over 40 years of earnest toil, I rest in the midst of family and friends, and can truly say I am content.

THE END.